THE PEOPLE'S SONGS

Also by Stuart Maconie:

Cider with Roadies
Pies and Prejudice
Adventures on the High Teas
Hope and Glory

STUART
MACONIE

THE PEOPLE'S SONGS

THE STORY OF MODERN BRITAIN IN 50 SONGS

EBURY
PRESS

5 7 9 10 8 6 4

This edition published 2014
First published in 2013 by Ebury Press, an imprint of Ebury Publishing
A Random House Group company

Copyright © Stuart Maconie 2013

Stuart Maconie has asserted his right to be identified as the author of this Work
in accordance with the Copyright, Designs and Patents Act 1988

Based on the BBC Radio 2 series © BBC 2013.
The radio series was produced by Smooth Operations (Productions) Limited

By arrangement with BBC. The BBC Radio 2 logo is a trademark of the
British Broadcasting Corporation and is used under licence

BBC Radio 2 logo © 2008

The Random House Group Limited Reg. No. 954009

Addresses for companies within the Random House Group can be found at
www.randomhouse.co.uk

A CIP catalogue record for this book is available from the British Library

The Random House Group Limited supports the Forest Stewardship Council® (FSC®),
the leading international forest-certification organisation. Our books carrying the
FSC label are printed on FSC®-certified paper. FSC is the only forest-certification
scheme supported by the leading environmental organisations, including Greenpeace.
Our paper procurement policy can be found at www.randomhouse.co.uk/environment

Printed and bound by CPI Group (UK) Ltd, Croydon, CR0 4YY

ISBN 9780091933807

To buy books by your favourite authors and register for offers visit
www.randomhouse.co.uk

For Ian Callaghan and Lorna Skingley

And with thanks of course to Bob Shennan

CONTENTS

INTRODUCTION

'Extraordinary how potent cheap music is'
NOËL COWARD

Upon finding out that you're a writer, people will often, after they've given you a look of pity and suspicion and checked for their wallet, ask if there's a book you really want to write. Usually this means a novel and they are rather surprised when you tell them that you have no more desire to write one of those than to design a range of microwaveable desserts or grow rubber in Malaysia. For a long time, though, I did have a stock answer to this entirely reasonable question. The book I would love to one day write would be a readable, authoritative one-volume history of British popular music that would redress some of the problems and prejudices, as I saw them, of rock scholarship; avoid rehashing the accepted wisdom, cast the net wider than the critical canon of the 'classic' albums and the 'iconic' bands and elevate to its rightful position pop music in all its giddy, daring, dazzling and diverse glory.

I should say that, for various reasons, the above isn't quite the book you have in your hand now. But it almost is. What happened is that in 2012 the controller of BBC Radio 2 and 6Music asked me would I be interested in writing a landmark year long series for the former network, a history of pop no less. Flattered and delighted, I said 'Yes, of course' and then immediately asked if I could actually do something a little different. What I would love to write and present was a social history of Britain as told through pop songs. We, after all, invented it. America can rightly claim to be the home of rock and roll, a 'wrong side of the sheets' offspring of the blues, gospel and country and a range of other rough, native American musics. Of that there's no doubt. And there are shelves of potentially ox-stunning tomes devoted to this revered canonical wellspring. Elvis, Robert Johnson, Hank Williams, etc. It is also the home of the great corpus of modern black music, from Coltrane to Stevie Wonder, Bessie Smith to Beyoncé.

But I'd argue that what we call pop music – that mongrel hybrid of rock, vaudeville, folk ballad, dance music, classroom hymns, street corner soul and classical music, that art form so plastic and pliable that it can embrace the wildest avant-garde experimentation and the most primitive and basic chants and beats – is a uniquely British invention. A music that has no one stylistic constant but a defiant, unsanctioned concept at its heart, the ability to speak to people, to affect people, to occupy people, to transform their lives or divert them for a moment, to console, to enrage, to amuse, to arouse. This then is a music that happens without the approval of critic or teacher or politician or pulpit. It both nods to history and makes history. But it happens without anyone's permission. Pop music runs like a seam of the coal we once mined, like the lettering in the rock we buy at the seaside, like a thread in a tapestry, through the warp and weft of the fabric of our daily life. No other art form, not film, not literature, not the theatre, gives the authentic whiff and flavour of the time like the pop charts of the day. I wanted to know which pop songs had actually shaped people's lives and formed the soundtracks to their world; the songs they'd fallen in love to, gone on strike to, danced at the school disco to, cried to, laughed to, made love to, sang in their Anderson shelters, on the terraces, in the pub. Not the ones that were endlessly regurgitated in well-meaning but partial and formulaic TV documentaries, broadsheets and rock magazines. A people's history of modern Britain told though our shared music.

Here's a handy way of summing up both what this book and its accompanying series are and are not. There are no Nick Drake songs in the list (although that beautifully melancholic singer and guitarist is mentioned in the chapter about the folk revival) even though I am a great fan of his music. The reason is simply that Nick's significance and impact on wider British culture and the lives of ordinary Britons has been negligible, whereas 'Y Viva España' and 'My Boy Lollipop' and 'Can't Get You out of My Head' and 'Bye Bye Baby's' are considerable. The Nick Drake story – and stories like his – have been told many times. It seems to me that the other story, the story of everyday British citizens and their relationship to pop music, has been overlooked, scorned even.

My idea was to take 50 records that in some way illustrate or illuminate a moment or an issue or a facet of British life since the Second World War and the dawn of the pop single. Some would capture a particular event: the Falklands, the Coronation or New Labour's 1997 landslide. Others would address a theme in our shared history, from dancing to industrial relations, sex to the countryside, school to immigration. At the heart of each chapter would be one emblematic record; a single made by a Briton, a member of the Commonwealth or with a significant UK input, and many other illustrative ones. The radio series does not run chronologically, whereas this book does, although of course you are free to dip in wherever you please.

One quote came back to me again and again while I was writing both book and series; the one by Noël Coward above about the potency of cheap music. I don't know exactly what Noël meant by cheap music. But I take it to mean pop music, which is far from cheap really, actually priceless, but which wears its demotic, romantic, exhibitionist heart on its sleeve. It belongs to all of us, all of us who've ever listened heartbroken late at night to the same song twenty times, sung on a picket line or at a wedding, danced in a muddy field at midnight by the light of a glowstick, pogoed in a mosh pit, spent time in their bedroom backcombing and spiking their hair, or putting gravy browning on their legs in lieu of nylons, or playing air guitar, or practising their rapping poses … or any of the other things a pop fan does.

We are all in this together, to coin a phrase. This is the People's Music. These are the People's Songs.

1. WE'LL MEET AGAIN

We are an island race, formed and bounded by the sea, steeped in salt and shingle and seaweed and song. At heart, we feel a little superior to and even sympathetic towards the Serb and the Slovak, the Paraguayan and the Mongolian, the Ugandan and the Swiss, landlocked and lugubrious, those for whom a border and a frontier means a checkpoint, a stamp and a road sign rather than the romance of the crashing surf and the far lonely horizon.

The White Cliffs of Dover are a range of sheer chalk cliffs stretching for some ten miles along the Kent coastline. Visible in good conditions from France, they are where Britain comes closest to continental Europe, just twenty-two briny miles or so distant; easily crossable by a strong swimmer with a decent coating of goose grease, from Captain Webb to David Walliams. But a political and cultural gulf stretches before them that has seen them come to mean something more than mere calcium carbonate and centuries of seagull droppings.

In *King Lear* the blinded and suicidal Gloucester tries to throw himself from this ageless symbolic headland:

There is a cliff whose high and bending head
Looks fearfully in the confined deep:
Bring me to the very brim of it

Matthew Arnold in his masterpiece 'Dover Beach' talks of where 'the cliffs of England stand/Glimmering and vast, out in the tranquil bay'. And at about 9 a.m. on 26 August 55 BC, Julius Caesar arrived to find the cliffs alive with fully armed and hostile natives so he nipped up the coast to Deal and began the Roman occupation of Britain there.

These cliffs have seen many things. But one thing they have certainly never seen is a bluebird. Take your pick: *Sialia sialis*, the Eastern Bluebird; *Sialia mexicana*, the Western Bluebird; or the Mountain Bluebird, *Sialia currucoides*. None of them has ever flown over the White Cliffs of Dover. Or ever will, unless something very strange happens to patterns of bird migration. This preposterous, unpatriotic, ornithological untruth tells you a great deal about this very British song. Namely, that almost everything about it is American: written by two jobbing Yank music hacks from Tin Pan Alley, Walter Kent and Nat Burton, based on a poem by Algonquin Round Table wit Alice Duer Miller, with a tune pinched from the tremulous, glutinous Judy Garland ballad 'Somewhere over the Rainbow'. Try singing the words from one to the tune of the other *I'm Sorry I Haven't a Clue* style and you'll see how similar they are.

So let's begin our story of post-war Britain in song here. Here on the misty English coast looking out to sea, hoping for better days, lulled and uplifted by the pure, stirring tones of a twenty-four-year-old London songbird called Vera Lynn. But with our roots very firmly in … Stockport.

Hughie Charles, or Charles Hugh Owen Ferry, as he was born on 24 July 1907 in Reddish, Stockport, turned down the chance to open the batting for Lancashire to seek his fortune as a plugger of sheet music and songwriter in Denmark Street, London's very own Tin Pan Alley. There, during the late thirties and early forties, he wrote a string of catchy sentimental numbers, at least two of which captured and chimed perfectly with the mood of the British people during the early days of the war. One was 'There'll Always Be an England', so stirring and strident that you could be forgiven for thinking it a Victorian paean to the glories of empire rather than written upon the outbreak of World War 2. Indeed so ramrod-backed and stiff upper lip is it that it's ripe for a kind of affectionate parody by talents as diverse as Tiny Tim at the Isle of Wight festival and the Sex Pistols, who used it as their entrance music. But Hughie Charles's other wartime smash, co-written with Ross Parker, was a very different affair and is perhaps even more indicative of the public mood back in the dark days of 1939, a time of uncertainty and fear laced with optimism and fortitude.

To understand quite how powerful and symbolic such music is, the same cheap music whose potency Noël Coward marvelled at, we need to remember that, at this crucial moment in the war, Britain stood alone against the might of Hitler and the Nazis, who had overrun and subjugated every other major European power. France had fallen in May 1940. The worst was coming to pass. Darkness was on our doorstep.

In its reference to blue skies coming after dark clouds there's an allusion – intentional or not, but certainly one that would have resonated with the audience of the early forties – to both the Luftwaffe and Messerschmitts that had darkened the skies over

England for two years and to Churchill's brilliant, Shakespearean speech on the eve of the Battle of Britain:

> The whole fury and might of the enemy must very soon be turned on us. Hitler knows that he will have to break us in this island or lose the war. If we can stand up to him, all Europe may be freed and the life of the world may move forward into broad, sunlit uplands.
>
> But if we fail, then the whole world, including the United States, including all that we have known and cared for, will sink into the abyss of a new dark age made more sinister, and perhaps more protracted, by the lights of perverted science. Let us therefore brace ourselves to our duties, and so bear ourselves, that if the British Empire and its Commonwealth last for a thousand years, men will still say, 'This was their finest hour.'

Broad sunlit uplands or new dark ages, blue skies or dark clouds, in the words of both Winston Churchill and Hughie Parker the same stark distinction between the evil of the Third Reich and the righteousness of the Allies is expressed in terms of dark and light that everyone could understand. And in that telling phrase of Churchill's about 'including the United States', there's a direct appeal to the Americans to enter the war and help us, exactly the same sentiment that Nat Burton and Walter Kent were expressing when they wrote about bluebirds over the White Cliffs of Dover, an explicit and heartfelt plea to their countrymen to come to Britain's aid. Popular music, in its own cheap and cheerful way, was echoing various shades of political opinion.

And of public opinion too. Because 'We'll Meet Again' meant much more than a glib 'see you around' to British men and women in 1939. The song resonated achingly with both soldiers going off to fight and their families and sweethearts. And while the message is defiantly optimistic – I know we'll meet again some sunny day, maybe on those broad sunlit uplands – the music has the same gently melancholic tone as '(There'll Be Bluebirds Over) The White Cliffs of Dover', and there is the sweet but distinctly eerie thought underpinning the sentiment, that the meeting may take place not in this world, but the next.

It's not quite a love song, not an erotic love song, anyway, to use the language of the poets of ancient Greece and the two kinds of love they distinguished, not eros but agape: companionship, friendship, devotion, support. It's a love song, maybe, but in the vein of 'He Ain't Heavy … He's My Brother', 'You've Got a Friend' or 'Bridge over Troubled Water' rather than 'Je T'Aime …' or 'Sexual Healing'.

Lynn's delivery is brilliant and in its own way as stirring as Churchill's speech. Pure and alluring, gorgeous without being remotely sexual. Not for nothing was she the Forces' sweetheart rather than the Forces' good-time girl. She was exactly the girl that our boys, as the nonagenarian Dame Vera still calls them, wanted to have waiting for them at home, these young men in dire circumstances. So popular was Vera's radio programme, *Sincerely Yours*, in which servicemen and their families provided requests, that at one point questions were asked in Parliament about whether it might stoke the homesickness and be bad for morale. As ever, the political class had shown how out of touch with its people it can be. Songs like 'We'll Meet Again', simple, touching, and maybe a little sentimental, were just what a beleaguered nation needed, alongside

the martial bravado of 'There'll Always Be an England' and the
jaunty glamour of Glenn Miller.

It's easy for us today, the generations born long after the Second
World War, to adopt a sneering or, even worse, condescending tone
towards some of the sentimental popular music of the 1940s. But
this is only easy because it is almost impossible for us to imagine the
day-to-day realities of that war, the daily hardships and loss and fear.
The most popular and requested songs on Forces radio today, the
ones enjoyed by the troops in Helmand province and Kosovo and
elsewhere, are singularly slushy.

Like the sentiments it expresses, 'We'll Meet Again' has endured
and survived. It was covered by The Byrds on their début album
and Pink Floyd's track 'Vera' on *The Wall* album refers to it 'Does
anybody here remember Vera Lynn?/Remember how she said that
we would meet again some sunny day?' On 13 September 2009
Lynn became the oldest living artist to make it to number one in
the British album chart, at the age of ninety-two, with an album
entitled *We'll Meet Again*, selling over 100,000 copies and ousting
The Beatles and the Arctic Monkeys from the top of the charts.

And the song has had a life on the big screen too. So popular
was 'We'll Meet Again' that it spawned a movie of the same name
starring Vera Lynn in 1943, by which time both America and the
Soviet Union had entered the war and the tide had turned against
the Axis powers. Many years later, Lynn's song was heard on screen
in a very different, much more ambivalent war movie: Stanley
Kubrick's *Dr Strangelove (Or How I Learned to Stop Worrying And
Love the Bomb)*. There it was used sardonically as the soundtrack
to a nightmarish plethora of nuclear explosions. And if as to prove
that real life is always stranger than satire, it emerged in the 1990s
that during the Strangelove era of Cold War paranoia Vera Lynn's

recording of 'We'll Meet Again' was one of the songs and shows held in twenty underground radio stations of the BBC's Wartime Broadcasting Service to boost morale in the immediate aftermath of an atomic war. And so Hughie Charles's little song would once again have been pressed into war service, in a world when right and wrong were much harder to distinguish, when anxiety rather than optimism was the dominant mood and the post-war world would not be a broad sunlit upland but an endless and desolate nuclear winter. But few Britons entertained such thoughts as they danced in the streets on VE day. Good had prevailed, though at a grievous price in terms of lives, as well as national stability and wealth. We would still be paying the price of our victory well into the next decade, until a young woman called Elizabeth Windsor came forward to helm and embody a national renaissance; a move perhaps towards those broad sunlit uplands.

2. CORONATION RAG

'*Hold the front page!*' they shout in those newspaper movies. Two headlines that *The Times* of London, 2 June 1953, was happy to hold the front page for positively bristled and swaggered with imperial pride: 'Thousands Spend Night on Coronation Route', and 'Everest Conquered: Hillary and Tenzing Reach the Summit'. As a double whammy of national pride and a piece of editorial chest-beating by the journal of record, it was hard to top. As a conjunction of events of national rejoicing and significance, it was impossible to make up. That same morning that a new, young Queen was crowned, a new Queen Elizabeth at that, on the other side of the world, at the top of the world, her new Walter Raleighs had achieved the last great dream of earthly adventure and exploration, the conquest of Everest, the world's highest mountain.

And so the British people, those of them that read *The Times* anyway, learned that Britannia ruled not just the waves but the roof of the world, and that a new Elizabethan era had begun. As they nibbled their toast and marmalade, with the wireless tuned to the Light Programme, they might have heard one of the unashamed cash-in hits of the day: one of two versions of a sentimental ditty called 'In a Golden Coach (There's a Heart of Gold)', written by Ronald Jamieson and sung by both slick crooner Dickie Valentine and avuncular shouter Billy Cotton and his band. Then, as now, everyone in pop from old guard to new breed wants to tug the forelock for Her Majesty.

You can almost feel the high sugar content of either version of the song furring your arteries. The lyrics, though, are a curious, slightly creepy mix of the obsequious and the Cromwellian:

> *As she drives in state through the palace gates*
> *Her beauty the whole world will see*
> *In a golden coach there's a heart of gold*
> *That belongs to you and me*

Now largely forgotten, the song was as ubiquitous in June 1953 as Band Aid was at Christmas 1984. Mass Observation, the social studies unit, reported the song being commonly sung in pubs and clubs, and a choir of East End schoolchildren clad in red, white and blue sang it as the Queen and Prince Philip passed along Parnell Road in Poplar.

The coronation of Queen Elizabeth II proved a rather nice payday then for songwriter Ronald Jamieson, as both Cotton's and Valentine's versions of his song were riding high at number two and number seven respectively in what was still the new fangled pop charts. The first official UK singles chart had begun just six months earlier in November 1952, compiled by the *New Musical Express*. The trade paper had been recently acquired by promoter Maurice Kinn and he had wanted a gimmick to give it an edge over the long-established *Melody Maker*.

Joint *NME* founder Percy Dickins came up with the idea of a musical league table as a reference to a record's sales success. He canvassed his contacts at approximately twenty music sales outlets, finding out what records were selling best and, on 14 November 1952, the first pop chart was born containing twelve entries. The very first number one was Al Martino with 'Here in My Heart'.

So the very idea of a pop chart was just a few months old when Coronation fever gripped the land. Wholesome entertainment giants of the day queued up to get aboard the bandwagon. The Welsh light tenor Donald Peers charted with 'Celebration Rag'. The B side, you've guessed it, 'In a Golden Coach (There's a Heart of Gold)', meant another few bob for Ronald Jamieson. Also in that chart of June 1953 was Vera Lynn with 'The Windsor Waltz', a slick and ruthlessly sentimental cash-in that trades in a kind of gauzy false memory syndrome for 'The Old Windsor Waltz', a fictitious dance invented to be nostalgic about.

Vera Lynn was still fondly remembered as the Forces' sweetheart of the Second World War. Those Forces were now demobbed, of course, but the Coronation inspired a glut of simple sentimental songs that harked back to and echoed the popular songs of the war – something which culturally and financially still hung over the chilly, austere, threadbare Britain of the early fifties, where meat, sugar and sweets were still rationed. Into this world the coronation of a new Queen burst like a sudden ray of sunlight. As James Morris (later Jan), the reporter who broke the news of the Everest triumph, said, it was a moment to 'restore the battered and shabby kingdom to its storied splendours'. There was something of the fairytale about it all. And from the scarlet of the liveried footmen to the gold of the coaches, it was as moment of Technicolor in a land of sooty greys and charcoal blacks.

Well, it was if you were in the Mall. If you were sitting at home in front of your newly purchased television it was still in black and white. But that didn't bother the many British people who bought the new-fangled contraptions just for this event. Television hadn't reached the north of England at all until 1951, so much of the country hadn't bothered with this expensive high-tech acquisition. But further south hire purchase and the Coronation combined to make a television set an affordable must-have for many ordinary people in the spring of 1953. Neighbours crowded into living rooms curtained against what little sun there was that wet day to watch the historic events. 'Put an H-aerial up over your house, and you will be astonished to find how many friends you have in the street,' said the *Manchester Evening News*.

The new Queen had agreed to the Coronation being televised so that as many people as possible could observe the ceremony, and an estimated 27 million people in Britain did via TV, while 11 million listened on the radio. There were more than 2,000 journalists and 500 photographers from ninety-two nations on the Coronation route. Thirty cameramen in the Abbey were chosen for their slightness of build, so as not to get in the way, particularly in the space above the organ loft. The BBC provided eleven hours of coverage, from the service itself to the two-hour procession through the streets of London, much of it soundtracked by the specially commissioned music provided by a talented social climber from Oldham called William Walton. And, after the young Queen herself, the star of the proceedings was by common consent one of the many guests from the Caribbean, Sālote Mafile'o Pilolevu Tupou III, the Queen of Tonga, an imperious lady, at 6 foot 3 inches and 350 pounds, who endeared herself to the spectators by riding through the streets in the pouring rain, refusing to put up the cover on her state coach, mopping water from her face with a handkerchief, beaming and waving at the delighted spectators. Such was her instant if brief popularity that a popular dance band leader quickly came up with a catchy tune in her honour, 'The Queen of Tonga'.

Winifred Atwell was another daughter of the Commonwealth who captured the hearts of the British in 1953. She grew up in a pharmacy on Jubilee Street, Tunapuna, Trinidad and Tobago, but in 1946 moved to London, where she had gained a place at the Royal Academy of Music. She became the first female pianist to be awarded the Academy's highest grading for musicianship. To support herself, she played ragtime and boogie woogie in London clubs and venues like the Casino Theatre where she caught the eye of impresario Bernard Delfont, who signed her up. It was the B side to her fourth single that made her a sensation in Britain, a honky-tonk tune called the 'Black and White Rag' which became a big radio hit and twenty years later became famous again as the theme to popular snooker show *Pot Black*.

By the time of the Coronation Atwell was an international star. Her hands were insured with Lloyds of London for a quarter of a million dollars, with the policy stipulating that she was never to wash dishes. More significantly, she was the first black artist to sell a million records in the UK. We may suspect that Britain in the 1950s was not the most enlightened or diverse of cultures but it's worth remembering and celebrating that Britain took Winifred Atwell to its heart in a way that America refused to. Bigotry prevented her ever becoming a star there. Her breakthrough appearance was to have been on *The Ed Sullivan Show* in 1956, but it was feared audiences in the South would simply not accept a black woman artist, least of all one who spoke like a Brit. The appearance was never recorded.

By contrast, Atwell became one of the biggest stars of mid-fifties Britain and Australia, with her own TV shows on both BBC and ITV. Hit after hit followed 'Britannia Rag' in 1952 and 'Coronation Rag', released to commemorate the Coronation of Elizabeth II in June 1953: 'Tiger Rag', 'The Poor People of Paris', 'Let's Have a Party', 'Let's Have Another Party', 'Let's Have a Ding Dong' ...

Atwell went on to play at three Royal Variety Performances at the specific request of the new Queen, who also asked her to play 'Roll Out the Barrel' as an encore. It would be easy to dismiss the jaunty, appealing music of Winifred Atwell as a period piece or a lightweight diversion. But the young woman from Tunapuna was hugely significant for several reasons. 'Black and White Rag' and those other big fifties' hits pricked the ears of many young British keyboard players in the same way that a generation of British guitarists looked to Bert Weedon and Hank Marvin. Young pianists like Rick Wakeman and Keith Emerson were thrilled by the verve and vitality of Winifred Atwell's playing. Emerson told *Keyboard* magazine later, 'I've always been into ragtime. In England – and I'm sure Rick Wakeman would concur – we loved Winifred Atwell, a fantastic honky-tonk and ragtime player.'

And remember that it was only five years before 'Coronation Rag' was riding high in the charts and Atwell a huge British star and favourite of royalty that the first few hundred anxious, cold and seasick immigrants from the West Indies had disembarked from the SS *Windrush* at Tilbury Docks. Winifred Atwell's music and its popularity in Britain are a potent symbol of a fast-changing society and a new kind of country, one in which a black woman played music of black origin to celebrate the crowning of a queen in a ceremony that was positively medieval – a be-frocked archbishop in

an ancient abbey placing a gold crown on a ruler by dint of birth –
and yet one that was watched by millions via the most up-to-date
technology imaginable. It had elements of both Shakespeare and
the space age.

And so the talk was of a new Elizabethan era, ushered in by
Atwell, the Archbishop of Canterbury and Dickie Valentine in the
UK, and Hillary and Tenzing on the summit of Everest. It was
a Panglossian, modernistic wave of national optimism and revival
that had begun with the 1951 Festival of Britain, a celebration of
British cultural vigour that spawned new buildings like the Royal
Festival Hall and the futuristic Skylon tower. It was the spirit of
Dan Dare and *Eagle* comic made real with rapid technological
developments. Just prior to the coronation, BOAC introduced
the first commercial jet service, from London to Johannesburg.
In October 1952 Britain exploded its first atom bomb near the
Monte Bello Islands in Western Australia: 'Today Britain is GREAT
BRITAIN again' was the *Daily Mirror* headline. Just four years
later Queen Elizabeth II would open the world's first nuclear
power station, Calder Hall in Cumbria. The *Sunday Graphic* ran a
comment piece on the changing role of women in society, 'At the
Dawn of the New Elizabethan Era', written by a twenty-six-year-
old trainee tax barrister called Margaret Thatcher.

Of course it wasn't all like that, and just as the Cool Britannia
of the nineties ended in anger over the Iraq war and weapons of
mass destruction, the new Elizabethan era gradually foundered in
the humiliation of Suez and the disillusionment of the angry young
men. But on that June day in 1953 the mood on the streets of
London was celebratory and optimistic. In the East End, traditional
heartland of support for the royals, there were street parties and

knees-ups. The children of Bow, Poplar and Cheapside dressed up and held their own coronations. Gaiety, light-heartedness, even silliness were back on our national agenda. They had never really gone very far away.

3. THE YING TONG SONG

We like a joke. In fact, as every boss or teacher or golf-club secretary will tell you, we like a joke as much as the next man. Particularly if the next man is British and not, say, German or American, and therefore someone with no sense of humour or understanding of irony. Neither of those slurs is true, of course, as anyone who's watched an episode of *The Simpsons* or *30 Rock* will tell you. But here in Britain we take humour very seriously. For the English, humour is a weapon, a crutch, an aphrodisiac, a social lubricant and a religion.

For as long as there have been songs, there have been novelty and comic songs. In fact, it took pop music quite a while to begin to take itself seriously, a development from which some would say it has never fully recovered. The musical publishing houses of Tin Pan Alley originally specialised in three types of song: ballads, dance and comic novelty songs. Even at the height of the First World War comic songs were among the most popular, perhaps as a welcome distraction from the horrors of the front. 'K-K-K-Katy', written by Geoffrey O'Hara, was billed as 'The Sensational Stammering Song

Success Sung by the Soldiers and Sailors'. The song tells the story of Jimmy, a young soldier 'brave and bold', who stutters when he tries to speak to girls. Finally he manages to woo, haltingly, Katy, the 'maid with hair of gold'.

> *K-K-K-Katy, beautiful Katy*
> *You're the only g-g-g-girl that I adore*
> *When the m-m-m-moon shines over the c-c-c-cowshed*
> *I'll be waiting at the k-k-k-kitchen door*

The 1920s was the heyday of the silly comic song. Audiences had had four years of carnage and a reaction against it was natural enough. Love and silliness became a kind of default setting, especially when combined. By the time of the Second World War humour and music often went together as a powerful propaganda tool. Making your enemy look stupid or foolish can be as effective as making them appear monsters. Hitler knew this as well too, despite his tin ear for music. During the summer of 1942 he suggested that propaganda broadcasts aimed at Britain and America should contain musical styles that appealed to those audience. For instance, after the first regularly worded verse of a song, a voice might say, 'Here is Mr Churchill's latest song.' The melody might be a familiar song known by both British and American listeners, but the words that followed were different:

> *I'm afraid of Germany, her planes are beating me*
> *At night, when I should sleep, into the Anderson I must creep*
> *Although I'm England's leading man, I'm led to the cellar by ten*
> *A leader in the cellar each night, that's the only damned way I*
>   *can fight.*

But the Allies topped the charts in propaganda parody. In the US the master of goofball music, Spike Jones, had a hit in 1942 with 'Der Fuehrer's Face', a song that literally blew a raspberry in the face of the Third Reich's absurd philosophies of racial purity and mastery, and, even more brilliantly, did it in the gloriously madcap mongrel musical vernacular of jazz and ragtime, two American musics of black origin.

In Britain, a famous piece of propaganda film cut up goose-stepping Nazis and a *Sieg Heil*-ing Adolf to the jaunty strains of 'The Lambeth Walk' and to brilliantly deflating effect. And, of course, though you'd never hear it on the radio, the people of Britain had their own unofficial propaganda anthem, the frankly implausible tale of the sundry missing appendages of the Nazi High Command and their possible locations sung to the tune of 'The Colonel Bogey March'.

We British have always enjoyed a smutty tune. From the ribald music-hall ditties like 'Oh! Mr Porter', a song about a young woman going too far couched as a train journey, to 'She's Never Had Her Ticket Punched Before' – yet more train-related innuendo – and later the saucy songs of George Formby such as the clearly non-confectionery-based 'With My Little Stick of Blackpool Rock'. (Clue: it's about his penis.)

At the opposite end of the scale from these broad and bawdy sing-alongs, the musical equivalents of Donald McGill's postcards, were some of the elegant and witty comic songs of the 1950s and early 1960s. The masters of this in the UK were Flanders and Swann, a duo whose clipped and proper musical style masked a waspish sense of fun and a vein of gentle satire evident in songs such as 'The Gasman Cometh', concerning the still enormously relevant topic of repair men causing havoc, and 'The Slow Train', their gorgeous, melancholic farewell to Britain's branch lines facing the axe from Dr Beeching. Across the Atlantic Tom Lehrer was mining a similar seam of piano-based satire and skittery. Lehrer's output was slight but hugely popular though his heyday was brief. Legend has it that he retired after Henry Kissinger was awarded the Nobel Peace Prize, saying 'satire was dead', but in fact he'd grown bored with performing some years before. He was, however, suspicious of the power of so-called satire. 'It's not even preaching to the converted; it's titillating the converted ... I'm fond of quoting Peter Cook, who talked about the satirical Berlin cabarets of the nineteen thirties, which did so much to stop the rise of Hitler and prevent the Second World War.'

In 1955 a twenty-nine-year-old record producer called George Martin became the head of Parlophone – the youngest head of a record company in the country. Martin spent the rest of the decade trying to give the ailing label an identity, and he found it through comedy records. The imaginative and experimental audio techniques needed for comedy songs would stand Martin in good stead for his next big career move with four young scousers. Before that, though, he produced period classics of the comedy genre such as 'Right, Said Fred' and 'Hole in the Ground' for Bernard Cribbins, as well as Rolf Harris, the *Beyond the Fringe* team and Peter Sellers and Spike Milligan of *The Goon Show*, whose surreal radio madness was a weekly fixture of British life from 1951 to 1960 and whose freewheeling fantasies called for absurdist sound effects such as 'set of false teeth hitting inside of bucket' and 'distant zither'. Indeed some of the later shows featured the work of the fledgling BBC Radiophonic Workshop.

He didn't produce the 'Ying Tong Song' though. In fact, the Goons signature tune had a curious gestation. It was originally the B side of 'Bloodnok's Rock 'N' Roll Call' which was the first British record to mention rock and roll and reached number three in the UK charts in 1956. Casting around for a flip side, Milligan claimed that he wrote this song as a bet with his brother: that he couldn't get a song with only two chords into the chart, which shows a fundamental misunderstanding of much pop music (see 'Jambalaya', 'Paperback Writer', 'Horse with No Name' and many more). The B side lingered longest in the public memory and affections, though. When reissued as the A side in 1973, it got to number nine. Interestingly only Sellers and Milligan actually sing on the record. As Harry Secombe was signed to Philips Records, he didn't sing on any of the Goons' Decca recordings of the 1950s, only speaking his words. Whenever famous Goon fan Prince Charles was parodied in latex form on *Spitting Image*, he would often be heard mumbling the song to himself. It's become something of a staple of the comedy song repertoire, covered by artists as disparate as the Muppets and Jon Anderson of Yes.

Within the world of serious rock, a sense of humour of the disdainful variety has sometimes been worn as a badge of honour. During the late sixties and early seventies, artists like Cheech & Chong, The Bonzo Dog Doo-Dah Band and Frank Zappa mocked the culture around them, hippy or straight, with a different kind of funny song: smart, knowing, even a little sneering, an in joke for the cognoscenti rather than fun for all the family. Zappa had both sides squarely in his sights for most of his career. Early albums like *Freak Out!* and *We're Only in It for the Money* satirise the rampant consumerism of modern America and the hippy left and, in particular, The Beatles' *Sgt Pepper* album. Later, 'Dancin' Fool' and 'Valley Girl' mocked various breeds of New York and LA hipster, the disco stud and the spoiled teenage girl, as played by his daughter Moon Unit. The Bonzos couched darkly seditious words in the comforting nostalgic settings of a palm court orchestra on songs like 'Canyons of Your Mind'. Sometimes, though, the love shines through these parodies as in the Bonzos' gloriously silly, cinematic 'The Intro and the Outro' and Neil Innes's masterful Beatles spoof, The Rutles.

Weirdly, some of the pioneers of British and American rock and roll have had their biggest hits not with their earnest and oft-discussed protean classics but with novelty songs. Lonnie Donegan is better known to many for 'My Old Man's a Dustman' (number one the UK) and 'Does Your Chewing Gum Lose Its Flavour (On the Bedpost Overnight?)' (top five here and in America) than for 'Rock Island Line'. Chuck Berry's only UK and US number one was 'My Ding-a-Ling', a risible few minutes of *double entendre* recorded at the Locarno Ballroom, Coventry in 1972. And while critics may eulogise Johnny Cash's despairing, deathbed version of Nine Inch Nails' 'Hurt', the truth is that far more people know and indeed bought the daft 'A Boy Named Sue' and 'One Piece at a Time', a moving account of chronic minor theft from an embittered car plant production line worker.

Ray Stevens, 'Weird Al' Yankovic, The Barron Knights, The Goodies … throughout the 1970s there were many acts with sizeable entries in *The Guinness Book of British Hit Singles* who specialised in novelty song and would appear regularly on *Top of the Pops* with varying degrees of embarrassment. We might think that, as rock and pop matures and grows, the essentially childish amusement of the novelty song would fade. In fact, the opposite would seem to be true. There have probably been more novelty hits since the 1980s onwards than in the sixties or seventies. The aforementioned *Spitting Image* team even had a hit with a song that was a parody of the comedy song. 'The Chicken Song' spoofs the 'Ying Tong Song' and others of its ilk, what the late writer Steven Wells called the 'ferret, nostril, outer Mongolia' school of comedy, a brand of lazy, tiresome wackiness.

If the gag-based humour of Benny Hill and The Barron Knights may have dwindled, it has been replaced by tracks that are even dumber and not even human in origin: Jive Bunny, Crazy Frog, and Mr Blobby, the Frankensteinian creation of former Radio One DJ Noel Edmonds, who in 1993 became the second novelty act to reach the coveted UK number-one spot, following Benny Hill with his 1971 chart-topper 'Ernie (The Fastest Milkman in the West)'. Novelty songs were a chart fixture throughout the eighties and nineties, and the ritual rolling of eyes at their embarrassing presence became a rite of passage for proper rock fans, as witnessed in Noel Gallagher's apparent disgust at the Mike Flowers Pops lounge version of 'Wonderwall', which was a bigger hit than his original.

And let's not forget that there's many a true word sung as well as spoken in jest. It's become received if half-baked wisdom to bemoan the fact that Ultravox's portentous 'Vienna' was kept from the top spot by Joe Dolce's piece of cod-Italian familial silliness 'Shaddap You Face'. But as music critics like Alexis Petridis and Pete Paphides, both the children of immigrant families, have pointed out, Dolce's song, about getting on and making a success of life in a new country with fortitude and good humour, was a great deal more relevant to them and others than 'Vienna', which, let's face it, meant nothing to Midge Ure or indeed most of us.

The long history of the novelty and comedy song proves that there is no accounting for taste and nor should there be. To a degree, you can hear them as a great leveller, a silly coloured thread binding us all. You can hear 'Right, Said Fred' and 'Hole in the Ground' in

'When I'm Sixty-Four' and 'Yellow Submarine', both fine examples of George Martin's studio expertise. And *The Goon Show*'s anarchic surrealism, itself an inheritor of Edward Lear, Lewis Carroll and Beachcomber, has filtered down to become one of mainstream entertainment's most lasting and popular tropes, very much with us in the zaniness of Vic and Bob and Paul Merton. Pop culture and pop music are much too important to be taken too seriously.

4. ROCK ISLAND LINE

Long before *The X Factor* or *Britain's Got Talent* or *Pop Idol*, long before *New Faces* or *Opportunity Knocks*, talent shows had been a staple of British TV. From 1952 to 1960 there was one for kids called *All Your Own* hosted by Huw Wheldon, later of arts show *Monitor* fame. By today's standards it was mild and genial, there was no sneering jury, no tears and rage, no competitive edge at all, in fact. Just nicely brought up kids harmonising or morris dancing or showing off their bonsai trees, stamp collection or matchstick model of Nelson's Column.

One teatime in 1958, Wheldon in his brisk but kindly style introduced a musical quartet from Epsom, one of whom, James Page, announces his intention, after school, to become a biological researcher and find a cure for cancer 'if it's not already been found'. In fact Jimmy Page was to put a great deal more time into chemical research in his early adulthood, while one of the biggest rock stars in the world with Led Zeppelin. But back in 1958 thirteen-year-old James was strumming along with his pals to a tune called 'Mama Don't Allow No Skiffle Playing in Here'. Like every other music-mad kid in Britain, he was in a skiffle band, playing what might well be called Britain's first homegrown pop style; the rangy, lonesome sound of itinerant American hobos transplanted to Blighty and played on homemade instruments and pieces of furniture in every parlour, shed and church hall from Berwick to St Ives.

We think of the 1950s as a time of austerity. Post-war Britain was a bankrupt nation, and the recovery was long and slow. It's fitting then that Britain's homemade, hand-me-down, make-do-and-mend musical mongrel of the fifties should be named after an earlier attempt to make ends meet. In 1920s Chicago a skiffle was a rent party; an informal, illicit knees-up held in someone's home where a hat was passed around or admission charged to help pay the host's rent. A handful of American bands and records of the pre-war era contain the word 'skiffle'. But the word was seldom heard again on either side of the Atlantic until the mid-1950s. Ken Colyer led a popular dance band of the time in Glasgow and his banjo player was one Anthony James Donegan ('Lonnie', to his friends), whose impromptu interval 'skiffle' sessions – lively, simplistic affairs with Lonnie on banjo and vocals with tea-chest bass and washboard accompaniment – soon became as popular as the regular dance band sets. The presiding spirit of these sessions came far from Glasgow, far from Britain, in fact. He was an irascible jailbird, labourer and guitarist from Louisiana called Huddie Ledbetter, or Lead Belly.

The musicologist John Lomax discovered Lead Belly and championed his music, making a record of him performing at the Louisiana State Penitentiary in 1933. A year later Lomax recorded the inmates of another southern jail, this time in Alabama, singing a song written by one Kelly Pace and telling the jaunty tale of a freight-train driver and his smuggling runs on the Chicago, Rock Island and Pacific Railroad.

In the 1940s Lead Belly himself recorded the song, slightly altered, under the aegis of Lomax again. And it was this version that young Lonnie Donegan heard, recorded and which became the blue touch paper for the British skiffle boom, the incendiary spark from which the whole conflagration of British rock music roared and crackled.

In the United States, 1955 was to prove a landmark year for several incidental but crucial moments in the story of popular music. The *Rock Around the Clock* movie was on general release, and Colonel Tom Parker became Elvis's manager. But no single event was as important for the future of British music as Lonnie Donegan's version of 'Rock Island Line'. Donegan had upped the tempo from Lead Belly's recording but kept the sparse instrumentation, the archetypal tea-chest bass and washboard rhythm section with Donegan's cheap driving guitar and wailing vocal over the top. But the sound cut through the schmaltzy orchestral light music that dominated TV and radio like a freight-train whistle. Slangy, hip, unstuffy, to a generation raised on rationed boiled beef and carrots and the prim, pinched formality of austerity Britain, even the sound of poor, rural America sounded exhilaratingly like freedom. But in Donegan – a cheeky everyman with a nasal voice and infectious stage presence – they also had a very homegrown hero. 'Rock Island Line', coupled with 'John Henry' on the B side, raced to the top of the UK charts, became the first début release to go gold and, in a wry coals to Newcastle by freight train fashion, even made the top ten in the United States.

This transatlantic musical trade was not without its scandal, though. Just as the 'Rock Island Line's engine driver was not entirely honest about his cargo, so Donegan, some claimed, was economical with the truth when it came to crediting the true originators of the song. Down the years Donegan often grumbled that, despite the song's huge success, he received merely a fixed studio fee of a few pounds from Decca Records. But he often failed to mention how he received publishing royalties on the song – his or any other version – by virtue of the fact that he was registered as the British copyright holder on a public domain song. This annoyed the likes of Pete Seeger – who recorded his own solo vocal version accompanied by the sound of chopping wood to demonstrate the song's older and simpler roots – and Alan Lomax, son of John and esteemed musical folkorist in his own right. In *The Penguin Book of American Folk Songs*, he states:

> John A. Lomax recorded this song at the Cumins State Prison farm, Gould, Arkansas, in 1934 from its convict composer, Kelly Pace. The Negro singer, Lead Belly, heard it, rearranged it in his own style, and made commercial phonograph recordings of it in the 1940s. One of these recordings was studied and imitated phrase by phrase, by a young English singer of American folk songs who subsequently recorded it for an English company. The record sold in the hundreds of thousands in the US and England, and this Arkansas Negro convict song, as adapted by Lead Belly, was published as a personal copyright, words and music, by someone whose contact with the Rock Island Line was entirely through the grooves of a phonograph record.

While Lomax is undoubtedly right, the peeved tone of this is sadly typical of the backbiting, infighting and skullduggery that runs through even the liberal and humane world of folk.

It should be said too that many of the British kids who were knocked out by the crazy new sound would go on to discover the likes of Lead Belly and Howlin' Wolf for themselves. Ironically, some of them – just like Donegan – would go on to become millionaire rock stars by purloining the older, poorer, blacker men's wares. But this is conjecture; and we are getting ahead of ourselves. Lonnie's uptempo reading of 'Rock Island Line' was to spend eight months in the chart, while the Busby Babes took the football league title and ITV took its fledgling steps, Hugh Gaitskell took control of the Labour Party and the Suez crisis darkened the horizon.

Skiffle was soon everywhere, a genuine grassroots phenomenon that spread from scout huts and classrooms to clubs, pubs and dancehalls. But its creative heart, at least symbolically, was a coffee bar on Soho's Old Compton Street called the 2i's, named after its owners the Irani brothers and run by two Australian wrestlers. Here, according to legend, as the Gaggia machine gurgled, the first generation of British rock and rollers learned their skiffle trade: Cliff and The Shadows, Joe Brown, Wee Willie Harris, Tommy Steele, Clem Cattini, Wally Whyton, The Vipers, Chas McDevitt, Johnny Kid, Jet Harris, Mickie Most, Screaming Lord Sutch, Paul Gadd (later Gary Glitter), Ritchie Blackmore (later of Deep Purple). Even its burly bouncer, one Peter Grant, was later to find a kind of rock and roll immortality as the feared and legendary manager of Led Zeppelin.

Out in the industrial towns and the leafy shires, kids acquired the rudimentary equipment needed to play this most joyous music: future rock and folk legends such as Mark Knopfler, Van Morrison, Roger Glover, Albert Lee, Martin Carthy and the aforementioned Jimmy Page all formed skiffle bands. And nowhere more so than in Liverpool, where a group called The Quarrymen were a popular local teenage outfit. At their gig at the Woolton church fête in July 1957, bandleader John Lennon first met a young amateur musician called Paul McCartney and they formed plans for a band together. George Harrison, then a local schoolboy, later reflected on the cultural impact of skiffle, as quoted in Andy Babiuk's *Beatles Gear*:

> There was this big skiffle craze happening for a while in England ... Everybody was in a skiffle group ... All you needed was an acoustic guitar, a washboard with thimbles for percussion, and a tea-chest – you know, the ones they used to ship tea from India – and you just put a broom handle on it and a bit of string, and you had a bass ... you only needed two chords: jing-jinga-jing jing-jinga-jing jing-jinga-jing-jing-jinga-jing. And I think that's basically where I've always been at. I'm just a skiffler, you know. Now I do posh skiffle, that's all it is.

Washboards and thimbles, string basses and broom handles ... there was an element of the quaint to all this, but there was also a deeper and more lasting significance to the skiffle boom. This was, to reiterate, a grassroots, local and defiantly amateur movement, existing outside of the establishment light entertainment world and the stifling strictures of the conventional music business. Witness the sometimes fraught beginnings of skiffle's very own flagship radio show, *Saturday Skiffle Club*. Initially, the prim commissars of BBC management were suspicious about the very notion of a radio show specifically for teenagers. But once this radical notion had been absorbed, auditions were held and early regular performers included the fledgling skiffle-arti: Chas McDevitt, The Vipers, George Melly and, of course, Lonnie Donegan (Cliff

Richard auditioned but was sadly turned down). The powers that be at Broadcasting House were not just concerned at the youthful recklessness of it all. They were also concerned with the material itself. Skiffle songs were often American in origin, even sometimes reflecting the black or working-class experience, and they often used religious themes in a breezy, faintly sacrilegious way. But their fears were allayed, the programme became a huge success and, as the sixties dawned, the 'skiffle' was quietly dropped from the title to become simply *Saturday Club* and Brian Matthew's show was to become a bulwark and mainstay of sixties' British pop life. This in itself was a nice, sweet analogy reflecting how skiffle itself developed into and was absorbed into the musical body politic of pop that was to dominate sixties' culture.

However gently and politely it did it, skiffle reacted against the drably consensual austerity of post-war Britain with homemade and improvised instruments being used to play rough and proletarian music. Soon, many of these skiffle-mad youngsters grew bored with the limits of this basic music. They became accomplished instrumentalists and sought out new avenues of expression. They became the British rock vanguard of the next decade. Something of skiffle's rough mongrel impulse would echo decades later in the upstart glee of punk. But before that, though, British rock would become a potent global force, and its first star was a son of Empire who brought something of the curled-lip sexiness of Elvis to the Lyons Corner House culture of post-war Britain.

5. MOVE IT

Someone once called it the easternmost city of the United States and, from the glittering blustery waterfront at Liverpool, you could see and hear why. Here was a bustling Atlantic seaport full of off-duty sailors, Irish, Chinese, Catholics, black marketeers. Liverpool turns its back on the rest of Lancashire, the rest of England, indeed, and turns its majestic face to Manhattan. Liverpool has always emulated the brash, wisecracking melting-pot mentality of the Big Apple and it was from New York and home to Liverpool that the merchant seamen, 'the Cunard Yanks', as they were known, brought back new and exciting music from across the Atlantic: blues, country, r&b and, most significantly from the mid-1950s onwards, rock and roll. Liverpool heard rock and roll pretty much before the rest of England, and among the first few British kids to hear this new sound would have been John Lennon, George Harrison, Richard Starkey, Paul McCartney and their various school friends. The effect was immediate and far reaching.

It's hard at this remove to understand the visceral shock that hearing the first rock and roll records gave to British teenagers in the

1950s. But even now, the early recordings of Elvis, Little Richard, Eddie Cochran and Jerry Lee Lewis carry an almost electrical jolt that must have fizzed like sodium and illuminated the grey day-to-day landscape of post-war Britain.

Rock and roll was an American mongrel born on the wrong side of the blues, country and gospel, distributed by the crackling new technology of radio stations, recording studios and primitive amplification. Its appeal was its carnal primacy: rock and roll was black slang for sex and the music positively reeked of sweat, perfume and booze, and that appeal was felt instantly by the pallid, hungry young of a bankrupt, bored Britain.

The rest of the country wasn't so sure, though. The establishment, in its various forms, denounced it as debauched, communistic, crude and alien. It wasn't just retired colonels, maiden aunts and shires curates who felt like this. The fledgling *New Musical Express*, faced with the choice of which new music to support – rock and roll or trad jazz – made the explicitly and deliberately political decision to opt for caution and go with Acker Bilk and Kenny Ball over Elvis and Jerry Lee. Its competitor the *Melody Maker* was no keener on rock and roll, calling it 'one of the most terrifying things to happen to popular music. The rock and roll technique, instrumentally and vocally, is the antithesis of all that jazz has been striving for over the years, in other words, good taste and musical integrity.'

By the way, in case you find this toe-curlingly British and fuddy-duddy, here's the hip view from the states on Elvis and rock and roll in 1957, as expressed by one Frank Sinatra in an article he wrote for the *LA Mirror News*:

Sung, played and written for the most part by cretinous goons; and by means of its almost imbecilic reiterations and sly, lewd – in plain fact, dirty – lyrics it manages to be the martial music of every sideburned delinquent on the face of the Earth. His kind of music is deplorable, a rancid-smelling aphrodisiac … it fosters almost totally negative and destructive reactions in young people.

As with so many things, and to misquote Willy Dixon, the men don't know, but the little girls – and lads – understand. Teenage Britain knew the power and worth of rock and roll instantly. The ground had been primed and seeded for the US rock and roll invasion for over a decade, of course. American troops had been stationed here since the Second World War, their glamorous, exotic presence echoed in the music of Glenn Miller: a thrilling source of attraction to British girls and fascinated exasperation to young British males. We shared a language, which not only helped rock and roll music find an audience here but may explain why an American movie with only a slender rock and roll connection would ignite a youth cultural ferment in sleepy post-war Britain.

By the time he put out 'Rock Around the Clock' in 1954 Bill Haley had already had hits with 'Crazy Man, Crazy' and 'Shake, Rattle and Roll'. But 'Rock Around the Clock' became the anthem of rebel youth, particularly in Britain. It was originally a B side that caught the ear of a young film writer/director called Richard Brooks and inspired him to make a film about youth and rock and roll. *Blackboard Jungle* premiered in March of 1955 and caused an instant sensation, earning four Oscar nominations, a Congressional inquiry, an 'X' rating in the UK and $8 million worldwide by 1957. More importantly, it was the film that introduced rock and roll to the world. Compared to *Rebel Without a Cause*, which opened the same year, this is not a movie about kids, but about those struggling to contain them and the perils of delinquency. Clearly, though, the audience took something entirely different from the movie, particularly here in Britain. There were riots at showings and the newly emergent Teddy Boys slashed the seats with razors as Bill Haley and His Comets performed 'Rock Around the Clock' over the opening titles of the film.

The Teddy Boy movement arose from working-class London in about 1953. The peacockery of their Edwardian-style garb – frockcoats, single-breasted, long, fitted and often featuring a velvet trim on the collars and cuffs, worn with narrow trousers, fancy brocade waistcoats, bootlace ties and colourful suede brogues – was a direct and deliberate affront to the wartime ethic of 'make do' and 'get by'. By incorporating elements of upper-class dress into their style, they were challenging the natural order beloved of adult society and the authority of what the Teds refused to accept as their 'social superiors'.

In his autobiography, the working-class Jewish playwright Steven Berkoff and former Ted recalls:

… you would always have your suits tailor-made even if it took a year of saving and many months of privation. A suit was your armour and your colours and further defined your sense of aesthetics. Thus costumed (in the fullest sense of the word), Berkoff the Teddy Boy was free to perform his image of himself on the dance floor. The jive was one of the greatest dance forms ever invented. And so all your arts were in some way fulfilled. You were the dandy, the mover and performer in your own drama, the roving hunter and lover, the actor adopting for the girl the mask of your choice.

At the Elephant and Castle, home turf of South London Teddy Boys, riots in the cinema were said to have led to 2,000 young people taking to the streets in an orgy of vandalism, according to lurid, excitable newspaper reports. By today's standards it seems to have been a fairly quiet riot: nine arrests, two policemen injured, some cups and saucers thrown about the streets and one or two £1 fines awarded. More seriously, Teddy Boys were very visible participants in the racial tension and violence which boiled over in the summer of 1958 in Nottingham and Notting Hill Gate.

Teddy Boys soon had their very own films too. A whole series of 'social problem' films about the Teddy Boy phenomenon were released at the end of the fifties and early sixties, such as *Cosh Boy*, *Violent Playground*, *Sapphire*, *The Angry Silence*, *Wind of Change*, *Flame in the Streets* and *The Boys* to name only the most prominent. *Blackboard Jungle* and the following year's spin-off *Rock Around the Clock*, from the Haley and His Comets tune, helped the song to top the UK chart in 1955 and, after a three-week break, again in 1956. It also ignited a moral panic as young cinema-goers ripped up and slashed seats and danced in the aisle, and rock and roll became associated in the minds of adult authority with the unruly and the delinquent. The *NME* stuck with trad jazz for the time being, but rock and roll simply would not be stopped. Elvis Presley reached number two in the UK chart with 'Heartbreak Hotel' in 1956 and had nine more singles in the top thirty that year. Soon would follow the first generation of rock and roll icons, Little Richard, Eddie Cochran, Jerry Lee Lewis, Gene Vincent, Chuck Berry and the rest.

Adult Britain couldn't stamp out rock and roll so it did the next best thing, it accommodated and absorbed it into the mainstream. Television in particular wanted to court these new adolescent rock and rollers. The BBC's *Six-Five Special* featured homegrown rock and rollers such as Adam Faith, Marty Wilde, Vince Eager and Johnny Gentle. Producer Jack Good wanted to drop all the non-musical elements from the show and concentrate on music. But the BBC refused, Good resigned and went to ITV to produce the first all-music teen TV show, *Oh Boy!*, which in 1958 gave a TV début to a future fixture of British entertainment and the third-biggest-selling artist in British pop history.

Harry Webb was born in Lucknow, India, in 1940 to British parents working in catering management for the Indian railways. On returning to England Harry became keen on skiffle and joined the Quintones, then the Dick Teague Skiffle Group, before getting a deal with legendary producer Norrie Paramor. For the B side of planned début single 'Schoolboy Crush', Paramor let Cliff sing 'Move It', a song written by a member of backing band The Drifters, soon to rename themselves The Shadows. The story goes that Paramor's daughter and *Oh Boy!* producer Jack Good both much preferred this original. Ahead of his performance on the show, Cliff said, 'It's wonderful to be going on TV for the first time, but I feel so nervous that I don't know what to do. I shaved my sideburns off last night ... Jack Good said it would make me look more original.'

Richard performed 'Move It' on *Oh Boy!*, and British rock and roll was born. The planned single was flipped, and climbed to number two in the charts, starting Cliff Richard on a career that continues to this day. We think of Cliff now, a little unfairly, as the Centre Court-serenading slightly prickly grand old man of bland. But the Cliff who sang 'Move It' was a brooding, animal presence who rightly drew comparisons with Elvis. And 'Move It', if lacking the feral darkness of 'Heartbreak Hotel', is a skeletal shuffling piece of proto-rock that still sounds lean and gripping.

Cliff and The Shadows were enormously influential on British rock, creating the drums, bass, rhythm and lead guitar template for generations of bands. The influence of bespectacled guitarist Hank Marvin cannot be overstated either. He owned the first Fender Stratocaster in the UK, serial number 34346, finished in Fiesta Red, with gold hardware, and imported into Britain by Cliff Richard. This Strat, with its tremolo arm, played through a few simple effects boxes with great verve and clarity by Marvin, made a generation of British males pick up a guitar, or at the very least a tennis racket.

After the urgency of 'Move It', Cliff and The Shadows soon transferred to a smoother, softer pop ballad style and starred in a series of prim, saccharine films which, if easy to mock, were vastly superior to Elvis's cheap, idiotic sixties movie output. But the die was cast. Rock and roll had gotten under the skin of British youth and it was an itch that had to be scratched. A young tugboat man on the Mersey, Ronald Wycherley, turned up at one of Larry Parnes's shows in Liverpool, blagged a backstage audition and found himself onstage within minutes. Rechristened Billy Fury, his 10-inch vinyl ten-track début *The Sound of Fury* – gutsy, infectious, and entirely self-penned – only scraped into the top twenty, but is now regarded as perhaps the first British rock album and a landmark in British music. Another *bona fide* British rock and roll classic of the period was 'Shakin' All Over' by Johnny Kidd and The Pirates, with its effects-heavy guitar playing by Joe Moretti and the drumming of the legendary Clem Cattini, the doyen of British session drummers, who has played on forty-four number-one singles. Like The Shadows, their line-up of bassist, drummer, single guitarist and sole non-guitar-playing singer became a classic British rock line-up used by, among others, Led Zeppelin (of whom hours of bootleg tapes exist of them covering Pirates' songs) and

The Who. It was after seeing The Pirates that Pete Townshend told Roger Daltrey to stop playing guitar on stage and concentrate on being a singing frontman.

British rock and roll then transmuted into British rock and the protagonists disappeared into history. Kidd and Fury both died young, one in a car crash, the other of heart disease. Cliff Richard went on to become an institution with hits through six decades.

Later, rock and roll came to be regarded as a somewhat curious antique fad, like morris dancing or brass bands, revived in vaguely comic style by Showaddywaddy, Shakin' Stevens or Alvin Stardust. Jiving was something that one's skilled aunt and uncle would perform at a wedding when their song came on, a song that might well be 'Move It' or 'Shakin' All Over'. Teds went on to be, to those of us who grew up in the seventies and eighties, the sworn enemies of punk rockers (for some reason), and find work mainly as bus drivers and conductors, or on the dodgems at funfairs. But as their inked tattoos would often say, as well as 'Mum and Dad' and 'love and hate', 'rock and roll won't never die'. And it didn't.

6. TELSTAR

It looked a little like a baseball, except a baseball about three feet high and weighing some 170 pounds, and on 10 July 1962 it was flung into space, into an orbit around the Earth, and into history. The launch of the satellite Telstar marked the beginning of the modern telecommunications era, maybe even the modern world. Around the globe that day, thanks to Telstar, the first vague wobbling images from the other side of the world emerged from a blizzard of interference onto black and white TV sets into the living rooms of Britain. In one such room sat a troubled, tormented, visionary record producer and musician savant called Joe Meek. Something in the mystery, optimism and otherworldiness embodied by the flight of that lonely piece of space hardware appealed to him, and inspired him to create a piece of music that still buzzes and crackles with the thrill and the promise of tomorrow.

Before The Beatles, before The Stones, before The Who or any of the more celebrated and perhaps credible British rock invaders, 'Telstar' by The Tornadoes was the first UK record to top the American charts. But that's just part of its significance. It was also a sonic revolution, provoked a famous legal battle, and tells a tale of mystery and tragedy. From The Beatles' tape loops to David Bowie to Depeche Mode; from the Aphex Twin to acid house to Kraftwerk; and from The Human League to Gary Numan to Grime, it points the way to the music of the future. But more than that it captured a new mood abroad in the Britain of the early 1960s, one which had started with the Skylon and Dan Dare in the 1950s and would reach its zenith with Harold Wilson's government and its almost fanboy worship of science and zeal for a Britain forged in what Wilson called 'the white heat of the technological revolution'.

David Egerton of Imperial College, London, states that, 'In 1960 Great Britain was, without doubt, the scientific and technological powerhouse of Western Europe.' By 1963 that scientific fervour had spread from the laboratories and workshops to the streets and pop culture. In the same autumn that Harold Wilson made his famous speech about the white heat of technology to the Labour Party Conference, Britain was also getting excited about a new TV show chronicling the adventures in space of a time-travelling eccentric, and the effects, both beneficial and worrying, of the dizzying speed of scientific advance. A huge part of the show's undoubted appeal was its fabulous theme tune, written by Ron Grainer and realised electronically by Delia Derbyshire of the BBC Radiophonic Workshop, home to the corporation's in-house boffins and pioneers of electronic sound. Here, as in so many other fields, Britain was forging ahead. The *Dr Who* theme thrilled (and continued to thrill) generations of young British musicians. With all due respect to John Cage and Karlheinz Stockhausen, it's no exaggeration to say that Delia's handiwork must be the most famous and influential piece of electronic music ever made.

As well as the dandyish Doctor, another idiosyncratic aristocrat became emblematic of Britain's rush into the technological future. Anthony Neil Wedgwood Benn, the second Viscount Stansgate, now plain Tony Benn, was Wilson's minister of technology and the man seen carving out a new meritocratic, technocratic open Britain in contrast to the class-divided, tweedy old United Kingdom of Harold Macmillan and Alec Douglas-Home. *Private Eye* lampooned Benn as Wedgie the Whizz and talked mockingly of 'Benn's Hover Britain'. But the truth was that Britain really was leading the world. A very visible symbol of this was the Post Office tower, a futuristic edifice that dominated the Bloomsbury skyline and appeared within weeks of construction in an episode of *Dr Who*, itself a part of the new sci-fi Britain.

The white heat of the technological revolution was not just burning in the West End, though. In a less salubrious part of North London, 304 Holloway Road, above a leather goods store, a troubled boy from Gloucestershire was changing the sound of pop for ever in a three-storey flat.

Joe Meek, the English Phil Spector, the lost genius of British electronic music, was born Robert George Meek in Newent, Gloucestershire, on 5 April 1929. A quiet, creative child, the rural lads regarded Joe's delicate artistic nature with suspicion. Even his own brother Eric claimed, 'We always said Joe should have been a girl. We used to call him a cissie. And he would usually fly into a tantrum and storm off up to the shed. He thought we were gross and mad. We thought he was feminine, rather than a boy, because he would rather dress up in some fancy clothes and be prancing about up the shed, doing a play or something.' The 'or something' often involved experimenting with any old gramophone or wireless kit he could take the back off.

Before he was ten he had discovered that yelling close to the pick-up of a gramophone during the run-off grooves produced a faintly audible recording there, and around the same time he constructed a short-wave radio out of junked parts. He subscribed to *Practical Wireless*, staged outdoor discos with speakers hung in the trees for the local cherry-pickers and made his first recording in his early teens – an acetate of brother Eric's girlfriend singing a popular dance tune. His national service in the Royal Air Force as a radar technician spurred a lifelong interest in electronics and outer space. From 1953 he worked for the Midlands Electricity Board before quitting to work as an audio engineer. Over the next few years he engineered and produced countless sessions for various UK record companies and worked on dozens of hit records: pop, skiffle, jazz, rock and roll, folk, blues, calypso and light orchestral works. Some of these period pieces are as odd and fascinating as his later experimental independent work. His 'Teddy Boy Calypso' was that most niche of compositions, a jaunty calypso advocating the return of naval-style capital punishment for unruly youths.

But his breakthrough came with his recording of Humphrey Lyttleton's jazz single 'Bad Penny Blues' when, against Lyttleton's wishes, Meek showed his experimental flair by modifying the sound of the piano, phasing the mikes, distorting the bass line and over-recording the brushed drums. Lyttleton was away while Meek mixed the track. He returned to find it finished and had to admit that, while he would never have approved it, it had something. The record became a big hit and an undoubted later influence on one Paul McCartney when he wrote 'Lady Madonna'.

After a stint at Denis Preston's Lansdowne Studios Meek struck out on his own as RGM Sound Ltd with toy importer Major Wilfred Alonzo Banks as his financial backer. He operated from his home studio which he constructed above the handbags and belts on Holloway Road. Most of Meek's early work here is undistinguished fare with one very notable exception. As the new decade began, Meek conceived, wrote and produced an 'Outer Space Music Fantasy' concept album called *I Hear a New World*. Marketed at the time as a stereo test disc, with less than 100 copies pressed, this bizarre sci-fi suite was perhaps the strangest artefact in a strange career: a whimsical, sweet, sinister electronic evocation of other-world civilisations called Globbots and Dribcots, recorded late at night and utilising sound effects like scraped combs, bubbles being blown in water, smashed glass, broken clockwork toys, radio interference, backwards tapes and toilets being flushed. Baffled record companies and their cutting engineers even refused to master some of his recordings from this period, claiming they would damage domestic speakers. The album was shelved for decades, apart from some EP tracks taken from it, but it became a cult item and is often cited by modern electronic musicians for its strangeness and far-sightedness.

Joe's next major venture was as successful as *I Hear a New World* was ignored and misunderstood. He teamed up with a Berkshire lad, initially with a view to making him a pop star called Anton Hollywood. But under his real name of Geoff Goddard he and Meek formed a songwriting partnership that soon found out that death sells, especially when draped in reverb, echo, ghostly girly vocals and high camp. Singer John Leyton remembers the recording: 'I was in the sitting room behind a little screen, and the rhythm section was in the room with me. The violin section was on the stairs, the backing singers were practically in the loo, and the brass section was underneath, on another floor altogether. And there was Joe next door, playing his machine like another musical instrument. It was quite bizarre.'

'Johnny Remember Me' spent fifteen weeks at the top of the chart in 1961. The insane DIY set-up Leyton remembers horrified the recording establishment. Arranger Martin Slavin railed in *Melody Maker*: 'A recording studio is the place to record. They are there for that specific purpose and they have the best technicians in their employ.' Joe responded in true punk maverick style: 'I would be a fool to listen to an arranger with a bee in his bonnet. I make records to entertain the public, not square connoisseurs who just don't know.'

Joe's obsessions were many and varied. Like Goddard, he was fascinated by the occult. He held seances regularly. But Joe never lost the childlike fascination with space evident on *I Hear a New World* and so, like the rest of the world, he watched in wide-eyed delight as, in early July 1962, the first shaky pictures from Telstar emerged. In the middle of the night Joe came up with a tune, which like all his compositions had to be *lah-lahed* at actual musicians to transcribe. In this case it was Dave Adams, summoned in the small hours to decipher Meek's warblings and subsequently rewarded with a co-writing credit. Meek's session band The Tornados, featuring George Bellamy, father of Muse's Matt, were called to London during a break from their summer season in Great Yarmouth. They laid down the basic instrumental track for 'Telstar' and its B side in a hectic session before having to leave for their next Yarmouth performance.

Meek added studio gimmicks galore, canyons of reverberation, reversed tapes, including another loo flushing it was said, but, most significant of all, Geoff Goddard added the thrilling lead keyboard line on a primitive electric valve organ called a clavioline, which produced a reedy sound and was capable of playing only one note at a time. It was Geoff's habit of wordlessly singing to himself while playing which produced the unearthly vocal echoes.

'Telstar' was released in August 1962, sped to number one in the UK and, astonishingly, emulated that feat in America before remaining at the top of the charts on both sides of the Atlantic for half a year. The record went on to sell 15 million copies.

But the stories of 'Telstar' the gleaming technological innovation and 'Telstar' the emblem of Joe Meek's success have weird echoes of each other. Initially both were on everyone's lips, on every front page and enormously successful. Meek had another huge number one with Heinz's 'Just Like Eddie', one of many tunes featuring future Deep Purple axe hero Ritchie Blackmore on lead guitar.

But then, without warning, AT&T's satellite fell silent and ceased operating. Radiation from a nuclear test back on Earth destroyed the delicate circuitry and the most cutting-edge technology became a chunk of space junk in an instant. Soon after, Meek's star began to lose its lustre. Lame 'Telstar' follow-ups 'Robot' and 'Joystick' were pale, and far less successful, imitations. Worse, a French composer, Jean Ledrut, claimed Meek had stolen the tune from an obscure piece of his own from a film called *The Battle of Austerlitz*. Meek's royalties were frozen at £29,000 and the case was mired in the French courts for years.

Like 'Telstar', Meek was falling to Earth. He was a gay man at a time when it was dangerous and illegal to be so, making him a hunted and haunted individual. He was arrested for importuning in a gents' toilet at Madras Place, just off Holloway Road. The fine of £15 meant little to Meek but the scandal tainted him at a time when homosexuality was regarded with fear and hatred by many.

After 'Have I the Right' by The Honeycombs in 1964, the hits dried up, he was viewed with some suspicion within the business and his personal life became more bizarre. The tantrums and pill popping increased. He was once spotting running down the Holloway Road in his pyjamas, screaming that someone was chasing him with a knife. He was found beaten, unconscious, in his famous red Ford Zodiac. It was said he was in contact with Aleister Crowley and Rameses the Great via occult ceremonies. If so, they were about the only people returning Joe's calls in 1967.

That year, on the morning of 3 February, Meek, by now broke, paranoid and dressing only in black (and convinced his studio was bugged by the police), was trying without much success to record a track with his assistant Patrick Pink. Sending Patrick out, Meek shouted for him to send his landlady, Mrs Shenton, up. An argument was heard, and then a gunshot. Joe had shot her with a gun belonging to Heinz. As Patrick Pink tried to tend to the dying woman, Joe calmly reloaded and blew his own brains out. Coincidence or not, it was eight years to the day since his idol Buddy Holly had died.

Two hundred people attended Meek's funeral in Newent. And in the intervening years the cult of Joe Meek has grown and grown. If he'd lived, he'd have been the same age as George Martin, a producer whose story is a very different one but with whom Meek can genuinely claim to share a kinship, as one of the great sonic pioneers of British pop. In one of pop's most tantalising might-have-beens, The Beatles almost allied themselves with the Meek stable but went instead with the *de facto* team of George Martin and Brian Epstein, a fact that caused Joe bitterness in later years. He later derided The Beatles as 'matchbox music' and 'just another bunch of noise, copying other people's music' but did show up for the occasional red-carpet invite from Epstein.

So we will never know what Joe's version of 'Strawberry Fields' would have sounded like. But we do know that 'Telstar' was a timeless slice of revolutionary pop. The same year Joe Meek died, the ones that got away elevated the recording studio itself to an instrument akin to a symphony, and brought effects, tape loops, sound collages and the like to their artistic and commercial acme with the release of *Sgt Pepper* ... Maybe this Meek didn't inherit the Earth, but British bedroom boffins like him did. From Tim Berners-Lee, inventor of the World Wide Web, to Jonathan Ive, the Newcastle Polytechnic student who designed the iMac, the iPod and the iPad, the geek inherited the earth. Joe Meek heard a new world, and forty years later that world is the one we live in.

7. SHE LOVES YOU

1963 was a year of change, upheaval and seismic shocks in Britain. True, we had nothing on this side of the Atlantic quite as traumatic and tragic as the November assassination of President Kennedy. But it was an eventful year nonetheless. We'd never had it so good, as Prime Minister Harold Macmillan told us, and the economic upturn went on. Some people still weren't getting rich quick enough. A bunch of them stole one and a half million pounds form a Royal Mail train in Buckinghamshire and earned themselves the name the Great Train Robbers – although, as has been said, they robbed one train, and they got caught. Not that great, really. On a more positive note American Express came to Britain, the Dartford Tunnel and the National Theatre Company opened, as did stretches of the M6 and M4. On these modern highways would soon run the newly manufactured Mini and Hillman Imp. When it stopped snowing, that is.

The year began with the country in the iron grip of the harshest winter for two centuries, a freeze that lasted from Boxing Day to March. But the thaw of that spring extended beyond the merely meteorological. Skirts got shorter, hair got longer, wages and hemlines went up, and famously, according to Philip Larkin, it was the year that Britain discovered sex, 'Between the end of the Chatterley ban/And the Beatles' first LP'.

And with sex came scandal. In 1963 a further blow to the old certainties and proprieties came with the shocking revelation that the minister for war, John Profumo, had been conducting an affair with a call girl by the name of Christine Keeler. Worse, Keeler had also been sleeping with the Soviet military attaché. And worst of all, Profumo lied about all this in the House of Commons. Shock waves ran through the establishment, Macmillan's government was permanently damaged and soon fell. Meanwhile, on the other side of the House, a pipe-smoker from Huddersfield called Harold Wilson became Leader of the Opposition. The North was on the rise, as seen with new TV shows like *Coronation Street*, in the writings of Shelagh Delaney, Keith Waterhouse, Stan Barstow, David Storey and Alan Sillitoe, and films based on their works, like *A Kind of Loving*, *Saturday Night and Sunday Morning* and *A Taste of Honey*. And perhaps most significant of all, that March, as the ice finally melted and the sun finally came out, a new, young, invigorating sound heralded a fresh post-ice age Britain.

You can almost see the change in British culture in the way The Beatles' image changed between their formation in 1960 and their global breakthrough in 1963. The quartet that played the clubs of Hamburg's Reeperbahn are sporting greasy quiffs, leather jackets and heavy-duty jeans with turn-ups. It is a style that is most definitely looking back to the fifties rather than towards the swinging sixties. Now look at The Beatles in 1963. The grease has been washed out, replaced by the softer mop-top cuts. The rocker uniform of denim and leather has given way to smart suits, Nehru jackets and a sharper, more modern aesthetic. Most of these moves had been masterminded by their new manager, Brian Epstein. But the biggest and most obvious change between The Beatles of Hamburg and The Beatles of *Ready Steady Go!* is that two members have gone – the brooding arty Stu Sutcliffe and the heartthrob drummer Pete Best – to be replaced by one Richard 'Ringo' Starkey, a sickly youth from the Dingle, part jester, part stooge and the man whose brisk, thrilling one-second drum roll ushers in one of the most exciting pieces of music the world had ever heard up to that point.

It's a common complaint of the serious, even snobbish rock fan that there are too many 'manufactured' bands around these days. Often such fans, generally male, contrast this contemporary phenomenon with proper classic rock bands like The Beatles. And yet, viewed by any sensible criteria, The Beatles were a manufac- tured band, manufactured largely by Brian Epstein, the Liverpool department-store entrepreneur who'd become their manager. The most obvious manifestation of this was the ruthless removal of drummer Pete Best. The reasons surrounding this are still pretty murky. Some say Epstein did it at the instigation of George Martin, who was unimpressed by Best's drumming at the early audition. George Martin himself disputes this, saying that he merely wanted a session drummer on the first recordings. Other versions say that Harrison, McCartney and Lennon were only too glad to be rid of a band member who had never really fitted in and was annoyingly popular with female fans. Whatever the truth, after much agonising, Epstein broke the news to Best that he was no longer a Beatle on 16 August 1962.

Some other pieces of skilful manufacturing were undoubtedly all Epstein's idea. Having always been a lover of the theatre and once nurturing an ambition to be a dress designer, Epstein had strong notions about clothes and presentation. He set about making the Beatles look less aggressive and more palatable to record companies and venues. According to Lennon, Epstein said:

> 'Look, if you really want to get in these bigger places, you're going to have to change … stop eating on stage, stop swearing, stop smoking …' We used to dress how we liked, on and off stage. He'd tell us that jeans were not particularly smart and could we possibly manage to wear proper trousers … it was a choice between making it or still eating chicken on stage.

Far from resisting this blatantly manufactured image, the band happily agreed. The firebrand Lennon's response to Epstein's request for the group to wear suits was, 'Yeah, man, all right, I will wear a suit – I'll wear a bloody balloon if somebody's paying me.'

Thus The Beatles turned up at Manchester's Playhouse Theatre in early 1962 for their first radio appearance wearing slim-fit grey mohair suits with skinny lapels, white shirts and thin black ties custom made by Beno Dorm, 'the Master Tailor for Impeccable Hand Made Clothes' in Birkenhead, and hair at Horne Brothers salon replacing their previous Tony Curtis DA cuts. Overnight the Fab Four had gone from brooding rockers to mop-topped mods.

It all paid off. Without Pete Best, without the quiffs and without the leathers, the newly made-over Beatles passed their audition, persuaded George Martin that their own song 'Love Me Do' was a better first single than the Mitch Murray song 'How Do You Do It?' (later taken to number one by fellow scousers Gerry and The Pacemakers) and the rest is history, not just of British pop but of the modern world. 'Love Me Do', 'Please Please Me' and 'From Me to

You' were all hits in quick succession. In ten hours, on 11 February 1963, they recorded their début album, *Please Please Me*. Eight of the songs were Lennon and McCartney originals, the band played all the instruments themselves and thus the template of the modern rock album was set. It was the first of eleven number-one albums over the next seven years. They were on tour for practically all of the first half of the year, and on 26 June 1963, sitting on their twin beds in a Newcastle hotel, John Lennon and Paul McCartney wrote the bulk of a new song which would be completed at the McCartney family home on Forthlin Road, Liverpool, the next day. The idea for the song was an unusual one in that the song is narrated in the third person, from an outside observer offering his point of view on a friend's relationship. Lennon later credited McCartney with the idea: 'It was Paul's idea: instead of singing "I love you" again, we'd have a third party. That kind of little detail is still in his work. He will write a story about someone. I'm more inclined to write about myself.'

This small but significant twist was indicative of the freshness and originality that the young band were bringing to pop. Five days later they assembled in studio two of EMI's Abbey Road Studios in St John's Wood to record the new song with George Martin and engineer Norman 'Hurricane' Smith, later to have hits of his own in the seventies with a series of camp retro sing-along numbers. Smith took a look at the lyric sheet and his heart sank: 'I was setting up the microphone when I saw the lyrics on the music stand. I thought, I'll just have a quick look. "She Loves You, Yeah, Yeah, Yeah; She Loves You, Yeah, Yeah, Yeah; She Loves You, Yeah, Yeah, Yeah." I thought, Oh my god, what a lyric! This is going to be one that I do not like.'

Doubts were assuaged, though, when the band began to play. George Martin remembers:

I was sitting in my usual place on a high stool when Paul and John ran through it on their acoustic guitars. George joined in on the choruses. I thought it was great but was intrigued by the final chord, an odd sort of major sixth, with George doing the sixth and John and Paul the third and fifths, like a Glenn Miller arrangement. They were saying "It's a great chord! Nobody's ever heard it before!" Of course I knew that wasn't quite true.

Martin thought this ending was corny. The band disagreed. Posterity was to prove them right. During the recording of the song there came a striking display of the mounting ferment that was already being called Beatlemania. Second engineer Geoff Emerick recalls in his book *Here There and Everywhere*:

On this particular day, The Beatles had, unusually, shown up hours before the session to pose for pictures in an alleyway behind the studio, giving the girls plenty of time to call their friends, and the crowd had swelled even larger than usual … somehow the huge crowd of girls had overpowered the police and broken through the front door. Dozens of rabid fans were racing around the EMI facility in desperate search of the Fab Four. 'It's a bloody madhouse out there. You've got to see it to believe it,' shouted Neil … There's no doubt in my mind that the excitement of the day helped spark a new level of energy in the group's playing … There was a level of intensity in that performance that I had not heard before and have rarely heard since. I still judge that single to be one of the most exciting performances of The Beatles' entire career.

On 23 August 1963 'She Loves You' was released in the United Kingdom. In less than a month it sold three quarters of a million copies, the fastest-selling record of any kind in UK history. It was the bestselling single of 1963 and remains the bestselling Beatles single in Britain today. It remained the bestselling single in the United Kingdom for fourteen years until overtaken by a song called 'Mull of Kintyre'. A hit for one Paul McCartney. At the time of 'She Loves You's release, there were more than a few wet blankets and naysayers around. The 'Yeah, Yeah, Yeah' refrain, slangy and clearly American, upset some, even Paul McCartney's dad. McCartney junior later remembered:

> We sat in there one evening, just beavering away while my dad was watching TV and smoking his Player's cigarettes, and we wrote 'She Loves You'. We actually finished it there because we'd started it in the hotel room. We went into the living room: 'Dad, listen to this. What do you think?' So we played it to my dad and he said, 'That's very nice, son, but there's enough of these Americanisms around. Couldn't you sing, "She loves you. Yes! Yes! Yes!?"' At which point we collapsed in a heap and said, 'No, Dad, you don't quite get it!'

But Jim McCartney was not alone. Many critics hated the 'yeah, yeah, yeah' refrain, including top DJ Brian Matthew, who dismissed it in the *Melody Maker* as 'banal rubbish'. East German Communist leader Walter Ulbricht famously claimed the song to be symbolic of the decadent culture of the West: 'The monotony of the yeah, yeah, yeah, and whatever it is called.'

The British Marxist historian Eric Hobsbawm, writing pseudo-nymously in the *New Statesman*, said that 'in twenty years, they will be forgotten'.

They were wrong. 'She Loves You' will be remembered long after Hobsbawm, Ulbricht and you and I, dear reader, are forgotten. It is perhaps the quintessential early Beatles song and quite simply one of the most explosive and exciting pop records ever made. And its sound is unmistakably that of a country shifting on its axis, turning away from a decade of conservatism and constraint to one of flamboyance and liberalism. The great American composer Aaron Copland understood this when he said, 'If you want to know about the sixties, play the music of The Beatles.' Even more specifically, if you want to know about England in 1963, listen to 'She Loves You'. And listen to another record from the same year, the sound of a young woman, a young music and a young country whose people would start to forge modern Britain.

8. MY BOY LOLLIPOP

It's become a modern commonplace for the professional grump to grizzle about Twitter, Facebook, email, Angry Birds and every other manifestation of the modern wired world. But even those churls rarely harrumph about the ways in which a cornucopia of varied cultural delights that once languished in reels in the basements of TV companies, only to be seen at the whim of a producer or scheduler, are now available to all. The past is a foreign country, they do things differently there, but thanks to YouTube we can see just how differently, and sometimes just how joyously.

Take, for instance, *The Millie Show*, first shown on Finnish television in 1964 and unlikely to have been seen much since until the coming of the internet. And what a loss that would have been. The production values are spartan: shot in monochrome, naturally, on a minimalist set adorned with the odd freestanding poster, foam plastic cubes and tetrahedrons, a few desultory go-go dancers. But at the heart of all this, and it truly it is its heart, is a young West Indian girl of sixteen, in Capri pants and a white mohair jumper, singing a song with the innocence of a nursery rhyme and the timeless exuberance of all great pop.

There have been deeper, more complex, more musically rich records in the history of British pop than 'My Boy Lollipop'. But there has never been a more joyous or a more significant one. For without this young girl, one of twelve children of a sugar plantation worker raised in a thatched shack in Milk River, Clarendon, Jamaica, the whole future of British music – from The Clash to Steel Pulse; from the sound systems of the Notting Hill carnival to stadium gigs by UB40 and The Police; from Madness to The Specials to ragga, dancehall and Tinie Tempah – the last forty years of pop would have been very different and much less colourful.

The only thing colourful on that grey, choppy, chilly day in 1948 at Tilbury when the SS *Empire Windrush* docked were the dazzling ties of some of the disembarking passengers, as reported in the *Thurrock Gazette*. The *Daily Mirror* reported with a hint of suspicion that 'many of the 492 Jamaican emigrants who arrived in Britain yesterday in the *Empire Windrush* wore expensive suits. There were even emigrants wearing zoot-style suits – very long-waisted jackets, big padded shoulders, slit pockets and peg-top trousers.' In fact, many of the arrivals had made their suits from high-quality Canadian blankets issued for bedding on the long crossing. The paper was characteristically even-handed, though, in its summing up: 'They are, then, as heterodox a collection of humanity as one might find. Some will be good workers, some bad. Many are "serious minded persons" anxious to succeed.'

Why had they come, then, these intrepid, wary travellers from a land of sunshine and warmth, to this bleak Thames Estuary port in a country still ashen and wounded from war? For a better life, as all immigrants do. The Jamaican *Daily Gleaner* newspaper had recently run an advert offering cheap transport to the UK (£28 10s for below-decks accommodation, forty-odd pounds if you wanted a cabin) for anyone who wanted to come to work in and help with the reconstruction of a Britain ravaged by six years of war. Many of the men who decided to make the journey on the *Windrush* were veterans of the war themselves, often RAF personnel who had served the 'mother country' in the fight against the Nazis. Some, not unreasonably, just wanted to see what this Great Britain place was all about. As one said much later, 'I wanted to see the Parliament where they decide my fate. I want to live there, man.'

Despite Britain's urgent, desperate labour shortage, and the fact that the immigrants had every legal right to come here, there were, from the moment of arrival, whispers, grumbles and outright hostility. 'No Irish, No Blacks, No Dogs' was the famously inhospitable sign in the windows of boarding houses. Questions were asked in Parliament about the legality of the 'invasion', as more than one paper called it, and about how long these fellows were intending to stay. Back home, the Jamaican colonial administration were also not keen on losing people in this way. The *Gleaner* itself reprinted a *Manchester Guardian* article that was cool on the notion, to say the least:

A large number of unskilled Jamaican workers, mostly men, propose to travel to the United Kingdom in the troopship *Empire Windrush* leaving Jamaica towards the end of the month, in search of work. The government of Jamaica desires to inform these travellers that the prospects of employment in England for unskilled labourers are very slight, and advises them to secure a definite offer of employment before leaving the island. It is made clear, however, to these men seeking to go on the *Empire Windrush* in search of employment in England … that no guarantee can be given that they will get the employment they seek.

Still, nearly 500 chose to make the month-long trip, each with a signature from the authorities confirming that they were responsible citizens and not 'trouble-makers'. The youngest was thirteen; there were fifteen stowaways; but three quarters were skilled workers, well educated and knowledgeable about the UK. On board were Euton Christian, destined to become Britain's first black magistrate, and Sam King, future black mayor of Southwark, whose family had sold three of their prize cows to pay for his passage. And from the very moment the ship docked part of its cargo was new and exciting music.

Two of the first of the new arrivals to make themselves known were the calypso musicians Lord Beginner and Lord Kitchener. The latter was a vibrant and voluble presence on ship who staged his own early one-man Live Aid during the crossing to pay the passage of a stowaway woman. Inspired by the promise of his new home, he was moved to compose 'London Is the Place for Me' which he serenaded the Tilbury quayside with from the *Windrush*'s gangplank.

Exactly a decade later, another boat headed in the opposite direction came ashore in a less controlled fashion on the island that the *Windrush* had sailed from. A young British man called Chris Blackwell, assistant to Sir Hugh Foot, governor general of Jamaica, was forced to swim for his life when his boat ran aground on a coral reef off Helshire Beach. The twenty-one-year-old made it to the shore where, exhausted, traumatised and dehydrated, he collapsed on the sand. Blackwell was discovered by a party of Rastafarian fishermen who nursed him back to health with natural remedies and Ital food. For the young Englishman it was a pivotal experience and the beginning of a lifelong love affair with the island's music, culture and spirituality.

Later that year, with a loan of £10,000 from his parents, Blackwell launched a record label intended to showcase Jamaican music to the world. He named it Island Records after Jamaica itself and Alec Waugh's novel and movie *Island in the Sun*, a hit song for Harry Belafonte. By 1962, when Blackwell returned to England, the fledgling producer had put out twenty-six singles and two albums which had attracted niche interest among the cognoscenti. That was all about to change when he discovered a fifteen-year-old-girl singer called Millie Small, who'd made a handful of singles in Jamaica.

Convinced of her appeal, he assumed legal guardianship of her with her mother's consent, paid for an economy class BOAC air ticket and brought the teenager to England along with guitarist and arranger Ernest Ranglin, one of the house band at Studio One, Kingston, known as the Motown of the West Indies. In a studio in unfashionable Forest Hill they recorded a cover version of Barbie Gaye's 'My Boy Lollipop' from 1956. Over the years a persistent and baseless rumour has circulated that a young Rod Stewart played the harmonica on 'My Boy Lollipop'. In fact it was Pete Hogman of The Pete Hogman Blues Band and Hoggie & The Sharpetones: 'The backing for "My Boy Lollypop" was recorded live in the studio. I played harmonica and Ernest Ranglin played a black Gibson. Several people have claimed to have played the harmonica break but I can promise you it was me, and it was all recorded in London.' The confusion seems to spring from a passing resemblance between Hogman and Stewart and both being sometime members of the 5 Dimensions, a UK blues outfit who provide backing on 'My Boy Lollipop'. Stewart himself has always denied ever being present at the recording.

When Blackwell heard the finished version, complete with Ranglin's staccato, bouncy guitar chops, sassy horn arrangement, chugging harmonica and Millie Small's deliciously infectious schoolgirl vocal, with its hiccups and yelps of delight, he knew he had a hit on his hands, thanks, in particular, to the unique sound, never heard before on a British record, as he told journalist Dan Daley:

> The reverb came from a sort of cupboard in the back of the studio that we used as a live chamber. It was a mono record, and we fed the sound in, adding a bit more of the reverb on Millie's voice. The record worked well for radio, but partly because it was a minute and fifty-one seconds. That was important for people at radio who were putting play-lists together. Also, Millie's voice was irresistible – for a certain length of time, anyway. So a short record worked well for her. I didn't put it on Island because I knew it was going to be so big. Independent labels in those days couldn't handle hits, because you couldn't pay the pressing plant in time to supply the demand, so I licensed it to Fontana, which was part of Phillips. It was a big hit all around the world, and I really wanted to look after Millie, so I went everywhere with her, which took me into the mainstream of the record industry.

Thus Millie's kittenish, lovable tune has a huge double significance in the history of British music. On a practical level for Blackwell, it was his entrée into the music business. Island would build on Millie's global success (number two here and in America, number one in Ireland and Australia, with seven million copies sold worldwide) and become the label that fostered superstars such as Bob Marley, Roxy Music, Traffic, Grace Jones and U2 as well as revered cult artistes like Richard Thompson and Nick Drake. (Bizarrely, in 1970, Millie would cover Drake's obscure 'Mayfair' in a ska style for a single, the B side of which was the overtly political 'Enoch Power'.) Long before Marley, though, Millie was the first Caribbean music superstar. In his memoir *White Bicycles*, Joe Boyd, manager and producer of many Island acts, recalls a sad postscript to Millie's sudden, global success:

> Licensed to Phillips, it became an international hit and Pepsi Cola invited Millie on a promotional tour of Africa and Latin America. Chris went along as chaperone and enjoyed every minute. At the end of the tour, a hero's welcome awaited Millie in Kingston. The motorcade wound its way through cheering, flag-waving crowds. This was Jamaica's first international success since independence. Finally, it reached Millie's shack. She jumped out of the limo and ran towards her mother with open arms. The older woman backed away fearfully from the most famous person in Jamaica and bowed low. 'Welcome Home, Miss Millie,' she said, holding out her hands. In that instance Chris's high opinion of himself plummeted. He felt his ambition had estranged a mother and daughter. In years to come, he would be an exceptionally protective manager.

But 'My Boy Lollipop' also marks the start of a rich cultural interchange between a generation of Afro-Caribbean artists, writers and musicians and the new UK 'homeland'. 'My Boy Lollypop' is an example of the bluebeat and ska music dominating Jamaica at the time. Millie was actually billed as 'The BlueBeat Girl' on the US single release. These catchy, sweet, rhythmically compelling genres would develop into the reggae, roots and dub of Toots and the Maytals, Lee Perry and, of course, Bob Marley. But in a more specifically British sense, Millie's opening of ears and minds to Jamaican music leads to all kinds of interesting, sometimes problematic cross-cultural fertilisation between the two countries. After Ska and Bluebeat, in the seventies, the skinheads and punks allied themselves to the music and rebel attitudes of roots reggae, stances also seen in the dub poetry of Linton Kwesi Johnson and Benjamin Zephaniah. In the eighties, Jamaican music in Britain took a softer turn with the coming of the first homegrown reggae style: lover's rock, gentle, rhythmic and sexy. Harder and more rambunctious were dancehall and ragga, which appropriated, sadly many thought, some of the worst aspects of hip-hop culture; its bling, sexism and homophobia. While all this was happening, white pop acts like The Police and UB40 pasteurised reggae into a hugely successful MOR commodity.

In a fascinating echo of the Millie Small story, nearly two decades later, unknown Jamaican schoolgirls once again lit up and invigorated the overcast British pop chart. Althea Forrest and Donna Reid had amused themselves in their Kingston bedrooms by putting new words to an earlier hit called 'Three Piece Suit' by Trinity and Joe Gibbs, itself a take on Alton Ellis's 'Still In Love with You'. Gibbs himself became aware of the girls' efforts and recorded Althea and Donna's answer version, which took the peacockery of the original and made it a fresh, funny declaration of female style and sexiness, albeit one that many UK audiences found incomprehensible.

Whether it understood the lyrics or not, the UK pop constituency certainly found the song irresistible, and once again Britain fell under the spell of Jamaican music thanks to the vitality and charm of young Jamaican women. Althea and Donna's take on the popular song 'Uptown Top Ranking', went to number one in February 1978.

Neither Althea, Donna nor Millie Small would ever repeat the success of their first and only real hit(s). Althea and Donna made a poor, formulaic album and disappeared, while Millie made a series of unsuccessful sequels, including the bizarre cover of Nick Drake's 'Mayfair' before exiting into the wings of pop history.

Millie Small's story is happy proof that history is not always written by the victors. Other performers had longer and more lucrative careers but no-one has been part of a more vital and engaging moment in pop, or a more historic one.

9. DEDICATED FOLLOWER OF FASHION

Manchester has not always been the vibrant city at the cutting edge of style that it is today. In 1796, when a fast-rising army captain by the name of George Bryan Brummell was told that his regiment was being sent from London to Manchester he immediately resigned his commission: 'I have heard that we are ordered to Manchester. Now you must be aware, how disagreeable this would be to me; I really could not go – think ... Manchester!'

He went on to cite the city's rough, uncultured reputation and lack of style. And style was hugely important to George Bryan 'Beau' Brummell: he was the archetypal dandy, a man who revolutionised men's dress in Britain. He introduced the modern suit and consigned to history the ludicrous knickerbockers, and such, of the past. He wore smart fitted clothes, changed five times a day and shocked society by washing daily.

Part of the reason why Beau Brummell was so loath to head north was that he was sure the city wouldn't suit his clothes. And he was probably right. London, along with Milan, Paris and New York, has always been one of the world's fashion capitals. Never more so

than at the beginning of 1966, when Pye Records announced the
release of a new single, 'a humorous, catchy, sing-along number'
by The Kinks. It got to number two in the charts and exhibited a
peculiarly British attitude towards ourselves and our role models.
Unlike 'England Swings (Like a Pendulum Do)' from the previous
year by Roger Miller, it was not a straightforwardly upbeat hymn
to our current national grooviness. No, like most of Ray Davies's
songs, 'Dedicated Follower of Fashion' was, once you'd licked
through the sweet coating, as sour as sherbet; a caustic put-down
of the affluent young things now 'flitting like butterflies' from shop
to shop along Carnaby Street and the King's Road. People who'd
never heard of The Kinks or their songs would soon know the
phrase 'Dedicated Follower of Fashion'.

As The Kinks' song climbed the chart, so England, or at least
London, basked in the knowledge that it was the pop cultural capital
of the world; a generation of musicians, artists, film-makers, actors
and photographers had combined to make it the most glamorous
and fashionable city on Earth. And fashion was right at the heart
of this imperial dominance. Later a disgraced Conservative MP,
Jonathan Aitken was then a young journalist who declared, 'The
fashion revolution was the most significant influence on the moods
and mores of the younger generation in Britain in the last decade
… it has seized the threads of all the contemporary cults and woven
them together in a strand that binds the entire younger generation
with a new sense of identity and vitality.'

Alongside the pop and rock stars who were making London
swing, models, designers and hairdressers were shaping the look of
the times, sweeping aside the fashion formalities of the New Look
and the stiflingly chic Paris fashion houses and bringing a fresh,
fun, youthful buoyancy to the catwalks and high streets. A young

designer called Mary Quant said that she wanted to make clothes that showed off the slim, fit bodies of the modern British girl, clothes that they could run for buses in and wash easily: 'I hated the clothes the way they were. I wanted clothes that were much more for life, much more for real people, much more for being young and alive in.'

In many ways Mary Quant embodied the classless dynamism of the times and of swinging London. She was the daughter of two Welsh schoolteachers from mining stock, who'd both gained first-class degrees at Cardiff University and come to London to teach. In 1955 she opened her first boutique, Bazaar, on King's Road. Back then this was a fairly ordinary West London thoroughfare, a quiet local high street full of bakers, greengrocers and fishmongers, and with just a small bohemian enclave of writers. She was to transform it into a catwalk, a glittering parade that the world would marvel at. Quant spearheaded a revolution without any real training in fashion, but with a finger on the pulse of everyday life. She broke with Paris and sold clothes that reflected the mood of the day: inexpensive, brightly coloured, simple; skinny rib jumpers, short skirts and dresses, sometimes in wool or PVC, coloured tights, hipster belts, sleeveless tops. She was every bit as much a rebel and a pioneer as The Beatles and The Stones, as much a convention-shattering iconoclast as Moon or Townshend.

Like many a swinging Brit, her favourite car was the Mini, designed by Alec Issigonis as fun, reliable, cheap and nippy transport for modern Brits. So when she raised the hemline of her skirts in 1965 to several inches above the knee, she knew just what to call this new skirt.

The miniskirt epitomised the spirit of London in the mid-1960s: free-spirited, unconventional, sexy and informal. When Jean

Shrimpton, one of the celebrity models of the day and a bona fide beautiful person, wore a miniskirt with no stockings, hat or gloves at the Melbourne Cup Carnival in Australia, she caused a sensation. The classic photo of the day showed a dramatic contrast in styles and outlook; behind the young, unaffected, beautiful Shrimpton – the Shrimp, as she was known – huddle a group of disapproving middle-aged bourgeois matrons in twin sets and pearls, a very potent image of the old and the new, and a geographical and generational shift that went much further than hemlines.

The colonies may have grumbled – the Aussie press was full of outrage and uproar about Shrimpton's 'childishness' – but generally the world was marvelling at what was beginning to happen on the streets and shops of W1 and SW3, the dance floors of The Bag o' Nails and The Scotch of St James, clubs like UFO and galleries like Indica. On 15 April 1966 *Time* magazine ran a cover story on 'London, the Swinging City'. The piece was almost gushing in its enthusiasm, a eulogy for a city that only fifteen years before had been a grimy and desolate bomb site:

In a decade dominated by youth, London has burst into bloom. It swings; it is the scene. This spring, as never before in modern times, London is switched on. Ancient elegance and new opulence are all tangled up in a dazzling blur of op and pop. The city is alive with birds and Beatles, buzzing with minicars and telly stars, pulsing with half a dozen separate veins of excitement. The guards now change at Buckingham Palace to a Lennon and McCartney tune, and Prince Charles is firmly in the longhair set ... In a once sedate world of faded splendour, everything new, uninhibited and kinky is blooming at the top of London life.

The theory went that the old order was being overturned by an explosion of vital young talent, often from outside the privileged classes. There were The Beatles, of course, and other working-class pop aristocrats like The Kinks, The Who, Eric Clapton and the Small Faces. There were the East End photographers David Bailey and Terence Donovan – and of course from the same patch the Kray twins, immortalised by Bailey in a famous portrait. From decidedly unglamorous Dagenham came Dudley Moore and Sandie Shaw. And with all due respect to the Shrimp, the face of the period was that of Lesley Hornby, or Twiggy, as she'd been nicknamed back home in Neasden for her 31–23–32 frame. Pictures of the teenager had been spotted by Deirdre McSharry, a fashion journalist from the *Daily Express*, who'd arranged for more photos and an article, which declared Twiggy 'The Face of '66'. The copy read: 'The Cockney Kid with a face to launch a thousand shapes … and she's only sixteen!'

There was tension and conflict too, of course. On one hand, the pill and changing social attitudes meant that women were enjoying a much greater sexual and economic freedom. But, on the other, the gamine beauties like Twiggy and the Shrimp that gazed out of the glossy magazines presented a very partial, some would say problematic, representation of womanhood which played on a 'schoolgirl' image. The London fashion industry soon came to be regarded as catering almost exclusively to young girls between the ages of fifteen and twenty. The models on all the popular catwalks and fashion magazines were skinny and androgynous, almost prepubescent figures in sharp contrast to the powerful Amazonian look of the fifties pin-up.

It was certainly a scene that celebrated itself, if sometimes with its tongue in its cheek. 'In my paisley shirt, I look like a jerk,' sang Syd Barrett of the Pink Floyd on 'Vegetable Man', while Pete and Dud satirised the trend for coded drug metaphors with the deliciously silly 'L. S. Bumble Bee'. Billy Nicholls's 'London Social Degree' had initials which also hinted coyly at one of the scene's most popular stimulants. Light entertainment stars like Petula Clark and Anita Harris got on board with delightful little oddities like 'Have Another Dream on Me' and 'London Life' – penned by Burt Bacharach – with its pertinent, perky declaration that 'While Paris sleeps, London just keeps right on a-swingin'.'

And then, in the more sardonic vein of Syd and Pete and Dud, there was 'Dedicated Follower of Fashion'. Given that it was written at the height of swinging London it displays a remarkable degree of sceptical distance from the whole florid, fabulous parade. It mocks the sixties fashion victim for his – interestingly it is his – fickleness, his effeminacy – think about those frilly panties – and his sheep-like consumerism. He can be found 'Everywhere the Carnabetian army marches on/Each one a dedicated follower of fashion.'

The Carnabetian army refers to Carnaby Street, an undistin-guished little cut-through just south of Oxford Circus that became synonymous with the public face of swinging London. Today, rents in that postal district are sky high, but back then, from the late fifties onwards, it had offered a cheap foothold in the West End for fashion entrepreneurs. Carnaby Street is now branded as Carnaby Village, a corporate theme-strip trading on its past. But even back in the days of 'Dedicated Follower of Fashion' it was a contentious address. In its mid-sixties heyday its two dozen shops, from boutiques like Domino Male to Lord John and Lady Jane, to Cranks health food store and Gear, a Victoriana bric-à-brac store, generated two million pounds a year in revenue, even if the real elite were elsewhere, probably up the King's Road. As George Melly said at the time, 'The real in-group wouldn't be seen dead in Carnaby Street.'

These were the contradictions at the heart of the classless democratic youthful revolution that made London the most swinging city in the world. The in-crowd, intentionally or not, were a small and exclusive set. *Private Eye*'s Christopher Brooker claimed that swinging London was in fact a court comprising about twenty people, most of them named already. David Bailey noted, even then, that it was 'a very elitist thing'. Twiggy herself commented of Mary Quant's King's Road boutique, 'It was for rich girls. Docker's daughters were rarely in evidence.'

These are the sort of sardonic sentiments that underpin 'Dedicated Follower of Fashion', a cynic's-eye view of swinging London that clearly resonated with millions who would never get inside the Scotch of St James or the chic boutiques of Kensington and Chelsea.

But a year on from 'Dedicated Follower of Fashion', Davies, in more tender mood and in a far, far better song, did leave us one of the loveliest, most reflective memories of those radiant few years. It's said that the Terry and Julie of 'Waterloo Sunset' are Terence Stamp and Julie Christie, two beautiful young film stars who embodied the glamour and brilliance of London in the mid-sixties. But in the song they become part of London's great teeming metropolis of workers, lovers and dreamers, rushing home to the suburbs, or to the city's glittering heart as the weekend begins.

Viewed romantically, in the summer of 1966, London, and by extension perhaps England, led the world; and on a beautiful late July day it was made official. 'Paperback Writer' was number one in the charts, *Born Free*, *Georgy Girl* and *Who's Afraid of Virginia Woolf?* were packing them into the cinemas of the West End; while the King's Road, Piccadilly and Carnaby Street were abuzz with youthful brio and the catwalks popped and dazzled with flashbulbs.

As the skirts shortened and the days lengthened, London town turned its sunlit face to the world. Like Renaissance Florence or Vienna at the turn of the twentieth century, England's capital city had become the cultural capital of the Western world: for music, fashion, design, theatre, literature and even sport.

On 30 July 1966 England beat West Germany 4–2 after extra time to win the Jules Rimet trophy and be crowned football champions of the world, right there in London, if not a particularly swinging bit outside the North Circular. But that's another story for another time. For now, let's just look back at those golden few years when London and England swung like a pendulum do. They think it's all over. It is now.

10. A WHITER SHADE OF PALE

If you'd been lucky enough to have been given a lift in John Lennon's car a month or two before the release of *Sgt Pepper* in June 1967, you'd have definitely heard a certain song and you'd have definitely been travelling in style. His multicoloured Phantom V Rolls Royce had been extensively customised to include a double bed, a TV, telephone and portable refrigerator. And it contained a state-of-the-art sound system on which all that spring and summer John played his favourite record, a dreamy, enigmatic piece of very British psychedelia whose meaning has never really been teased out but whose opaque, intoxicated atmosphere, both radiant and sinister simultaneously, seems to sum up that first summer of love and the coming of new sounds, new styles, new attitudes and new stimulants to pop music and the country at large. In its willingness to experiment and embrace Bach, r&b, rock and the new abstract shapes of pop, it summed up the sense of limitless possibilities and artistic freedoms felt by even an unknown band from Southend on their very first release.

'A Whiter Shade of Pale' by Procol Harum was number one during the early weeks of that luminous, transcendent summer of 1967. 'Everything about this record is an overwhelming gas,' said *Melody Maker* on its release. Soon it could be heard everywhere: in shops and schools, pubs and parties; in bedsits and halls of residence, and in the new-fangled discothèques. It soared from transistors on those daring, thrilling pirate radio stations such as Radio London and Radio Caroline and, later in the year, on the BBC's new pop network Radio One. And it was undoubtedly playing in the canteens and corridors of Abbey Road as The Beatles and Pink Floyd put their finishing touches, in adjoining studios, to two other defining masterpieces of the era: *Sgt Pepper* and *The Piper at the Gates of Dawn*,whose 'See Emily Play' had shared the charts with Procol Harum's début single.

'See Emily Play', 'A Whiter Shade of Pale', *Sgt Pepper* ... all of these and more formed a soundtrack to that brief glorious season in pop when youth in all its gilded glory was at the vanguard of cultural change. Love was in the air, and something else was in the air besides, something just as sweet and intoxicating.

Is 'A Whiter Shade of Pale' a drug song? The lyric's writer, non-performing Procol Harum member Keith Reid, has always claimed that its central images are taken from an incident at a party of the day, and an overheard comment that a girl's face had turned a whiter shade of pale. But any decent party back then would have had more than Watneys Red Barrel on offer and, like The Beatles' 'Lucy in the Sky with Diamonds', whether the lyrics refer explicitly to a drug experience or not, the imagery and ambience are soaked in the blissed-out, baffling, dreamlike and sometimes nightmarish images of the time, heavy with the new, altered moods of the day.

Since Siberian shamen used the fly agaric mushroom to achieve the right state of mind for their ritual chanting, people have been making music under the influence of drugs. The musician tribesmen of pre-Columbian America used peyote and other psychedelic cacti. Performances of the Eleusinian Mysteries – musical rituals of ancient Greece involving harps and lyres – are thought to have involved the use of Psilocybe and other psychoactive fungi like ergot, a potent hallucinogen used in the making of LSD. Put simply, these guys were out of it.

Much later, in the nineteenth century, French composer Hector Berlioz produced what we might think of as the first modern piece of drug music when he wrote the lurid, fantastical *Symphonie Fantastique* about the effects of opium. With the coming of jazz, major figures such as Charlie Parker, Miles Davis and John Coltrane were regular and heavy heroin users. But with the coming of the hippy era drugs such as LSD and marijuana became not just a private vice of the performers but a key component of the scene, shaping its tenets of free love and free expression, personal liberation, the quest for enlightenment and guilt-free pleasure. Paul McCartney openly admitted to LSD use, saying: 'It opened my eyes. It made me a better, more honest, more tolerant member of society.' It also changed the sound of the music, from Hendrix and the Jefferson Airplane's far-out sonic adventures to The Beatles' studio and tape trickery, the musical equivalent of an acid trip. And it changed the lyrics, too, from the romantic platitudes and well-made witticisms of Tin Pan Alley to a kaleidoscope of surrealistic, allegorical and sometimes wilfully nonsensical imagery. One man more than any other was the pioneer in this regard.

Bob Dylan famously introduced The Beatles to marijuana on 28 August 1964 in their suite at the Delmonico Hotel, New York. When the lads sheepishly informed Dylan that they had never tried it before, he said, 'But what about that song, "I get high, I get high"? Lennon then even more sheepishly informed him that this was not the actual lyric to 'I Wanna Hold Your Hand' but 'I can't hide, I can't hide'. Dylan had been expanding his mind and his lyrics for a year or so. One of his latest songs, 'Mr Tambourine Man', had a childlike dreamy lyric widely thought to refer to a drug dealer. Dylan's influence in this regard was enormous, not least on Procol Harum's Keith Reid, as he explained to *Uncut* magazine:

My main influence was Dylan. I could see how he did it, how he played with words.

I used to go and see a lot of French films in the Academy in Oxford Street. *Pierrot le Fou* made a strong impression on me, and *Last Year in Marienbad*. I was also very taken with surrealism, Magritte and Dali. You can draw a line between the narrative fractures and mood of those French films and 'A Whiter Shade of Pale' … I was trying to conjure a mood as much as tell a straightforward, girl-leaves-boy story. With the ceiling flying away and room humming harder, I wanted to paint an image of a scene. I wasn't trying to be mysterious with those images, I wasn't trying to be evocative. I suppose it seems like a decadent scene I'm describing. But I was too young to have experienced any decadence, then. I might have been smoking when I conceived it, but not when I wrote it. It was influenced by books, not drugs.

Soon a whole cottage industry was to grow up around the deciphering and analysis of cryptic lyrics like 'A Whiter Shade of Pale'. The clarity and precision of the classic popular songwriters was becoming replaced by deliberate obscurity, symbolism and elaborate metaphors. The Bonzo Dog Doo-Dah Band in their ridiculously florid 'The Canyons of Your Mind' satirised this trend brilliantly.

In the movie of Roddy Doyle's *The Commitments*, there's a scene in which the merits of 'A Whiter Shade of Pale's lyric are discussed between two members of the young band: 'Poxiest lyric ever written: "One of sixteen vestal virgins who were leaving for the coast." What does that mean?' To which they are surprised to hear a listening Catholic priest reply, 'I never understood that bit either, it's a very peculiar lyric.'

The 'Vestal Virgins' were, by the way, the six holy priestesses of Vesta, the goddess of the hearth and home, whose duty was to maintain the sacred fire of Vesta in the circular Temple of Vesta at the eastern edge of the Roman Forum. No record exists of any seaside excursions in the literature of ancient Greece, nor any mention of a bonus ten virgins available for such trips.

The line 'As the miller told his tale' would seem to refer to 'The Miller's Tale', from Chaucer's *The Canterbury Tales*, a bawdy story that could indeed make a young woman's face turn a whiter shade of pale. However, Keith Reid claimed, 'I'd never read "The Miller's Tale" in my life. Maybe that's something that I knew subconsciously, but it certainly wasn't a conscious idea for me to quote from Chaucer, no way.'

But what mesmerised Britain in the May of 1967 was not just the song's mysterious words. Gary Brooker's blue-eyed soul vocal, honed by his time in various Southend r&b bands, gave a ragged

edge of feeling to the impenetrable verses. 'It's equal parts Dylan
and Stax,' he later remarked in *Uncut* magazine. And his music
blended a variety of musical styles to brilliant effect:

> I'd been listening to a lot of classical music, and jazz. Having
> played rock and r&b for years, my vistas had opened up.
> When I met Keith, seeing his words, I thought, 'I'd like to
> write something to that.' They weren't obvious, but that
> doesn't matter. You don't have to know what he means, as
> long as you communicate an atmosphere. 'A Whiter Shade
> of Pale' seemed to be about two people, a relationship, even.
> It's a memory. There was a leaving, and a sadness about
> it. To get the soul of those lyrics across vocally, to make
> people feel that, was quite an accomplishment. I remember
> the day it arrived: four very long stanzas, I thought, 'Here's
> something.' I happened to be at the piano when I read
> them, already playing a musical idea. It fitted the lyrics
> within a couple of hours. Things can be gifted. If you trace
> the chordal element, it does a bar or two of Bach's 'Air on
> a G String' before it veers off. That spark was all it took. I
> wasn't consciously combining rock with classical, it's just
> that Bach's music was in me.

There's a charming, rather naïve film made to accompany 'A White
Shade of Pale' that is sweetly typical of such pop promos of the
era. Made using the Scopitone format, we see the band running
and jumping around in the grounds and ruins of Witley Court
in Worcestershire in their floral shirts, flares and facial hair in the
self-consciously goofy way of the period. But intercut with these

shots are the customary visual furniture of the era: Piccadilly Circus, Routemaster buses, bobbies on the beat in the West End and girls in miniskirts on the King's Road; in other words, a parade of exclusively London iconography. When we think of Britain in 1967, the images that come to mind are invariably centred around London. It was the city that was swinging, not London as a whole. Even the quartet of Northerners who had done more than any other to usher in this new era were now part of the glitterati of the London scene (or at least Paul McCartney was), *habitués* of the Bag o' Nails, the Scotch of St James, the galleries and restaurants of Soho and Mayfair.

It's possible to date the start of what became known as swinging London to the Colin MacInnes books of the mid-1950s, with their cool tales of the capital's *demi-monde*. But whether swinging London ever swung much further north than St John's Wood is debatable. The summer of love produced little in the way of provincial flower power, and if we think of the movies of the day, they are all London based, with the North taking an extended summer of love break between the grit of *A Taste of Honey* and *A Kind of Loving* and the bleakness of *Kes* and *Get Carter*. Long hair, kaftans and bells on a bloke were also much more likely to receive a warm reception at the UFO club or the Indica gallery than the pubs and factories of Bradford, Bury or Bolsover.

Almost half a century on, 'A Whiter Shade of Pale' still resonates with echoes of that golden summer. In 2009 it was still Britain's most played record on the radio. The runner-up was Queen's 'Bohemian Rhapsody'. The two songs both contain the unusual word 'fandango' in the lyrics.

A rather sad postscript perhaps indicates how much the times have changed from the belief that all you needed was love.

Matthew Fisher, organist on the recording, filed a lawsuit claiming he deserved songwriting royalties for his distinctive organ melody. In 2006 a judge agreed and awarded Fisher part of the copyright. The ruling means that he now receives a share of future royalties for the track. One of the five judges who heard the case, Baroness Hale, said: 'As one of those people who do remember the sixties, I am glad that the author of that memorable organ part has at last achieved the recognition he deserves.'

11. JE T'AIME

The British Broadcasting Corporation has not always been the crazy, freewheeling, anarchic scene setter it is today. Down the years Auntie Beeb could be accused of being a little prim, banning records from its airwaves for what might seem rather mild breaches of taste. In 1952 it banned Frankie Laine's 'Answer Me' for the line 'Answer me, Oh Lord!' It banned the main theme from the Frank Sinatra movie about heroin addiction, *The Man With the Golden Arm* ... even though it was an instrumental. It not only banned Paul McCartney's 'Give Ireland Back to the Irish', a rather jaunty call for Troops Out and Irish Nationalism, DJs could not even mention the title on the chart run-down, referring to it as 'a record by Paul McCartney and Wings'. Best of all, in 1942 it banned 'Deep in the Heart of Texas' because the infectious clap-along chorus was causing munitions workers to join in and make mistakes.

Times change, as do cultural sensitivities. Some songs, though, will always remain slightly shocking, simply because of the way they sound. Listen to 'Jungle Fever' by The Chakachas, or 'Love to Love you Baby' by Donna Summer, and unless you believe the late

Ms Summer that those moans and groans were the result of a bad toothache, you will know just why Auntie Beeb banned both of the above. What is happening, or what is supposed to be happening, on both these records is unmistakable. It is the sound of sex. And, although it was 1969, the BBC would rather you didn't hear it.

Back in the late 1960s the two sexiest countries in the world were separated by twenty-two miles and a thousand years of mutual hostility and suspicion. But as any self-respecting Mills and Boon or Shakespeare fan will tell you, dubiousness and dislike are often just a front for seething passions that will come to the fore when opposites attract.

Through the forties and fifties, the more obvious slick, widescreen machismo of Latino and Yank heartthrobs – from Elvis to Mario Lanza, Rock Hudson to Marlon Brando – may have brooded and brawled their swoonsome way into the hearts of the world, but by the 1960s a new definition of cool held sway, one based on style, youth, sophistication, glamour and wit. Paris and London were the centres of world fashion, art, music and film and the *habitués* of this world – models, photographers, painters, writers, singers, directors, actors – were the new sex symbols. On our side of the channel, we had The Beatles, Michael Caine, Mick Jagger, Jean Shrimpton, Terence Stamp, Julie Christie, David Hemmings, Twiggy, Sandie Shaw and the rest. In France there was Catherine Deneuve, Alain Delon, Françoise Hardy, Sacha Distel and, of course, Brigitte Bardot. In the winter of 1967 Bardot was in the middle of a short but passionate love affair with the goatish French songwriter Serge Gainsbourg, who'd made his name writing for Juliette Gréco and then having hits with the teeange France Gall, a so-called yé-yé girl. Yé-yé was a kind of lightweight catchy chart pop that Gainsbourg initially dismissed as 'banal'. When he realised he could make money from it, and Gall, he changed his mind: 'I am a turncoat,' he said. 'I turned my coat and I now see that it is made of silk.' One of those hits actually won the Eurovision Song Contest in 1965, 'Poupee de Cire, Poupee de Son'.

By 1967 the thirty-four-year-old Bardot's film career was waning and her second marriage was on the rocks. But she was signed to Gainsbourg's record company and both were booked to appear on Sacha Distel's prime-time Saturday night TV show. A disastrous date followed during which the drunken Gainsbourg's usual quirky charm deserted him. But Bardot phoned the next day and demanded as recompense that he write her 'the most beautiful love song you can imagine'. The result, written that night, was 'Je T'Aime ... Moi Non Plus'.

Late one winter night Gainsbourg and Bardot went into a dimly lit studio in Paris and under the auspices of hip arranger and producer Michel Colombier recorded 'Je T'Aime ...' in an intimate two-hour session. The two singers were squashed into a cramped and presumably steamy glass booth; engineer William Flageollet witnessed what he described as 'heavy petting'. Rumour soon circulated that it was an '*audio vérité*' recording of Bardot and Gaisnbourg actually having sex, with the newspaper *France Dimanche* reporting that the four minutes and thirty-five seconds of 'groans, sighs, and Bardot's little cries of pleasure [gave] the impression you're listening to two people making love'.

When reporters told Bardot's husband, the German industrialist Gunter Sachs, of the recording, he was incensed. Bardot, fearing bad publicity before her new movie *Shalako* rather than her husband's wrath, pleaded with Gainsbourg not to release the record, and reluctantly he agreed, protesting, 'The music is very pure. For the first time in my life I write a love song and it's taken badly.'

The affair ended and the pair went their separate ways. On the set of a movie called *Slogan*, Gainsbourg met a modishly coltish English actress called Jane Birkin, recently divorced from composer John Barry. A wild night out in Paris ended with Gainsbourg passed out drunk on his bed. Birkin left a copy of 'Yummy, Yummy, Yummy, I Got Love in My Tummy'. The pair soon fell in love and became inseparable. Shortly after filming ended, Gainsbourg asked Jane to record a new version of 'Je T'Aime ...', which they did in a Marble Arch studio under the direction of Arthur Greenslade, who at one point asked Birkin to calm down.

'I only sang it because I didn't want anybody else to sing it,' said Birkin, who also claimed that Gainsbourg asked her to sing an octave higher than Bardot, 'so you'll sound like a little boy'. Gainsbourg and Birkin rushed back to Paris with it, where Gainsbourg slipped the disc on in the background in a hotel restaurant. Birkin recalled, 'Everybody's knives and forks were in the air, suspended. Nobody went on eating.' Gainsbourg added, 'I think we've got a hit.'

The old goat was right. Released in February 1969 in a sleeve that teased '*interdit aux moins de 21 ans*' (forbidden to those under twenty-one), and despite being banned or heavily restricted almost everywhere, it went to number one in Austria, Norway and Switzerland and in the UK, where it was the first banned number-one single as well as the first single in a foreign language to top the charts. It stayed in the UK chart for thirty-one weeks, and was a bigger hit here than anywhere else in Europe.

Why? Well, we in Blighty have always liked a cheeky song, of course. But a certain traditional mistrustful fascination with the French may explain some of our enthusiasm for 'Je T'Aime ...' Also, in its pairing of the older continental seducer–Lothario and the wide-eyed English rose, 'Je T'Aime ...' was buying into a very

British scenario beloved of comedians, TV writers and music-hall songs such as 'The Spaniard Who Blighted My Life'. It also traded on a long if furtively held belief that the French and Latins are obsessed with, more comfortable with, and better at sex than us.

Writer Sylvie Simmons summed it up nicely in her biography of Gainsbourg, *A Fistful of Gitanes*:

> Certainly 'Je T'Aime ...'s languid, almost over-pretty, chocolate-box melody contained some surreal images for a love song ... but the lyrical subtleties were lost on late-1960s Brits. What they heard was an expertly stroked organ, orgasmic groans and a soft-focus melody, the musical equivalent of a Vaseline-smeared *Emmanuelle* movie. It was confirmation that life across the Channel was one of unchecked lubriciousness, and 'Je T'Aime ...' became as essential a part of any successful seduction as a chilled bottle of Blue Nun.

But by 1969 Britain was becoming a different country. A long-standing trope of our national self-image had it that British men were repressed, frightened of sex and probably secretly homosexual while British women were sex-starved and frustrated. This persisted into the 1970s and underpinned the 'humour' of saucy postcards, comic songs and TV sitcoms like *George and Mildred* and *On the Buses* and a long-running, rather dreary comedy of the day called *No Sex Please, We're British*. But this was the view from the middle-aged, male-dominated light entertainment establishment. It was a younger, less uptight generation who bought 'Je T'Aime ...' which, with its moody, heady organ vibe, was a musical cousin to 'A Whiter Shade of Pale'.

The title of the song is enigmatic. It translates as 'I Love You
... Me Neither', adapted from a remark by Salvador Dalí about
Picasso: 'Picasso is Spanish, me too. Picasso is a genius, me too.
Picasso is a communist, me neither.'

Gainsbourg himself, ever the Frenchman, was keen that the
song's philosophy should be properly understood, as quoted by
Simmons in her biography of Gainsbourg:

It expresses the superiority of eroticism over sentimentalism
... there exist millions of songs devoted to romantic,
sentimental love, encounters, discoveries, jealousies, illusions,
disillusions, meetings, betrayals, remorse, hates, etc. So why
not devote a song to a kind of love much more current
these days, physical love? It is not an obscene song, it seems
reasonable to me and fills in a gap. The explanation is that
the girl says 'I love you' during love and that the man, with
the ridiculousness of virility, doesn't believe it. He thinks that
she only says it in the instant of enjoyment, of pleasure. I
happen to believe that, and it's a bit my fear of being had,
but it's also an aesthetic move, a search for the absolute.

And of course, it just sounds sexy, as does everything French to the
Anglophone ear, because of all those liquid consonants, breathy
fricatives and soft slurred non-guttural syllables, even when it's
saying, 'You are the wave, I the naked island ... Physical love goes
nowhere ... Like the irresolute wave ... I go, I go and I come ...
Between your kidneys.'

In the end, perhaps the most telling fact about how we as a
nation, like Jane Birkin, fell hard for the steamy, sensual mutterings
of the priapic Frenchman is that, of the dozens and dozens of

covers, most have been comic, defusing the song's erotic force with an embarrassed chortle from the likes of Frankie Howerd and June Whitfield, Judge Dread, and Gorden Kaye and Vicki Michelle of *'Allo, 'Allo*, itself an example of our ongoing obsession with the otherness of the French. Good Moaning indeed.

In 2012 Madonna performed the song live during her exclusive concert at the Olympia in Paris. She was eight when the record was released and is unlikely to have heard it on the radio as most US stations branded it obscene. In America it got to number 69, appropriately.

12. LIVING IN THE PAST

It's an ill wind that blows nobody's mind. One of the unexpected benefits to emerge from the economic hardships experienced by Britain in the early 1970s – energy crisis, fuel rationing and three-day week – was for fans, presenters and creators of weirdo music. As striking miners picketed the coke depots and put the squeeze on fuel and electricity reserves, all of the nation's TV channels (yes, all three of them!) ended transmissions at 10 p.m. One immediate effect of this, if by immediate you mean nine months later, was an upsurge in the birth rate, as bored Britain had an early night and sought other amusements. But people also turned to the trusty old wireless and there many of them were introduced to the *sotto voce* late-night delights of Whispering Bob Harris and John Peel and *Top Gear*, then a long-haired groovy heads' music show rather than a long-haired middle-aged show for car bores. Ratings for these niche shows went up and a minor sales spike followed for the kind of music they often played, music that embodied a massive and wonderful contradiction. Progressive thumbed its nose at commerciality – it said explicitly and implicitly that it wanted nothing to do with the sordid world of hits and charts – and yet it sold in its millions and made its non-breadhead, just-in-it-for-the-music artists into millionaires with Rolls Royce collections and private jets.

For a long time, love of progressive rock was the love that dare not speak its name, especially after its banishment to the back of record collections and to the ash-heap of history during the year-zero scorched-earth policy of punk. At least, that's the time-worn story as told and retold by the official rock histories. In fact, Pink Floyd and Genesis were to sell even more records after the coming of punk had supposedly put their heads in the revolutionary tumbril. There is some truth in this version of history, though. The whole musical and aesthetic framework of progressive rock – technical virtuosity, hi-falutin' conceptual conceits, the album as grand artistic statement as opposed to the flimsy novelty of the single – was torn down by the punk iconoclasts in 1977. Rick Wakeman, florid, cape-wearing keyboardist of Yes, once compared the advent of punk to being made redundant from one of Britain's many failing industries of the era: 'Overnight you were told, we don't need your kind of thing any more, here's your cards.'

After punk, progressive rock was definitely anathema for a long time, at least according to punk's high church in the music press. But actually progressive rock had never been properly cool within the UK music press. Even in the seventies, it was never popular with the hipper critics, who preferred the simpler poses struck by 'real' rock and rollers, taking their cue from American blues and country rather than European folk and classical. Though they sold far, far fewer records, Little Feat would always get better reviews than ELP. Prog's popularity with the rank and file meant that it was covered. But it had never had the cachet the London press gave to The New

York Dolls or The Velvet Underground – American, faintly sordid and therefore cooler even if they sold almost no records and had never even been heard by the average *NME* reader.

If prog had a heyday at all then it ran from roughly 1969 to 1975. 1969 saw the release of what is generally regarded to be the first progressive rock record: *In the Court of the Crimson King* by King Crimson. But there's an argument to be made, one with which King Crimson, Yes, Genesis and their progressive peers of the day would maybe agree, that the prototype for prog rock was an album as popular, accessible and adored as anything in music's history. The Beatles' *Sgt Pepper* contains all the seedlings of what would flower as progressive rock: adventurous, experimental, richly diverse musical settings, multi-part songs, the influence of non-pop musics, diverse instrumentation, impressionistic lyrics on subjects other than boy meets girl, and the studio as compositional tool. The clearest and most concise example of all this was the closing track, 'A Day in the Life', whose influence on other sixties musicians was swift and far-reaching.

The young London-based King Crimson were part of what might be called the post-*Pepper* generation. They had broken on to the rock scene with their performance at The Rolling Stones' Hyde Park free festival in July 1969 in front of an estimated half a million people. By the time they played that momentous gig they had already begun recording their début album, a cornerstone of progressive rock. The sessions were long and intense, produced by the band themselves, and a prodigious, pioneering feat of eight-track recording, densely built up over many hours of overdubbing with layers of instrumentation, including violin, saxophone and the eerie woodwind and string ensembles produced by a Mellotron keyboard. Even before record buyers had heard a note they knew this was a striking and different offering: the anguised and haunted face of the Schizoid Man adorning the record's cover was also the subject of the album's arresting opening track. *In the Court of the Crimson King* was dark, eerie, complex and polyrhythmic, and ventured into scales, tonalities and time signatures where most pop feared to tread. It featured non-performer Pete Sinfield's fantastical, grotesque, prolix lyrics, such as '21st Century Schizoid Man's infamous opening couplet: 'Cat's foot, iron claw, neuro-surgeons scream for more at paranoia's poison door.'

If *Sgt Pepper* was a radiant, beatific hymn to the possibilities of the summer of love, then this was its dark side: the scary but compelling landscape that lay beyond 'A Day in the Life' from a band named, appropriately enough, with a term for the devil. This was pop music that had largely excised the blues and r&b element that was the kernel of all rock and roll and replaced it with stylings from jazz and the classics. The critical response was largely adulatory – Pete Townshend of The Who later called it 'an uncanny masterpiece' – and the album reached number five and went gold in the States.

There was another DNA strand running from *Pepper* to the prog era. From 1957 to 1960 John Lennon had attended Liverpool College of Art, one of the network of British art schools that nurtured a host of British rock musicians: Syd Barrett, Brian Eno, John Cale, Bryan Ferry, Jimmy Page, to name a few. It's interesting to note that many of the products of art school went on to mainstream success largely as singles artists – Ian Dury, Ray Davies, Eric Clapton, Adam Ant, Joe Strummer – while most of the defining players of the more grandiose and symphonic prog bands – Emerson, Lake and Palmer, Yes, Jethro Tull – were working musicians from their teens from blue-collar backgrounds who'd served an apprenticeship in hard-gigging r&b and soul bands.

Emerson, Lake and Palmer were the next band of King Crimson's singer and bassist Greg Lake – in consort with Carl Palmer, a young Brummie drummer with form in Atomic Rooster and Arthur Brown's bands, and Keith Emerson, a fearsomely talented keyboardist who played in P. P. Arnold's soul band before forming his own band The Nice, early prog contemporaries of Crimson. They made their début at the legendary Isle of Wight festival of 1970, where they stunned the crowd but were shunned by media tastemakers. John Peel airily and wrongly dismissed them as a waste of electricity. Several million disagreed and went on to make them one of the biggest bands globally of the 1970s, filling the stadiums of the world with their huge muscular take on Mussorgsky's *Pictures at an Exhibition* and their dystopian sci-fi fantasies *Tarkus* and *Brain Salad Surgery* with its famous H. R. Giger sleeve (Giger was later the designer of the *Alien* set in the Ridley Scott movie).

Emerson's position as progressive rock's premier 'keyboard wizard' was challenged from various sources – Tony Banks of Genesis, Kerry Minnear of Gentle Giant, Dave Greenslade of Greenslade – but his main friend and rival was Rick Wakeman, a larger-than-life character whose seemingly contradictory enthusiasms for beer and fart jokes and glittering capes and concept suites taken from Jules Verne and Arthurian myth made him one of the most high-profile proggers. Wakeman had studied at the Royal College of Music and served time as a session man before becoming part of the classic line-up of Yes. The quintet welded awesome instrumental power to the piping-voiced lyrical extravagances of former Accrington milkman Jon Anderson. Anderson was something of a Napoleon figure in the band, according to drummer Bill Bruford, but even he acknowledged his drive and the unique appeal of his idiosyncratic, enigmatic, perhaps nonsensical lyrical flights, which ran like a bamboozling thread through albums like *Close to the Edge*, *Fragile* and their mad *magnum opus, Tales from Topographic Oceans.*

Another of progressive rock's driving personalities was Ian Anderson of Jethro Tull. Anderson and the band had served time on the seaside dance hall, r&b circuit of Blackpool and beyond before arriving at a musical style that melded hard rock, folk and early music and a singular lyrical vision and world view. Unlike his namesake Jon, Ian Anderson was no questing adherent of various Eastern mysticisms. Anderson's delivery was dry, throwaway and sardonic, and his words smart, superior and sarcastic. From the start he set himself and his band subtly but sharply apart from their whey-faced and softer-headed hippy colleagues, as on the early hit single 'Living in the Past'. Along with the ambitious structure, 5/4 time signature, wild flute soloing and instrumental flair came a dry, aloof state-of-the-nation address, a wry personal take on the calls for 'revolution' from the perfumed, beaded youth of the day.

'Living in the Past' was a very palpable hit, particularly in the US, where it reached number eleven in 1969 and started Tull's march to superstardom. They marched largely alone, since after 'Living in the Past', their music grew more arch and structurally complex, a trend that reached its apogee on the two *magnum opi,* *Thick as a Brick* and *A Passion Play*, the critics generally loathed and poured scorn upon them. With only 60 million album sales to console them, Tull continued on to the present day. Their last album was *Thick as a Brick* too, updating their epic album-length song suite of 1972 for a new century.

It cannot be overstated that despite its difficult time signatures, fantastical sleeves and outlandish concepts and costumes, prog was enormously, insanely popular all over the world. Stadiums full of fans lapped up the difficulty of it all, relished the uncommerciality and thus paradoxically made it far more commercial than much pop of the day. Released early in 1973, Rick Wakeman's purely instrumental solo album comprising quasi-classical pieces about long-dead English Tudor queens, *The Six Wives of Henry VIII*, sold 15 million albums. Bill Bruford captured this nice contradiction brilliantly when he said that, as a creative musician, being in Yes, King Crimson and other prog acts was great because you could play in 15/8 time and still stay in good hotels.

Maybe the best example of this central irony of prog is the story of the glorified bedroom project-cum-instrumental solo album made by a troubled teenager from Reading, which not only became one of the most famous albums of all time but also launched a business empire that grew to include music, films, soft drinks, cinemas, telecommunications, vodka, personal finances, aviation, the heart of the English rail network and commercial space travel.

When the young Richard Branson rang the even younger Mike Oldfield, the latter was sitting on the stairs of his parents' home looking in the phone book for the number of the Soviet Embassy with a view to becoming a citizen of the USSR. He'd been told that the state there supported unusual music on government-run record labels. Oldfield was at his wits' end, having sent his demos everywhere he could think of and being told on every occasion that a lengthy, complicated instrumental suite with no drums and no vocals – unless you counted some caveman grunting – performed by an unknown kid playing bass in Kevin Ayers's band was never going to sell. Just as he was leafing through the yellow pages, fledgling Virgin label boss Branson rang offering some downtime in his manor. Oldfield eagerly availed himself of Branson's offer, and made his album in the dead of night and at weekends, sleeping under the mixing desk when necessary.

The result was *Tubular Bells*, a record that is indisputably, emblematically progressive in genre and scope, looking to the minimalism of Philip Glass as well as older symphonic masters like Sibelius, heavy metal, folk and what would become known as world music. *Tubular Bells* went on to sell 17 million copies around the world, launched a series of successful spin-offs and has charted again at some point in every decade since its original release.

Perhaps you can understand the reluctance and suspicion of conventional label bosses and A&R men. Rick Wakeman aside, until the tills started ringing, progressive rock was viewed as a ridiculous non-starter. Once it had proved to be a money-spinner you could maybe forgive the hubristic excesses and pretentiousness that became synonymous with prog – as far as professional critics were concerned, if not paying fans, of course.

ELP took to travelling around with their gear, of which there a was considerable amount, in three individual pantechnicons, each emblazoned with their respective surnames. Greg Lake's lorry contained a Persian carpet worth £2,000 – about a year's wages in 1972 – which he sat on for his acoustic spot. In the liner notes for Yes's *Tales from Topographic Oceans*, Jon Anderson explains how 'while backstage at the Madison Square Garden, I was leafing through the Paramahansa Yoganda's *Autobiography of a Yogi* and became caught up in a lengthy footnote on page 86'. Similarly, Gentle Giant announced on the sleeve of their second album:

> It is our goal to expand the frontiers of contemporary popular music at the risk of being very unpopular. We have recorded each composition with the one thought – that it should be unique, adventurous and fascinating. It has taken every shred of our combined musical and technical knowledge to achieve

this. From the outset we have abandoned all preconceived thoughts of blatant commercialism. Instead we hope to give you something far more substantial and fulfilling.

And, of course, there was the vainglorious defining folly of Rick Wakeman's staging of his King Arthur concept album on ice at Wembley. But was any of this more fanciful or hateful than the weary self-absorption of most rock artists? Prog revelled in the unusual, tended to look outwards, to story, myth and sci-fi for inspiration, rather than inwards, as many rock singer-songwriters did, to their own love life or half-baked politics.

The lazy, regurgitated cud of most rock criticism is that prog rock was all about trolls, wizards and capes. In fact, there are about four records like this, and none of them the very biggest sellers. Prog's big hitters follow a different pattern. *Tubular Bells* is instrumental and non-programmatic. *Dark Side of the Moon* and *The Wall* are gloomy existential confessionals about real-life issues with not a dungeon or dragon in sight. Yes albums lean towards furious jazz-rock workouts, with some yoga and Eastern mysticism thrown in. The Groundhogs offer bleak, psychological self-examination. Genesis' *Selling England by the Pound* and *The Lamb Lies Down on Broadway*, and Jethro Tull's *Thick as a Brick* and *A Passion Play* are all swingeing satires on modern Britain, while Gentle Giant's *Power and the Glory* is a post-Watergate critique of governmental corruption. A whole strand of late progressive rock – bands like Matching Mole, Henry Cow and what came to be called the Rock in Opposition movement, involving a network of bands across Europe – was Marxist, activist and explicitly political. Progressive rock may not have been about moon and June or boy meets girl but the notion that it was all about sword and sorcery is a myth.

Prog, like folk, is always having a revival and so it is now alive and well in the music of a new generation of tricky, clever pop acts who have made the polyrhythm and the contrapuntal hip again. There will always be musical crusaders, caped or otherwise.

13. PARANOID

If you'll forgive a variation in spelling, there are two John Osbornes whose influence on British culture since 1945 has been profound. One of them wrote *Look Back in Anger*, the post-war theatrical bombshell that gave us the concept of the angry young man, a disenfranchised provincial intellectual hell-bent on upsetting the complacency of the staid, middle-class, middle England around him.

The other John Osbourne was a disenfranchised provincial too, though intellectual might be stretching it by his own admission, and maybe not so much an angry young man as a confused and hopeless one. He was one of six kids growing up on the breadline in Lodge Road, Aston, a bleak, bomb-ravaged suburb of Birmingham.

'I always felt crappy and intimidated by everyone,' he later recalled. 'So my whole thing was to act crazy and make people laugh so they wouldn't jump on me.' He left Birchfield Road Secondary Modern without qualifications and turned unsuccessfully to petty theft, serving a short term in Winson Green prison after his dad, John senior, refused to bail him out. By now known as Ozzy, Osbourne then tried his hand at a variety of different jobs

including slaughterhouseman, funeral home worker and horn tester
in the local Lucas car factory where, some say, he got the taste
for the bleak, wailing monolith of sound that would later make
him a millionaire and change the world. In the 1970s Britain was
in decline as a manufacturing power, but Osbourne, Tony Iommi,
Bill Ward and Geezer Butler were a firm of Midlands industrialists
who would take and market a very British invention, like the steam
engine or the spinning jenny, to every corner of the world.

Heavy metal may also be the most maligned, misunderstood
music in the world. Sneeringly regarded as the province of adolescent
geeks and provincial plebs, it has always lacked any critical cachet;
it was largely ignored for years by music papers and radio networks,
and the Sunday broadsheets would never sully their spreads with
it, except with a heavy dose of irony and anthropological distance.
And even then, the media would invariably concentrate on antics
and make-up rather than the music's massive global appeal to
communities as varied as hairy bikers in Cumbria and tanned
teenagers in São Paulo.

Existing on its own terms, a collection of thriving subcultures
that don't need subsidy, scholarship, the approval of opinion
formers, TV advertising, self-serving awards ceremonies or any of
the cluttering paraphernalia of pop, and drawn from the blue-collar
classes of industrial towns, hard rock and metal have never been
fashionable but they may be the ultimate People's Songs.

Iron, cobalt, copper, zinc, mercury, lead, cadmium, tungsten,
plutonium, uranium. Chemists and metallurgists have been into
heavy metals for centuries. These compounds were at the heart of
the steel, smelting, iron and leather industries that had brought
muck and brass to the West Midlands – places like Walsall, West
Bromwich, Tipton, Dudley, Cradley Heath; the great flaming,

belching foundries and furnaces that stretched between Birmingham and Wolverhampton – and made the area famous (and infamous) since the Industrial Revolution. In *The Old Curiosity Shop*, published in 1841, Dickens described how the chimneys and forges 'poured out their plague of smoke, obscured the light, and made foul the melancholy air'. In 1862 Elihu Burritt, the American Consul in Birmingham, said the region was 'black by day and red by night'. Some say that J.R.R. Tolkien, who grew up in Birmingham and based the Two Towers on two of the city's landmarks and the Shire on the area around Sarehole Mill, used the Black Country as the model for the grim region of Mordor in the *Lord of the Rings*.

But that term of chemical classification – heavy metal – slipped into the language of pop with William Burroughs back in 1961. In his book *The Soft Machine*, also destined to be become a phrase known to underground rock heads, he introduced us to 'Uranium Willy, the Heavy Metal Kid'. The term then crept into rock culture in the US. It appeared in a *Rolling Stone* review by Barry Gifford of San Francisco band Electric Flag in May 1968. It first appeared in a song the same year: 'Born to Be Wild', written by the splendidly named Mars Bonfire and later performed by Steppenwolf in the biker road movie *Easy Rider*.

But whatever you call it, the sound that constitutes heavy metal, like heavy industry itself, is a British invention. Yes, the poor rural counties of the United States were the cradle of the blues, gospel and rock and roll – that is the seedling of hard rock. But British beat bands amplified it, slowed it down, turned it up and turned it around and added the key element of the monumental, monolithic riff.

In 1964 The Kinks released their third single, 'You Really Got Me'. American musicologist Robert Walser has called it 'the first hit song built around power chords', a kind of basic two-note voicing of a chord from octaves and fifths that is neither major nor minor. It's been described as the blueprint for modern hard rock and metal. Contrary to persistent rumour, Jimmy Page, later of Led Zeppelin, did not play the solo in 'You Really Got Me' – that's Dave Davies – but Page does contribute rhythm guitar. Ray Davies wrote the song while trying to work out the chords to 'Louie, Louie' by The Kingsmen, and the distorted guitar sound was produced by Dave slashing the speaker cones with a razor blade.

'You Really Got Me' was aggressive, urgent and hugely influential. The Kinks themselves revisited it on 'All Day and All of the Night' and Pete Townshend has admitted that The Who tried to emulate that sound on 'I Can't Explain'. The protean sound became heavier yet in the hands of Cream and a tranche of US bands like Vanilla Fudge, Blue Cheer and Iron Butterfly.

Whether much of this filtered back to the pubs of Birmingham is not known. The members of Black Sabbath, or Polka Tulk Blues Band or Earth as they were formerly known, were initially drawn together by their love of The Beatles. Like their idols, they made several trips to Hamburg as a struggling heavy blues band. The need to flesh out their eight-song repertoire with extended jams and riffs informed their signature sound. That, and a bizarre workplace accident to guitarist Tony Iommi. Aged seventeen, Iommi decided to quit his day job at the sheet-metal factory to give the musician's life a serious go. He came home for his lunch on his last day and mentioned to his mum that, as he was leaving, he may as well stay at home and skip the afternoon shift. She berated him for this and he grudgingly returned to the shopfloor, only to slice the top off two of his fingers in a machine. He was initially despondent but, inspired by the example of Django Reinhardt, he made himself two thimble-type false fingers from the leather-coated tops of washing-up bottles and tuned his guitar lower using much lighter strings. The result was the sludgy subterranean rumble that defined Sabbath.

As well as Iommi's guitar, the other key elements of Sabbath's sound that set them apart from their contemporaries were Osbourne's desolate wail of a vocal, the thunderous rhythm section and the lyrics of bassist Geezer Butler, a sci-fi and Tolkien fan and something of a backstreet hippy philosopher obsessed with environmental issues, geopolitics and the occult. He'd suggested the name change to the arresting Black Sabbath, after a Boris Karloff movie of that name (Butler had noticed the crowds of people queuing for a showing of the film across the road from their rehearsal rooms and pointed out, 'Isn't it funny how people love to be frightened'), and he had a hand in the stark opening to their début album *Black Sabbath*.

Rain falls heavily, dully. In the distance a lone church bell tolls forlornly. Ominously, a peal of thunder, and then emerging from the murk, an enormous, jagged, lurching zombie of a riff.

Geezer Butler was a fan of Holst's *The Planets* and was fooling around at rehearsals trying to play the tritonal main theme from 'Mars, Bringer of War'. This pricked Tony Iommi's ears and he came up with the band's second composition and their defining early piece, 'Black Sabbath', a riff based on the Devil's Interval – notes actually banned by the medieval Christian church for their satanic powers – and featuring a masterful opening line straight from M.R. James, or Bram Stoker, 'What is this that stands before me?'

Black Sabbath's début album appeared on the hard rock imprint Vertigo, beloved of 'heads' and hippies for its optical illusion logo, which when rotating on the turntable made for a psychedelic experience – especially if the listener was in a suitably altered state.

And many of Sabbath's listeners were. But Sabbath's audience were no floral hippies from the perfumed gardens of St John's

Wood or Hampstead. They were in many ways the authentic voice of the young British working class, a mirror image of the skinheads that they were a strange parallel to. Unlike the grammar school constituency who favoured Genesis or Cat Stevens, Sabbath's fans were often in manual, unskilled or semi-skilled work. As with the band themselves, hard heavy music, along with beer, football and a bag of cheap dope or speed, provided a release from long days in the factory or foundry.

In an article in a 1973 anthology called *Rockfile*, a young writer called Andrew Weiner wrote perceptively and sympathetically about Sabbath's fans:

> These kids in the audience they'd all like to play like Iommi. Not like Hendrix or Clapton or any other silver-fingered guitarist God you could mention. They want to play like Iommi. WHAM, WHAM, WHAM. And they could too. Or at least they think they could. And that again is one of the main virtues of Black Sabbath. Send any four kids up from the floor and they'll try to play like that. Send Black Sabbath back into the depths of the audience, and this is the music they'd go and see ... The kids believe it, and Sabbath believe it. Black Sabbath remain, in present circumstances, the nearest thing to a people's band we have.

Sabbath's status as a people's band was cemented instantly when their début album went top ten. Returning from yet another Hamburg trip and being told this, Ozzy Osbourne assumed there had to be two Black Sabbaths, telling *Esquire* magazine, 'I got my first royalty cheque for a hundred and five quid. I couldn't believe it. I gave my mum a fiver, got pissed on the rest, bought some shoes, bought some Brut smelly stuff. It was like someone winning the fucking lottery. It changed the family structure, because now everybody was looking for a handout.'

Further success was to come in the most extraordinary way. The title track of their second album, *Paranoid*, became an unexpected hit single in the summer of 1970, nestling behind Elvis's 'Wonder of You' and Smokey Robinson's 'Tears of a Clown'. Unexpected, since the song is a bleak, primitive proto-punk lament about isolation and insanity. Ozzy alternatively grinned and grimaced his way all through their *Top of the Pops* appearance and Iommi told *Record Mirror*, 'We're really pleased about getting on TV. People complain about groups like us selling out when we go on *Top of the Pops*, but they also complain about the sort of record which is normally in the charts. When a group like us make the charts they start to complain about selling out. They don't seem to be able to make up their minds.'

After the success of 'Paranoid', the rock intelligentsia went even cooler on Sabbath, who had never exactly been the critics' darlings, as Andrew Weiner pointed out in the book *Rockfile 3*: 'Any third-rate support act has a better chance of getting an album track played on *Sounds of the Seventies* or a gig on the *Whistle Test*, or even a moderately sympathetic write-up in the music weeklies.'

One-time champion John Peel promptly dropped them, and other bands shunned them as guitarist Iommi reflected ruefully to the doyen of sixties publicists Keith Altham in *Record Mirror*:

> We got on really well with John to begin with but something seems to have upset him. It's very difficult to say what gets into these people. There are certain musicians ... who seem to actively dislike us although we've given no cause. Some

groups or individuals seem to go out of their way to be unpleasant to us. Maybe it's a kind of jealousy of our success but it's not been an instant thing – we had to work for it and we struggled for a couple of years before we achieved anything worthwhile … The people who really matter to us are our audiences and it is what they think and how they react which really concerns us.

Ozzy added, 'When we played the Fillmore recently, for example, in the States, the Faces just didn't want to know us. Well that's OK if that's the way they feel – we obliterated them anyway.'

The crowds at the Fillmore were typical of the way America embraced the band. US critic Lester Bangs called them 'the Milton of Rock and Roll', stern electric moralists warning man of the wages of sin and the end result of his greed and lust for power. To teenagers disillusioned by Watergate and terrified of being sent to Vietnam, 'War Pigs', 'Children of the Grave' and 'Paranoid' were cogent anthems of daily dread and celebrations of hedonistic release. Put simply, America went mad for them. Sabbath, in turn, went mad themselves, on a long journey into excess that took in drug and alcohol abuse and biting the heads off several small birds and mammals, all of which is chronicled elsewhere.

But what was the lasting legacy of 'Paranoid' and Black Sabbath? The cognoscenti may have turned their backs on them but as Sabbath's rise was paralleled by that of fellow West Midlanders Led Zeppelin, and in a poppier way Slade, so British hard rock became a global influence and a distinct subculture. Indeed, Zeppelin became the world's biggest rock band. And a couple of miles down the A4123 in West Bromwich another young steel worker, named Glenn Tipton, formed a band called Judas Priest: 'The factory I worked in was a massive steelwork labyrinth, riddled with polluted canals, massive grimy workshops, foundries and steam hammers. It doesn't take a great leap of imagination to realise why metal ended up sounding the way it did.'

Judas Priest also went on to conquer America, and with their studded leather S&M look and the radio-friendly sound of albums such as *British Steel* shaped the template of stadium hard rock, later often maligned as 'hair metal' or 'poodle rock'.

In the UK, Black Sabbath became the motherlode for a sound and culture that proliferated, spread and diffused into scene after scene. Later in the decade, from other British heartland cities and towns, emerged the New Wave of British Heavy Metal, a less bluesy, more punkish variant of the classic sound, exemplified by Sheffield's Def Leppard, Saxon from Barnsley and the Tygers of Pan Tang from Whitley Bay. Once again, America was welcoming, particularly to Def Leppard, whose *Pyromania* and *Hysteria* albums sold over 30 million copies there.

At the other extreme, the late 1980s saw the emergence of new strains of metal, all heavily influenced by Sabbath's original mood and direction. Napalm Death hailed from Birmingham, Extreme Noise Terror from Ipswich, Bolt Thrower from Coventry; and many others were based around Nottingham's Earache label, which produced several extreme variants of the metal sound in a bewildering array of new genres: speed metal, hardcore, grindcore, thrash, doom metal, sludgecore, even pornogrind.

'Paranoid' defined modern heavy metal. In its own way it is one of the most influential records ever made. And belatedly it has even received a degree of intellectual and artistic respectability. In 2011 Birmingham staged a Home of Metal series of artistic events. Artist Mark Titchner's *Be True to Your Oblivion* occupied four rooms at

Walsall's New Art Gallery and featured a giant installation of the Napalm Death founder Nic Bullen's disembodied mouth, while the leather museum, also in Walsall, staged an exhibition named after Judas Priest's *Hell Bent for Leather* telling the story of fetish gear, homosexuality and heavy metal.

And the song has become a national inside joke in Finland, where at least once during any concert, regardless of the type of music being played, someone will shout, '*Soittakaa* "Paranoid"!' ('Play "Paranoid"!')

The bleakest hit single in our history, forged in the dying embers of declining industries across the British Midlands, turned out to be one of our greatest exports to the world.

14. LIGHT FLIGHT

Perhaps the most famous quote about folk music is that of the great American jazzman Louis Armstrong, who said, 'All music is folk music. I ain't never heard no horse sing a song.' Nice line, although a lot of folk fans don't think so. On discussion boards since the internet began, they will cry (or post) 'horse' or 'horse alert' whenever they think the quote is about to be wheeled out and used against them.

The purists problem with Louis' catchy quote is that it implies there's nothing distinct or unique about folk music. But why not read it another way, as a testament to the power of folk, saying that what folk music does so well is what all music should do, namely articulate the human condition and the human experience with voices and instruments. Folk can claim to be the original people's music: not the sanctioned music of the court and salon, but the music of the multitudes. It is the music people have sung to themselves and each other for centuries, to tell of their loves and labours and losses, their struggles and victories – as well as a surprising number of tales concerning people being murdered down by the river, having their maidenhood taken by inconstant lovers and unfaithful knights, going on whaling expeditions, seeing sudden apparitions of drowned lovers, being robbed by good-time girls in the middle of the night, and prospecting for gold.

The ongoing story of folk music is how successive generations take the subject matters, the tunings, the sounds and styles, the wellsprings of traditional music, and re-invent and re-energise them.

From Cecil Sharp and Vaughan Williams in the early twentieth century, to Martin Carthy, Bert Jansch and others in the sixties and seventies, to twenty-first century talent like Kate Rusby and Bellowhead ... it was as wise a man or woman as Louis who said, 'There's always a folk revival going on.'

In the 1840s the German poet Heinrich Heine toured England and concluded, 'These people have no ear either for rhythm or music and their unnatural passion for piano playing and singing is all the more repulsive. Nothing on Earth is more terrible than English music.' Heine's haughty words were quoted in an infamous German book of 1904 by Oskar Schmidt called *Das Land Ohne Musik*, *The Land Without Music*, a jingoistic dismissal of English musical culture. It was a chauvinistic and tub-thumping time in Britain as well, and in 1906, reflecting a growing nationalism, the Board of Education officially sanctioned the teaching of folk songs in schools. Composers like Vaughan Williams, Percy Grainger and George Butterworth and enthusiastic academics like Cecil Sharp travelled through rural Britain collecting the indigenous songs of mainly agricultural workers.

Folk reinvigorated English classical music, creating a new national or pastoral school that was completely distinct from and unburdened by the dead weight of European romanticism. It produced masterpieces by Vaughan Williams, Holst, Delius, Grainger, Butterworth and more. Sharp has been accused by some, like the Trotskyite critic Dave Harker, of gentrifying these people's songs and romanticising the arduous lot of the agricultural worker. But in recent years these views have themselves been criticised and fallen out of fashion, while Sharp is being reassessed as a giant of British music.

After the Second World War there was a further British folk revival. This time the impetus came, to a significant degree, from the United States. The touch paper was lit by the great American musicologist and folklorist Alan Lomax, who'd arrived in Britain to escape McCarthyism. This new folk revival was much less traditional in focus; it was unashamedly leftist and encouraged contemporary songs and singers. One of the key figures in England at the time was Ewan MacColl, born Jimmy Miller, in Salford – the 'Dirty Old Town' of one of his most famous songs – into a family of expatriate Scottish activists, trade unionists and singers. MacColl originally worked in left-wing theatre with his first wife Joan Littlewood before, inspired by Lomax, turning to folk music. MacColl's approach, and that of other important revivalists like A.L. 'Bert' Lloyd, was very different from Cecil Sharp's. Rural romanticism was replaced by gritty ballads of industrial labour, sea shanties and work songs. Topic Records were a pioneering label here, born out of the Workers' Music Association, and their 1963 album *The Iron Muse: A Panorama of Industrial Folk Music* was a defining collection, sung by the likes of MacColl, Newcastle's High Level Ranters, The Oldham Tinkers, Anne Briggs and Dick Gaughan.

MacColl, Lomax and the rest, through such groundbreaking work as the and the *Child Ballads* Folkways set of 1961 and

Charles Parker's rightly legendary social/musical history series the *Radio Ballads* of 1958–63, were, along with the homespun folkish vim of Lonnie Donegan, inspiring a generation to sing and play roots music.

An informal network of live sessions, pub nights and clubs began to flower all over Britain. There was MacColl's own Ballad and Blues night in the Scots Hoose pub in Soho (now the Spice of Life), Les Cousins on nearby Greek Street, the Bristol Troubadour, the Jug o' Punch in Birmingham, run by Ian Campbell, father of the UB40 brothers, and many more.

Soon every major city in Britain had its own folk club. It's thought that by the mid-1960s there were over 300 in Britain, a circuit of venues that, as well as offering open-mic spots and floor-singing for amateurs, provided a living for professional musicians playing folk. Musicians who were regulars at these clubs included Bert Jansch, John Renbourn, Sandy Denny, Ralph McTell, Nick Drake, Al Stewart, John Martyn, The Watersons, Davy Graham, the Incredible String Band and more. Young US musicians like Joni Mitchell, Julie Felix, Jackson C. Frank, Tom Rush and Tom Paxton were also drawn to the clubs. A young Paul Simon famously wrote 'Homeward Bound' on Widnes station while on a tour of one-night stands in British folk clubs and 'borrowed' Martin Carthy's arrangement of 'Scarborough Fair'.

Audiences were small but passionate, if often somewhat doctrinaire. Some clubs had strict policies which demanded only traditional songs and unaccompanied singing. Others were more liberal in nurturing talent. Following his conversion to electric music at the Newport Folk Festival 1965, Dylan got short shrift on his tour of the UK. A heckler shouted 'Judas' at his Manchester

Free Trade Hall gig, to which he replied, 'You liar.' In Liverpool one man shouted, 'Where's the poet in you? What's happened to your conscience?' Jeers of 'traitor' and 'phoney' rang out regularly at gigs, and *Melody Maker* said of the Dublin show, 'It was unbelievable to see a hip-swinging Dylan trying to look and sound like Mick Jagger. For most it was the night of the big let-down.'

But this 'neanderthal mob', as Dylan biographer Robert Shelton described them, were standing Canute-like against the electric tide. With the fluid intermingling of ideas across the Atlantic and the loosening hold of the purists, a new sound called folk rock or, as it was sometimes known in Britain, electric folk, began to emerge, taking as its template The Byrds' cover of Dylan's 'Mr Tambourine Man'.

In Britain the trailblazers of the new sound were a handful of bands merging folk idioms with American rock, blues and jazz. Fairport Convention initially drew comparisons with Dylan and the Grateful Dead, but with the arrival of singer Sandy Denny and fiddler Dave Swarbrick for their second album the band turned to more traditional English music for their inspiration. They weathered a traumatic car crash in which several people were killed to produce the masterpiece of British folk rock, *Liege & Lief*, and their body of work includes two precocious bona fide classics of folk rock: 'Meet on the Ledge' and 'Who Knows Where the Time Goes', written by the young Richard Thompson and Sandy Denny respectively. After the success of *Liege & Lief*, founder Ashley Hutchings left to form Steeleye Span, who forged their own brand of electric folk and hard-edged rock arrangements of traditional ballads.

Other talents like Shirley and Dolly Collins, The Watersons and Anne Briggs produced stark, austere yet haunting music in a more traditional vein, often featuring unaccompanied solo or harmony vocals or in the case of the Collins sisters, one's keening, unearthly, very English voice set against the chilly beauty of the small portative pipe organ. Shirley, the singer, had, as a teenager, been introduced to Alan Lomax at a party of Ewan MacColl's and gone on a road trip of America's South with him collecting music and field recordings from many performers. Recordings from this trip were issued by Atlantic Records under the title *Sounds of the South*, and recreated in the film *Oh Brother, Where Art Thou*.

Then there were the guitar heroes of the scene: Martin Carthy, John Renbourn, Davy Graham and Bert Jansch. Graham's instrumental 'Anji', as covered by Jansch, became the 'Stairway to Heaven' or 'Apache' of the folk guitar scene. Every amateur guitarist worth their salt had to have a bash at it and even now you can hear it ringing out from the tents and guitar stalls at folk festivals the length of the land.

Two of these crack players, Renbourn and Jansch, recorded a duet album called *Bert and John* and shared a flat in St John's Wood. Out of this, and boozy Sunday night sessions at the Horseshoe Hotel in Tottenham Court Road, emerged a fully fledged band with the addition of Danny Thompson and Terry Cox on double bass and drums and Jaqcui McShee on vocals. The result was a breathtaking mix of different influences: folk, blues and jazz. As there were five of them they named themselves Pentangle and they soon became the talk of the London folk scene, daring, unusual and brilliant.

While Pentangle were honing their style over their first two albums and selling out the Royal Festival Hall, there was similar excitement in the BBC drama department. The corporation was planning its first ever colour drama serial, a tale of three young women sharing a flat in heady late-sixties London. *Take Three Girls*, starring Liza Goddard, Susan Jameson and Angela Down, though light and accessible, did explore some pertinent issues of the day, like single motherhood, sex and drugs. Pentangle's 'Light Flight', from their popular *Basket of Light* album, was the perfect choice of theme: airy, bright, with a tricky rhythm that skips between 5/8, 7/8 and 6/4, sung with girlish insouciance by Jacqui McShee, it's achingly of the period and effortlessly, enduringly catchy and appealing.

Pentangle also provided incidental music for the series and the resultant publicity and acclaim made 'Light Flight' a surprise hit single and took *Basket of Light* to number five. A period in the limelight followed with constant TV outings, and appearances at the Isle of Wight festival in 1970 and Carnegie Hall.

With hindsight, these few years at the cusp of the sixties and seventies were the high tide of the British folk revival and folk rock. Pentangle, Fairport Convention, John Martyn, Steeleye Span, Richard and Linda Thompson were all big names on the gig circuit and in the music press. Albums by Nick Drake and Vashti Bunyan, though overlooked and underrated at the time, are now seen as classics. Waiting in the wings, though, was a rough Larrikin music that would make folk seem very old, out of time and in the way.

Punk sent folk underground for a while, back to the clubs that had always sustained it. Despite its earthiness and violence, folk seemed to represent everything punk was out to destroy: beards, bucolic revelries, acoustic instruments, real ale and morris dancing. Folk enthusiast, actor and comedian Ade Edmondson has talked of 'having to hide all his Pentangle and Steeleye Span albums' once he'd become a punk. But if the musical profile of folk dwindled during the New Wave upheaval, folk and the folk clubs were to have an unexpected influence on the culture of Britain in the seventies and eighties. Folkies like Billy Connolly, Mike Harding, Jasper Carrott, Bernard Wrigley, Bob Williamson and Richard Digance who'd always interspersed their club sets with patter and digressions found that their humour was as popular as their music, and they became light entertainment fixtures on TV.

In the nineties and first decade of the new century there followed a resurgence in traditional and roots music, inspired by new, young artists and a reappraisal of the best of the past. Hip guitarists from the worlds of indie and rock like Johnny Marr of The Smiths, Graham Coxon of Blur and Bernard Butler of Suede became regulars at folk awards and festivals, citing their respect for musicians of the ilk of Martin Carthy and Bert Jansch. The music of the sixties veterans underwent a critical and commercial renaissance as did that of Nick Drake, Vashti Bunyan, Nic Jones, the Incredible String Band, Donovan and more.

And new young folk musicians like Kate Rusby, Seth Lakeman, Bellowhead and The Unthanks fused the best of the past with a modern edge and vitality. Largely these acts met with approval from the folk community, but sometimes the folk world can belie its cuddly bearded image by being unapologetically stubborn and entrenched. Take folktronica or laptop folk, a variant of acoustic music intercut with samples and processed effects that enjoyed a brief spell of popularity in the new millennium, as practised by bands like Adem, Tunng and Jim Moray. Some warmly welcomed this new development; others grizzled, stuck their fingers in their ears literally and metaphorically, and declared that it wasn't folk. This prompted a neat response from one of the folk aristocracy himself, Martin Carthy, who remembered the days when even using a guitar was seen as a dubiously modern use of technology:

> I don't really know what to do about bringing the two scenes together, except to try and get myself invited to play at some of their festivals. I don't think people are scared off by their using computers or whatever. You'd call me part of the folk establishment, and I think it's the most important thing to have happened in the past few years. That was the argument when I was twenty. Should you be allowed to accompany yourself on a guitar? Was it tasteful? I hate that word. I hated it then and I hate it now. If this music has survived flood, fire, plague, pestilence, war, it can survive someone plugging a computer in. It can stand anything. You can do anything with this music.

Another leading light of the folk world, musician and presenter Mike Harding, took a rather different view, remarking after a folk awards ceremony that, in the new acoustic and folk scenes, there were 'too many songs about love and not enough about whaling'.

But as Martin Carthy said, folk can survive anything, and part of that survival is about adaptation and renewing the old archetypes and tropes. A wonderful example of that is one of the best original folk songs of the twenty-first century: Chris Wood's 'Hollow Point'. When the song begins, we seem to be very much in a traditional ballad mode: a young man is walking out into the world on a beautiful summer's morning. But as the song goes on the focus becomes more modern and the mood chills as we realise that this is a contemporary story, that of John Charles Menezes, the innocent Brazilian electrician murdered in a tube train shooting by Special Branch officers using hollow-point bullets, shells that cause maximum trauma and damage to the body and are illegal in warfare.

For a millennium or more, these are the stories that folk has been telling directly and beautifully. And that's why there's always a folk revival going on.

15. STARMAN

It's the evening of 6 July 1972. Britain has not long had its tea, possibly eaten off its lap, while watching news footage of picket lines, plane hijackings or explosions in Belfast. The nation is having a snooze or getting ready to go the pub or doing its homework when, into its living rooms through the television comes a smiling, benevolent, alluring, mysterious alien who is going to change the way we look and the music we listen to for ever – in the process dragging the monochrome Britain of *Coronation Street*, muddy football pitches, bovver boots, woodchip and drab certainties into a kaleidoscopic and confusing place where, not only was it not possible to say whether these pop stars were boys or girls any more, you couldn't even be sure what planet they were from.

Up until the single 'Starman', taken from the album Ziggy Stardust (or more accurately *The Rise and Fall of Ziggy Stardust and the Spiders from Mars*) and this legendary, folkloric appearance on *Top of the Pops*, David Bowie was known to the world – if at all – as the curious fellow who'd had a hit called 'Space Oddity' three years before, a topical near novelty that chimed in with, cashed in with even, the *Apollo* Moon landings of 1969. That was about a spaceman too. But Major Tom was an Earthman venturing into space. 'Starman' reversed the story. Here was an alien who was coming to Earth to change us – a strange, sexy, ambiguous presence who was going to release us from the drab and the everyday, a bit like David Bowie himself.

It might be argued, without too much hyperbole, that David Bowie invented, or at least laid the groundwork for, our modern pop culture on that summer Thursday in 1972. To understand how thrilling this moment was, it needs to be seen in context – in the context of the chart music around it, the novelty acts, the balladeers, the teen heartthrobs, Hurricane Smith and 'Puppy Love' and Gilbert O'Sullivan's 'Ooh Wakkadoo Wakkaday'.

From the first moment – the diaphanous B-flat chord played on that blue acoustic guitar, the first shimmering appearance of Bowie's face, ghostly, wan, mischievous, resplendent in his spiky carrot-orange *coiffure*, drawling his words with sleepy obliqueness – this is clearly different. Wonky of grin and stick-thin, he sings a song full of drowsy narcotic cool, a song of a friendly alien come to save the world, making his first contact, not with the authorities but with the kids via the late-night radio, 'a slow voice coming over on a wave of phase'.

Then that glorious chorus. The octave leap at the start of 'Starman's refrain is borrowed from 'Somewhere over the Rainbow', as Bowie will later candidly acknowledge when he melds the two songs in performance later in 1972. The bond between the two lies deeper than just the notes, though: 'Starman' evokes a strangely similar emotional dimension to Judy Garland's showtune; both are hymns to childlike hope, joyous, vulnerable, wistful, voices from a dream.

Song aside, two things about the performance that night remain perfect and imperishable. Firstly, there's the way that in the line 'I had to phone someone so I picked on you ... hoo ... hoo' Bowie turns, glances, looks straight down the camera, smiles flirtatiously, points and twirls a beckoning finger at every mesmerised, outsider kid in the land. Everyone who'd ever been bullied, overlooked, teased or picked last for games just found a friend, a cool friend telling you that his alien army of starmen needed you just like Kitchener had once recruited Tommy Atkins. Then, as that soaring euphoric chorus begins, guitarist Mick Ronson appears at Bowie's slender side. Seeing him, Bowie drapes a limp, louche arm around Ronson's shoulders, pulling him softly into the embrace, the near kiss of the harmonies. Kids gasped, mums all over Britain tutted over their knitting and dads in lounge doorways muttered something unrepeatable.

What had happened to Bowie in the three years since 'Space Oddity'? He had slowly evolved from a quintessentially sixties psychedelic folkie in thrall to Syd Barrett and Anthony Newley to a rock performer steeped in the harder sound of The Stooges and The Velvet Underground. Two transitional albums followed, *The Man Who Sold the World* and *Hunky Dory*, before he emerged in 1972 with a new band, the tightly rocking Spiders from Mars comprising Mick Ronson, Woody Woodmansey and Trevor Bolder, and with a highly contrived and constructed new persona: Ziggy Stardust, a messianic rock-star ambassador from Mars based loosely on two outsider artists, Vince Taylor and The Legendary Stardust Cowboy. This new look and band was unveiled to around sixty people in the unlikely surroundings of the rear function room of the Toby Jug pub in Tolworth, near Kingston upon Thames. Arriving on stage to a tape of *A Clockwork Orange*, to which a clear aesthetic debt was owed, the small show was a triumph. Like an extraterrestrial touching down almost unnoticed in a farmer's field or suburban backwater, Ziggy had fallen to Earth with a minor but definite splash.

As for Bowie's new look, he'd been dabbling in the outrageous for a year or two, posing in a dress for the cover of *The Man Who Sold the World* and undertaking a US promo tour similarly attired, for which he attracted bemusement, praise and downright hostility in roughly equal measure.

Of the new Ziggy get-up, Bowie later said, 'It was a cross between Nijinsky and Woolworth's, something cobbled together from whatever was lying around.' Somewhat surprisingly for a trio of burly blues players from the rugby league stronghold of Hull, the band also adopted the look with gusto. Bowie commented at the time, 'Actually, I'm a bit worried about the way that the band have fallen into it so easily! Remember they were into hard blues, but now they enjoy the costume bit.'

In the wake of that famous *Top of the Pops* appearance, thousands of kids debated and discussed this new pop phenomenon in playgrounds at bus-stops and in factories across the land the next day. Some thought Bowie was a freak, a pooftah, a queer. But many others had found him and his song transfixing, spellbinding, so utterly other and different that it cast the rest of the charts, the rest of the living room, the rest of humdrum seventies life into sharp relief. Here was something stranger and darker and more joyous all at once. It was a moment of epiphany, of revelation, for a generation – for kids gay or straight, male or female, of whatever class but particularly from the nation's estates and provincial towns. It was a validation of the right to be strange, to be unusual, to be you.

Ian McCulloch, later of Echo and the Bunnymen, as quoted in David Buckley's *Strange Fascination*, remembers watching it at home in Norris Green, Liverpool:

> As soon as I heard 'Starman' and saw him on *Top of the Pops* I was hooked … In 1972, I'd get girls on the bus saying to me, 'Eh, la, have you got lippy on?', or 'Are you a boy or a girl?' Until [Bowie] turned up it was a nightmare. All my other mates at school would say, 'Did you see that bloke on *Top of the Pops*? He's a right faggot, him!' And I remember thinking, 'You pillocks,' as they'd all be buying their Elton John albums, and Yes songs and all that crap. It made me feel cooler.

Five days before Bowie and the Spiders appeared on *Top of the Pops*, the first Gay Pride march had taken place in London. But British culture was still bullishly yet nervously hetero. From John Inman's Mr Humphries to Larry Grayson, effeminate men were comic staples. Even in the supposedly progressive rock and underground culture, homosexuality was invisible. Swaggering, ringleted Vikings like Roger Daltrey and Robert Plant were the template for a rock front-man. 'Birds' were there to be leered at and lusted after. Even John Peel's column in rock weekly *Sounds* was routinely illustrated with a picture of him in the bath with a pouting naked woman or a sexy schoolgirl. There were no gay rock stars. The Stones and The Beatles may have pushed the envelope with drugs and nudity and oddball politics, but the notion of one of them being homosexual was unthinkable. But the Ziggy persona was both ultra-cool and sexually ambiguous. Normal Earth rules did not apply for the Starman. And Bowie's genius was in allying this daring, sci-fi fantasy to catchy, driving rock and roll that every brickie in the land could enjoy.

It should be said that there was nothing explicitly or politically homosexual about Bowie's 'Starman' aesthetic. His producer Tony Visconti told David Buckley,

> He was never camp ... I think he was being more flamboyant and theatrical rather than making a sexual statement ... I think he suddenly realised that he could do something outrageous to get noticed – he was ignored for years until he appeared on the front pages of the tabloids, pushing a pram and wearing a dress. It was a clever move – the first of many.

Bowie himself has always been teasingly vague on the subject. To coincide with the first Ziggy promo pictures he told *Melody Maker* in 1972 that he was bisexual. Four years later he told *Playboy*, 'It's true – I am a bisexual. But I can't deny that I've used that fact very well. I suppose it's the best thing that ever happened to me.' Then, in 1983, he recanted all the above in *Rolling Stone*, saying his earlier declarations had been 'the biggest mistake I ever made'. In 1993 he coyly admitted that he had always been a 'closet heterosexual'. He has spent his latter years in a close and contented marriage with the Somali former supermodel Iman.

But the nuts and bolts of gender and sexuality are not really the point here. It's the unmistakable, glamorous, heady whiff of a new order that you can scent on that summer's breeze. Essentially, the significance of 'Starman' is the emergence of the alien androgyne, an inscrutable emissary from the outer limits, the great beyond – from the future, another world, another way of doing things – into the still largely boy meets girl, beer and skittles universe of pop. After this can come Adam Ant, Johnny Rotten, Phil Oakey, Gary Numan and Boy George. And Bowie, consciously or not, was also extending a trope of English art with the Starman long cherished in literature and entertainment: Peter Pan, Sherlock Holmes, Dr Who … the attractive, ambiguous, aloof outsider with a heart (or two) of ice and gold. Bowie's travelling spaceman reverses the concept of the alien from fifties US culture and H.G. Wells – the cruel, inhuman invader – and replaces it with the notion of the extraterrestrial as style warrior and saviour. Bowie may look outlandish in his multi-coloured faux snakeskin jumpsuit and his *Star Trek* boots, but his message is one of reassurance and optimism, whispered like a late-night DJ into the ears of teenagers glued to their radios. As well as 'Over the Rainbow' there are nods to other great moments in popular song: the staccato Morse Code guitar line hints at both 'Wichita Lineman' and the Supremes 'You Keep Me Hangin' On' while the circular la-la'ed outro recalls T. Rex's 'Hot Love' and The Beatles' 'Hey Jude'.

Bowie came to fully inhabit the Ziggy persona and toured the world with the show for the next year or so, spreading Ziggy's message of intergalactic love and revolution to the rest of Britain, America, Japan, Australia and beyond. But the new stardom and schedule took its toll and, as he prophesied in the song 'Ziggy

Stardust', 'Making love with his ego Ziggy sucked up into his mind
... When the kids had killed the man I had to break up the band'
– which Bowie did onstage at the Hammersmith Odeon on 3 July
1973. But he had changed the world of pop by then.

He had taken notions of fame and sexuality from the modern
art of Warhol and his ilk and introduced them into the heart of
the UK mainstream. Unlike Warhol's US protégés The Velvet
Underground, Bowie sold records in their millions, and sold them
to ordinary British teenagers who would never be quite so ordinary
again – and nor would the country they would come to adulthood
in. The 'Smalltown Boy'(s) and girls were on the rise.

16. GIVE IRELAND BACK TO THE IRISH

Van Morrison, Thin Lizzy, Sinéad O'Connor, Westlife, U2; these are some of the names that might come to mind when we think of Ireland's pop music heritage as well as perhaps Dana, Josef Locke, John McCormack, The Virgin Prunes, Horslips, The Divine Comedy, My Bloody Valentine, Microdisney and others in what is a fine, eclectic list. But when Morrissey sang of his 'Irish Blood, English Heart', he could have been talking of a whole other family tree, a separate canon of British pop with its roots in the old country: Lennon and McCartney, Boy George, Johnny Rotten, Kate Bush, Oasis, Mike Oldfield, Elvis Costello, Shane MacGowan, Johnny Marr and, of course, Morrissey himself, all second-generation Irish, the children of immigrants, often driven and inspired by their feelings of displacement and community.

From St Patrick to Oliver Cromwell, Ireland's pre-twentieth-century relationship with England is murky, complex and bloody. In the early part of the last century, battle lines were drawn between the Irish Republican movement and their desire for home rule and forces loyal to the crown, such as the Ulster Volunteer Force and the English militia of the Black and Tans. Art wrestled with the difficulties of this relationship in different ways – from the sweet, sentimental beauty of Anglo-Irish composers like Bax, Moeran and Hamilton Harty, to poetry like Yeats's 'Easter, 1916', which talks of a terrible beauty being born from the struggle for Irish independence.

Out of this period came some of the most visceral, contentious songs in the history of British music. On the one hand, the fiery rebel songs of the Republican movement such as the 'Rifles of the IRA',' Go On Home British Soldiers', 'The Bold Fenian Men' and 'The Foggy Dew'; on the other, Loyalist ditties such as 'Lurgan Town', 'The Sash My Father Wore' and 'The Boyne Water' which date back to even earlier struggles like the victory of King William of Orange at the Battle of the Boyne in 1690, and which reflect just how entrenched and desperate the stories they tell are.

Generations grew up singing these songs, both in Ireland and in the cities of England where the Irish made their home. They would sing them in pubs and clubs, at weddings and on the terraces, often with only the dimmest of understandings of the events and issues they commemorated. This was how Paul Gascoigne came to cause a furore when playing for Glasgow Rangers in 1997, as he celebrated a goal in the highly sectarian 'Old Firm' derby match by dancing a jig and playing an imaginary flute, unaware, he said, that it was an inflammatory salute to the Loyalist pipe bands.

As rock and pop made the sixties swing across most of Britain, Ireland had its own more genial, conservative take on the beat group revolution. Showbands were a cross between the big dance band and the small pop combo, usually about six or seven in number and mixing the hits of the day with old standards, presented in a lively, crowd-pleasing style, sometimes with patter and comedy. Van Morrison and Rory Gallagher were among the musicians who cut their musical teeth in showbands, and Roddy Doyle's Commitments are clearly in the tradition. Some 700 of these bands were thought to have been gigging across Ireland in their late-sixties heyday. One of the most popular, on both sides of the border, was The Miami Showband. Three of the band were murdered by loyalist paramilitaries and members of the Ulster Defence Regiment at a bogus checkpoint in 1975. The showband phemomenon dwindled after this, a massacre which *Irish Times* writer Frank McNally called 'an incident that encapsulated all the madness of the time'.

Those times were the height, or should we say the depths, of 'the Troubles', a deceptively anodyne phrase for a period of seemingly intractable horror and violence. There's no definite agreement about when the Troubles began, merely that, after a fairly peaceful decade in the fifties, unrest and political ferment developed around 1966, the fiftieth anniversary of the Easter Rising. This was the year that the illegal Loyalist paramilitary UVF formed, and civil rights marches swiftly followed, demanding an end to discrimination against Catholics in jobs and housing. But the flashpoint came in 1969 with the clashes in Derry that became known as the Battle of the Bogside and, on 14 August, the deployment of British troops on the streets of Northern Ireland.

The events of 1969 ushered in three decades of bloodshed, which went largely unacknowledged in mainstream Irish rock, from Horslips to Thin Lizzy, Rory Gallagher to Van Morrison, and the folk music of Christy Moore and Planxty or the pop ballads of Waterford's Gilbert O'Sullivan.

It took the massacre of unarmed Catholics by the British army, on what became known as Bloody Sunday, for pop to finally take note of the growing mayhem in the province – and even then the response was largely from musicians across the Irish Sea. Both

Beatles of Irish descent wrote songs about the troubles. On his patchy, polemical *Some Time in New York City* John Lennon included two songs about the situation, 'Sunday Bloody Sunday' and 'The Luck of the Irish'. But the most controversial and high-profile musical response to the troubles came from Lennon's erstwhile Beatle partner.

Astoundingly, 'Give Ireland Back to the Irish', was the début single by Paul McCartney's new band Wings, his response to the Bloody Sunday massacre. That he chose such a provocative song to launch his new band's career is a testament to how strongly McCartney felt about the matter. He later told Beatle historian Mark Lewisohn,

> From our point of view it was the first time people questioned what we were doing in Ireland. It was so shocking. I wrote 'Give Ireland Back to the Irish', we recorded it, and I was promptly phoned by the chairman of EMI, Sir Joseph Lockwood, explaining that they wouldn't release it. He thought it was too inflammatory. I told him that I felt strongly about it and they had to release it. He said, 'Well, it'll be banned,' and of course it was. I knew 'Give Ireland Back to the Irish' wasn't an easy route, but it just seemed to me to be the time. All of us in Wings felt the same about it. But [veteran Irish showband guitarist] Henry McCullough's brother, who lived in Northern Ireland, was beaten up because of it. The thugs found out that Henry was in Wings.

As you might imagine, McCartney's musical response to the Irish troubles was more reasonable, affable and tuneful than Lennon's:

Great Britain you are tremendous
And nobody knows like me
But really what are we doing in the land across the sea?

But even such emollient sentiments didn't placate the authorities. The song was censored in a blanket way: it was banned by the BBC, ITV and commercial radio. As we've seen, the BBC declared that it was unsuitable for broadcasting and even refused to mention the title: on the chart run-down *Pick of the Pops* the venerable Alan Freeman had to refer to it as 'a record by the group Wings'. Despite this, the song was in the charts for eight weeks and got to number sixteen. It also climbed to number twenty-two on the *Billboard* Hot 100 and reached number one not only in the Republic of Ireland but also in Spain. 'I'm very proud of that,' said McCartney, years later. 'The Basque separatists loved it.'

Another song released as a direct response to events in the province was Barleycorn's 'Men Behind the Wire' written by Paddy McGuigan about the British government's policy of internment, the imprisonment without trial of suspected Republican sympathisers. Released on 14 December 1971, the song spent five weeks at number one in Ireland, sold more copies than any other Irish single till then and remained in the charts for months. Royalties were donated to families of the internees. It became a rebel standard covered by other Republican musicians such as The Wolfe Tones, Liam Clancy and the Flying Column. Years later, bizarrely, the English singer Dido quoted the famous refrain – 'Armoured cars and tanks and guns/Came to take away our sons/But every man must stand behind/The men behind the wire' – on a track on her largely innocuous album *Safe Home*.

The forces' sweetheart Vera Lynn and 'our boys'.

Lonnie Donegan, the face of the 'rough, mongrel' music that was skiffle.

The British love of the madcap and zany made unlikely pop stars of the Goons, pictured here in 1951.

Very much a 'young one' at this point, the former Harry Webb hits the floor at Elstree Studios for his screen debut in the 1959 movie *Serious Charge*.

The thin blue line meets Beatlemania in full hormonal frenzy outside Buckingham Palace in 1965.

Millie Small, the first superstar of Jamaican music, with DJ Alan 'Fluff' Freeman.

The Kinks
in 1967.
Dedicated, if
not discerning,
followers of
fashion.

Two icons of the swinging sixties:
model Jean Shrimpton poses in a mini.

The Woburn Abbey Festival during that luminous, transcendent summer of 1967.

Mods and rockers enjoying a moment of moral panic.

Serge and Jane; the older continental seducer-Lothario and the wide-eyed English rose in 1970. Their duet 'Je T'Aime' was the first number one to be banned by the BBC.

Pirate radio; rakish, buccaneering and happening without the grown-up world's permission. Robbie Dale, self-styled Admiral of the Beat Fleet on board Radio Caroline.

Prog-caped crusader Rick Wakeman relaxing at home

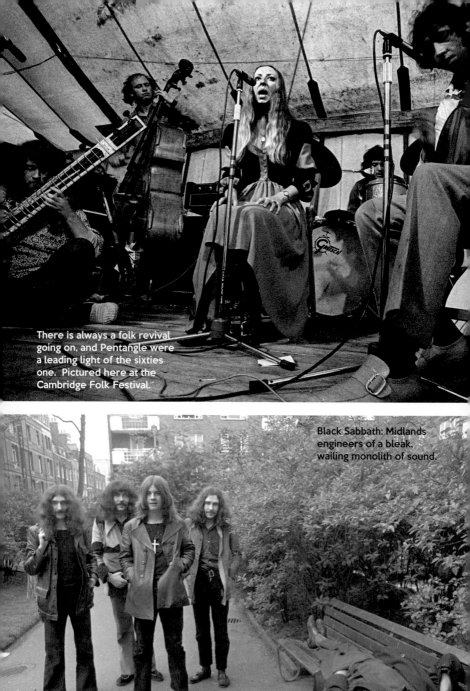

There is always a folk revival going on, and Pentangle were a leading light of the sixties one. Pictured here at the Cambridge Folk Festival.

Black Sabbath: Midlands engineers of a bleak, wailing monolith of sound.

An armed British soldier patrols a street in Londonderry at the height of the Troubles.

NO SURRENDER

Bowie in 1973 as Ziggy
– a smiling, benevolent,
alluringly mysterious alien.

The Sex Pistols sign their short-lived contract with A&M outside Buckingham Palace, 1977.

WHAT PRICE NOW FOR OUR MINERS?

KERESLEY MINERS WIVES UNITED NO RISE NO RETURN

Union of Mine

Part of the Union. Miners' wives protest at the Tower Hill rally in 1972.

Rollermania: part football hooligan, part Andy Stewart's *White Heather Club*.

'Men Behnd the Wire' was from Dublin, though. From Ulster itself came Seamus Heaney's 1975 poem 'Whatever You Say, Say Nothing', a written rather than musical response that summed up a reticence born of fear or intransigence. With the coming of punk, however, magazines like *Hot Press* and labels such as Good Vibrations fostered New Wave culture on both sides of the border and young Northern Irish bands began to emerge and engage through this newly politicised idiom. A Belfast schoolboy band called Highway Star (named after the Deep Purple song) was one of many that underwent a Damascene conversion to punk. Changing their name to Stiff Little Fingers (this time, after a Vibrators' song), they began to write and play material directly inspired by their experience of the Troubles. Their first single, 'Suspect Device', was followed by 'Alternative Ulster', a song that doesn't just condemn the British troops 'and the RUC dog of repression' but demands that the youth of Northern Ireland of both communities transform their own lives and 'alter your native land'.

The Undertones were a similar bunch of proletarian kids from strife-torn Derry, a city whose very name was a ethno-political flashpoint: Londonderry to the Unionists, Derry to the Republicans. The Undertones came from the Catholic community but their music generally eschewed any easy taking of sides, preferring instead to chronicle the mundanity, as well as joy, of working-class life in urban Northern Ireland, where high unemployment was a fact of life. Singer Feargal Sharkey was the only Undertone with a job, delivering TVs for Radio Rentals.

As their music developed from its three-chord roots, the song-writing became more subtle too. 1981's 'It's Going to Happen!' was deceptively upbeat considering its subject matter: Margaret Thatcher's battle against the Maze prison hunger strikers. Ten prisoners ultimately died from starvation, including Bobby Sands, elected as a Member of Parliament during his fast. The Undertones performed it on *Top of the Pops* on the night Sands died, and guitarist Damian O'Neill wore a black armband. Later he wondered whether this might have alienated the band's Protestant fans, of whom there were many.

The Pogues emerged from the punk scene too, but in the pubs and clubs of London. Their place in the music of the Troubles is more than a little problematic. None of The Pogues was actually Irish, and singer Shane MacGowan was a prep-school boy from Kent. But Irish roots and tradition clearly informed their music and one song in particular, 'Streets of Sorrow/Birmingham Six', told the story of innocent Irishmen framed by the British police for pub bombings they didn't commit. But many other of The Pogues' songs seemed more concerned with presenting what could be seen as a clichéd 'Oirishness': a romanticisation of booze, brawling and poetry.

Two of the biggest stadium rock bands of the eighties addressed the Irish question in typically grandiose style. Glasgow's Simple Minds came from that divided city's Catholic community and their track 'Belfast Child' was a folkish lament for all the Troubles' victims. But their arena rock peers U2 had the most direct impact of any rock band on the history of the Six Counties.

'Sunday Bloody Sunday' from 1983 is probably the most famous and recognisable pop song about the troubles. But it isn't just about the 1972 atrocity. According to the band, it also refers to the Bloody Sunday of 1920, a massacre of Irish civilians at a football match in Dublin's Croke Park during the Irish War of Independence. And U2's involvement in Northern Irish politics went beyond the merely musical. Post-Live Aid, Bono had become perhaps the ultimate rock statesman, involved in various charitable and political endeavours, confidant of the Pope and various world leaders. In 1998, as the Peace Process moved slowly towards establishing some kind of calm in Ulster, Bono staged a significant and symbolic moment at a gig at Belfast Waterfront Hall for 2,000 sixth formers ahead of a referendum on the Good Friday agreement. He invited the Unionist hardliner David Trimble and the SDLP leader John Hume on to the stage, where they appeared in shirtsleeves, and, arms locked together, hailed their 'leap of faith out of the past and into the future'. It was a moment of reconciliation across the sectarian and political divide. Hume and Trimble were later awarded the Nobel Peace Prize for their efforts. Maybe Bono should have been included too.

An uneasy peace has prevailed in Northern Ireland since then, with only sporadic outbreaks of violence. We are beginning to see the province as an ordinary part of the British Isles, subject to the same economic and political ups and downs as the rest of us, rather than a war zone. That's the small humane point of a song by Billy Bragg on his *William Bloke* album of 1996. It's called 'Northern Industrial Town' and is a description of a place 'Where the front doors of the houses open into the street/There's no room for front gardens, just a two up, two down'.

The city Bragg describes could be seen as a neighbour to Sheffield, Leeds, Manchester or Glasgow, rather than Kabul, Baghdad or Beirut. But the city is Belfast, and maybe we should come to think of it as just a 'Northern Industrial Town'.

17. PART OF THE UNION

Considering that most of us spend half of our lives (or more) engaged in it, are obsessed with it, addicted to it, dependent on it, and worry if we're not getting it, there are not many pop songs about work. There are even fewer about industrial relations. Enter the words 'British pop' and 'union' into your favourite search engine and you will find many references to The Jam, The Who, Geri Halliwell and Britpop, but not so many to USDAW, Arthur Scargill or Transport House. It's the Union Jack not the Trade Union Standard that seems to flutter over the rock and roll stage in the UK.

We are very different to our American cousins in this respect. And the way that the notion of work is reflected in British and American pop would seem to speak volumes about deep-seated cultural attitudes in the two countries. There's many a true word spoken in jest, and there's many a truth found in the most trivial and unlikely places.

Like Dolly Parton and Bernard Cribbins, for instance. Before George Martin got distracted by those scouse beat-poppers and their tape loops and sitars, he had a proper job making comedy records. The best remembered of those are probably the two hits he made with genial railway stationmaster Bernard Cribbins: 'Right, Said Fred' and 'Hole in the Ground'. Like much British comedy, the humour in these ditties is a sly celebration and satire on the British workman and industrial relations. In 'Right, Said Fred', two hapless removal men spend most of their time drinking tea, complaining and not actually doing much work before clocking off for the day. On the curiously jazzy 'Hole in the Ground', however, there's a hint of sedition as the workman who is digging the titular hole receives some unwanted advice from a 'grand and official' bowler-hatted toff whom he eventually – spoiler alert – kills and buries in the said hole.

In these two little songs a whole mindset and culture is revealed: British workers are essentially lazy, incompetent and opinionated; bosses are aloof and out of touch; and work is pointless and demoralising. In Dolly Parton's 'Nine to Five', the office girl is harassed and overworked and has a similarly unhelpful boss but, chasing the American dream, she pours herself 'a cup of ambition … jump[s] in the shower and the blood starts pumpin'.'

Contrast Dolly Parton's wage slave with the narrator of another song, 'Morning Train (Nine to Five)' by British songstress Sheena Easton. They were both US number ones within months of each other and initially had identical titles. But they could not be more different in spirit. Unlike Dolly, Sheena is not going out to work with her blood pumpin' but spends her day idly and passively dreaming of her baby who takes the morning train, works, and then comes home to her.

Not only is work not seen as fulfilling or meaningful in many pop songs, it's often regarded as actively damaging and stifling to one's natural creativity. There has even been a rich and enduring strain in

British pop reviling work and sneering at guinea pigs treading the wheel. You can hear it in Cat Stevens's 'Matthew & Son', where the office worker is seen as a servile, harried drone. You can hear it in Elvis Costello's 'Welcome to the Working Week', in The Jam's 'Smithers-Jones', in John Lennon's 'Working Class Hero', where the proletariat are 'still fucking peasants as far as [Lennon] can see'. It is also there in many songs by The Kinks, perhaps most explicitly in 'Shangri-La'. In the 1960s the sociologists John Goldthorpe and David Lockwood posited a concept called 'embourgeoisement' in which affluent manual workers such as those in the car plants of Luton and Coventry became more home-centred, less class conscious and more concerned with material wealth for themselves and their families. In 'Shangri-La' Ray Davies seemed to be mocking the commuter who gets on the train every morning while worrying about his mortgage and his hire-puchase agreements.

Compare this with perhaps the greatest song about work ever written. In Jimmy Webb's glorious 'Wichita Lineman', sung definitively by Glen Campbell, we are invited, compelled in fact, to identify with the telegraph engineer testing the lines in the Kansas flatlands, as he works quietly and with dignity thinking about his holiday, his girl and whether that stretch down south will stand the strain of the winter. In an interview with US website Songfacts Jimmy Webb has said of 'Wichita Lineman':

My characters were all ordinary guys. They were all blue-collar guys who did ordinary jobs. As Billy Joel likes to say, which is pretty accurate, 'They're ordinary people thinking extraordinary thoughts.' I always appreciated that comment, because I thought it was very close to what I was doing or what I was trying to do. And they came from ordinary

towns. They came from places like Galveston and Wichita
and places like that.

That lineman in Wichita was probably unionised, in the Commun-
ications Workers of America union, the largest union in the world.
Considering that friendly societies and trade unions began here, with
the Steam Engine Makers' society in the early nineteenth century,
and the first Trades Union Congress was held in Manchester in 1868,
the labour and union movements have been far more prominent
in American music. Pete Seeger, Phil Ochs and Woody Guthrie
have all written and sung songs celebrating and encouraging union
membership. Guthrie's most famous of these is 'Union Maid',
written when he and Seeger were part of the Almanac Singers as
a response to a request for a song encouraging women to join a
union. Seeger later said in his book *The Incompleat Folksinger*:

> I'm proud to say I was present when 'Union Maid' was written
> in June, 1940, in the plain little office of the Oklahoma City
> Communist Party. Bob Wood, local organiser, had asked
> Woody Guthrie and me to sing there the night before for
> a small group of striking oil workers. Early next morning,
> Woody got to the typewriter and hammered out the first two
> verses of 'Union Maid' set to a European tune that Robert
> Schumann arranged for piano ('The Merry Farmer') back in
> the early 1800s. Of course, it's the chorus that really makes
> it – its tune.

Guthrie's 'Union Maid' is part of a tradition of American folk
music that has explicitly encouraged collectivism and organisation.
In Britain, liberals made to feel smug by televangelists, Fox News

and the like tend to rather patronisingly characterise the US as an innately conservative country. But America was a nation forged in revolution and the violent overthrow of a foreign dictator – namely us. And American folk has often been more directly agit-prop than its English counterpart.

The great inheritor of Woody Guthrie's legacy was, of course, Bob Dylan, who had often addressed the issue of work, bosses and the machinations of industry. His song 'Maggie's Farm' was at the centre of a controversy when Dylan performed it at the 1965 Newport Folk Festival in an aggressive, electric version, to the consternation of assembled folkies like the great Pete Seeger. But what's often forgotten in all the hullabaloo of Dylan 'going electric' is the song itself, and Dylan's identification of himself as little more than a service-industry worker shackled to the demands of profit and marketing. Two decades later he was still interested in the myth and travails of the American working man. In the song 'Union Sundown' from his album *Infidels* he bemoans the drain of jobs away from American manufacturing to cheap labour in the developing world:

> *They don't make nothin' here no more*
> *You know, capitalism is above the law*
> *It say, 'It don't count 'less it sells'*
> *When it costs too much to build it at home*
> *You just build it cheaper someplace else*

Thirty-three years after Dylan's guiding light Woody Guthrie wrote 'Union Maid' in those Communist Party offices in Oklahoma, Richard Hudson and John Ford, two members of the British band the Strawbs, used it as the basis for their own wry and ambivalent take on the union movement. 'Part of the Union' was composed in the strife-torn, candlelit Britain of 1973 at a time when, ironically, workplace relations within the band were far from cordial. Strawbs founder Dave Cousins was unhappy with the way that Hudson and Ford's songs were taking the band away from its folk roots as the Strawberry Hill Boys towards a more radio-friendly pop sound. Hudson and Ford were originally going to release 'Part of the Union' themselves under the name The Brothers – the fraternal union greeting – but the record company saw its topical appeal and insisted the Strawbs release it against band leader Cousins's wishes. 'Part of the Union' was seen by hardcore fans and critics as an aberration, but it still became their biggest hit, only kept from the number-one slot by the might of Sweet's 'Blockbuster'.

To understand just why 'Part of the Union' was so successful we have to look beyond the naggingly catchy sing-along tune and to the candlelit hinterland of Britain at the time. As it climbed the charts, Edward Heath's Conservative government introduced a pay freeze in a desperate attempt to curb inflation and shore up the collapsing economy. Soon after it charted over one and a half million workers struck in protest. Unions led by TUC General Secretary Jack Jones were in daily conflict with Edward Heath's government. The waves of industrial action, including a work to rule by the powerful mining union the NUM, plus a global oil crisis, resulted in a severe energy and fuel shortage in Britain. To conserve supplies, Heath's government announced that commercial users of electricity would be limited to three specified consecutive days' consumption each week and prohibited from working longer hours on those days. TV networks would cease broadcasting at 10.30 p.m. It was into this gloomy, darkening winter that the Strawbs appeared on *Top of the Pops* with Hudson banging on an outsize drum emblazoned with The Associated Union of Strawbs Workers singing a song that seem to both mock and celebrate the entrenched conflict and the national crisis.

A famous US labour protest song of the 1930s, written by Florence Reece, covered by Seeger, Guthrie and others and now a staple of the political folk scene, asks 'Which Side Are You On, Boys?'. And the question is, which side were the Strawbs on? Many commentators at the time thought that the song was sarcastically anti-union, a common trope in British comedy and satire from Peter Sellers's Fred Kite to Mike Yarwood's repertoire of seventies union leaders such as Jack Jones, Len Murray, Clive Jenkins and Vic Feather. But the band themselves always maintained that the song was a raucous and wry celebration of the working man and the union movement, albeit a tongue in cheek one. As so often, the British response to a crisis was to ally with not ideologues of left or right but to roll our eyes and have a laugh.

A few months later, though, in May 1974, with the country still reeling from the strikes, power cuts and three-day week, Alan Price had a hit with his 'Jarrow Song', which seemed to advocate a much harder line. In Price's song, based on the events of the thirties, the north-east hunger marchers are encouraged, often by their wives, to fight for a decent wage and freedom and told to 'burn down' the London establishment if they refuse. The song's basis was historical but its contemporary relevance to mid-seventies Britain was obvious.

With its brass-band backing and earthy good humour, 'Jarrow Song' is clearly rooted in a British folk music tradition rather than rock. When the working man and woman have found a sympathetic voice in the people's songs it's usually in the folk and traditional sphere. 'Blackleg Miner' is a nineteenth-century composition that's been covered by many folk stalwarts like Dick Gaughan and Richard Thompson. But most vividly and memorably, Steeleye Span played their version of the song live at Nottingham's Theatre Royal in 1985 during the miners' strike. Many of Nottingham's miners hadn't supported the strike and continued to work. In this charged atmosphere the song ceased to be a quaint historical curio and became a confrontational political act, arguably far more 'punk' than anything the Sex Pistols ever dared.

Folk music today is still far more likely to get its hands dirty with the world of the workplace than its chart-pop or album-rock cousin. Modern folk act The Unthanks recently worked on an album and film project about the history of the Tyneside shipyards of their native north-east. *Songs from the Shipyards* is not a period piece or a rose-tinted romanticisation of what was a tough, dangerous, precarious way to earn a living, though. The Unthanks celebrate hard physical work and the communities for whom it was a way of life without sentimentalising matters.

Back in 1973 when the Strawbs rode high in the charts with 'Part of the Union', those communities were often in daily conflict with the government and their representatives were on TV as often as the Strawbs. With the coming of Thatcherism at the decade's end, though, union leaders were less likely to be seen as freedom fighters and more as treacherous fifth columnists. Speaking of striking miners during her first term, Margaret Thatcher even went as far as to claim they were traitors: 'We had to fight the enemy without in the Falklands. We always have to be aware of the enemy within, which is much more difficult to fight and more dangerous to liberty.'

So dangerous were these enemies within that the full force of the law and the state was mobilised against them. There were roadblocks on the motorways, identification-demands by uniformed men, cars turned back on the Queen's highway, security checks on motorway exits near Mansfield, the free movement of free citizens curtailed, Nottinghamshire villages under curfew, phones tapped and diaries seized and photocopied. All of this to stop the movement of flying pickets, mobile units of workers who would travel to reinforce the picket lines of other strikers elsewhere in the country. It is an era long gone. Look now in the history books or on the internet and the first mention you will find of Flying Pickets is with regard to the charts of Christmas 1983 when five old-school Marxist activists, veterans of the left-wing 7:84 theatre company, had a small, bitter revenge on Margaret Thatcher by calling themselves The Flying Pickets in tribute to their striking brethren and having a huge number one with 'Only You'. Elvis Costello said of 'Only You' that he wasn't terribly keen on the music, but that it was always nice to have Communists at number one at Christmas.

In 1998 'Part of the Union' resurfaced as a television advert-isement for insurance company Norwich Union. But by then the long years of Conservatism were over and a new mood was abroad. Smoother, younger, more saleable, it spoke with a classless, well-modulated, regular guy kind of voice. 'Call me Tony,' it said.

Our youth now love luxury. They have bad manners, contempt for authority; they show disrespect for their elders and love chatter in place of exercise; they no longer rise when elders enter the room; they contradict their parents, chatter before company; gobble up their food and tyrannise their teachers.

Obese, lazy, argumentative and disrespectful, Socrates, it seems, had young people sussed some two and a half thousand years before the *Daily Mail* even rolled off a press. Hesiod did too, another Greek, but writing four hundred years earlier, in the 8th century BC:

I see no hope for the future of our people if they are dependent on the frivolous youth of today, for certainly all youth are reckless beyond words. When I was a boy, we were taught to be discreet and respectful of elders, but the present youth are exceedingly wise and impatient of restraint.

Feckless, self-indulgent, workshy, violent and probably on drugs, in other words. And just what is it that makes them like that? Once again, millennia before we'd even thought of Facebook, junk food, body piercings or bad parents, a guy called Plato knew exactly where the blame lay: 'When the mode of the music changes, the walls of the city shake.' As long as there has been fashion, music and young people in search of an identity, there's been a whole lotta city wall shakin' going on.

In Britain we've been spotting trends, gangs and scenes among those crazy young people since at least 1590, when the Jacobeans noticed a young people's scene – the 'roaring boys' – made up of noisy gangs of aggressive street louts who intimidated passers-by. In Victorian Manchester, gangs called scuttlers, identified by their fringed hair, tilted caps and bell-bottomed trousers, would patrol their favourite music halls and attack members of rival gangs with their sharpened belt buckles. Members were recruited from the age of fourteen up to twenty-one, and included girls as well as boys. The females often took an active part in fights between rival gangs.

Flappers and bright young things aside, early twentieth-century Britain, experiencing two world wars, left little room for young people to dwell on the building of subcultures. To an extent the military provided a sense of belonging, a language and a look. But after 1945 a creature called 'the teenager' began to appear courtesy of the youthquake built on the post-war baby boom. Social historian Steven Mintz has claimed that until about 1955 youth subculture did not exist, as children aspired to (or were forced into) adulthood as fast as their physical development allowed. But new social attitudes combined with better diet and living conditions meant the first generation of post-war teenagers were fit, healthy and physically adult while remaining largely free from adult roles and responsibilities. They had disposable cash but often didn't have to do hard physical work to earn it. This freedom and privileged position gave them the opportunity to react, respond and revel in their surroundings in new ways, and music and fashion were a major part of that vibrant response.

In September 1953 the *Daily Express* described a new youth phenomenon they called the Teddy boy, Teddy being short for Edwardian, the Teddy boy's clothes style of choice – a dandified throwback to the aristocratic styles of Edward VII's reign. To dress well in this style was not cheap in 1908 or 1958. The clothes were often tailor-made and paid for on HP, but a commitment to looking smart and dressing well has often been a characteristic of working-class style.

Teds were the first youth group in England to differentiate themselves through their age, look and love of a certain kind of music. They helped create the notion of a youth market that remains today.

Ten years or so later, the mods, another fastidiously dressed working-class youth cult, began to emerge, like edgy urban butterflies, on the streets of London. Mods took their cue from the earlier modernists, described in the 1959 novel *Absolute Beginners* by Colin MacInnes as young modern jazz fans who dressed in sharp modern Italian clothes. But this soon came to mean sharply dressed working-class youth who collected r&b, Motown and jazz records, watched French and Italian art films and read Italian magazines, popped pills, rode scooters and danced.

The mods, whose heyday was the early and mid-1960s, loved black American music and continental chic. But the movement also sprang its own homegrown bands, chiefly The Who, The Small

Faces, The Spencer Davis Group, The Action and The Creation. Recreationally, they were committed hedonists who worked and played hard. Major store was set around getting things just right, be it the music, the scooters – Vespa or Lambretta – or the clothes, Italian labels, Sta-Prest, Ben Sherman, Fred Perry.

At the opposite end of the aesthetic spectrum from all this were the rockers. They'd been around since the 1950s, sometimes called ton-up boys or leather boys (as in the British movie of the same name) for their penchant for customising motorcycles and taking them for 100 m.p.h. spins on arterial roads, stopping to hang out at transport cafes, tea stalls and truck stops. Out of practicality, their clothes were functional and often dirty: heavily patched and decorated leather and denim jackets, T-shirts, jeans, boots, Brylcreem. This defiantly unchic look meant rockers were often not welcomed into clubs, pubs and dance halls. This pushed them further towards outsider status and an identification with the undomesticated, itinerant lone biker, a romantic image from Marlon Brando to *Easy Rider*. The initial British rockers favoured the simple rock and roll of Chuck Berry, Gene Vincent and Eddy Cochran, what George Melly called 'smash and screw music'.

Rockers were likely to work in dead-end manual labour or factory jobs. Mods often worked in offices or some kind of white-collar occupation. Rockers saw the mods as effeminate, consumerist and phoney; mods saw the rockers as boorish, naïve, conservative and ugly. As cultures, they were diametrically opposed to each other's taste and lifestyles and some of them took those differences to the seaside in the spring of 1964.

After the fashion of Churchill, they fought each other on the beaches, with coshes, razor blades, bike chains, flick-knives and knuckle-dusters, then the promenade at Clacton over the Easter weekend, 1964. By Whitsun the trouble had spread to Margate, Brighton and Bournemouth. But we should be wary of exaggerating the depth and breadth of the mod and rocker clashes. As film crews and journalists arrived, the battles were smaller but better publicised. But they never spread much further that a few south-coast resorts. There were no clashes worth the name in Blackpool, Filey or Colywn Bay.

However geographically constrained, the brief, bruising summer of the mods and rocker violence left an indelible stamp on our cultural landscape. It's still shorthand for the reckless, casual, tribal nature of youth and the potential for madness that pop brings with it. It was helped in this by being mythologized in music by perhaps the most significant of all the mod bands, The Who, in their sprawling concept piece or 'rock opera' *Quadrophenia* and its flagship single '5.15'. While The Who started off in 1964 as card-carrying members of the London mod scene, making their name with muscular rebellion anthems like 'My Generation', *Quadrophenia* was actually recorded at the reflective distance of 1973. As such, it is both nostalgic for the thrills of the era and yet wise to the pitfalls of youthful excesses. In '5.15', the confused, vulnerable protagonist Jimmy falls into a drug-induced reverie, albeit an angry and fragmented one, on the titular train to Brighton – scene of some of his most life-affirming moments during that febrile summer of 1964. Out of his brain on the 5.15, as the song has it, he rages internally against the vapidity and sterility of ordinary life, and how the youthful promise of the mod culture has let him down, as he feels his own life and psyche collapse to the sounds of throaty brass fanfares and a driving beat.

Thus, thanks to The Who, the iconic images of fighting among the deckchairs and our endless appetite for nostalgia, the brief flaring of mod and rocker violence is still seen as emblematic of youth subcultural conflict by generations of pundits and documentary makers. The *Birmingham Post* said in 1964 that mods and rockers were 'internal enemies' who would 'bring about disintegration of a nation's character'. It was a moral panic and described as such by the young sociologist Stanley Cohen, who hung out with the kids and in the courts and from it produced the landmark sociological study *Folk Devils and Moral Panics*.

The harder end of the mod aesthetic gave rise to one of the seventies' most recognisable, feared and misunderstood youth cults, the skinhead. Skinheads, too, valued smartness and style, but they rejected the artistic and cultural aesthetic of the mods. Theirs was a more macho, conservative and aggressive attitude to the world around them. Eventually, and ironically, what began as a celebration of characteristic working-class style and self-assertion curdled into a narrow cult of nationalism and violence against perceived outsiders: hippies, immigrants and gay people. But the ugly, ultra-nationalist right-wing skinhead of today, snarling in his fatigues and piercings, is a world away from the seventies' rude boy in a Crombie with a folded handkerchief, white Levis and Harrington jacket.

Cultural critics, writers and sometimes even kids themselves have long argued about just what youth cults really are and what they're for. Twentieth-century sociologists of the functionalist school like Talcott Parsons – who first used the term 'youth culture' – benignly thought that youth cults and teenage groupings were a place to break with parents and a space to work through issues of identity before the demands of work and family bore down upon young people. Youth culture, then, is a rite of passage. Marxist theorists have argued among themselves over whether youth culture is a radical critique and rejection of wider, consumerist society or an integral part of capitalism, whereby young people are encouraged to buy themselves a lifestyle and an identity. Shari Benstock and Suzanne Ferriss made the fascinating claim that the mods' obsession with fashion and shopping was the 'ultimate affront to male working-class traditions', since traditionally shopping was usually done and certainly only enjoyed by women. Browsing the racks for your two-tone suit was, in fact, a quietly revolutionary act of gender politics.

Glam rock, punk rock and New Romantics, the great music cults of the seventies and early eighties, were highly visible but it's arguable how genuinely counter-cultural any of them were. And since the eighties the routine complaint of the ageing pop fan is that there is no youth culture that stands for anything now – a total lack of angry confrontation with the authorities that bespeaks only apathy and conformism. Others would argue that no youth subculture has ever provided any challenge to the powers that be, merely a warm glow of identity and purpose to a generation of pop fans.

But what a glow. And those of us who aren't part of today's teenage music subcultures should be wary of claiming to know or understand them. Youth cults still cause a moral panic. Witness the recent hysteria over hoodies. A glut of British films over recent years has demonised, sometimes literally, young hooded street males from *Harry Brown* to *Eden Lake* to Philip Ridley's *Heartless*. Happily, Joe Cornish's brilliant *Attack the Block* bucks this trend and attempts to understand the lives a of its sink-estate tribe and portray them with humour and a dash of heroism.

Senior lecturer in sociology and criminology, Dr Jack Fawbert, located the genesis of the great hoodie panic in the June 2005 decision by the Bluewater shopping centre in Kent to ban customers wearing hoodies. Prevously, the mainstream media had hardly ever used the word hoodie. Suddenly it became the *de rigueur* headline applied to any negative behaviour by young people, even when there was no evidence that hoodies had actually been worn. Moral entrepreneurs like former Metropolitan police commissioner Sir John Stevens called for longer prison sentences for 'thugs wearing hoods'. As with the mods and rockers, ironically, and somewhat hilariously, the condemnation saw hooded tops become a must-have fashion item: sales soared in Bluewater, even though customers couldn't wear them out of the shop. As Dr Fawbert pointed out,

> Today, nobody is scared of mods and rockers and, despite the impression having been given that hoodies terrorising British society was almost the beginning of the end for civilisation, in twenty years' time, the same attitude will prevail with regard to hoodies.

And, one imagines, to Street Rats, the Get Paid Crew, trackies, Young Alts, Indie Scenesters, Craft Kids, Rahs, or any of the other youth tribes Channel 4 has identified in a project that's been running over the last few years. Two forces have driven the great turbine of pop music and social change more than any other, and both are forms of conflict. Wanting to be like everyone else is good for the makers of uniforms but bad for the makers of art. All human progress is based on dissent, choice, and what San Francisco's musical mavericks The Residents call 'the globe-wrenching power of difference'. It is the grit in the oyster that becomes the pearl.

In a nice example of the cyclical and serial nature of these things, some concerned, well-meaning voices decided that boredom, as was ever the case, was to blame for the violent teenage cult of the scuttlers, who once caused panic on the streets of Manchester to the sound of music-hall ditties. Accordingly, the philanthropic folks set up a series of clubs in the poorest and worst areas of the city, offering sport and healthy recreation as an alternative to robbery and street fighting. One of these 'lads' clubs' was in Salford. Many years later Graham Nash of the Hollies would hang out there, and the club would be immortalised in the striking image of the legendary Manchester group The Smiths on the cover of *The Queen is Dead*.

Music, in all its diversity, runs through the story of British youth culture like the streak of lime in a punk's hair or the stitching on a button-down Ben Sherman. It is the business of youth to get on with the business of baffling their elders and sometimes their friends. As the sick, mod-cult spokesmen turned elder statesman of British letters, Pete Townshend, once said, 'The kids are alright.'

19. Y VIVA ESPAÑA

There's an old gag that says that the British weather is the world's most powerful colonising influence. Whether it's down to the rain, or our supposedly terrible food, or even our restless and inquiring minds, there's no doubt that we Brits invented the notion of leisure tourism. Firstly, it was Oxbridge graduates on the Grand Tour, essentially a seventeenth-century gap year spent in France and Italy admiring the Grand Canal and the treasures of Renaissance art. Then, with the coming of the railways in the 1840s, travel and tourism became a much more democratic endeavour. Given the later associations of Brits on holiday – lager, Bacardi Breezers, vomiting in tavernas, and stomach pumps – it's somewhat ironic that the first organised excursion, or package holiday, took place on 5 July 1841, when Thomas Cook chartered a train to take some temperance campaigners to a rally in Loughborough to campaign against the evils of drink.

Pretty soon, though, the trains were driving holidaymakers to drink, not from it. With cheap mass transit and better conditions of employment, the Victorian working classes found themselves able to enjoy the pleasure palaces of burgeoning seaside resorts such as Southend, New Brighton and, infamously, Blackpool. Attractions included zoos, opera houses, theatres, lagoons, pleasure gardens and, of course, music halls.

Music hall, like the seaside in general, was popular, vulgar and vibrant. A playground for the working classes, and a welcome release from the arduous monotony of labour, music halls were the clubs and venues of their day, and music was at the heart of their appeal. Songs like 'Daisy, Daisy' and 'The Boy in the Gallery' were the big pop hits of the time. In *The Making of Modern Britain* Andrew Marr says:

> There were plenty of teenage stars tearing their way towards ruin with drink, promiscuity and even drugs … The rewards could be spectacular, particularly for the singers who were prepared to go on tour to Australia, South Africa, Paris and New York. But for most music-hall performers, like most rock bands, life was an endless trail from provincial date to date, always on the road, sleeping in lousy rooms, dreaming of a hit.

'Abroad is bloody,' said George VI, a remark later expanded upon by the second Baron Redesdale and father of the Mitford sisters into, 'Abroad is unutterably bloody and foreigners are fiends.' Ironically, some of the first foreign holiday tours were developed after the First World War for families wishing to see the battlefields on which their husbands and brothers had died. But as the great wars of the twentieth century gave way to peace and prosperity, it didn't take long for the average Briton to change George VI's remark to 'Abroad is bloody great.'

After the Second World War, as British seaside resorts embarked on a long, slow decline, Thomas Cook began promoting foreign holidays on the Continent. In the early 1950s, when only one in a hundred Britons had ever been abroad, the company showed information films in town halls, encouraging holidaymakers to visit Spain, Italy and Switzerland. It worked. A craze for foreign travel caught on and within a decade demand rocketed.

Horizon, founded by Vladimir Raitz, offered trips from Gatwick to the Mediterranean. At Calvi, in Corsica, there is still a Club Horizon railway station on the coast, but the crowds soon moved on to Mallorca and the Costa Brava. Other companies – Lunn Poly, Clarksons and more – joined in offering these so-called 'package' holidays, which combined transport and accommodation arrangements into a single deal. By the late 1950s and 1960s, cheap package holidays were giving a generation of ordinary Britons an affordable chance to travel abroad. One of the first charter airlines was Euravia, which began flights from Manchester Airport in 1961 and Luton Airport in 1962. Once distant and mysterious destinations like Crete, Corfu and the Costa Brava became as familiar as Clacton, Cleethorpes and Colwyn Bay. Millions of working British folk began a giddy annual summer pilgrimage to the Continent: the 1938 Holidays with Pay Act had guaranteed workers paid leave from their jobs, and they set off, clutching their Ambre Solaire and Harold Robbins's paperbacks, in search of sun, sea, sex and fun in general.

Music was a big part of that fun, hand in hand with drink, of course. Sometimes this will have meant the indigenous music of the holiday destination, and maybe a few albums of bouzouki or flamenco made their way back to Britain along with the ouzo, sombreros and Mateus Rosé. But the first real holiday pop hit is a great example of that weird, sweet, baffling yet simple musical Esperanto that we might call Europop.

Despite winning *Opportunity Knocks* a couple of times, the Latin-flavoured Scottish four-piece Los Caracas couldn't get a hit in Britain. So they decamped to Italy, changed their name and their style, but were still living on corned beef on a campsite outside Rome until a song by a Merseysider called Lally Stott gave them a massive hit across Italy, then Spain, then the rest of the Continent. Naggingly catchy with a queer, nursery-rhyme lyric, bumptiously danceable, especially with a few vinos or Nastro Azzurros inside you, package holidaymakers returning from Rimini and Rhodes sought it out on their return to the UK. Championed by Tony Blackburn, it was the hit of the summer of 1971, remaining at number one for five weeks from early June. Critics loathed it, of course, and even the band weren't keen, initially. Band leader Ken Andrew said, 'We were as disgusted with the thought of recording it as most people were at the thought of buying it. But at the end of the day, we liked it.'

As well he might. 'Chirpy Chirpy, Cheep Cheep' sold over ten million copies worldwide. 'Y Viva España' sold fewer and only reached number four here three years later, but whereas Middle of the Road's holiday hit was essentially a piece of memorable pop doggerel, 'Y Viva España' wasn't just for the peeling package-holiday popsters. It was about them.

Oddly, the song was originally written by two Belgians, Leo Roozenstraten and Leo Caerts, in 1971, and was a hit across Europe in various versions with a straightforwardly romantic, even clichéd celebration of Spain.

How beautiful is the Mediterranean Sea,
the Costa Brava and the Costa del Sol.

The fandango and the sardana excite me
because in your notes there's life and there's heat.

For its UK release, though, a former advertising man called Eddie Seago added a lyric that's also a kind of celebration; a wry and pungent anthem to the new meeting of minds and more between the cultures of Britain and Spain in the bars and bodegas of Benidorm and Marbella.

Musically 'Y Viva España' is a cheesy, perhaps unsubtle pastiche – the musical equivalent of those bullfighting posters adorned with your own name – albeit one with Seago's funny, *risqué*, technically adept lyric. But the rhythm is a *paso doble*: the dance of the bullring and the meter of the lyric cleverly follow that.

And in some ways it is pure music hall, with its blushing British belles and saucy Latin Lotharios. There are seaside postcard references to kissing him behind the castanets and rattling his maracas. And the broken rhyme of 'chat a matador' is straight out of the Hollywood songbook. But we shouldn't over-egg this crème Catalane. It's not an imperishable pop classic by any means, although as a tack-sharp period piece, it's as insightful as 'Ghost Town' or 'God Save the Queen'. To compound the cross-cultural fertilisation, it was sung by a sexy Swede called Sylvia Vrethammar. It hinted at, in its own way, a very successful, very cordial kind of European Union.

Of course, there is an actual European Union of pop, one that's every bit as exasperating and controversial and that conjures up even more Euro-scepticism than the one in Brussels.

The European Broadcasting Union was formed on 12 February 1950 by twenty-three broadcasters from across the continent at a conference in Torquay. It wasn't long before the director of Swiss

TV, Marcel Bezençon, proposed a song competition between the member EBU nations, both as a technical experiment in broadcasting and as a symbolic gesture of unity from a continent not long since riven by war. The first contest was held in Lugano, Switzerland in 1956, and was won by the host country.

Since then, Eurovision has grown into, depending on one's point of view, an annual spectacular of good-natured fun or a grisly camp monstrosity built on terrible music and factionalism. The continuation of war by other dreadful means. Well, not always dreadful.

If ABBA's 'Waterloo' is the best Eurovision winner ever, it's not for want of other nations trying. The United Kingdom has won on five occasions, been runner up on fifteen and finished last three times. Our relationship with the contest is as conflicted as our relationship with the Continent. We want to be loved and respected by them and yet we do not trust them; we mock them but envy them, think them ungrateful and duplicitous ... but are desperate to be accepted, and also want to take our ball home and see how they like it then.

The Eurovision Song Contest has never been cool, which has possibly been its charm, at least to us cynical Brits. But from the late 1980s onwards, the music that drew thousands of young Britons to the package resorts of the Mediterranean was hip and underground. These sounds were cool in a way Sylvia and Middle of the Road had never been. Music now was not just a part of the trip, it was the trip. And a new kind of trip in every sense.

Fifty miles offshore from Valencia, the third largest of the Balearic islands, Ibiza, had long been a draw for night owls, dreamers and clubbers. In the sixties hippy idealists saw it as a paradisiacal playground of nature, peace and drug taking, as seen in the movie *More*, with music by Pink Floyd. Ibiza enjoyed a freedom unthinkable in the rest of Franco's fascist Spain. In 1973, marshland was drained on an old *finca*, or rural estate, called Pacha to make a kind of discothèque that became popular with locals and, later, foreign jetsetters. In the 1980s a club called Ku became a kind of outdoor Studio 54, attracting sun-seeking celebrity party animals like Roman Polanski, Grace Jones, Freddie Mercury and Jean Paul Gaultier.

But towards the end of that decade the club scene became less exclusive, more enthusiastic; less about designer labels and being seen and more about a delirious love for the music, the vibe and losing oneself in the crowd. Ibiza became the holiday destination of choice for working Britons intoxicated by the new club sounds of acid house and the so-called second summer of love.

At his legendary nights at the Amnesia club DJ Alfonso would spin a playful mix of everything from Cyndi Lauper to Henry Mancini to Art of Noise, an eclectic approach that fed back into the clubs of Manchester and London: Shoom, Phuture and the Haçienda. In late 1987 and late 1988 a succession of English visitors including London DJs Nicky Holloway, Paul Oakenfold and Danny Rampling, and Northern musicians like New Order and Happy Mondays would be influenced by the new Balearic beats, an influence you could hear on Happy Mondays' tracks like 'Hallelujah' and New Order's *Technique*, an album recorded in a party atmosphere on the island itself.

Before long, though, resorts like Ibiza, Magaluf, Ayia Napa on Cyprus, and Zante and Kos off Greece became victims of their own success. As hordes of young Britons, many younger and less discriminating about music or DJ mixes, flocked to these summer destinations, so the resorts became synonymous with drunken excess, exhibitionism, vulgarity, and even violence.

Blur's emblematic mid-ninetiess hit 'Boys and Girls' celebrates the phenomenon, after a fashion, and talks of 'following the herd down to Greece on holiday'.

In 2012, smart US weekly the *New Yorker* ran a fair-minded if mildly horrified piece about the young Brit on holiday abroad. It acknowledged that, as a nation, we are more outgoing than Americans, noting that 'eighty per cent of the British population possesses a passport, versus America's thirty-five', but then pointing out that we have 'transformed Spain's Magaluf into "Shagaluf" and the Costa del Sol into the "Costa del Concrete", where steak and kidney pies outnumber paellas'.

The American website AskMen recently listed its favourite drinking holiday destinations, but was at pains to point out, 'No, we're not talking about a list for binge-drinking boozing Brits here. You won't find Malia, Magaluf or Kos on this run-down. These suggestions aren't for the uneducated drinker who doesn't care which bourbon is being poured, or who thinks that house wine was created by Paul van Dyk. This is a list of locations where lovers of beer, wine and spirits can truly enjoy the finer aspects of their drinks.'

Faced with this kind of smugness, it's hard not to fancy a cheeky Vimto, head for the nearest foam party and ask the DJ for some Whigfield. We may not know our Grey Goose from our Smirnoff Ice, but we do know how to make Saturday night last for two weeks self-catering.

20. DON'T CRY FOR ME ARGENTINA

What were the golden years of rock music in Britain? A subjective question, of course. But there's a wealth of learned critical opinion and popular feeling that would say that those charmed and fertile years between 1965 and 1968, when England swung and British rock was the most imaginative, adventurous and appealing scene in the world, were rock's *anni mirabiles*. Just think of the albums to come out of this era. In fact, think of one album, the one album that incredibly was the bestselling album of 1965, 1966 and 1968.

Can that be right? One album. Yes. And it wasn't any of those ones you'd think. Had it not been for those pesky upstarts The Beatles and their one solitary year at the top of the album charts with *Sgt Pepper* in 1967, the biggest album throughout the golden age of British Rock would have been not by Lennon and McCartney, nor Jagger and Richards; not by Townshend or Ray Davies or Pink Floyd, but by Rodgers and Hammerstein, Julie Andrews, Christopher Plummer and the seven Von Trapp kids. Yes, *The Sound of Music* was the bestselling album of the mid-sixties. Rock didn't rule those golden years in Britain; musicals did.

And did this rankle with the aforementioned Townshend, Davies and Floyd? Well, if it did, it didn't stop any of them trying to get on the bandwagon. For what are *Tommy*, *Quadrophenia*, *Arthur* and *The Wall*, or for that matter Lou Reed's *Berlin* or David Bowie's *Ziggy Stardust* ... if they are not musicals – outlandish, outsized fictions staged in song? You can call them rock operas but in their plush, velour, fire-curtained hearts, from the one and nines where the ice-cream lady proffers her choc ices, they look and sound exactly like the sound of musicals.

The very beginning, it's a very good place to start, as the delightful Julie Andrews herself sang in *The Sound of Music*. Telling stories via songs dates back to time immemorial. The ancient Greeks included music and dance in their stage comedies and tragedies as early as the fifth century BC, and we know that the great Athenian playwrights, Aeschylus and Sophocles, composed their own music to move along the action in their works. In other words, showtunes have been around for twenty-five hundred years. As with much else, the Romans borrowed from and developed Greek theatre. The comedies of Plautus included song and dance routines performed with orchestral accompaniment. In Europe in the Middle Ages strolling players, minstrels and troubadours toured their musical productions, and the Renaissance saw the heyday of Commedia dell'Arte, an Italian tradition where raucous clowns improvised their way through familiar stories with musical interludes and devices. By the 1700s ballad and comic operas like John Gay's *Beggar's Opera* were the hot tickets of the day in England, France and Germany. All of these pre-date and then run parallel to the development of grand and classical opera. They are in some ways the loam of pop music.

Though they are often elevated with terms such as operetta, Gilbert and Sullivan's works are to all intents and purposes musicals.

And in their light, catchy, entertaining handling of social, moral and political themes, they prefigure the musicals and pop compositions to come. The great American songsmith Johnny Mercer said, 'We all come from Gilbert.' Alan Jay Lerner saw Gilbert as the father of the modern pop lyric, who 'raised lyric writing from a serviceable craft to a legitimate popular art form'.

> I was born into a generation that still took light music seriously. The lyrics and melodies of Gilbert and Sullivan were hummed and strummed into my consciousness at an early age. My father sang them, my mother played them, my nurse, Emma, breathed them through her teeth while she was washing me, dressing me, undressing me and putting me to bed. My aunts and uncles, who were legion, sang them singly and in unison at the slightest provocation.

Sweetly, this is an experience successive generations of British pop kids will remember, perhaps replacing Gilbert and Sullivan down the years with Gracie Fields, Irish tenors, then The Beatles or Take That, the power of what Coward once called cheap music being reinforced by being handed down orally in a DIY fashion that pre-dates and can still sometimes trump technology.

Noël Coward's brittle, elegant music, like that of his friend and mentor Ivor Novello, came to define English musical theatre between the wars, a curious mixture of cut glass and sentiment. Although saying little, in their light, gossipy parade of aristocrats and socialites, about how ordinary England lived, they did come to embody a certain kind of Englishness to the extent that even today the respected Internet Movie Data Base opens its biography of him: 'Noël Coward virtually invented the concept of Englishness for the twentieth century. He was indeed the first Brit pop star, the first ambassador of "cool Britannia".' All of which would be news to George Formby, The Beatles, Winston Churchill, the Sex Pistols, Margaret Thatcher, David Beckham, the Spice Girls, Adele and many more.

Late in his career, Coward did write a musical called *Ace of Clubs* set in a Soho nightclub populated with sailors, gangsters and chorus girls, quite unlike any other Coward musical. It was clearly, if lightly, influenced by the new breed of pacy, accessible, demotic musical coming out of the United States; productions like *Oklahoma* and *South Pacific*, which had premiered the year before, even containing a song called 'I Like America'.

The musicals coming out of America, in their engagement with race, sex, crime and politics, and their increasing use of a musical vernacular rooted in black music, gospel and blues, were creating an auspicious climate for the sound if not the concept of rock and roll, which would go on to abandon the notion of a well-told fiction for a howl of expressive rage and lust. American rock and roll films like *Blackboard Jungle*, *Rock Around the Clock* and *The Girl Can't Help It* married the two worlds to a degree with cinematic grit.

Over here, even three years after *West Side Story*, arguably the first hint of a rock and roll musical, *Oliver!* was the toast of the West End, a hundred-year-old tale set to music by Lionel Bart that was more Edwardian parlour than West End discothèque. Later, though, ironically Damon Albarn of Blur – who we should point out first met guitarist Graham Coxon when they were both in a secondary-school version of *Guys and Dolls* in Colchester – would do much to rehabilitate Bart. When asked about Liam Gallagher's jibe concerning Blur's 'chimney sweep music' he told *Q*'s Adrian Deevoy:

Well, I do have a big *Oliver!* problem. I'm completely besotted by Lionel Bart. There's a great story about him: he'd made a fortune, he was richer than any of the pop stars, worth something like £50 million in 1964, and when he was at his most wealthy and bon vivacious he hired this chateau in France and flew fifty or sixty friends out there for this amazing weekend party. Then he just disappeared, and a year later he got a bill and none of the people had left the party. They'd stayed for a year and he hadn't noticed. Then he sold all the rights to his songs. But I just think he's wonderful … The man was on it big time.

Bart may have lived the rock and roll lifestyle but musicals were seen as occupying a different, older and more establishment milieu than rock bands, until, that is, developments in the mid-sixties.

In July 1966 Toronto music magazine *RPM* ran a news story noting that Canadian songwriter Bruce Cockburn was working on a 'rock opera', working on the premise that to write such a thing you need only have 'something to say'. Nothing more seems to have been heard of this, though. Or it's said that one night round at Pete Townshend's house, The Who guitarist played a spoof ten-minute comedy piece called 'Gratis Amatis' to his manager Kit Lambert and some friends. 'It sounds like a rock opera,' said one, to which Lambert responded, 'Now there's an idea!'

But The Who were beaten to the first rock opera credit by several other bands. Released in October 1967, the English Nirvana's *The Story of Simon Simopath* is probably the first entire album by a rock band to comprise a single story, although whether this qualifies it as a concept album or a musical or opera is hard to say. Then in December 1968 The Pretty Things released *S.F. Sorrow*, an album which told the story of protagonist Sebastian F. Sorrow's 'Solomon Grundy'-style journey from cradle to grave.

But then in May 1969 Pete Townshend and The Who released *Tommy*, the first musical work explicitly billed as a rock opera. Its tale of pinball and destiny was both grandiose and homespun – and enormously successful, with concert, film, ballet and theatrical productions mounted over the course of the next four decades.

The Who would venture again into rock opera four years later with the story of a mentally fractured mod that was also filmed and staged: *Qudrophenia*. But in between The Who's two *magna opera*, several of their peers within rock and very much outside rock would attempt something similar.

In October 1969 The Kinks released their attempt at the form: *Arthur (or the Decline and Fall of the British Empire)*, intended as a Granada TV production that never materialised. Clearly this gave Ray Davies the bug, as he followed it with several others: *Preservation, Act 1* (1973), *Preservation, Act 2* (1974), *Soap Opera* (1975) and *Schoolboys in Disgrace* (1975), all staged with varying degrees of success and lavishness.

But *Tommy* and The Who's most direct and far-reaching influence would be on a budding composer in London, Andrew Lloyd Webber, and his lyricist, Tim Rice. It inspired them to write a fifteen-minute school piece which begat *Joseph and the Amazing Technicolor Dreamcoat*, which in term begat *Jesus Christ Superstar*. This was first recorded and released as a concept album, but such was the success and profit from the record sales that it funded a subsequent stage production in late 1971, which had been Lloyd Webber and Rice's real idea all along. It was in this form, as an explicitly billed 'rock musical', that it stunned Broadway and is running to this day, currently in a production featuring former Radio One DJ Chris Moyles and Spice Girl Melanie C.

That was almost it for Lloyd Webber and Rice as a working unit. They were to produce just one more musical collaboration. The doubting Thomases who'd thought *Jesus Christ Superstar* a bizarre and niche proposition were even more convinced that their latest venture would be a flop; a Broadway musical style production, with pop singers, telling the little-known tale of an Argentinian politician's rise and fall. *Evita* too was originally a 1976 album, featuring Paul Jones, Barbara Dickson and Julie Covington, spotted in the *Rock Follies* TV show. Rock performers Steve Marriott and John Fogerty were approached but weren't interested. In most of the world, except the United States interestingly, *Evita* the album outsold *Jesus Christ Superstar*. The single 'Don't Cry for Me Argentina' went to number one and was a huge hit abroad, as were several other tracks from the album. When it became a show, it was nominated for five Tony Awards, including 'Best Musical'. When it became a film, the world's biggest pop star, Madonna, took the title role.

Post-Tim Rice, Lloyd Webber's various lyricists have filled West End theatres ever since, in a symbiotic relationship with pop. And Jeff Wayne's *The War of the Worlds* and Pink Floyd's *The Wall* were both hugely theatrical pieces from within the rock fraternity that eventually became elaborate stage shows.

In recent times we have seen the rise of the jukebox musical, a kind of retro-engineered production where a story is created from the back catalogue of a band. The most famous examples of the trend are *We Will Rock You*, a sci-fi yarn written by Ben Elton around the works of Queen, and the hugely successful show and film *Mamma Mia!*, based on the songs of ABBA. Benny Andersson of the band later said that he and Björn had obviously written an ABBA musical but just didn't know it until someone put them all together.

At the time of writing, Guy Garvey of the fêted Mancunian rock band Elbow is planning to decamp to New York to begin work on a *King Kong* musical and hopes to succeed on the Broadway stage where a 2011 *Spiderman* musical written partly by Bono and The Edge of U2 somewhat underperformed. The rock star of old may be an unlikely candidate for the bouquet, the dressing-room mirror with the light-bulb frame, the good-luck telegram and the curtain call, but they also know that the tills are alive with the sound of music.

21. BYE BYE BABY

'Belieber', 'Durannie', 'Apple Scruff' ... down the years there have been any number of nicknames given to the devoted teenage-girl fans of various pop idols. There are 'Wannabes' and 'Little Monsters' too, acolytes of Madonna and Lady Gaga. Usually, though, the object of their adoration is of course male, and at least part of the allure is physical and emotional as well as musical. Which may be why this fanaticism is often trivialised and humorously demeaned by the invariably male opinion formers and gatekeepers of the media, even if that media is just the playground or common-room bush telegraph of gossip, rumour and ridicule. A 2012 *Daily Telegraph* piece on Beliebers captioned a picture of the singer 'Justin Bieber, a rugged hunk of beefcake if ever there was one, and complete with detachable Lego-style hair, too' – the implication being that this odd little guy was no real man nor real rock star and certainly not worthy of girls' attentions, unlike say Thom Yorke or Nick Cave.

Staying with those Beliebers, there are no comparable names for male obsessives, be they fans of Oasis, Muse, Kasabian or whoever, which is interesting given that there is a clear element of the bromance and man-crush from the stadiums packed full of males at their gigs. Male fans' appreciation of, say, Kate Bush always comes couched in terms of an informed appreciation of her work, even when the giddiness, lack of perspective and proprietorialness clearly spells a crush.

But girl fans of boy bands and teen heartthrobs are not thought to possess this kind of considered and credentialed appreciation. For the guys, it's respect, passion and good taste. For the girls, it's a silly, immature phase they'll grow out of.

Let's hope not, because the teen-idol crush has always been one of those great generational engines that move pop forward, if not always in the way it was intended. When The Beatles could no longer hear themselves over the auditoria of screaming girls, they gave up playing live and retreated to the recording studio and turned Abbey Road's Studio 2 into their version of the artists' garrett. Scott Walker's disenchantment with pop-idol status sent him underground into the furthest reaches of experimentalism. With each of his solo releases he moved further away from the romantic ballads of his heyday, through Brel and Bergman and finally into musique concrete and atonality.

Even before there were posters, there were poster boys. Niccolò Paganini's flowing locks and virtuosity on the violin made women faint and men suspect that he was in league with the devil. Few of Rudolph Valentino's fans ever heard him speak since he was the greatest film star of the silent era. But 100,000 people, mainly women, lined the streets of New York for his funeral.

With the invention of the phonograph and the talkies, singers like Mario Lanza and Gordon MacRae captivated female fans with their widescreen handsomeness and rich tenor and baritone voices. But, in contrast to the beefy machismo of such types, the first pop singer to hold a generation of young women in his thrall was Francis Albert Sinatra, a skinny crooner from Hoboken, New Jersey, who came to fame with the Tommy Dorsey band just prior to the Second World War. Sinatra changed the entire way the music business was structured. Before Sinatra-mania, popular music had been largely consumed and enjoyed by adults. But after the war, the coming of relatively cheap phonographs and the new 45 r.p.m. singles meant that adolescents could enter the market.

Sinatra was the first performer to appeal to – maybe even create – a powerful new constituency of teenage girls. Comedian Jack Benny said of the opening night of Sinatra's stint at the Paramount Theatre in 1942, 'I thought the goddamned building was going to cave in. I never heard such a commotion ... All this for a fellow I never heard of.' When he came back two years later, riot police were called to contain the 35,000 fans who couldn't get in.

Sinatra's legions of fans formed pop music's first self-defined fan group, the first teenyboppers, if you will. Outfitted in bobby socks, saddle shoes and poodle skirts and with their own cutesy slang including phrases such as 'jeepers', these 'bobby-soxers' were patronised by the media as vapid little girls rather than acknowledged as a powerful consumer group. Shirley Temple gave the definitive onscreen performance as one in the 1947 movie *The Bachelor and the Bobby-Soxer*. Psychologists warned parents about the almost hypnotic allure of Sinatra's voice that led one besotted bobby-soxer to attend fifty-six performances over an eight-week period.

These, and more, were the worries that attended the rise of the phenomenon known as Elvis Presley. It has become a matter of historical amusement that TV companies could only film him from the waist up for fear of what his pelvic gyrations would do to young female sensibilities. It sounds ludicrous, but the fear was absolutely real. By contrast, The Beatles were seen as less sexually threatening, perhaps, but posed an even bigger danger to global sanity simply by virtue of the sheer scale of the response they created wherever they went. There was even a word for it, of course: Beatlemania, the attendant hysteria of which has formed the deep bedrock of our very notions of what pop stardom means. In the same way that all lengths and areas must be described in comparison to football pitches or the size of Wales, so quantities of pop madness – be it The Osmonds, Take That or One Direction – must be measured in Beatle units. The Beatles' dominance of the discourse of pop became almost total in the sixties, crossing gender, generation and to an extent even race and creed. But Beatlemania was at least initially, and in its wildest, most joyous manifestation, a girl thing – until pop music developed a critical language to keep pace with the band's musical development. Even then it was no more heartfelt or worthy than the sobbing and madness of Beatlemania. As the poet Patrick Jones once said, there is eloquence in screaming.

Outside the UK, the fever of early Beatlemania seems to have affected both sexes equally. Look at footage of Beatle shows in Scandinavia or the Netherlands from 1963 and 1964 and you'll be struck by the touching, boundless, giddy enthusiasm of the young men in the audience. The United States was similarly affected. Dennis Locorriere, singer with Dr Hook and the Medicine Show, once said, ahead of The Beatles' first appearance on *The Ed Sullivan Show*, that him and his classmates, male and female, kept their ears tuned to clandestine transistor radios in lessons while excited announcers would give regular updates such as, 'The Beatles are now over Greenland' and 'touchdown in an hour for The Beatles'.

After that show, a night that changed American popular culture for ever, a generational fault-line cracked open across America. While the kids went nuts, adult America responded with wrongheaded hauteur that now appears laughable. *Newsweek* said:

> Visually, they are a nightmare: tight, dandified, Edwardian/ Beatnik suits and great pudding bowls of hair. Musically, they are a near-disaster: guitars and drums slamming out a merciless beat that does away with secondary rhythms, harmony, and melody. Their lyrics (punctuated by nutty shouts of 'yeah, yeah, yeah!') are a catastrophe, a preposterous farrago of Valentine-card romantic sentiments ... the odds are they will fade away, as most adults confidently predict.

One reviewer bemoaned the fact that the girls in the audience were clearly smitten by these effeminate oiks rather than another *Ed Sullivan* regular, the singer Robert Goulet, viewed as far more 'virile and mature'.

Some have said that The Beatles' swift conquest of America was down to a bereaved nation desperately hungry for joy and release from mourning its young President Kennedy, assassinated just months before. But *Slate* magazine has rightly taken one look at the audience that night and dismissed this theory:

> It's extremely doubtful that any of these teenage girls were cheering, screaming, palpitating, even crying with joy as some sort of catharsis to their anguish over Lee Harvey

Oswald's deed in Dallas. Meanwhile, their parents, who were the ones more likely traumatised by the death of the president, remained tellingly immune to Beatlemania. The Beatles took hold of our country and shook it to a different place because they were young, because their music had a young, fresh feel, and because – this is the crucial thing – our parents didn't get it.

The quote about Goulet's virility and maturity goes right to the heart of the strange psychology of the teen-heartthrob phenomenon. It is almost exactly equivalent to the *Daily Telegraph*'s caption on Justin Bieber, displaying the same tone of baffled condescension about the kind of fellow these silly girls are smitten by rather than, presumably, captains of industry or captains of the first eleven.

Donny Osmond was a doe-eyed Mormon from a conservative family who positively radiated unsexiness, and yet he was phenomenally popular. Maybe for this very reason. The theory, generally espoused by adult males (so we should be a little wary), is that these boy-men, hairless and pre-pubescent, are sexually neutral and unthreatening. Donny was a snog-object, not a sex object. David Cassidy, while slightly more worldly, was a model of bruised androgyne vulnerability. He was incredibly popular during his *annus mirabilis* of 1973, when he sold out Wembley Arena six times in one week and caused such madness among the 33,000-strong crowd at Melbourne Cricket Ground that there were calls for him to be deported. Apart from Cassidy himself, his entourage and security guards, it's doubtful whether there was one male in these audiences. The dark side of the teen hysteria was seen at his White City Stadium show of May 1974 when a mass stampede led to the death of fourteen-year-old Bernadette Whelan.

We had our homegrown heartthrobs too. David Essex had a roguish, gypsy twinkle that was positively lascivious in comparison to Donny and Marie. But perhaps the most unlikely heartthrobs of all, at least to baffled males, then and now, were a quintet of sallow Scottish lads with bog-brush haircuts and half-mast trousers.

The appeal of the Bay City Rollers – and their appeal was phenomenal – was that they were the boys next door, on the next street, on your bus or in your class: real, normal city lads.

They chose their name by throwing a dart at a map of America. The dart landed on Bay City, Michigan, so, conceivably, they could have been called the Rabbit Hash Kentucky Rollers. They had a hit in 1971 with 'Keep On Dancing' but then promptly disappeared, only to resurface with the classic line-up – Les, 'Woody', Eric and brothers Alan and Derek, under the auspices of manager Tam Paton – and enjoyed a string of hits throughout 1974. 'Remember (Sha-La-La)', ' Shang-a-Lang', 'Summerlove Sensation', 'All of Me Loves All of You' … by early1975 Britain was in the grip of Rollermania, with the band starring in a twenty-week UK television series, *Shang-a-Lang*. They had a number one in the States and their début album *Rollin'* knocked *Tubular Bells* from the top slot in the States.

The band were visually striking, to say the least, with a look that was part football hooligan, part Andy Stewart's *White Heather Club*. It's ridiculousness was much commented upon and much mocked, but its blend of glam-rock camp and street edge was irresistible and became ubiquitous among legions of fans. And the nature of that fandom was often terrifying in its intensity. When the Bay City Rollers appeared on Australian TV show *Countdown* the director, Ted Emory, recalled:

There were hundreds of kids done up in tartan pants that didn't reach the tops of their shoes, constantly bashing on the Plexiglass doors. They would do anything to get into that television studio ... two hundred kids bashing on the door and a total eclipse of the sun occurred. I'd never seen one. On this day we all stopped in the studio and the Rollers went up on the roof. We stood out there and watched the flowers close up and all the automatic street lighting come on. It was chilling, the most fantastic thing you'd ever see. Downstairs the kids never turned around, staring into the Plexiglass waiting to see the Rollers come out of the studio, go down the corridor and into the canteen. [They] never noticed the total eclipse of the sun.*

Whether it was the mania, the stress or the half-mast trousers, the Rollers story soured almost as soon as it had begun. In early 1976 bassist Alan Longmuir, the oldest Roller, decided to quit. A man in his late twenties, he had always looked the least at ease with his teen-idol status. Eventually the teens turned to something new, punk, and the band fractured into several competing versions of the Rollers which are still touring to this day. Then came the inevitable royalties disputes, which also still rumble on, along with a legacy of acrimonious disputes with Arista Records and manager Tam Paton.

Paton was the son of a potato merchant from Prestonpans, a small town east of Edinburgh, who assumed an almost monstrous level of control over the band, at least according to some of their members, two of whom accused him of seriously sexually assaulting

---

* From Peter Wilmoth's *Glad All Over: The Countdown Years*.

them. When Paton died aged 70, the response from former singer Les McKeown was cool to say the least: 'I'm delighted he's dead. He ruined a lot of people's lives, including mine. I've planned a nice day of celebration with my wife and mates. We will rejoice. It's been a long time coming and it's closure for me. Tam Paton is dead, long live the future, the future's bright.'

The Bay City Rollers story, with its sad, seedy air of exploitation, is a very 1970s entertainment parable. But the phenomenon of the teen heartthrob seems as perennial as pop itself. Take That's is a particularly satisfying version of the archetype; cute boys from Manchester and the Potteries put together by a gay manager with a clear eye on the pink pound who then become the teenage girl obsession of the nineties, a generational crush of massive proportions. The band call it a day at the height of their fame, they each go solo and their controlling, driven creative leader Gary Barlow finds himself gallingly eclipsed by the group's jester, Robbie Williams, once labelled a 'fat dancer' by Oasis's Liam Gallagher but who goes on to become the biggest pop star of *fin de siècle* Britain; part Gazza, part Sinatra. As his star fades in turn, Take That return without him and become bigger than ever, buoyed by the still-burning desires of young girls who are now labelled yummy mummies. Prodigal Robbie returns and Gary reinvents himself as the don of the TV talent show and pop impresario by royal appointment.

At the time of writing, One Direction are not only proving that the heartthrob boyband concept is still pop's most potent force but proving it on a scale that forces Beatle comparisons, however much that grieves some. No act since the Fab Four has managed this level of success internationally and not even The Beatles managed to top the Billboard chart with their first album, a feat 1-D, as they are known, pulled off in 2012.

Enoch Powell once said that all political careers end in failure, and it's tempting to say that, by their very nature, all teen-idol stories end in disillusionment, loss of innocence, looks and money. Scott Walker, ageing well, respected as an artist and working on his own terms, may be the exception that proves the rule. We shall watch that rugged hunk of beefcake, Justin Bieber, with interest, and wait eagerly for his dark, knotty classical pieces about dictators and plague due some time around 2040.

22. YOU SHOULD BE DANCING

During the week Vincent sold paint in a houseware store.
All day, every day he stood behind a counter and grinned.
He climbed up and down ladders, he made the coffee, he
obeyed. Then came the weekend and he was cut loose.

Thus wrote Nik Cohn in a 1976 article for *New York* magazine
called 'The New Tribes of Saturday Night'. It was a piece about
a growing aspect of the Big Apple's nightlife, the young working-
and middle-class people who swarmed to the city's new disco clubs
every weekend, lured by the promise of sex and romance, booze
and drugs, but also by the transcendent thrill of music and dancing.

An entirely unscientific survey of most pop songs – based on
some desultory web browsing, recourse to memory and flipping
through the racks – would seem to reveal that, after 'love', the
words 'dance' or 'dancing' crop up the most frequently in song
and album titles. Sometimes, they even get a little smoochy and
become intertwined. Tina Charles, you may remember, loved to
love but her baby just loved to dance. The Human League even

had an album called *Love and Dancing*. And after that, the word 'weekend' must come in third or thereabouts. Dancing and the weekend are indissolubly knit in the people's songs: an escape from the nine-to-five, the end of the working week, the sweet giddy release of loud music, lights and the dance floor. That's what Nik Cohn's famous piece of reportage from the streets of New York was about; that was what Vincent was looking for in the clubs of Manhattan after a hard week at the paint store, although by the time the article was transformed into one of the greatest music movies ever, Vincent had become Tony Manero, as played by John Travolta, and the New Tribes of Saturday Night had become *Saturday Night Fever*, one of the biggest-selling albums and most potent musical phenomena ever.

People have danced to music as long as they have made music – indeed, that was why people first made music, as a background to chant, dance and ritual. Later, young folk would gavotte, quadrille and galliard their courtly way down the centuries, through the plays of Shakespeare and the novels of Jane Austen.

Then, in the twentieth century, dance bands came to be precisely that: ensembles playing music for dancing and live entertainment as opposed to the rarefied listening experience of the concert hall. These were the extended forerunners of the modern pop group, playing live in clubs and halls, with a backline rhythm section and fronted by a singer. Usually known by their band leaders' names – Henry Hall, Joe Loss, Ted Heath and, of course, Glenn Miller –these were the Stones and Beatles of their day.

The Nazis banned Glenn Miller and other decadent American music, so members of the French underground met in secret cellars and basements they called discothèques, where a single turntable would provide the night's entertainment. When the discothèques could go literally over-ground after the war, they proliferated, and some became infamous: the Cotton Club in Harlem, Régine in Paris, and, much later, Annabel's in London and the Peppermint Lounge in New York.

Such places would play host to a raft of fad and novelty dance crazes, the creation of which, for most of the fifties and sixties, was an almost weekly occurrence, from the famous – the Twist, the Locomotion, the Mashed Potato and the Frug – to the less well remembered, like the Batusi (Batman's version of the Watusi) and the Freddie, Freddie and the Dreamers' contribution to choreography. Teen magazines would print guides to choreography and records would come complete with printed sheets marked with footprints and the steps to be followed.

By the mid-sixties even those who couldn't afford the prices at Annabel's hops could dance in their own towns and cities, as bops held in youth clubs and dance halls were superseded by the coming of the city centre nightclub-discothèque, a far more sophisticated, adult environment, where dressing up, copping off and getting down was the evening's agenda. No movie of the day was complete without its discothèque scene, with obligatory oil slides, light show and miniskirted girls. And there is almost as much footage of George Best in his medallion, white polo neck and Italian leather blouson as there is of him taking on Ron 'Chopper' Harris down the wing.

If you wanted to catch a glimpse of George Best's body swerve on the dance floor rather than Old Trafford's pitch, the place to be was a club on Brasenose Street, Manchester, called the Twisted Wheel. There were more sophisticated, more expensive, more aristocratic clubs in Britain at the time, but none more influential than the Twisted Wheel, a sweaty, smoky, noisy basement in the industrial north. This was where r&b and soul found a gateway into

Britain, where Britain's most vibrant, purist sect devoted to dancing began; it was the birthplace of Northern Soul.

Northern Soul records were obscure, flopped US releases, on labels like Revilot, Mirwood, Okeh and Ric-Tic (and occasionally the bigger rosters like Motown and Stax), prized for their driving beats and danceability and, as the scene blossomed at the start of the seventies, for their rarity and exclusivity. The early DJ pioneers of Northern Soul – Russ Winstanley, Richard Searling, Keith Minshull among others – would often find these obscurities remaindered in the warehouses of US record labels, and literally cover them: put sticky tape over the artist and title so that the real identity of the work could be hidden and the tunes would become their private calling cards; their signature tunes. This led to many tracks having two names: 'Festival Time' by the San Remo Strings was also 'Double Cookin'' by The Checkerboard Squares.

The heartland of this profoundly underground scene, a real music cult if ever there was one, was the north-west and the Midlands; in temples like the Golden Torch in Tunstall, Stoke, the Blackpool Mecca, Va Va in Bolton and, of course, Wigan Casino, a sprung-floored 1940s dance hall that became the crucible of Northern Soul, drawing thousands of devotees from the length and breadth of Britain to dance the night away – literally – at the famous all-nighters, to exultant, impassioned torch songs like Gloria Jones's 'Tainted Love' or Frank Wilson's ultra-rare 'Do I Love You (Indeed I Do)', quirky instrumental grooves like 'Afternoon on the Rhino', Bok to Bach and the Just Brothers' 'Sliced Tomatoes', later remade for a different generation of dancers as 'The Rockafeller Skank'.

Dancing was Northern Soul's *raison d'être*, its be-all and end-all. The dance moves were quick, nimble and athletic, involving gymnastic pirouettes, flips and backdrops. Dancing was solo and by both sexes. The tunes would be classified according to the dances that best fitted them: Wigan stompers, 100 m.p.h. dancers and floaters. And the scene's distinctive clothing style was tailored to hours of dancing in sweaty clubs – singlets, baggy bowling shirts, voluminous flares, bar towels worn off the belt as sweat wipes. In darkened corners, on Wigan Station at dawn or in the café of the swimming baths, where dancers would congregate after the all-nighters, records would be swapped and sold, lists compared, treasures acquired. American soul and r&b artists like Sandi Sheldon, Dean Parrish and Tommy Hunt were amazed to learn that records of theirs they'd thought long flopped and forgotten were anthems of the Northern Soul scene. When they came to Wigan to play, the response was ecstatic.

As word spread about this unique phenomenon, TV crews also arrived in Wigan to make earnest, bemused documentaries featuring belching chimneys and cobblestoned streets intercut with whirling, gyrating clusters of dancers. The London music industry became interested, scenting sales, and put out tacky remakes and quick cash-ins that regularly charted through 1973 and 1974, tracks like Wayne Gibson's 'Under My Thumb', 'Ski-ing in the Snow' by Wigan's Ovation and 'Footsee' by Wigan's Chosen Few that were hits but scorned by the purists of the scene. And it was a scene built on purism, as hard-line as a Maoist cell or a religious cult in its demands on its adherents. By 1975 Northern Soul had gone underground again, to the delight of most of its loyalists, and found new homes in Cleethorpes, the home counties and London's 100 Club, where it still thrives today.

Just as Northern Soul was fading from public view, a new sound was emerging from the clubs of America, one that would have its imperial phase with the release of *Saturday Night Fever*. The movie and album didn't invent disco, but revived a style of music that had been around for several years, nurtured in small clubs in New York and Miami, the preserve of marginalised groups in dark, subterranean lairs: gays, blacks, Latinos and women. Music like The Hues Corporation's 'Rock the Boat' (from the West Coast), and George McCrae and KC and The Sunshine Band from the Florida stable of T.K. Records. Travolta and the Bee Gees took this music over-ground, where light flooded from a glitterball and reflected off a dazzling white suit.

The high priests of disco, to the general public at least, were a toothy trio of brothers from Chorlton, Manchester via the Isle of Man, then, later, Australia, who'd enjoyed great success with their tremulous, melodramatic ballads in the sixties but who'd spent several years in the wilderness before manager Robert Stigwood drafted them in to write the music for the movie version of Cohn's article, now fictionalised as *Saturday Night Fever*. Their *Children of the World* album had seen them experiment with disco grooves and a keening falsetto, and its crowning glory was a tune that would be pressed readily into service as a highlight of *Saturday Night Fever* and a kind of manifesto. Life was tough in the mid-seventies, what with terrorism, economic recession and football violence, but there was a way to forget it all. 'You Should Be Dancing'.

The Bee Gees only became involved in *Saturday Night Fever* very late in the production's process. According to John Travolta, 'The Bee Gees weren't even involved in the movie in the beginning ... I was dancing to Stevie Wonder and Boz Scaggs.' When they got the commission, they decamped to a château in France and came up with the bulk of the songs in a single weekend. Barry Gibb recalled the reaction to the demos:

They flipped out and said these will be great. We still had no concept of the movie, except some kind of rough script that they'd brought with them ... You've got to remember, we were fairly dead in the water at that point, 1975, somewhere in that zone – the Bee Gees' sound was basically tired. We needed something new. We hadn't had a hit record in about three years. So we felt, 'Oh, Jeez, that's it. That's our life span' – like most groups in the late sixties. So, we had to find something. We didn't know what was going to happen.

What was going to happen was that their next three singles – 'How Deep Is Your Love', 'Stayin' Alive' and 'Night Fever' – all reached number one in the United States and many countries around the world. The age of disco was here. The Bee Gees gave the B side of 'Stayin' Alive', 'If I Can't Have You', to Yvonne Elliman and she had a number one with it. Two different versions of 'More Than a Woman', the Bee Gees' and Tavares', were played on the radio. Gibb brothers' songs were at number one for twenty-five consecutive weeks in the States. The movie soundtrack was the highest-selling album in recording history at that point. It's now sold more than 40 million copies and is presently the seventh highest-selling album of all time.

For a music that was so ubiquitous, so inclusive in spirit, disco could wield a very exclusive door policy. Unlike the cheap functionality of Northern Soul venues and dress sense, disco studs and divas dressed or aspired to dress in the Halston, Gucci and Fiorucci that Sister Sledge drooled over in 'He's the Greatest Dancer'. The clubs were nakedly elitist. The chorus and title of Chic's 'Le Freak' was originally 'Fuck Off', a response to Nile Rodgers and Bernard Edwards not being let into Studio 54, the New York nightclub, forbidden city and imperial epicentre of disco, where Bianca Jagger had once turned up on horseback. And if the Bee Gees and Travolta were disco's public face, Chic were its geniuses: intelligent, witty, aspirational, sensual, visceral, irresistible ... the writing team and guitar/bass duo of Rodgers and Edwards were its Shakespeare, Bach and Einstein rolled into one (or rather two).

As a wise man or woman once said, 'All things in moderation.' And as someone even wiser added... 'including moderation'. When the working week is done, girls and boys just want to have fun; Cyndi Lauper nearly said. And finally someone else said that dancing is 'the vertical expression of a horizontal desire'. It certainly can be that, but look at the faces of the dancers at any Northern Soul night then or now and it's obvious that the rapt, entranced expressions are not just about sex or showing off, they're about self-expression, liberation, escape and getting your kicks, as Dobie Gray sang, out on the floor.

23. GOD SAVE THE QUEEN

It was, in its own way, fittingly Elizabethan, with echoes of the first era to bear that name. On 6 June in the year of Our Lord 1977, on a fine summer's evening in rural Berkshire, Elizabeth Mary Alexandra Windsor, reigning monarch of the United Kingdom, lit a bonfire beacon in the ancient surroundings of Windsor Castle, built as a seat of the Norman conquerors a millennium before and where one of her predecessors, Charles I, had been imprisoned prior to his execution. But this was a happier night, full of all the pomp and ceremony of state, the beginning of a week of celebrations to commemorate her twenty-fifth year on the throne.

The lighting of the great bonfire beacon was echoed across her realm by the lighting of other bonfires, on high Lake District fells, on the bandstands of market towns in the shires, along Hadrian's Wall and on the ramparts of sundry other of her royal castles. The next day she processed in glory cheered by her subjects to the clamour of trumpets in her gold state coach to St Paul's Cathedral and a service of thanksgiving. Here she made a speech with echoes of an England long gone worthy of her namesake, good Queen

Bess: 'When I was twenty-one I pledged my life to the service of our people and I asked for God's help to make good that vow. Although that vow was made in my salad days, when I was green in judgement, I do not regret nor retract one word of it.'

The final event of the week of celebrations was a stately river progress down the Thames from Greenwich to Lambeth. After the Queen opened the Silver Jubilee Walkway and the new South Bank Jubilee Gardens, the journey ended with a firework display, and a procession of lighted carriages took the Queen back to Buckingham Palace where Her Majesty and the Royal Family appeared on the balcony to a cheering crowd. Across Britain, from village green to council estate, toasts were raised at hundreds of street parties. This was a kind of national rapture, at least for some of the nation, the 'England's dreaming' that a new breed of barbarian now gathering at the gates of the palace with their own flaming brand called punk rock was to determine to light a purgative fire under and rouse us all from our slumber.

The word 'punk', in its archaic meaning as a 'prostitute', first appeared in print in England in 1596, and was soon in common use. Linguist Eric Partridge says it was 'a very frequent word in Elizabethan and in Restoration plays'. Shakespeare uses it four times, twice in *Measure for Measure*. But in the twentieth century it acquired a new meaning in the US as a petty criminal, especially a young male hoodlum. Both these outsider senses of the word made it ideal to be co-opted by the rock critic Dave Marsh, who used it in 1970 in rock journal *Creem* to sum up that magazine's particular approach to rock culture:

Our point of view was vulgar, belligerent, often less respectful to rock's major institutions ... with the result that all of us – and especially me – were frequently assaulted with the epithet: 'You are such a punk.' I decided this insult would be better construed as a compliment … in order to emphasise our delight in rock's essential barbarism.

And it was this sense of the word 'punk' – anti-establishment dissenter, Roundhead rock rebel, wilful iconoclast – that was soon being spouted by every teenager and tabloid editor in Britain.

In the mid-1970s, 15 per cent of Britain's population – eight million people – were between the ages thirteen and twenty-one. Two-thirds of them were working class, and a quarter of their total were on the dole. Many of these young people had grown up in new towns, sink estates and declining industrial cities, often against a backdrop of the kind of brutalist high-rise, high-intensity housing developments designed by the kind of pioneering architect who would never have to live in them. The Britain in which punk rock developed was a grim and squalid place: economically bankrupt, socially fissile, blighted by strikes, the occasional bomb and urban decay.

'Our place in the world is shrinking, our economic comparisons grow worse. We shall end up with wage controls … even a breakdown of democracy. Sometimes when I go to bed at night I think that if I were a younger man, I would emigrate.' The man in the pub? A tabloid opinionater? No. James Callaghan, foreign secretary and later prime minister.

At supposedly opposite ends of the TV music spectrum, both *Top of the Pops* and *The Old Grey Whistle Test* gave a striking snapshot of the conditions that forged punk, that made it so necessary. On *Top of the Pops* a parade of novelty hits, anodyne ballads, cabaret soul and mawkish muzak was presented by smirking, self-congratulatory DJs clearly more interested in their latest supermarket opening. Whereas *The Old Grey Whistle Test*, the corporation's supposedly progressive alternative, was a showcase for the dreariest of MOR, AOR and limp country rock framed in an atmosphere of ossified complacency.

It has become a cliché to say that the music superstars of the day were out of touch, but that doesn't mean it wasn't true. These truly were the cake-eating inheritors of Marie Antoinette, a super-elite of rock aristocrats, surrounded by courts and retinues of hangers-on, who wore their excess as a badge of success: Eric Clapton toured Europe on a customised train attached to the *Orient Express* while unemployment, strikes and riots played out in inner cities back home; Emerson, Lake and Palmer's individualised pantechnicons have been discussed; Joe Walsh satirised the situation, and earned another speedboat for his pains with 'Life's Been Good', sung with wry cheek from the point of view of a pampered rock star ('I have a mansion, forget the price/Ain't never been there, they tell me it's nice'). *Melody Maker*'s Caroline Coon summed it up neatly when she wrote, 'Millionaire rock stars are no longer part of the brotherly rock fraternity which helped create them in the first place.'

Britain was ripe for a cultural revolution, and, as with many revolutions, its shock troops were a curious, combustible mix of theorists, intellectuals, strategists and brawny footsoldiers. At its theoretical vanguard were the likes of Malcolm McLaren and Vivienne Westwood, King's Road intellectual fashionistas with a liking for scandal and the Situationist movement. McLaren had tried his luck as a rock entrepreneur with American band the New York Dolls who are sometimes cited as one of the American originators of punk. But, in truth, British punk was a very different beast from American variety. Bands like Blondie and the Ramones were essentially nostalgists, reviving the tropes of fifties' and sixties'

AM radio, while Television and Talking Heads were cerebral art rockers. British punk was nihilistic, political, sardonic, and basically a great deal edgier, as McLaren's next gambit illustrated.

Received wisdom has it that McLaren was the omniscient, manipulative Svengali to whom the Sex Pistols owed all of their notoriety and success. They were actually much more proactive in their own destiny than this. In July 1973 guitarist Steve Jones and drummer Paul Cook stole an entire PA system from the Hammersmith Odeon that was due to be to used by David Bowie in his final concert as Ziggy Stardust. The pair were *habitués* of McLaren's King's Road clothes store and hassled him into providing the funds for instruments and practice facilities. McLaren became their manager – at this stage they played Roxy Music and Faces covers with rough energy but little else. A teenage scenester called John Lydon rechristened himself Johnny Rotten and auditioned as singer for the band, miming Alice Cooper's 'Eighteen' in a Chelsea pub. Now named the Sex Pistols, they were soon to become the most infamous and important British band for a generation.

Punk rock, aggressive, transgressive and even a little regressive, simmered and fermented through the hot summer of 1976, its message spread through a bush telegraph of small but now legendary gigs in places like St Martin's School of Art, the 100 Club and the Lesser Free Trade Hall, Manchester; sympathetic radio DJs like John Peel and a samizdat fanzine network including such publications as *Sideburns*, which ran the legendary illustration later reprinted in Mark Perry's *Sniffin' Glue* proclaiming 'This is a chord, this is another, here's a third, now form a band', summed up the new aesthetic. The traditional weekly rock press soon caught up. Charles Shaar Murray in the *NME* claimed that 'this music is coming from the straight-out-of-school-and-onto-the-dole deathtrap which we seem to have engineered for Our Young; the '76 British terminal stasis, the modern urban blind alley.' Although The Damned beat the Sex Pistols to the making of the first UK punk single with 'New Rose' in November 1976, Malcolm McLaren's band remained very much the leaders of the UK punk movement. Other bands blossomed in the Pistols' wake: the Buzzcocks and The Clash, whose Joe Strummer talked of the effect that Rotten and the rest had had on him: 'Yesterday I thought I was a crud. Then I saw the Sex Pistols, and I became a king.'

But the next year, 1977, was to prove punk's high water mark, coinciding as it did with an event utterly antithetical to punk's trenchant, revolutionary zeal. Rather like the Sex Pistols and The Clash, Her Majesty Queen Elizabeth was about to embark on a large-scale British tour of her own, having decided that she wanted to mark her silver jubilee by meeting as many of her subjects as possible. Six mini-tours in three months, covering thirty-six counties, was an itinerary most rock bands, even punk ones, would balk at. By the time she reached Lancashire there were a million people on the streets to greet her.

The Sex Pistols had been the most talked-about band in Britain after their début release, 'Anarchy in the UK', and an expletive-filled, unforgettable appearance in December 1976 on a London teatime magazine show hosted by Bill Grundy. That they were just a pop group seemed to have been forgotten. Instead they were now seen as a sustained attack on the nation's morals and civilisation in general. In the wake of the Grundy appearance councils had pulled the plug on tour dates, tabloid editorials demonised them. One London councillor, Bernard Brook-Partridge, declared, 'Most of these groups would be vastly improved by sudden death. The worst of the punk rock groups, I suppose, currently are the Sex

Pistols. They are unbelievably nauseating. They are the antithesis of humankind. I would like to see somebody dig a very, very large, exceedingly deep hole and drop the whole bloody lot down it.'

Before February 1977 was out, EMI had dropped them and bassist Glen Matlock had left to be replaced by one Sid Vicious. In March they signed to A&M records outside Buckingham Palace, were dropped ten days later, albeit £75,000 richer, after an outcry from some of the label's older guard and alleged incidents of vandalism and threatening behaviour at the A&M offices. CBS dallied with them, then thought better of it, before Virgin eventually signed them, prompting walk-outs and the downing of tools at the vinyl pressing plant.

But a month ahead of the Monarch's jubilee celebration, the Sex Pistols released 'God Save the Queen', their own piece of filthy bunting waved in mock celebration, and one of the most incendiary rock singles ever released – thanks mainly to the coldly visceral and imaginative attack of Rotten's lyrics and delivery. Without Rotten's leering, accusatory delivery, God Save the Queen would be quite a conventional rock song, albeit a thunderously good one. With it, it become a nightmarish anthem of dissent from the lower reaches of serfdom. Snide, scornful and nihilistic, it is also ambiguous. Writer Simon Hattenstone has suggested, 'There was always something of a nationalist in Lydon. If you listen carefully enough to the lyrics of "God Save The Queen" you realise he was having it both ways.' Rotten has always maintained that it was not the Queen herself, but the docile, herd-like British public and establishment that were his targets. The song concludes with a bleak repeated refrain of 'No future'.

The immediate future, though, held a spectacular clash of cultures. Jon Savage, author of the magisterial history of punk

England's Dreaming, states that for the more superheated punks the Queen's jubilee was 'vaguely fascist, and a return to a past that had never really existed. This was enthusiastically backed by the media, in which almost no dissent against the jubilee was allowed.' 'God Save the Queen', then, gave the nascent punk scene its own anthem, and its own jubilee regatta.

On 7 June Sex Pistols manager Malcolm McLaren and Virgin records chartered a private boat and had the Sex Pistols perform while sailing down the River Thames, passing the Houses of Parliament. The event was intended as a mockery and riposte to the Queen's official river procession planned for two days later. The Pistols' version ended in chaos and confrontation, as the police, whose launches forced the boat to dock, surrounded the gangplank at Embankment pier. While the band members and their equipment were bundled away, McLaren, Westwood and many of the band's entourage were arrested in a nasty mêlée.

Many newspapers and pundits predicted, indeed, steeled themselves for, 'God Save the Queen' reaching number one in that jubilee week. As it turned out, the Pistols failed to dislodge Rod Stewart's 'The First Cut Is the Deepest' from its third week of four at the top. To this day many believe that 'God Save the Queen' far outsold Rod Stewart but that the chart was rigged to prevent embarrassment. McLaren later claimed that CBS Records, which distributed both singles, told him the Sex Pistols were actually outselling Stewart two to one. There is evidence that an exceptional directive was issued by the British Phonographic Institute to exclude sales from certain shops, such as Virgin, for that week only.

These events have all now passed into history too, part of the pageant of British cultural life. Punk rock itself is now viewed nostalgically and sentimentally by its ageing adherents. Yesterday's punks are today's granddads and now often exhibit the same conservatism and reactionary hostility to modern pop culture. The safety-pinned, mohicanned punk has become as much part of the souvenir postcard and tea-towel iconography of England as the Beefeater, the Pearly King and the Chelsea pensioner. But punk's rupture with the past did bring genuine change: a new freedom and energy, a new inclusiveness towards race and gender, and new avenues of opportunity in writing, design, art and music for young working-class talent. Ironically then, 'God Save the Queen', the Sex Pistols and punk rock showed that there was a future in England's dreaming and that it might embrace men, women, gay, straight, rich, poor, white and black.

24. SOLSBURY HILL

When I was about eight years old, my primary school teacher, Mr Moore, took us for our regular Friday afternoon music session. Normally he would sit at the piano and we would bellow along tunelessly to 'Lord Of The Dance' and 'Kumbaya'. One day he played and sang a new tune, and was visibly moved by the words and melody. When he finished he was quiet for a moment, and then said, haltingly, 'That's such a beautiful, moving piece of music. You won't understand now. But one day you will.'

The song was 'Linden Lea' by the great English composer Ralph Vaughan Williams. It is a beautiful song, not just for its sweet, limpid melody but because of the words, taken from a poem by William Barnes. It's a song about the beauty of nature and the countryside, and the powerful balm and solace they provide. The last verse is, I think, the one that really got to old Joe Moore:

Let other folk make money faster
In the air of dark-roomed towns,
I don't dread a peevish master;

Though no man may heed my frowns,
I be free to go abroad,
Or take again my homeward road
To where, for me, the apple tree
Do lean down low in Linden Lea.

Rock and roll, on the other hand, is surely, as the title of Charlie Gillett's famous book had it, *The Sound of the City*. It's the sound of neon lights and nightclubs, freeways, tower blocks, shops and factories, the urban *Sturm und Drang*. But running under all this, as cool as a mountain stream, is a strand of popular music about the countryside and the natural world. Pop's perspective on our green and pleasant land may be an idealised one, more sylvan glades and dancing streams than polytunnels and agro-barons. But it certainly speaks to something deep in our national character.

Cecil Sharp and Vaughan Williams roamed England in the early part of the twentieth century collecting folk ballads and village songs. Sharp's agenda was explicitly rural. He didn't think the songs of the industrial classes or factory workers constituted 'real' folk music. Right from the very start of recorded music and modern song, the countryside had been idealised as a prelapsarian idyll. And it was to stay that way right the way through the tumultuous rock era of the 1960s.

On the surface, there couldn't have been a more urban outfit than Traffic. They emerged from the r&b scene in Birmingham, maybe England's biggest industrial city, and were even named after the stream of cars that stopped them crossing the road once outside London's Dorchester Hotel. But Traffic will forever be remembered as the band who pioneered the concept that became one of the great clichés of seventies rock. After early jams at the Elbow Room club in Aston, Birmingham, the band took the unusual step of renting a cottage near the village of Aston Tirrold, Berkshire, to write and rehearse new music for two years. Their first album was hatched there and the sojourn created a template for many of their peers that came to symbolise unfettered creativity and artistic freedom, or 'getting it together in the country'. Steve Winwood recalled, in a 1994 interview for *Q* magazine:

> The cottage thing came about for practical reasons, really. We were staying in a house in London, and whenever we wanted to play, the neighbours would be banging on the walls. We wanted somewhere where we could just play whenever we wanted. We found this cottage in the Berkshire Downs. It was a big estate with a sort of hovel for the gamekeeper, which was what we rented. Actually, it was a beautiful place and we set up a sort of mud stage where we could just play in the open air. It was very cut off with no road to it, just a track, and there were only about three weeks in the year when you could get a car up there. The rest of the time it was just a quagmire.

Traffic's Berkshire retreat became a celebrity crash pad. Jim Capaldi:

> I think we endeared ourselves to our contemporaries. People would come and hang out with us – Bonzo, Leon Russell, Stephen Stills, Ginger Baker, Pete Townshend, Eric Clapton – the hours would just drift into days. I suppose, looking back on it, they were all in cities in hotel rooms, going to the Bag o' Nails and all those clubs and getting out to the country was a nice break for them. You'd call it a hippy

commune now, but at the time it was just a practical thing, but very inspirational. When I hear Traffic records and look back on those years, I don't really think of festivals and clubs and rock and roll, I think of tracks on the Berkshire Downs, crows over a coppice. It was a very powerful experience.

Winwood added, 'Camping out, cooking over an open fire: it was like William and the Outlaws.'

Getting it together in the country soon became *de rigueur* for serious rock bands. When Led Zeppelin came home after a punishing US tour in 1970, Robert Plant and Jimmy Page holed up in a cottage called Bron-Yr-Aur near Machynlleth in southern Snowdonia, where singer Plant had spent childhood holidays in the fifties. It had neither electricity nor running water, which only added to the isolation and the mystique. Page described their time there with great affection in the same interview for *Q*:

Robert and I went to Bron-Yr-Aur in 1970. We'd been working solidly right up to that point. Even recordings were done on the road. We had this time off and Robert suggested the cottage. I certainly hadn't been to that area of Wales. It was the first time I really came to know Robert. Actually living together at Bron-Yr-Aur, as opposed to occupying nearby hotel rooms. The songs took us into areas that changed the band, and it established a standard of travelling for inspiration ... which is the best thing a musician can do. So we took our guitars down there and played a few bits and pieces. This wonderful countryside, panoramic views and having the guitars ... it was just an automatic thing to be playing. And we started writing.

Many of the songs for *Led Zeppelin III*, *Houses of the Holy* and *Physical Graffiti* were written at Bron-Yr-Aur. And the house itself gave its name to two songs, 'Bron-Yr-Aur Stomp', in which Robert Plant sings touchingly of walking in the surrounding woods with his dog Strider, and 'Bron-Yr-Aur', an acoustic instrumental from *Physical Graffiti*. Wales, too, provided a solace and refuge for the young Mike Oldfield. The massive and unexpected success of his début album *Tubular Bells* threatened to overpower the young musician, who'd always been somewhat delicate. He quit London and took himself away to a cottage called The Beacon, on Hergest Ridge, a hill in Herefordshire that straddles the English–Welsh border. He flew his glider there, rode his horse, drank Guinness in the local pub and walked his sheepdog, Bootleg, who would later grace the cover, on top of the hill, of *Hergest Ridge*, his second million-selling album. On his next album *Ommadawn*, he referred to the place rather sweetly on the short song 'On Horseback': 'So if you feel a little glum/To Hergest Ridge you should come ...'

This trend of 'getting it together in the country' reached its absurd apotheosis with the recording of Yes's *Tales from Topographic Oceans*. The band couldn't agree on whether the recording should take place in the city or the countryside. In the end a compromise was reached. The album would be recorded, over five months as it turned out, in Morgan Studios, London, which would be decorated and dressed to give it a rustic ambience. A white wooden fence was erected, along with a small barn, complete with bales of hay strewn about. A model cow with electronic udders provided the finishing touch.

It did become rather easy to chortle, especially when a new breed of rock-star country gentlemen began to emerge. Paul McCartney had always been the Beatle with the outdoor sensibility, expressed in songs like 'Mother Nature's Son'. The cover of his solo album *Ram* showed him wrestling with a recalcitrant sheep, a pose that John Lennon mimicked callously on the *Imagine* album, where he is pictured holding a pig by its ears. Later, of course, McCartney would record the staggeringly popular 'Mull of Kintyre', a windswept love letter to his remote Scottish retreat. It seemed for a while in the seventies that, along with the private jet and expensive drug habit, it was *de rigueur* for rock stars to become farmers, or at least be engaged in some sort of agricultural entrepreneurship. Trout farming was particularly popular. Jethro Tull's Ian Anderson became one of the country's major fish suppliers, and The Who's Roger Daltrey could be seen on a TV advert for American Express strolling around his trout farm in green wellies and Barbour jacket like a rock-star version of Bernard Matthews. It is a rock archetype that still pervades: witness Bryan Ferry's public support for the Countryside Alliance and Blur's Alex James's country-squire lifestyle of cheese-making.

The vast majority of pop music created in or about the British countryside tends to view it uncritically and romantically as a place of joy and escape, unsullied by the grime and stress of inner-city life, the traffic jams, shopping malls and high-rises. Very occasionally, though, some songs from more politically engaged performers have looked beyond the idealised picture of bucolic bliss.

The Housemartins' 'Me and the Farmer' boasts a picture-postcard image of a lovely English dale, but the song, typically of the band, juxtaposes an irrepressible beat and melody with a sour and sardonic lyric, in this case a portrait of the farmer not as benevolent John Bulll-ish countryman but as a mean-spirited capitalist exploiter of people and the environment who's 'Ripped up fields, bullied flocks/And worked his workers right around the clock', and is even hated by Jesus since 'Jesus gave what the farmer took'. Robert Wyatt's 'Pigs ... (in There)' begins as a description of a drive through the beautiful Wiltshire countryside on a summer's day that turns gently to horror as Wyatt realises that, in contrast to the fresh and invigorating feel of the day outdoors, the squat concrete bunkers he sees in the distance, baking in the heat, are full of pigs. His repeated disbelieving 'Pigs ... in there?' is a kind of anti-chorus, all the more disturbing for its simplicity.

Fascinating though these songs are, they're in the minority. There aren't many songs which take this grim view of the countryside as ruthless, exploitative factory floor. Most are personal declarations of genuine feeling for its beauty, often born of dissatisfaction with the urban rat race. When a young model and singer called Vashti Bunyan grew tired of London in the late 1960s she travelled north in a gypsy caravan to Scotland and a life of rural simplicity, writing songs as she went. These songs became her album of 1970, *Just Another Diamond Day*, overlooked at the time but now recognised as a lost (happily rediscovered) classic and one of the loveliest albums of its era, filled with the changing of the seasons, birds, insects, dusks and dawns and the quiet round of the rural day.

In mid-1977 Peter Gabriel, lead singer of Genesis, was in the grips of a crisis. He was increasingly weary of the treadmill of touring, rehearsing and recording, and torn between the demands of a successful rock group and domestic commitments to his wife and sick daughter. One evening he took himself for a solitary walk from his home in the village of Box to the top of a local beauty spot, Solsbury Hill. His reverie there and his internal dialogue about his future became his first solo hit, titled, appropriately enough, 'Solsbury Hill', from where he 'could see the city light' and 'an eagle that flew out of the night' – probably a buzzard – and ponder his situation. The finished song, airy and sweeping, is filled with a sense of revelation and inspiration from nature, familiar to anyone who has ever taken a problem for a long walk or climbed a hill to gain some perspective on life. For all it's tricky 7/4 time signature, soft-rock arrangement and hoarse, impassioned vocal, it is really a modern version of 'Linden Lea', a hymn to the transformative power of landscape and nature and 'getting it together in the country'.

25. ARE 'FRIENDS' ELECTRIC?

In 1779 a Leicestershire youth called Ned Ludd is said to have smashed two spinning frames in a fit of anger. During the Napoleonic wars new automated looms workable by cheap unskilled labour resulted in the loss of jobs for many skilled textile workers. They responded by smashing and burning the new machines. Taking Ned as their figurehead, they were known as Luddites, and many wool and cotton mills were destroyed before the government suppressed the movement.

Luddites were concerned for their jobs, but in the centuries to come the dizzying speed of technological growth left many concerned for their souls. Mary Shelley's *Frankenstein*, Aldous Huxley's *Brave New World*, Fritz Lang's *Metropolis*, even Charlie Chaplin's *Modern Times* – all expressed a fear of the dehumanising effects of technology and science. *Doctor Who*'s chilling adversaries the Cybermen were inspired by scientific consultant Kid Pedler's fear that, with the increased use of artificial limbs and medical technology, men could become machines. Debates about cloning and stem-cell research still rage within the fields of science and ethics.

From *2001: A Space Odyssey*'s Hal to the Daleks, from *Transformers* bad guys the Decepticons to Gort in *The Day the Earth Stood Still*, robots, computers and the scientists who program them have been as much a source of fear and suspicion as awe, and the future has not always been something to look forward to.

It's 1969. Neil Armstrong takes a giant step for mankind as he becomes the first man on the Moon. But, just seven years on from the wide-eyed enthusiasm of Joe Meek's 'Telstar', the new rock generation are less easily impressed by white-coated boffins and the activities of what American sociologist C. Wright Mills called the 'military-industrial-scientific complex'. Zager and Evans's hit 'In the Year 2525' is perhaps the first dystopian sci-fi pop single. Each verse takes us further and further into the far future, a horrifying one at that, where our minds are controlled by chemicals and our bodies by machines. By the year 6565, they predict, 'You'll pick your son, pick your daughter too/From the bottom of a long glass tube'. That line may well have inspired the media's demeaning term 'test tube baby' for little Louise Brown, born a decade later by IVF, the first such birth in the world.

Zager and Evans were destined to be one-hit wonders, but the same year a young man called David Bowie was beginning a long and distinguished pop career with an opportunistic sci-fi ditty called 'Space Oddity'. Compared to his later output, the track feels a little gimmicky, not least because of its use of the currently faddish Rolf Harris-sanctioned toy instrument, the Stylophone.

At the time 'Space Oddity' was widely seen as a rip-off of '2525'. But it is a much more opaque and human song about the isolation of an astronaut, a man floating in a tin can far above the world. Bowie later said, 'Here we had the great blast of American technological know-how shoving this guy up into space, but once he gets there he's not quite sure why he's there. And that's where I left him.'

The loneliness of the long-distance spaceman was the subject, three years later, of a hit by another grand dame of British rock, Elton John. In his 'Rocket Man', Bernie Taupin's lyric tells of an astronaut whose daily grind is as unglamorous and routine as anyone's, and who states, 'It's just my job five days a week.' Interestingly, though Bowie's and Elton John's songs are both pieces of speculative science fiction, neither is particularly imaginative or futuristic in style, both being pretty conventional seventies' ballads. But an electrical engineering boffin in New York, Dr Robert Moog, was doing his bit to take the pop song into the space age, developing his famous synthesizer at the Columbia–Princeton Electronic Music Centre. His early customers included Wendy (at that point still Walter) Carlos whose *Switched-On Bach* album, featuring Moog interpretations of Bach classics, sold a million copies and won three Grammies at the turn of the seventies. Inspired by *Switched-On Bach*, keyboardist Keith Emerson of The Nice bought the second commercially available Moog synthesizer and used it extensively in his next band, Emerson, Lake and Palmer. One of their *tours de force* was, naturally, a grim vision of a nightmare future robot dictatorship called 'Karn Evil 9'.

Malcolm Cecil and Bob Margouleff of Tonto's Expanding Headband introduced Stevie Wonder and soul music to the Moog, where it featured extensively on albums like *Music of My Mind*, *Talking Book* and *Fulfillingness' First Finale*. But no one explored the possibilities of the new instrument as extensively as Bach's descendants and countrymen in modern Germany. Berlin's Tangerine Dream constructed albums full of dreamy, romantic, mysterious musical suites played entirely on synthesizers, Mellotrons and sequencers. Meanwhile, over in the GDR in Düsseldorf, another group of young Germans were building new sounds that chimed ambiguously with a new Germany.

Autobahn was Kraftwerk's breakthough album internationally, a wry electronic hymn to Germany's motorway network which nodded to the US pop of The Beach Boys but did so in a deadpan *Vorsprung Durch Technik* style. Here in the land of Newport Pagnell services and Spaghetti Junction, Kraftwerk proved hugely influential on both established stars like David Bowie, whose music soon took a distinctly electronic turn, and young fans and bedroom dreamers like Slough Grammar schoolboy Gary Anthony James Webb.

Webb played in various teenage bands before forming Tubeway Army with his uncle Jess Lidyard. At the time he had adopted the artistic *nom de plume* Valerian. But on signing a deal with Beggars Banquet, he changed this, inspired by a plumber in the *Yellow Pages*, to Numan. While recording his first album for the label, he made a discovery that was to change the sound of his band and many others. In the studio was a Mini-Moog awaiting collection by a hire company. Numan absent-mindedly hit a few keys and was astonished by the keyboard's power and timbre.

This new stark, electronic sound was perfect for the lyrical content of Numan's new songs. His second album *Replicas* was a concept album based around a book idea of Numan's, set in a future metropolis, where androids known as Machmen subdue and dominate the human population on the orders of a shadowy cabal called The Grey Men. Numan has always acknowledged the influence of his favourite writers on the *Replicas* album, as he told *Mojo* magazine:

'There's a lot of Philip K. Dick in there. I love him. There's a lot of [William S.] Burroughs, too. The songs on *Replicas* were musical versions of short stories I was writing. Each story was about an aspect of what I thought London might be like in twenty or thirty years' time. There's a lot of violence, so they get this big super-computer in to work out a solution. It quickly realises that people are the problem, so it starts the 'Quota test', where people have to get to a certain level of intelligence, or they're taken to be re-educated – got rid of.

One of the central songs of this ambitious collection, 'Are "Friends" Electric?' owed its alienated ambience to serendipity according to an interview with the *Guardian*

I was trying to write two separate songs and I had a verse for one and a chorus for the other, but I couldn't finish either, [then] I realised they sounded all right stuck together. That's why it's five minutes long. Before I recorded it I was playing it back and I hit the wrong note and it sounded much better. That harsh note is probably the crucial note in the hook. It transformed it from almost a ballad into something quite unusual … I didn't expect the [huge] success, because you couldn't dance to it and it didn't have a definable chorus.

The success of 'Are "Friends" Electric?' meant that Numan (who would quickly became a solo act under his own name) was soon selling out far bigger venues than the Marquee. Released in the May of 1979, it went to number one and stayed there for a month, buoyed by Numan's robotic TV performances and a release on the modish picture-disc format.

In much the same way that punk fellow travellers The Boomtown Rats were a much bigger singles group than The Clash, or that The

Shamen sold more records than the pioneers of house and techno, Gary Numan became popular with the public but a figure of mild fun for the press, who reviled his support of the Conservative Party and delighted in his often hapless aviation exploits while preferring the work of the German originators such as Kraftwerk, Neu! and Tangerine Dream or cooler UK antecedents Bowie, Roxy Music and Brian Eno. But Numan undoubtedly did more than any other musician to popularise electronic music and introduce a pop generation to sounds that had once been the preserve of the *conservatoire* or the underground. In an interview with Songfacts website he explained his position:

> At the time I felt like I was waving my flag, fighting for a cause. But now I look back on it, I think very differently. So I'm just glad that it's evolved the way it has. I'm glad that the stuff I did in those days gets some recognition. I'm glad that the whole electronic thing found its feet and became a totally established part of music in general, and has been now for a good couple of decades or so. I think there's better music around [now] because of it. The technology itself has come on in leaps and bounds. It's made a dramatic contribution to music in general, and I'm just proud that I played a small part in that.

As the eighties dawned, other bedroom knob twiddlers with hire-purchase synths became part of the fabric of British pop. From industrial Sheffield came The Human League, whose witty and intelligent mix of dystopian sci-fi futurism with electronic glam and disco was initially a cult hit, before a line-up change saw singer Phil Oakey recruit two teenage girls he'd seen dancing in a disco, and huge success on both sides of the Atlantic followed. From suburban Basildon came Depeche Mode, who went from fresh faced electro-poppers to purveyors of stadium-filling gothic, dark techno. After quitting Depeche Mode, Vince Clarke formed Erasure who, in the late eighties along with the Pet Shop Boys, made synthesisers the sound of hedonism (rather than alienation), the true legacy of Giorgio Moroder and the house sounds of Chicago and New York.

But the nineties and beyond have seen the return of what we might call dystopian pop, as exemplified by the bleak futurism of Radiohead's *OK Computer*, possibly the most influential album of recent decades. This was described by music writer Tom Moon as a 'prescient ... dystopian essay on the darker implications of technology ... oozing [with] a vague sense of dread, and a touch of Big Brother foreboding that bears strong resemblance to the constant disquiet of life on Security Level Orange, post-9/11.'

Gary Numan rarely attracted this kind of critical eulogy. But musicians from Prince to Lady Gaga, techno pioneers like Juan Atkins and Afrika Bambaataa, and industrial bands like Nine Inch Nails have all cited Numan as an influence. He may never have been as cool as Bowie or Eno, but the picture disc of 'Are "Friends" Electric?' still lurks in many a record collection, possibly even Radiohead's.

26. ANOTHER BRICK IN THE WALL

School, the happiest days of your life according to many, our first introduction to the austerity of duty according to the sociologist Émile Durkheim. Einstein said that education consisted of forgetting all the things you learned in school, while Mark Twain, who can always be relied upon to say something, claimed he never let school interfere with his education.

Given that, like falling in love and growing old, education is an experience that it is common to pretty much all of us, it's not surprising that there should have been so many songs about school. Maybe what is surprising is that so many – the vast majority – have been so negative, so critical, so down on the old Alma Mater.

The British education system has been in a state of permanent revolution under successive governments since the Second World War, so perhaps it's no surprise that songs about the specifics and structure of school are extremely thin on the ground. No one can keep up; and every generation has a slightly different sort of schooling. Thus you won't find many stadium rock anthems or dancefloor classics about the Butler Education Act of 1944 and the setting up of the tripartite school system, nor the introduction of the GCSE.

What you will find is school used generally either as a cipher for repression, boredom or the power of the state or, less often, a handy metaphor for a lost world of innocence. These last are the *Goodbye, Mr Chips* of pop, and the fifties and sixties were full of them, in both Britain and the United States.

The Beach Boys' 'Be True to Your School' was a song so alien in concept to British ears, even in 1963, that it serves as a metaphor for some crucial transatlantic differences. It's hard to imagine The Beatles or The Kinks or even Cliff Richard singing a song that asks, 'Ain't you heard of my school/It's number one in the state', and whose chorus demands that the listener shows a loyalty to their educational establishment, 'Just like you would to your girl ...' Its *naïveté* and good faith is both touching and slightly disturbing. 'The New Girl in School' by fellow surfing scenesters Jan and Dean is by comparison positively louche in its description of a school-wide male crush on the titular new girl. Interestingly, there's a premonition of films like *Mean Girls* and the songs of Taylor Swift in the line about 'The chicks are jealous of the new girl in school/ They put her down and they treat her so cruel' . Whereas in Britain we had Cliff's 'Schoolboy Crush', a goofy, drippy song about, well, a schoolboy crush full of wince-inducing references to 'record hops' and 'graduation' that was to be his début single until wisely it was flipped for 'Move It', which of course went on to kick-start British rock and roll.

Almost all of the golden generation of British rock in the 1960s were products of the state education system set up in 1948. As late as the 1970s, Genesis were an exotic and frankly posh oddity, having been educated at Charterhouse public school. Rock and roll was a working-class pursuit; ex-public school boys in the music industry were more likely to be in management, or the media. Andrew Loog Oldham and Brian Epstein were both privately educated, and John Peel attended Shrewsbury public school. Their charges, though, would often sing of the joys and trials of the humble state school system. The Hollies were masters of the nostalgic first-love-in-the-playground ditty, but there's a more adult subtext to their May 1967 'Carrie Anne'. Though the song conjures up a romance begun in a Manchester primary school, it's actually about a very late-sixties dalliance. In 1995 Nash revealed that the song was about Marianne Faithfull, whom he was close to but who was having an affair with The Hollies' married singer Allan Clarke. 'If it felt good, you did it. It would have been hypocritical not to sleep with someone simply because he or she was involved with someone else!' said Ms Faithfull. Nash was too shy to use her real name so he changed it from Marianne to Carrie Anne, which surprisingly threw people off the scent for three decades.

Their hit of the following year, 'Jennifer Eccles', is actually the exception to the rule that there are no songs about the specifics of the school system. In this song the protagonist hopes that his sweetheart will pass her eleven-plus, as he has, so she will follow him to the same (grammar) school.

The name 'Jennifer Eccles' is both beautifully evocative of sixties Lancashire (in the same way Victoria Wood's Kelly-Marie Tunstall was the perfect eighties Northern name) and based on two real people: Allan Clarke's wife Jennifer and Graham Nash's wife, whose maiden name was Eccles.

The very British notion of the playground, that asphalt jungle of fights, football, rough and tumble and slap and tickle, is celebrated in a number of songs. 'Remember the Days of the Old Schoolyard' was inspired by the playground at St Joseph's in Camden, London, where Cat Stevens went to school. It was an appropriately nostalgic song for a crucial turning point in Stevens's life. It was his last hit before he became a Muslim and changed his name to Yusuf Islam.

Looking back, as the bright, youthful buoyancy of our swinging sixties childhood gave way to the harsh realities of the seventies and eighties, it seems our view of many things changed, including school. Lennon's 'Working Class Hero' posits ordinary people as hapless dupes brainwashed by television and the products of a heartless education system where "They hate you if you're clever and they despise a fool.'

It's a long way from the sunny innocence, the satchel carrying and chalk hearts of Jennifer Eccles. The school as the domain of the bully resonated in The Smiths' 'Headmaster Ritual'. It's another almost painfully autobiographical account of Morrissey's school days at St Mary's secondary modern in Stretford, a school, like all Manchester schools, run by 'belligerent ghouls ...[and] spineless swine with cemented minds'. What saves this from being as dour a song as Lennon's is Johnny Marr's cascading, whirling guitar arrangement and Morrissey's black humour. He describes the headmaster's ancient threadbare suit, his penchant for doing 'the military two-step down the nape of [his] neck'.

Another northern indie band of the era, The Housemartins, wrote a different kind of anti-school song in 'Bow Down' from their album *The People Who Grinned Themselves to Death*. Here the narrator is a child dwarfed and confused by the school and its systems who, in a beautiful image, moulds his Plasticine into a little man who looks just like him. 'His limbs were so weak and he couldn't move his mouth to speak/And I could bend him into any shape I wanted him to be.' It's the same affecting mood of frightened vulnerability heard on Supertramp's 'School' a place of 'don't do this and don't do that' or the Devil might come to put out your eyes.

But none of these is quite the sustained attack that Pink Floyd's Roger Waters levelled at the education system in 'The Happiest Days of our Lives/Another Brick in the Wall Pt II'. They should be seen in context, as part of *The Wall* album, a bleak disquisition on isolation and alienation caused by the loss of Waters's father when he was a baby and his disenchantment with the stadium-rock status of the band. Various issues get it in the neck from Waters over the course of *The Wall*'s four sides: the military, rock stardom, fascists, marriage and, of course, teachers.

Waters was a grammar-school boy from Cambridgeshire High School for Boys, the only one of Pink Floyd not to go to private school, contrary to what many people think. But his grammar-school experiences were clearly far from happy. In the song, and even more vividly in the film, with its Gerald Scarfe animations, the teacher is a brutal – and Scottish – tyrant who is cruel and contradictory, bellowing 'Wrong! Do it again!', 'If you don't eat yer meat, you can't have any pudding! How can you have any pudding if you don't eat yer meat?!'

'Another Brick in the Wall' was just as caustic, but couched in a disco beat at the brilliant suggestion of producer Bob Ezrin. A natural single, its highlights included Dave Gilmour's tremendously liquid, funky solo and a kids' chorus. This was also Ezrin's idea; he'd pulled a similar trick on Alice Cooper's 'School's Out'. Music teacher Alun Renshaw of Islington Green School, close to Floyd's original Britannia Row Studios, was approached. Ezrin wanted a mixed bag of pupils, kids with different voices: 'Twenty-four tracks of cockney, posh, everything. Fill 'em up.'

The end result confounds our expectations. After years of nymphs and shepherds and St Winifred's, kids' choirs on records tended to be cute to the point of cloying. The effect of the choir on 'Another Brick in the Wall' is chilling, partly because of the words – 'We don't need no education/We don't need no thought control' – but also because of the cold, hostile and defiant tone.

Of course the notion of a multi-millionaire grammar-school rock star declaring that no education was needed for the plebs in the comprehensive system was unpalatable to many. Waters defended himself in a 2010 interview with *Mojo* magazine, saying the song was ironic and satirical:

> You couldn't find anybody in the world more pro-education than me. But the education I went through in a boys' grammar school in the fifties was very controlling and demanded rebellion. The teachers were weak and therefore easy targets. The song is meant to be a rebellion against errant government, against people who have power over you, who are wrong. Then it absolutely demanded that you rebel against that.

It didn't help, though, when it was later revealed that Islington Green school had received just a lump sum of a grand for their crucial contribution to a single that sold over four million copies and was the last number one of the 1970s. A later lawsuit saw them win considerably more in royalties. A year later another gang of North London tearaways produced their own response to the Floyd's grim account of school life.

Madness had grown up not far from Islington Green, in Camden, and over the first three years of their existence had grown from being cheeky rudimentary ska poppers to a great English observational band in the vein of The Kinks and The Beatles. The first single to be taken from their *Absolute Madness* album was 'Baggy Trousers', a jerky, fairground, vaudevillian romp back to their Camden school days, depicting pupils and a colourful parade of skiving teachers down the pub 'passing round the ready-rubbed'.

Singer and lyricist Suggs said in *Uncut* magazine in 2008:

'Baggy Trousers' was sort of an answer to Pink Floyd, even at that age I thought the line 'teacher leave them kids alone' was a bit strange, sinister – though I think Floyd are a great band. It sounded self-indulgent to be going on about how terrible schooldays had been; there was an inverted snobbery about it too. You went to a posh public school? You wanna try going to my school. I remember thinking that Pink Floyd's 'Another Brick in the Wall' showed a very different school experience to ours. In my school, I generally felt sorry for the teachers who were given a hard time because we were all up to no good. So I tried to redress the balance a little bit with this song. The title refers to the high-waisted Oxford bags we used to wear with Kevin Keegan perms – the worst fashion known to humankind.

'Baggy Trousers' was such a hit with the very schoolkids whose world it captured so evocatively that the band had to undertake a matinée tour just for school-age fans.

One can see Suggs's point. The trouble with the more po-faced of the anti-school diatribes down the years is that they verge on well-fed self-pity, and American folkie Tom Paxton's 'What Did You Learn Iin School Today?' may be the worst offender here:

a holier than thou, this hurts me more than you castigation of schools and teachers for pretty much every social ill. The people's songs that will last longer have a little more warmth about them, like Janis Ian's 'At Seventeen' and, more recently, Taylor Swift's 'Fifteen', both of which are tender and sympathetic songs about how frightening and exhilarating high school can be for a teenage girl. And then there's 'Wonderful World' by Sam Cooke, an achingly beautiful song that contrasts Sam's passion for his girl with an exhaustive list of his academic shortcomings, including his incompetence *vis-à-vis* the slide rule.

As popular music grows older as an art-form, so do its laureates and lyricists and so school becomes a distant memory for the established and credentialed performers. The cultural climate is different too. The notion of grown men like Alice Cooper singing from the point of view of schoolkids now seems weird at best, if not downright creepy.

Undoubtedly the pithiest song about school is to be found on Nirvana's début album *Bleach*. Titled simply 'School', the lyric, which in its entirety runs 'Won't you believe it?/It's just my luck/ No recess!', probably says more about school than any Ofsted report ever will.

27. GHOST TOWN

The Locarno Ballroom, Coventry, an airy modernist tower of glass and steel, was one of the most striking buildings of the new Coventry that arose after the city's destruction by bombing during the Second World War. The Locarno was built during the city's post-war boom, a boom that rolled on four wheels and on names like Jaguar, Triumph, Hillman, Humber, Talbot and Commer. Coventry was Britain's Motor City, its Detroit, and its huge, well-paid workforce reaped the benefits of the town's wealth in new houses, a go-ahead football club run by Jimmy Hill, an Olympic-sized swimming pool, Britain's first pedestrianised shopping precinct, theatres, galleries, and clubs like the Locarno, where through the swinging sixties and into the seventies you could have seen everyone from Brian Poole and his Tremeloes to Pink Floyd and, where in 1972, as noted in Chapter 3, Chuck Berry recorded his only UK number one, 'My Ding-a-Ling'.

By 1981, though, Coventry was taking a battering again – not from the Luftwaffe this time but from the chill wind of economic blight that saw its manufacturing base collapse, its car plants close

and its golden age of prosperity end in rocketing unemployment
and urban decay. Coventry's plight was mirrored in cities all across
the Midlands and the North, from Liverpool to Newcastle, from
Birmingham to Leeds. But Coventry's dark ages of the early 1980s
are remembered differently from those of those other beleaguered
cities, not so much in newsreels of riots and petrol bombs as in the
eerie sing-along strains of a very unlikely chart topper.

'This town is coming like a Ghost Town,' sang the town's
most famous musical sons, The Specials, 'All the clubs have been
closed down.' RIP the Locarno, opened 1960, closed 1981, and
commemorated in British pop's strangest and most sombre number
one, which managed to dampen the party spirits when *Top of the
Pops* celebrated its 900th edition. As its mournful sounds died away,
veteran pop presenter David Jensen said, 'Oh, dear, that wasn't
very cheery, was it?'

The Specials actually had two number one singles. Seventeen
months before 'Ghost Town', a live version of a very different
number, 'Too Much Too Young' — simplistic and boisterous — had
topped the chart. This was very much the defining mode of the
early Specials. They emerged from multiracial Coventry outfit The
Automatics, who fused punk and reggae to clumsy but riotous effect.
But the band's keyboardist and creative lynchpin, Jerry Dammers,
had more ambitious plans. After seeing first hand a violent attack
on the crowd and support act by right-wing skinheads at a Sham 69
concert in Bracknell, he wanted to use music as a force for good as
he explained to the *Guardian* in 2002:

> It was obvious that a mod and skinhead revival was coming,
> and I was trying to find a way to make sure it didn't go the

way of the National Front and the British Movement. I saw punk as a piss-take of rock music, as rock music committing suicide, and it was great and it was really funny, but I couldn't believe people took it as a serious musical genre which they then had to copy. It seemed to be a bit more healthy to have an integrated kind of British music, rather than white people playing rock and black people playing their music. Ska was an integration of the two.

As The Specials and via their manager Rick Rogers, they brokered a deal with Chrysalis Records to have their own label and creative freedom. That label was 2-Tone, a phrase coined by Jerry Dammers who, along withwith bassist Horace Panter and graphic designer John 'Teflon' Sims, created the striking Walt Jabsco logo that adorned every 2-Tone release (a man in a black suit, white shirt, black tie, pork pie hat, white socks and black loafers, and based on a Peter Tosh album sleeve). Its first release was a split seven inch, 'The Selecter' by The Selecter and 'Gangsters' by The Specials, which is still as darkly exhilarating as it was in 1979.

2-Tone recruited like-minded bands from across working-class multi-ethnic Britain, and the next four singles, by Madness, The Beat, The Selecter and The Specials again, all made the UK top ten. Britain was in the throes of a fully fledged youth revival and in pubs and playgrounds across the country, the Rude Boy look – Ben Shermans, Sta-Prest, pork pie hats, braces, Crombies – became *de rigueur* with the nation's streetwise youth.

2-Tone's heyday was glorious but brief. Dammers's visionary but reputedly autocratic style was not to everyone's liking. The other hit bands quickly left 2-Tone. The Specials continued through

1980 with a tranche of brilliant seven-inch singles like 'A Message to You Rudy' 'The Special A.K.A. Live EP', 'Rat Race' and, from their second album *More Specials*, 'Do Nothing' and 'Stereotypes', which indicated a move into a stranger, darker, richer musical palate, taking in jazz, lounge music and film soundtracks, and a bleak, sardonic view of their own communities and countrymen.

Touring the *More Specials* album was to open their eyes to another reality of contemporary Britain, a more politicised and sympathetic view which culminated in their masterpiece. Though the band were hugely successful, they were ragged and overworked and internal relations were strained. Gigs in Newcastle, Leeds and Cambridge descended into violence. Dammers and guitarist Roddy Radiation were arrested and charged with incitement to riot in Cambridge. Dammers later recalled:

Everyone was getting under pressure and the band was getting tired. It wasn't just that: the country was falling apart. You travelled from town to town and what was happening was terrible. In Liverpool, all the shops were shuttered up, everything was closing down. Margaret Thatcher had apparently gone mad, she was closing down all the industries, throwing millions of people on the dole. We could actually see it by touring around. You could see that frustration and anger in the audience. In Glasgow, there were these little old ladies on the streets selling all their household goods, their cups and saucers. It was unbelievable. It was clear that something was very, very wrong.

Dammers wanted to convey this vision of modern Britain in a song but met with initial scepticism over the musical setting:

I had to practically get down on my knees and beg them to do it. The overall sense I wanted to convey was one of impending doom. The sound was a very important part of it: the Yamaha home organ, those weird Japanese fake clarinet sounds. I love anything in music that's fake and wrong and weird. I think that's what gave it that haunting feeling. 'Ghost Town' wasn't a free-for-all jam session. Every little bit was worked out and composed, all the different parts. I'd been working on it for at least a year, trying out every conceivable chord. It was a combination of the first album and the second album, the complete history of the band gelled in one song. I can remember walking out of a rehearsal in total despair because Neville would not try the ideas ... I remember Lynval rushing into the control room while they were doing it going, 'No, no, no, it sounds wrong! Wrong! Wrong!' In the meantime, Roddy's trying to kick a hole through the wall from the control room to the studio room. It was only a little studio in Leamington and the engineer was going, 'If that doesn't stop, you're going to have to leave!' I was saying, 'No! No! This is the greatest record that's ever been made in the history of anything! You can't stop now!'

'Ghost Town' is like a fairground ride through a nightmare, a fractured and fragmented slideshow of images from an urban hell played out to the lush but demented strains of a Dario Argento horror movie. For a tantalisingly brief moment there is a ray of sunshine, a flicker of light in the form of a nostalgic reverie when Terry Hall takes the lead vocal and remembers the peace and prosperity of boom-town Coventry. But this is shattered within seconds, and we are back, zombie-like, on a trip through the darkened underpasses of a deserted, strip-lit city. As the writer Alexis Petridis put it in a 2002 piece for the *Guardian* about 'Ghost Town':

> Despite their complaints that London was burning with boredom, most punk bands had retained a whiff of metropolitan glamour. Terry Hall's vocals, however, described a grimly provincial world of shopping precincts and shabby ballrooms in a deadpan Coventry whine. The album also displayed the band's ability to define the preoccupations of post-punk youth – the NF are on the march, Teddy boys and punks punch it out, 'boot boys' lurk in the shadows, waiting to strike. It was a talent that would come to its fullest fruition on 'Ghost Town'.

Tom Watson, now Labour MP for West Bromwich East, was a teenager in the Midlands at the time:

> I was fourteen years old. 'Ghost Town' spoke to me and every other teenage kid. I remember the school careers officer telling me that if I didn't smarten up I wouldn't get a job in the local carpet factory. My 'Ghost Town' was Kidderminster, but it could have been any Midlands town. We all wore our Fred Perrys and worshipped The Specials. A quarter of a century later, Conservative politician Sir Peter Tapsell said that what Thatcher and Howe did in 1981 was 'financially and economically illiterate'. 'Fuck you,' I thought when the careers office door closed. I joined the Labour Party.

Even the recording of 'Ghost Town' was appropriate to the era and the surroundings. Bassist Horace Panter is still proud of the fact that 'it was recorded in the small basement of a row of terrace houses in Leamington. It was around the time bands were going to Montserrat to record albums in ninety-six-track studios. The Specials went to a little town in the Midlands and recorded on eight-track.'

In Coventry that spring, an Asian teenager, Samtam Gill, was murdered in a racist attack. In the ensuing violence between skinheads and Asian youths, eighty people were arrested. On the day of 'Ghost Town's release, The Specials announced they would play a benefit concert for racial unity. The National Front said they would march through the city on the same day. This was the Britain that 'Ghost Town' was born into: violent, depressed, riven with political strife; a country under siege.

'Ghost Town' soundtracked this Britain to eerie perfection. It managed to be both edgy and beautiful, urban and spectral. It was also starkly, mesmerisingly different from the shiny synthesiser pop prevalent in the charts of the day, and soon made its way to number one. It stayed there for three weeks and became the harbinger of a summer of flames and broken glass, a summer of violence and destruction as, fanned by unemployment and police oppression, riots broke out across Britain. 'Ghost Town's timing was both perfect and terrible. As those unforgettable strains wafted from cars and radios and jukeboxes there was rioting in Brixton and Toxteth, in the Chapeltown district of Leeds and St Paul's in Bristol, in Handsworth and Streatham; all were inner-city areas with simmering tensions.

But there were also disturbances in Cirencester and High Wycombe, Aldershot and Bedford, in the very heart of Middle England. These events left Dammer energised but also appalled:

I'd planned a band from the age of ten that was going to cause a revolution. And when it actually happened, I suppose you're entitled to think, 'Oh my God. Maybe I actually had something to do with it.' It was scary, because I'm not a person who likes violence in any way. But I put the blame on Margaret Thatcher and the Tories. The riots didn't happen because of The Specials; they happened because of the way Thatcher was treating people. That's the way it's always worked in this country. People are pushed until they snap. And then things change, a little tiny bit.

Something was about to snap in The Specials too. The band were in meltdown and at the *Top of the Pops* appearance for 'Ghost Town' the band's three vocalists, Neville Staple, Terry Hall and Lynval Golding, announced they were leaving to form a new band the Fun Boy Three. They went on to have a succession of chart hits. The Specials continued without them and made a critically well received but modestly successful album called *In the Studio*. But neither band ever enjoyed as big or as significant success as 'Ghost Town'.

Thirty years after 'Ghost Town' was a hit, a re-formed Specials, as is the way of things in our nostalgia- and revival-obsessed age, returned to play a sell-out reunion show at the Ricoh Arena, the home of Coventry City football club, named after a corporate printer and photocopier manufacturer. A partial reunion anyway: Jerry Dammers was conspicuous by his absence. The reasons are far from clear but can be raked over online. It's all rather sad.

Perhaps better to remember them by their swan song and their finest three and a half minutes that may be, if not the greatest record ever to make number one, then the least likely to and perhaps the most powerful. Even if you wouldn't go that far, few would argue that there has ever been a more timely number one; a record that reflected its era, like a cracked and distorted hall of mirrors reflecting a country on the edge of collapse.

28. SHIPBUILDING

Here's a joke that did the rounds in the North of England in 1982 or 1983. An ex-army type is walking along a city street when he sees a man with no arms and no legs sitting on the pavement playing a mouth organ. A sign beside the chap reads 'Veteran of the Falklands War'. Touched, the passer-by peels off a twenty-pound note and drops it in the ex-soldier's hat. The veteran looks up and says, 'Muchas gracias, señor.'

I think this joke reveals plenty about the heartfelt but complicated feelings that ran through the British people at the time of the Falklands War in 1982. The invasion of the South Atlantic islands was an act of naked aggression by a fascist state and thus had to be resisted, said the patriot and the fair-minded of left and right. But for many on the liberal left, that meant allying oneself with a loathed, hard-line bogey woman and taking arms against the wretched conscripts of a bankrupt state. But then Britain was wretched and bankrupt in 1982 too, and to let General Galtieri's jackboots trample British soil would be a final indignity.

In late March of that year, Argentine marines posing as scrap-metal dealers had planted a flag on South Georgia, and, on the back of centuries of largely British sovereignty and quietly rumbling dispute, Argentine forces soon mounted amphibious landings, swiftly overcoming any resistance by the islanders. The British government were spectacularly unprepared for these events, despite several years of warnings from the Royal Navy over the simmering issue. In truth the British had recently been ambivalent over the islands, until, that is, the Argentine junta came to power, and Prime Minister James Callaghan hardened his line. 'I'm not handing over one thousand eight hundred Britons to a bunch of fucking fascists,' was his trenchant verdict. The British public were less clear about all this. Pretty much no one knew where the Falkland Islands were. When, in late 1981, the former colony of Belize was granted independence, the *Daily Mirror* ran a helpful list of what remained of the British empire: Hong Kong, Gibraltar, the Virgin Islands, Montserrat, St Helena, Diego Garcia, the Cayman Islands, Pitcairn and the Turks and Caicos. It actually forgot about the Falkland Islands.

Come the invasion, the Argentinians were rather hoping that the British government had forgotten about them too. Like Argentina, Britain was in an economic mess, and the military junta had taken note of substantial defence cuts in the United Kingdom before launching its invasion.

Bellicose and adamantine, Mrs Thatcher was in no doubt that British resolve would win the day. When told that it would take three weeks for a Task Force to reach the Falklands, she replied, 'Three days, you mean.' When she was corrected, the enormity of the task was brought chillingly home. The commander of the Task Force, Admiral Sir John Fieldhouse, said privately, 'I hope the people realise that this is the most difficult thing we've attempted since the Second World War.'

In the spring of 1982 the nation talked of little else other than the Falklands, and disagreements, cracks and arguments ran through every school class and workshop, office and salon bar, right to the heart of Westminster. When the passionately left-wing Labour leader Michael Foot got to his feet in the chamber in the wake of the invasion and talk of a Task Force being sent to repel the Argentines, few thought they would hear him utter such supportive sentiments: 'There is the longer term interest to ensure that foul and brutal aggression does not succeed in our world. If it does there will be a danger not just in the Falklands but to people all over our dangerous world.'

And we didn't just talk about the Falklands War, we sang about it, as well. The launching of the Task Force inspired Elvis Costello to write the definitive song about the Falklands conflict, and one of the most moving and subtle artistic responses to any war. As plans were being made to deploy troops in the South Atlantic, Nick Lowe was having a party at his London home, where in-demand producer Clive Langer played a new jazzy tune he'd written to Elvis Costello, whose new album he was about to start work on. Langer wasn't happy with the lyrics he'd come up with, but Costello loved the chords and, within days, came up with a newsworthy set of 'the best lyrics I've ever written'.

'Shipbuilding' is sung from the point of view of a worker at one of Britain's great declining shipyards – Tyneside, Belfast, Barrow or the Clyde – who knows that war can bring prosperity as well as tragedy to the families there. The boy who may get the bicycle for his birthday is also the son who may get taken to task, that is sent to lose his life with the Task Force. The genius of the song lies in its personalisation of the dilemma, and the reminder that underlying the rhetoric and grand narratives of war are small human stories of tragedy, compromise and waste. 'Is it worth it?/A new winter coat and shoes for the wife?' The song's beauty is that it lets that question hang unanswered rather than provide the obvious, opinionated, didactic answer. Technically, it is a deft piece of songwriting as well; the rhymes of 'filled in', 'killed in' and 'shipbuilding' serve to hammer home the point that not wholeheartedly supporting 'our boys', as the Thatcherite press dubbed them, was regarded with suspicion by some. Even Task Force Admiral Sandy Woodward condemned the 'lunatic nationalistic pride' being exhibited by some. 'GOTCHA!' was the *Sun*'s headline printed by editor Kelvin MacKenzie as a response to the sinking of the Argentine light cruiser the *General Belgrano* with the loss of 323 lives.

Costello offered 'Shipbuilding' first to the cult British singer and musician Robert Wyatt, formerly of Soft Machine but then in the throes of a fascinating solo career conducted after a fall from a window at a mid-seventies party that had rendered him paraplegic. His wheelchair-based hit rendition of The Monkees 'I'm a Believer' in 1974 remains one of the highlights of *Top of the Pops*. Wyatt was an inspired choice by Costello and Langer, for his unique voice, his love of jazz and his communist sympathies. When he received the demo of the song with guide vocals by Costello, Wyatt, struggling to quit smoking to protect his already fragile voice, said his first thought was, 'Ooh, I can't sing that.' But then he was seduced by what he called 'Clive's beautiful chords. I hadn't really thought about the issues. Plus I'm not good at anger. I saw my role as a messenger, just a canary, really. The singer's job is not to interfere. I simply shadowed the demo.' And that original demo, with Steve Nieve from Elvis's band the Attractions on piano and Madness's

Mark Bedford on double bass, became the single, with the addition of just Wyatt's vulnerable, doubting vocal.

Other musical responses to the situation in the South Atlantic were less nuanced and more direct in every way. The anarchist punk collective Crass wrote several angry polemical tracts about the conflict on their album *Yes Sir, I Will*. There was little of 'Shipbuilding's melancholy contemplation on the singles 'Sheep Farming in the Falklands' and 'How Does it Feel to be the Mother of 1,000 Dead?' The latter title was intended as an accusation levelled at the Prime Minister and led to questions in Parliament. Other punkish acts like New Model Army and The Exploited recorded visceral, often unrepeatable diatribes against the war effort. But Billy Bragg's 'Island of No Return' was sung from the point of view of a Task Force squaddie advancing on the Argentine-held capital, Port Stanley. Bragg himself was a soldier briefly in 1981 before buying himself out of the army for £175. His squaddie, one of 'our boys' too, is a bewildered, frightened everyman, who

> *Never thought that I would be*
> *Fighting fascists in the Southern Sea*
> *I saw one today and in his hand*
> *Was a weapon that was made in Birmingham*

This last line was of course a reference to the fact that the British government had many lucrative arms contracts with dictatorships in places like Argentina. Pink Floyd's gloomy anti-war swansong 'The Fletcher Memorial Home' also specifically refers to the Falklands War and the sinking of the the *Belgrano* outside the 'exclusion zone'.

There was, perhaps unsurprisingly, very little in the way of support for the government's military stance from the musical community. The defiantly un-PC Macclesfield-based punk band The Macc Lads chose to eulogise the British fighting man and his lifestyle when compared to that of the Argentinian. Interestingly, the metre and sentiments of 'Buenos Aires' are reminiscent of the kind of barrack-room ballad that's been sung in Aldershot, or shanty sung in Portsmouth, for hundreds of years:

Costa Mendez lives in fear of real men who can hold their beer
Fray Bentos and cheap red wine is all they eat in the Argentine
But after a scrap with the English Navy, they'll ask for the recipe
for chips 'n' gravy

And of course, there were Argentinian songs about the war. Charly Garcia and Raúl Porchetto had popular hits critical of the British stance, while punk bands like Los Violadores expressed anti-junta sentiment in songs that were often banned.

By the time Robert Wyatt's version of 'Shipbuilding' was released in the summer of 1982 the Falklands War was over, the Argentinians having surrendered two months previously. It has been called the 'the last old-fashioned war' in that both sides were evenly matched, using the same fairly primitive technology and military hardware, and where Britain last fought alone for its own cause. Its chief impact was to revive the ailing fortunes of Margaret Thatcher and her government. The Falklands victory confirmed to her supporters and convinced some doubters of her steely resolve. Buoyed by the victory and a new mood of national pride, she won the next two elections and remained in power for the rest of the decade. Prior to the Falklands, the political journalist Tom Nairn wrote:

> Britain needs another war. This alone would recreate
> the peculiar spirit of her nationalism, rally her renegade
> intelligentsia like in the thirties, and reconcile the workers
> to their lot. Unfortunately, war of that sort, like her empire,
> is a lost cause.

He was wrong. For many – though perhaps not the 'renegade
intellegentsia', the Falklands was almost exactly that kind of war,
although the events of spring 1982 were so odd and unexpected
that no one could have predicted that the national psyche would
be transformed by scrap-metal dealers and ships at the bottom of
the world.

As for 'Shipbuilding', it remains one of the great social
observational songs of our time. Radiohead said that it was the
piece of music they would most like to see reach an alien civilisation
on the *Voyager* space probe. Costello himself, when asked in 2008
whether it was still his best lyric, remarked:

> It's a pretty good lyric, yeah. The key line for me is, 'Diving
> for dear life/When we could be diving for pearls'. That we
> should be doing something beautiful, better than this. I
> wrote the lyric before the *Belgrano* sinking. I've been to see
> the monument, stood and read the names of all the men …
> well, boys, who died. Whatever you say about the conflict of
> war, that crime alone will see Thatcher in hell.

As a response to the horror of war, it's to be hoped that 'Shipbuilding'
will be remembered when 'GOTCHA!' is forgotten.

29. OUR HOUSE

An Englishman's home is his castle – literally for some Englishmen, of course. The rest of us have to make do with something more modest. But house and home, what they mean, the difference between the two and the emotional push and pull of them have been inspiring and exasperating artists for centuries.

Home is a shorthand in most art forms for security, love, solidity, all that's good, enduring and true in what Phillip Larkin called our 'intricate, rented world'. Home is where the heart is; home, sweet home; keeping the home fires burning; even if you're *Home Alone* it's still a place to be defended and treasured, and the invasion of the home as the ultimate affront is a staple of Hollywood, from *Key Largo* to *Halloween* to *The Panic Room*. After three volumes and several thousand pages of perilous, fantastical life and death adventures, the last words of Tolkien's *Lord of the Rings* trilogy, as a relieved Sam Gamgee enters his own front door, is, 'Well, I'm back.'

But I'd argue that pop music is perhaps an art form built on the rejection of home. Rootless, nomadic, escapist, pop often rejects the domestic in favour of the new and the faraway. 'The Wanderer',

'I Can Never Go Home Any More', 'Born to Run', 'Born to Be Wild', even 'I Was Born Under a Wanderin' Star': all reflect the impulse towards freedom and escape – the frontier mentality – in American rock. There are as many songs in which home acts as a metaphor for torpor and suffocation as for safety and solace, a prison rather than a sanctuary.

That may be a modern notion, though. The Victorians were an energetic, sentimental lot. When they weren't conquering far-flung continents or building enormous bridges, they were busy composing mawkish, lachrymose parlour-ballad paeans to hearth and home: 'There's No Place Like Home', 'Home, Sweet Home', 'I Want to See the Dear Old Home'. These songs were manifestly manipulative and arch in their sentimentality, even then. And that's before we apply any hindsight to the Victorian domestic sphere: in truth, it was a place where women and children were subjugated by men, where domestic violence, abuse and alcoholism went on behind the closed doors of respectable houses.

The Victorian era saw a housing boom. Huge numbers of new homes were built to keep pace with a changing demographic; between 1801 and 1911 the population of Britain almost quadrupled. But supply and demand were often unevenly matched, and the poor and lowest paid often had to make do with cramped, insanitary accommodation and life at the whim of unscrupulous landlords.

Until the beginning of the twentieth century 90 per cent of all houses were rented from private landlords. Among those who could afford it, though, there was a solidifying of the nuclear family and a drawing away of this small social unit from wider society, class and community. It was something the ever-observant Charles Dickens incorporated into *Great Expectations*, with the clerk Wemmick leaving behind the pressures of work and the city in his mock castle in Walworth, his pride and joy. Charles Pooter, along with his 'dear wife' Carrie, resident at 'the Laurels', Brickfield Terrace, Holloway, in *Diary of a Nobody*, was the gently comic embodiment of the contented home-owner taking trivial things too seriously. We may chuckle at his small-minded absurdity ('Pooterish' has entered the language, as John Major found to his cost) but we also fondly recognise ourselves in him too. As Charles Pooter has it in the opening pages: 'After work in the City, I like to be at home. What's the good of a home, if you are never in it? "Home, Sweet Home", that's my motto.'

As the city became increasingly frenetic, stressful and impersonal, people craved space. The coming of the omnibus and the railway allowed an escape to the quiet and fresh air of the countryside. New, smart terraces were built on what were then the outskirts of town. It was the birth of the suburbs.

In popular culture, particularly in America, the suburbs have always been a shorthand, possibly a lazy one, for repression and conservatism. 'A place of wide lawns and narrow minds,' as Ernest Hemingway rather ungraciously put it. Almost as soon as the American suburbs had been built they were being sneered at. Pete Seeger's 'Little Boxes' was an airy put-down of the suburbs of Daly City, California and its inhabitants, criticising their taste, their attitudes and their opinions, which somehow the writer and singer seems to know simply by driving though their estate. As it made the *Billboard* Hot 100 in 1963, it must have been bought by some of the very people it so contemptuously dismissed. Singer-songwriter Tom Lehrer, a satirist who picked his targets rather more acutely, said that it was 'the most sanctimonious song ever written'.

The same attitudes were heard haughtily expressed in scores of pop hits of the day. Suburban domesticity was seen as the stultifying cultural opposite of the radicalism and free expression of the counterculture, although what was the hippy-rock enclave of Laurel Canyon if not a gigantic suburb, rife with one-upmanship and wife swapping. Not even the great Gerry Goffin and Carole King were immune from the temptation to judge and mock. Their 'Pleasant Valley Sunday', a dig at the consumerism and small-mindedness of life in West Orange, New Jersey, was one of The Monkees' biggest hits and took a Seegerish view of 'Rows of houses that are all the same/And no one seems to care'.

John Betjeman was cut from very different cloth than Pete Seeger – flannels rather than denim – and his take on suburbia was much less judgemental, much more affectionate. Betjeman sneered at Slough, of course, and in doing so inspired Morrissey's 'Every Day Is Like Sunday', but his poems of suburbia are almost proto-pop in their economy, catchiness and chiming rhymes. English lyricists like Ray Davies, Suggs, Damon Albarn and Paul Weller are far closer to Betjeman and Larkin than Hunter S. Thompson or Allen Ginsberg.

The dwellings in Betjeman's *Metro-Land*, the greenbelt estates and the new British suburbs spreading out from London, were much more than just little boxes made of 'ticky-tacky' to those who were happy to call them home. Slum clearance and the building of modern out-of-town estates meant that many workers and their families could leave behind their dirty and inadequate back-to-back housing and move into new, clean homes with gardens and inside lavatories, and even have somewhere to park the new cars and enjoy the labour-saving household devices bought on new hire-purchase schemes. The Ray Davies-penned Kinks' song 'Shangri-La' is less cynical and acerbic than some of its American counterparts, but the overall impression is that the suburban Shangri-La is an empty, illusory paradise unworthy of all the hard work that's been necessary to attain it. Again, it might seem a bit rich for a millionaire rock star to mock ordinary working people's desire for a clean home and inside toilet, but then again rock and roll has never been slow to judge. In Manfred Mann's 'Semi-Detached, Suburban Mr James', the singer's former love is castigated for spurning his bohemian charms for domestic life in the 'burbs, asking,

> *Do you think you will be happy, buttering the toast*
> *Of your semi-detached suburban Mr Most?*

Some songs were more generous, though. The Small Faces' 'Lazy Sunday Afternoon' is a genial slice of life in a London manor, and The Beatles' 'Penny Lane' is one of the best examples of McCartney's genius for finding the strange and mysterious in the everyday, a surreal, impressionistic portrait of suburban Liverpool on a busy, hallucinogenic afternoon.

McCartney also provides us with perhaps the most beautiful exploration in song of another aspect of home, sweet home. While the Victorian middle-aged man like Dickens's Wemmick might have seen it as a castle, a refuge and a personal fiefdom, for the young, the confined and the restless, home could mean a place of boredom and despair, a claustrophobic cage far away from the real world – where adult life was taking place, in all its multifarious, exciting glory. 'She's Leaving Home' was described by the late Ian MacDonald, a great writer and Beatle authority, as being 'among the finest work on *Sgt Pepper* – imperishable popular art of its time'. It is one of the few Beatle tracks on which the group do not play a note and which George Martin did not arrange; it was done by Mike Leander for a small string orchestra. McCartney had seen a story about a teenage runaway in the *Daily Mirror*, and in the song, which alternates elegantly between Paul's lead vocal and John's Greek chorus, the perspective shifts between the young girl's desire for fun and freedom and the parents' misguided love. The actual story concerned a girl called Melanie Cole, who was seventeen at the time. She didn't leave to meet a man from the motor trade but a croupier. She was found ten days later and returned home. She was pregnant and later had an abortion. In Lennon and McCartney's hands, this simple, rather ordinary tale of a domestic upset becomes a work of art that shows how the gulf and the faultline between the generations was clearly seen in many a British living room.

The notion of the home as a prison that the young want to flee from has perhaps never been better expressed than in 'She's Leaving Home', but there are echoes of it in such songs as Lene Lovich's 'Home':

Home is just emotion, sticking in my throat
Let's go to your place
Home is so suspicious, home is close control

Similarly, in The Smiths' anthemic 'There Is a Light That Never Goes Out', Morrissey begs of his love, 'Please don't drop me home/ Because it's not my home, it's their home.' However, peers of The Smiths sometimes alluded to the cold realities of life outside the parental home. In both Soft Cell's 'Bedsitter' and Squeeze's 'Up the Junction', the 'room of one's own' desired by Virginia Wolfe and her protégé Morrissey is a new start but a squalid, cheerless one.

Looking down now on Britain's housing landscape in the day of The Smiths, Soft Cell and Squeeze, we would see a very different nation. Almost a half of Britain's housing was social housing, provided by the council, a legacy of the Atlee government's post-war drive to provide 'homes fit for heroes'. Margaret Thatcher's similarly zealous drive to turn Britain into a 'property-owning democracy' in the 1980s would change all that. But social housing as characterised by the brutalist estates of the fifties and sixties provided an urban iconography that would seep into and colour the background of pop. The high-rises of Hulme in Manchester, where Tony Wilson's Factory Club met in a grim council-estate pub called the Russell, would shape the bleak, urban aesthetic of Factory Records, the music of Joy Division and the sound world of producer Martin Hannett. The Trellick Tower in London's North Kensington, near Goldborne Road and Ladbroke Grove, has loomed large in the work of Damon Albarn. It featured in the video for Blur's 'For Tomorrow' in 1993, standing for a kind of cheery consensual London idyll, the band backed by a chorus of pensioners, schoolchildren and mothers in and around the tower block, with The Trellick offered as a model of urban inclusivity. Seven years later Albarn returned to make a video for his Gorillaz project, 'Tomorrow Comes Today', but this time the imagery was nocturnal, strip lit and the tower blocks were unpeopled, the office blocks backdrops for graffiti art in the manner of Bansky. This was social housing not as community but as catwalk, a fashion accoutrement with the right note of modern edginess.

Between those two records, at the height of the temporary madness called Britpop, Blur released a single called 'Country House', famous now for its role in the chart battle with Oasis's 'Roll With It'. Here the Englishman's home as castle metaphor was extended to become a cipher for affluent out-of-touchness, the very big house in the country as artistic dead end. Blur were often seen as inheritors of the tradition of shrewd, catchy observational pop that began with songs like The Kinks' 'Shangri-La' and was continued in the early eighties by Madness. Their 1983 song 'Our House' was one of their numerous UK successes but their only sizeable hit in America where, like Dexy's Midnight Runners with 'Come On Eileen', they are regarded as a novelty-ish one-hit wonder. That 'Our House' should be their US calling card was more than a little baffling. MTV was growing increasingly powerful and Madness were famed for their witty, idiosyncratic videos. But the promo film 'Our House' is as British as an Andy Capp cartoon strip. In fact, the band look very like Andy Capp in their flat caps and workshirts, as they disport themselves in a tiny English terraced house beneath a railway line. There is more than a hint of Benny Hill or *Are You Being Served?* about it both of which, now we come to think about it, were enormously popular in the States.

Or maybe they just liked the record. It's very hard not to. 'Our House' can hold its head up proudly in the company of the 'Penny Lane'-era Beatles that it would seem to aspire to: dazzling, playful, economical, catchy, imaginative, brilliantly crafted – 'the kids are playing up downstairs' is a lovely little verbal gag thrown in almost offhand – and rich with meaning without a whiff of self-importance. It's a sort of love song to home and family, but sung by someone who had to leave: the heartfelt, plaintive voice, in the midst of the parlour singsong, quietly, passionately interjects, 'Something tells you that you've got to get away from it.'

The push and pull of home, the love of it and the need to leave it, resonates through the classic British pop song book. Another laureate of everyday life was Swindon's Andy Partridge, writer of many domestic English pop classics for XTC. His song 'Respectable Street' is a lovely example of the ambivalence about hearth and home that runs through 'Our House'.

'Respectable Street' both rages against suburban life and seems to quietly acknowledge the singer's dependency on its quiet civility. Partridge said, 'I can't write mid-Atlantic airport-lounge music. I can't talk about my hot babe with her leather and whip or meeting my cocaine dealer. I like to write about what's going on around the town. I'm not from Memphis, Tennessee: I don't know what it's like to be out on the highway in a Buick. I used to go round the Co-op with my mum's dividend number. That's still my language.'

30. GOLD

The point is, ladies and gentlemen, that greed, for lack of a better word, is good. Greed is right, greed works. Greed clarifies, cuts through, and captures the essence of the evolutionary spirit. Greed, in all of its forms – greed for life, for money, for love, knowledge – has marked the upward surge of mankind.

So proclaimed Gordon Gekko in his stirring, enraging defence of the avariciousness of capitalism in Oliver Stone's totemic eighties movie *Wall Street*. On this side of the Atlantic, too, a revolution just like the one Gekko was championing swept though the offices, factories and boardrooms of Britain in that decade. For better or worse, Britain was never the same again, and we are still living with the consequences.

In 1979 Sunny Jim Callaghan, having fatally delayed calling a general election, suffered a 'winter of discontent' of strikes and unrest, and ceded power to Margaret Hilda Thatcher. As this political sea change was taking place XTC were riding high in the charts with 'Making Plans for Nigel'. The song is more personal than political, the tale of a dull youth and his overbearing parents. But one line chimed with the times. Nigel, we're told, has a future with British Steel: 'Nigel's whole future is as good as sealed.'

In fact, neither Nigel nor British Steel had much of a future. Margaret Thatcher's response on taking office was swift and brutal. By the time it was sold off a decade later, British Steel had shrunk by 80 per cent. Former Labour MP Woodrow Wyatt said that he admired Thatcher because, 'She is not a conservative. She's nothing like those wets ... She is a radical making a revolution which horrifies many Conservatives.' Bob Geldof would later say, 'The way she took on the trade unions ... She was a punk. Eighteen-year-olds with Porsches and red braces and mobile phones the size of a back pack thinking it was cool. Actually, I think it was cool.'

Geldof would probably not have said that back in 1979, when it would have been PR suicide for a pop star. As the recession bit and the economy flatlined, Margaret Thatcher was the most unpopular prime minister since the war, with a 70 per cent disapproval rating. Some of her most vocal critics came from the pop fraternity and not just from the usual suspects, punk bands like Crass or The Exploited. UB40's 'One in Ten' was a lament for the unemployed; Wham!'s 'Wham Rap (Enjoy What You Do)' was a witty and defiant celebration of life on the dole. Most blunt of all, The Beat's 'Stand Down Margaret' was an infectious plea for her to fall on her sword, possibly literally.

Pop acts prepared to say a good word for the Iron Lady were few and far between. ELO's Bev Bevan was one; another was Gary Numan, who was a public supporter of Thatcher initially, perhaps after falling foul of a faintly ridiculous Musicians' Union campaign against tapes and synthesisers. Even he later had his regrets, though:

'The support for Margaret Thatcher was blown out of all proportion. I only voted Conservative once, but it has stuck with me for ever. I said I didn't believe anyone who would rather have a Mini than a Ferrari,' later adding, 'I'm not socialist, I know that. I don't believe in sharing my money.'

Though her ratings were at rock bottom, far from standing down Thatcher attacked her revolutionary programme with zeal and vigour, slashing, selling and deregulating as she went. Buoyed by the Falklands War, she went further down the road of *laissez-faire* capitalism. She privatised British Telecom, the National Bus Company, airports and water companies and plcs like Jaguar and Rolls Royce. Perhaps her most famous privatisation was British Gas, flogged off with the slogan, 'If you see Sid, tell him!'

All of which was music to the yuppie ears of affluent urban professionals getting rich quick under Thatcherism. A new aspirational acquisitiveness – avarice – was reflected in the films, books and TV of the time as well as subsequently: from Jonathan Coe's *What a Carve Up* to Caryl Churchill's *Serious Money* at the Royal Court, to Harry Enfield's distinctly unserious but wickedly accurate Loadsamoney character, a crass, self-employed Essex plasterer getting rich during the property boom and described by one critic as 'Thatcherism's shameless golem'.

The morally dubious entrepreneur who dabbled in a bit of this and a bit of that became a staple of TV comedy, most famously in *Minder*'s Arthur Daley or *Only Fools and Horses*' Del Boy Trotter. Set alongside this, of course, were the era's real entrepreneurs and innovators, like Clive Sinclair, and principled hippy capitalists such as Anita Roddick of the Body Shop and Virgin's Richard Branson.

In 1984, the year that Branson launched his Virgin Atlantic flight service, 40 per cent of Virgin's profits had been made by a pop group, one led by a colourful and controversial cross-dresser called George O'Dowd, or Boy George. Culture Club, like Virgin, were making huge commercial inroads here and in America and George later mused, 'The music scene was healthier than it had been in a long time. Suddenly it was OK to feel rich, famous and no shame. Some saw it as a natural consequence of Thatcherism.'

Money, status, style, power; the songs of the day and their videos reflected a padded-shouldered world of surface and prestige: Elton John hoofing it in a boater on the French Riviera; OMD driving around Blenheim Palace and Stowe public school in a classic convertible sports car; Duran Duran's 'Rio', the acme of all this, where the Birmingham band, dressed in elegant, unstructured and frankly unseaworthy designer-label clothes, disported themselves offshore on a seventy-foot sailing ketch. Even bands from councillor David Blunkett's socialist paradise of Sheffield toyed with the imagery to ironic effect – ABC in their gold lamé suits, striped blazers and boaters; and Heaven 17's knowing satirical corporate packaging aesthetic bolstering the message of songs like 'Crushed by the Wheels of Industry' and 'I'm Your Money'. Singer Glenn Gregory explained, 'Let's get rid of all this hypocrisy of "We're artists, we don't care about the money." Let's strip the face bare and look what's underneath – handshakes, signing contracts, business.'

Only a few short years on from the year-zero anger of punk – Dave Rimmer's book on the Culture Club phenomenon was titled *Like Punk Never Happened* – pop was re-entering the mainstream entertainment life of the nation. It was photogenic, catchy, upbeat and ambitious, and the popular press and TV could easily incorporate it into their world view. While sales of specialist, earnest rock inkies like *Sounds* and *NME* fell, the *Sun* launched its own pop and entertainment section. It was called 'Bizarre' and by the sound of its opening day manifesto it was a well-chosen name: 'Simply the first column ever published in a national newspaper which encompasses every aspect of being young in Britain today. Bizarre is about Pigbag and hang-gliding. Space Invaders and pacy paperbacks. The Rolling Stones and Zoot Suits. Bizarre will be a must every day for everyone with a zest for life.'

Smash Hits never went really big on Pigbag or hang-gliding, but the clever, self-consciously breezy pop magazine was the bible of the day, a less precious version of *The Face*, with its tongue in its cheek and its eye firmly on the charts. Its deputy editor was Neil Tennant, later one half of one the eighties' most interesting acts, Pet Shop Boys, who, while obsessed with style and club culture and blithely aloof from the standard rock poses, nevertheless made some slyly political points of their own in songs like 'Opportunities' and 'Shopping', a barbed comment on insider dealing in the City, Thatcher's deregulated square mile.

One of the bands that *Smash Hits* would have, in their inimitable style, both lionised and mocked was Spandau Ballet. They emerged from the scene that coalesced around the Blitz nightclub in Covent Garden, initially, like all pop cults, an outsider movement of misfits and eccentrics. Spandau Ballet's Gary Kemp described it as, 'Bright young people on a shoestring. A bunch of people who were media hungry, trying to be special at a time when things were quite dark and gloomy. Maybe it was all puffed up out of all proportion. The overblown shoulder pads, the money, the hair, but there was great pride in where we came from. This sense that fifty people in a room did change the landscape.'

But as the New Romantic sound and look became more successful and absorbed into the bloodstream of eighties pop, so it became more self-congratulatory and self-absorbed. It's said that

The Smiths chose their deliberately prosaic name as a riposte to the preposterous, empty flamboyance of names like Spandau Ballet and the preening nature of the New Romantic ethos. But is that quite fair, or quite the full story?

Asked whether Morrissey was a spokesman for youth, the Style Council's Mick Talbot replied, 'Only those youth who've been to college or university.' There was some truth in this, particularly perhaps in the South, where The Smiths' gritty Northern romanticism found less of a natural home. But Spandau Ballet's Gary Kemp has always maintained that their vision, one rooted in the capital's soul-boy scene, was just as authentic and true to its class and community background. Pictures and profiles of the band and their peers would appear initially in the new 'style press', magazines such as *The Face*, *ID* and *Blitz*, rather than the resolutely monochrome rock weeklies. He told Dylan Jones in 201,

> We didn't talk to the music press, as we had no interest
> in trying to persuade them that what we were doing was
> good. They didn't believe we were working class and tried
> to paint us as middle-class Tories. The music papers at the
> time were full of middle-class white boys who didn't like
> the fact that we were from council estates. They wanted to
> believe something else. They wanted to believe that we were
> right wing when we were anything but. We all came from
> the Essex Road in Islington and we had no sympathies with
> anything remotely Thatcherite. We were also commercial,
> which in those days was a political act in itself. We just
> wanted to get on and improve our lot. We wanted to be
> successful, we wanted to be famous, and we didn't see why
> we should be embarrassed about it.

'Gold' was released as Margaret Thatcher roared back into office in imperial pomp galvanised by the Falklands victory and the lack of a realistic opposition. It reached number two on the charts, held off by KC & The Sunshine Band's 'Give It Up'.

Precisely what 'Gold' is about is anyone's guess, the opening lines certainly offer little clue: 'Thank you for coming home/I'm sorry that the chairs are all worn'. But the chorus positively shouts, and in Tony Hadley's case it's at the top of a not inconsiderable voice, of self-belief, dynamism, ambition and a thrusting sense of getting on which, fairly or not, given its timing and the band's aesthetic, makes it appear at least the ultimate Thatcherite pop anthem.

Margaret Thatcher was to stay in power for the rest of the decade, despite from 1985 onwards the best efforts of a coalition of left-wing pop acts keen to re-engage young people with politics, especially in support of the Labour Party. They named themselves Red Wedge and their number included Billy Bragg, The Housemartins, Elvis Costello, the Style Council, The Communards. And Gary Kemp.

31. THE LOVE CATS

We shall start naturally with the great pop culture vulture, the Roman diplomat and historian Jordanes and his *magnum opus Romana*:

> Now from this island of Scandza, the Goths are said to have come forth long ago under their king Berig in three ships. As soon as they disembarked and set foot on the land in Scythia they pitched camp, joined battle and drove others from their homes ... Now Mars has always been worshipped by the Goths with cruel rites, and captives were slain as his victims. They thought that he who is the lord of war ought to be appeased by the shedding of human blood. To him they devoted the first share of the spoil, and in his honour arms stripped from the foe were suspended from trees.

On the other hand, the journalist Mark Ellen gives the best definition of the modern goth that I know:

Heading from the south, drive up the M6 through the Midlands and north Lancashire till you reach the south of the Lake District, say Silverdale, at about dusk on an autumn night. Leave the motorway and head left for the coast on an A road till you reach any small market town or big village. Find the war memorial. On it there will be a young man and woman with violet hair huddled together drinking a bottle of cheap supermarket cider, smoking and laughing. These are goths.

How did perhaps the gentlest of all Britain's post-war youth cults come to bear the name of one of Europe's most feared, destructive and warlike tribes, a race chiefly responsible for bringing down the Roman empire? The answer lies not in music but in books.

In 1764 a book by Horace Walpole, *The Castle of Otranto*, started a craze in England for a kind of melodramatic and exciting fiction that combined horror and romance. Readers loved these tales in the way a modern audience might enjoy a horror movie; they were titillated and thrilled by the gore and ghostliness and dash of sex, all in the comfort of their own parlour or boudoir. Walpole was obsessed with gothic architecture and history and his novel was subtitled 'a Gothic Story', and the term stuck for writing and art of this nature. Writers like Clara Reeve and Ann Radcliffe developed the form and it spread like wildfire across the Continent and beyond: Mary Shelley's *Frankenstein*, the lurid tales of the Marquis de Sade, Edgar Allan Poe and, transplanting the gothic to the Yorkshire Moors, Emily Brontë's *Wuthering Heights* all followed. Gothic romance became so popular that it even inspired a very smart and successful parody, Jane Austen's *Northanger Abbey*.

But it was in Yorkshire again, a little further north and west than the wild Pennine moors where Cathy and Heathcliff brooded and emoted, that the most significant event in the history of modern goth music and culture made landfall, when the Russian schooner *Demeter* ran aground at Whitby and Count Dracula, in the form of a dog, slipped into the town to wreak bloody havoc. Repressed Victorian England was initially lukewarm about Bram Stoker's novel but gradually a Dracula cult developed, drawn like innocent virginal Lucy Westenra by the titular count's sinister sensuality; a demonic force at large in a world intent on eroticising and enslaving women. Stoker's models for the count were said to be a Romanian prince called Vlad the Impaler and, interestingly for our purposes, the seventeenth-century Hungarian torturer and serial killer Elizabeth Báthory, who later gave her name to a deeply gothic Swedish black-metal band.

The vampire craze really bit, however, in 1922 when German film director F. W. Murnau adapted Stoker's tale for his silent classic *Nosferatu*. It was an unlicensed version which led to Murnau being sued and all copies of the film destroyed. The fact that we have it today is down to painstaking reconstructive detective work in the nineties. *Nosferatu* embedded the notion of the vampire in our minds, and the dark thread of what would become goth in our culture. Bernard Sumner of Joy Division and New Order would later say of *Nosferatu*, 'The atmosphere is really evil, but you feel comfortable inside it,' which would seem an excellent short definition of goth in general.

There are some who say you can hear the first bat-like stirrings of goth in the music of Gary Numan, Ultravox and The Damned. But the first use of the term, as applied to a strain of post-punk, would seem to be by one Anthony H. Wilson of Factory Records. Being interviewed along with Steven Morris on the TV show *Something Else* in September 1979, Wilson described Joy Division as 'gothic' compared with the pop mainstream, in much the same way that gothic architecture was starker and darker than the elegance of the classical styles. Around the same time, Joy Division's producer Martin Hannett proposed, 'It's dancing music, with gothic overtones.'

The shadowy nocturnal bleakness of the band's début album *Unknown Pleasures* and the austere, chilling beauty of its follow-up *Closer*, allied with singer Ian Curtis's dark and tortured lyrics and his eventual suicide, would seem to give Joy Division a solid claim to being the wellspring for modern goth. But there are those who would claim that title for Siouxsie and the Banshees. They had been the last of the punk bands of '76 to be signed, and their début album *The Scream* was far darker and stranger than the records of many of their punkish peers. As one listener remarked, 'When *The Scream* came out, I remember it was much slower than everybody thought [it was going to be]. It was like the forerunner of the Joy Division sound, it was just big-sounding.'

That listener was one Robert Smith of Crawley. His band Easy Cure were in the process of shortening their name to The Cure, and shading their edgy new-wave pop into something more gloomy and abstract. Their first album was a nervy, wiry slice of post-punk, but the next three releases – *Seventeen Seconds, Faith* and *Pornography* – perhaps constitute the ultimate goth cannon: tortured, murky, yet grandiose. Writer Dave Hill coined the aphorism 'Phil Spector in Hell'. Any record that begins, as *Pornography* does, with the line 'It doesn't really matter if we all die' (from 'One Hundred Years') is surely a key text of goth. Looking back on this period, in an interview in *Propaganda* magazine in 1992, Smith recalled: 'It's like it happened yesterday. I felt a special camaraderie with certain bands like the Banshees and Joy Division. The first crop of punk bands had faded from the scene, and a new crop came up 'round '79 and '80, who were much darker and moodier – less anarchic. Bands like Joy Division, us, Gang of Four, Echo and the Bunnymen. The only early punk bands who survived were the ones able to make that transition, like Siouxsie and the Banshees and The Damned.'

By the time they released 'The Love Cats' in 1983, Smith was growing bored of the band's self-imposed straitjacket of gloom. Compared to the stifling claustrophobia of *Faith* and *Pornography*, 'The Love Cats' breezes along all 'ba-ba-bas', swinging double bass and sassy horns. But the mood is still faintly sinister, based, said Smith, on Patrick White's morbid novel *The Vivisector*. 'The Love Cats' also has that feline playfulness that is a key element of goth: a certain sado-masochistic sexiness, all hissing and claws.

Goth, though, has always been about much more than just the music. There is what we might call its philosophical preoccupations: death, doomed love, the supernatural, suicide, decay, horror and sex. And then there was the visual aesthetic, which grew out of punk: monochrome, Mohicans and silver jewellery, a look which slowly became more elaborate and recherché: fishnets, PVC, leathers, crushed velvet, silk, dyed hair backcombed into a bird's nests or crimped, and, of course, make-up – the cadaverous white skin, rouged lips, darkened, hollow eyes. Writer Cintra Wilson believes, 'The origins of contemporary goth style are found in the Victorian cult of mourning.' And certainly Dickens's Miss Havisham can be read as a goth icon, along with Nico, Morticia Addams, Bettie Page and Bela Lugosi.

The last of these, the famed Hungarian horror actor, was
the subject of one of goth's great early singles; a song released
in the last few months of the seventies with a sound that would
set the tone for goth in its coming, perhaps definitive, decade.
'Bela Lugosi's Dead' by Bauhaus comes perilously close to being
ludicrous – 'The bats have left the bell tower/The victims have
been bled' – but that in some ways is the whole point of what can
be called 'high goth': a profound and rumbling earnestness that
trembles on the lip of camp.

After Bauhaus came a trail of classic eighties' goth bands: The
Sisters of Mercy, Gene Loves Jezebel, Fields of the Nephilim, Sex
Gang Children, All About Eve. Goth has proved to be one of the
most enduring strains of modern pop too. The Cure are still one of
the world's biggest live bands. And you can hear the dark echoes of
goth in modern bands like The Horrors and in the global popularity
of a music called emo, with bands like My Chemical Romance,
Jimmy Eat World and Dashboard Confessional. Emo kids celebrate
the drama and anguish of life, the loneliness of being an outsider,
the superficiality of the modern world; and they do so in eyeliner
and with cerise fringes. Emo is goth by any other name.

This music still adorns a thousand black-painted and candlelit bedrooms, along with copies of Kafka, nail varnish and bottles
of cider. Goth and its acolytes were always easy to caricature
and mock, and that's exactly what the British music press did
for twenty-odd years, but, in truth, goth was a subculture that
provided real identity and solace to a kind of vulnerable, outsider
kid. It found beauty in unlikely places and said that in your lonely
and miserable moments you are not alone. It offered the feeling
of belonging, even if that very thought would have horrified the

goths who felt themselves unique, tortured and isolated. It could be argued that, with its emphasis on the fantastical and bizarre and the cult of the individual, goth is the most escapist and non-political music cult ever. But that is to ignore the fact that the personal is the political; and to express difference without fear is an inherently political act – a right that should be enshrined and protected in any healthy society.

Which is why the murder of Sophie Lancaster in a park in Bacup, Lancashire, in 2007 was so horrifying and cruel. Sophie and her boyfriend were attacked by a gang of thugs simply because they were goths, because they were different. Ade Varney, creator of an online petition calling for action on hate crime, said that Goths

get verbal assaults every day, and not just from young people. But now younger teenagers have the mentality of hardened criminals, and I definitely sense this violent aspect getting worse … Sophie's death has made people think, and I have heard of teenagers, especially girls, modifying the way they dress when they walk through certain areas.

The reaction to Sophie's death was as compassionate as her death was senseless. There have been plays, films, art installations, documentaries and music. There was a twelve-hour tribute concert at her local football club, and songs were dedicated to her at festivals all over the world. There's the Sophie Lancaster Stage at the Bloodstock heavy-metal festival and a memorial bench on the cliffs at Whitby, site of Bram Stoker's fictional horror. It reminds us that real wickedness, real evil, doesn't reside in emo, goth or the subcultures that celebrate darkness and mystery. It often comes from the people who pride themselves on being 'normal' and fear and hate those who are different, who just want to be themselves. Pop music, joyously, is a place where you can be.

32. TWO TRIBES

The Kelvedon Hatch Secret Nuclear Bunker, nestling in a wood just off the A128 Ongar–Brentwood road, must be Britain's creepiest tourist attraction. It's a drab, anonymous bungalow on some unremarkable farmland, but one hiding a remarkably dark and eerie secret. Behind and below it, built deep into a small hill, lies a three-floored bunker complex to which 600 people, including the prime minister and his cabinet, would have retreated in the event of a nuclear attack on Britain.

Here they'd have tried to run what was left of the country, while the rest of us took our chances above ground. They'd have slept as best they could, eaten their emergency rations, visited the grim sick bay, tried to keep calm and carry on underground, far beneath a scorched and blasted England. To reach their quarters, a 100-yard tunnel stretches before you, ahead of the bunker itself. Strip-lit and utilitarian, the reason for its inordinate length is simple. The guards stationed at the other end would have had ample time to aim and fire on any intruders before they got halfway along its stark, lonely, echoing length.

And once inside, among the chosen ones, a chilling mockery of normal life would have gone on, complete with entertainment from the playlist of the Wartime Broadcasting Service. There, along with tapes of The Beatles and old editions of *Hancock's Half Hour*, was a recording of Vera Lynn's 'We'll Meet Again'. It's unlikely there would have been a copy of Frankie Goes to Holllywood's 'Two Tribes' lying around, though. As the politicians and military cowered below, and we burned above, the last thing any of us would have wanted was five sarky, seditious, sexually charged scousers, who'd already had one run in with the authorities, reminding us that we were living in a land where sex and horror were the new gods, and, more to the point, that when two tribes went to war, a point was all that you could score.

To use the contemporary parlance, Frankie Goes to Hollywood owned 1984. By the time 'Two Tribes' entered the chart at number one in June, with all the ruthless power and accuracy of a guided ICBM laying waste to all before it, many observers knew they were trouble. An earlier appearance on the rock show *The Tube* with a sleazy lo-budget promo for their track 'Relax' hinted at a band rougher than a Croxteth boozer at closing time. For that performance, filmed at Liverpool's State Ballroom, the band sported the peaked-cap, leather-boy gay-clone look with varying degrees of success. Singers Paul Rutherford and Holly Johnson seemed to the manor born, but Peter Gill, Mark O'Toole and Brian Nash ('the lads', as they became known) looked decidedly uncomfortable. And the song has a weird, lumpy middle section that seemed to have been badly spot-welded on from another song. But 'Relax' had something. Certainly Trevor Horn thought so. The former Buggles singer turned hi-tech production guru was intrigued and signed the band to his fledgling ZTT record label.

ZTT stood for Zang Tumb Tuum, a phrase borrowed from the Italian Futurist artist Filippo Tommaso Marinetti. It was a typically erudite and striking reference from the former *NME* writer Paul Morley, hired by Horn as a kind of resident ideologue-cum-*agent provocateur* for his new label. Zang Tumb Tuum, Morley claimed, was the sound of a 'drum machine going into battle' and it was immediately apparent that ideas, outrage and controversy would be part of Frankie's and ZTT's armoury. Morley announced that ZTT would launch 'a strategic assault on pop' and that the Frankie Goes to Hollywood singles would address the biggest themes and taboos head on: sex, war and religion.

First then, sex. From the video to the sleeve to the lyrics – 'Relax, don't do it/When you want to suck it, do it/Relax, don't do it/When you want to come' – the lubricious thrust of 'Relax' was obvious to anyone, even disc jockeys, and thus Radio One's Mike Read took it upon himself to remove the single from the turntable halfway through a play, branding it 'obscene' and engendering a BBC-wide ban for the record. The ensuing furore was just one of the reasons why the single entered the chart at number one and went on to become the seventh bestselling UK single of all time. It was also, and remains, a great tune. And so, to war.

For almost as long as there had been an atomic bomb there had been songs about it. In the wake of the detonations of the bombs on Hiroshima and Nagasaki there was a glut of songs like Homer Harris's 'Atomic Bomb Blues', 'The Hydrogen Bomb' by Al Rogers and 'Atomic Power' by the Buchanan Brothers, all of which expressed a kind of grateful shock and awe in the face of a new weapon that could end war but could also end humanity. Later came 'When They Drop the Atomic Bomb' by Jackie Doll and his Pickled Peppers, a vile country ditty encouraging a nuclear strike in the Korean War. But with the coming of a new generation and a youth cultural revolution in pop, glee and awed respect turned to fear and paranoia. In Britain music was crucial to the Ban the Bomb movement and the Aldermaston marchers. Journalist Eric Winter wrote in the folk magazine *Sing*, 'The hydrogen bomb may be able to destroy singers but cannot destroy songs – songs are stronger than the hydrogen bomb ... we believe that song has a powerful role to play in the struggle of the British people for peace and socialism.' The duffle-coated protesters marched to anthems such as John Brunner's 'The H Bomb's Thunder', Ewan MacColl and Pete Seeger's 'That Bomb Has Got to Go' and the Ian Campbell Folk Group's 'The Sun Is Burning'. That was later covered by Simon and Garfunkel, and as the protest movement and rock culture developed across the Atlantic, so the anti-nuclear songs came forth from the likes of The Byrds, Crosby, Stills & Nash, Dylan and Barry McGuire. 'I Come and Stand at Every Door', 'Wooden Ships', 'Masters of War', 'A Hard Rain's a-Gonna Fall' and 'Eve of Destruction', all are full of biblical dread and apocalyptic imagery.

This was the height of the first Cold War, the era of Stanley Kubrick's black satire *Dr Strangelove, Or: How I Learned to Stop Worrying and Love the Bomb* and the children's nuclear defence movie *Duck and Cover*. But what some historians call the Second Cold War began in the late 1970s with the Soviet invasion of Afghanistan. That ushered in a decade that was as much about paranoia as it was about padded shoulders, and where 'mutually assured destruction' and 'upward mobility' were two sides of the same shiny aspirational coin. From Nena's '99 Red Balloons' to Ultravox's 'Dancing with Tears in My Eyes', from Sting's 'Russians' to Prince's '1999', from Iron Maiden's '2 Minutes to Midnight' to 'Breathing' by Kate Bush with its chilling line about 'Chips of plutonium/Are twinkling in every lung', the pop aristocracy of the 1980s, particularly in Britain, was seemingly obsessed by the arms race and the dark prospect of nuclear war. In this they were merely reflecting a low-level thrum of fear in wider society, seen in TV dramas like *Threads*, children's literature such as Raymond Briggs's *When the Wind Blows*, even the ubiquitous student poster parody of *Gone with the Wind* featuring Reagan and Thatcher ('She promised to follow him to the end of the earth. He promised to organise it!').

It's not made clear exactly what apocalypse has befallen the world in the scenario for the *Mad Max* films, the first of which was released in the same year that Margaret Thatcher came to power in the UK and the Soviet Union invaded Afghanistan. But a nuclear war is the most likely explanation for the movie's bleakly violent, dystopian setting. The opening narration for the second film talks of what happened 'when two mighty warrior tribes went to war'. The phrase resonated with a young Holly Johnson, eager, following the enormous global success of 'Relax', for the next big topic, the next big sound and the next big controversy. Frankie and the creative minds of ZTT chose the biggest of them all, the mighty warrior tribes of the world's warring superpowers and the spectre of the end of the world.

When producer Trevor Horn told his colleagues at ZTT that 'Two Tribes' was to be the follow-up to the phenomenon that was 'Relax', they were unconvinced of the song's merit. But Horn was right. 'It's all about the bass line,' he said, correctly. The relentless, funky motif provides the song's spine and, said Johnson, symbolised the United States, while overlaid are various Cossack swirls and flourishes redolent of Russia. Whether this was true or a nice piece of *post hoc* rationalisation is debatable, though it was a clever idea.

But the real genius of 'Two Tribes' is that it captured the prevailing *Zeitgeist* of techno-fear and the colossal madness of nuclear war by mirroring it. Whereas the stereotypical anti-war song of the past had generally involved a strummed acoustic guitar, a wheezing harmonica and some mournful, hippy Cassandra bewailing mankind's plight, 'Two Tribes' was sleek, futuristic and awe-inspiring. It sounded like the apocalypse: an enormous inhuman clamour made by machines every bit as powerful and complex as an intercontinental ballistic missile – baffling cutting-edge musical technology such as the Synclavier sampler and the Sony 3324 digital multitrack recorder. 'Two Tribes' was the first record to be recorded entirely digitally. It took three months, the combined talents of ZTT's state-of-the-art production team. And cost almost £200,000.

In June 1984 Britain was bombarded with at least seven different versions of the song spread over several seven- and twelve-inch releases and featuring myriad refinements and variations, such as Chris Barrie's Ronald Reagan impression, sirens, orchestral interludes and parodies of the *Protect and Survive* civil defence films recited, in a glorious irony, by the same actor, Patrick Allen, who had voiced the original official versions. Paul Morley denied that this glut of versions was merely cynical marketing. He later said, 'You were supposed to buy them all because they were all pieces of magic and they all created a story. One part was just one chapter. I wanted them to be constantly different and constantly worth the money and worth the wait and fill people's lives with this absolute magic.'

Frankie's strategic assault on pop was waged on many flanks, not just the musical. The video for 'Two Tribes', directed by Kevin Godley and Lol Creme, featured lookalikes of Ronald Reagan and Soviet premier Konstantin Chernenko fighting in a bear pit while Frankie and a baying audience, featuring various other world leaders, laid bets on the outcome. The fight spreads, becoming a widespread brawl, and finally Earth itself is seen to explode.

With song, video and band ubiquitous, the Frankie war machine opened up another front. A range of T-shirts went on sale designed by Morley and based on the work of hip UK fashionista Katharine Hamnett. Each of these bore slogans such as 'Frankie Say Relax', 'Frankie Say War! Hide Yourself!' and, best and most provocative of all, 'Frankie Say Arm the Unemployed'.

'Full Spectrum Dominance' is a modern doctrine of warfare espoused by the United States military. It states that the aim of military operations should be complete control and dominance of every facet of the battle-space – land, sea, air, information, the electro-magnetic spectrum, outer space. In the appropriately Orwellian year of 1984 Frankie Goes to Hollywood achieved Full Spectrum Dominance.

33. SMALLTOWN BOY

There are many reasons to remember Howard Hawks's classic screwball comedy of 1938, *Bringing Up Baby*. It's a triumph of elegant and witty film-making from Hollywood's golden age. Katharine Hepburn and Cary Grant are every bit as good as you'd imagine they'd be, and the film is routinely and correctly cited as one of the finest comedies of all time.

But there's another, odder but just as significant reason why *Bringing Up Baby* is a movie landmark. It occurs in a scene about halfway through. Cary Grant, the happy-go-lucky palaeontologist, has contrived via a laundry mishap to lose his clothes and is forced to answer the door in one of Hepburn's négligés, where he is met by an outraged battle-axe visitor. When she asks why he's dressed this way, he replies, 'Because I just went gay ... all of a sudden!'

Of course, most cinema-goers of the time would assume he meant flighty or frivolous. But 'gay' had been used in secret Hollywood circles to mean something entirely different for over a decade. So it seems very likely that Grant's quirky ad lib, accompanied by a little jump, is the first time in mainstream popular culture that the word gay came to have homosexual connotations before a mass audience.

The Manic Street Preachers had a famous T-shirt slogan which proclaimed 'All Rock and Roll Is Homosexual'. But it took a while for popular music to catch up with film, art and literature, where same-sex relations were concerned. As usual, there was the odd *risqué* blues ballad back around the time of *Bringing Up Baby*, such as Kokomo Arnold's 'Sissy Man Blues', a plaintive tune with the explicit request 'I woke up this morning with my pork grindin' business in my hand …/Lord, if you can't send me no woman, please send me some sissy man.'

In the forties and fifties songwriters Ivor Novello and Noël Coward were widely known within the entertainment business to be homosexual. But Novello's last musical, *Gay's the Word*, was about a failing impresario called Gay Daventree and was in the tradition of musicals such as *The Gay Lord Quex*, *The Gay Divorcee*, *The Gay Dog*, *The Gay Cavalier* and *The Gay Invalid* in using the word to mean carefree rather than anything to do with sexual orientation.

Similarly in 1966 when Graham Gouldman wrote the top ten hit 'No Milk Today' for Herman's Hermits the line 'The company was gay, we'd turn night into day' was merely a rueful reference to past happy times between a boy and a girl.

But when Ray Davis sang about 'David Watts' the next year, the schoolboy hero of the song was jokingly named after a homosexual promoter in Rutland who had designs on guitarist Dave Davies. Hence 'All the girls of the neighbourhood try to go out with David Watts/They try their best but can't succeed', and the line 'he is so gay and fancy free' is deliberately ambiguous even if most of the people who bought the record wouldn't have understood the term 'gay' in this sense.

The subtext of 'David Watts' very much sums up the discreet, not to say secretive, even furtive status of homosexuality in British culture in the 1960s. Contradictions abounded. There were, for instance, a plethora of gay showbiz managers. There was Larry Parnes with his stable of working-class male rockers like Billy Fury, Tommy Steele and Marty Wilde; there was Kit Lambert of The Who, and, of course, The Beatles' Brian Epstein, whose plight as a closeted gay man is said to have inspired John Lennon's 'You've Got to Hide Your Love Away'. And there was Simon Napier-Bell, latterly Wham's manager, but who in the sixties managed The Yardbirds and once explained, 'At a time when being gay was illegal, and the only way to live as an out gay man was to work in the theatre or as a hairdresser, pop management offered a new opportunity. So a lot of gays started to dabble in it.'

But front of stage there were few openly gay performers. Funny men Frankie Howerd, Kenneth Williams and Charles Hawtrey all masked their true selves behind conspiratorial, comedic camp. In the world of pop music, a few high-profile performers wrestled with issues around their sexuality, often against a backdrop of rumour and gossip.

Dusty Springfield was sometimes amazingly candid about her personal life, as when she told the *Evening Standard* as early as 1970, 'Many people say I'm bent, and I've heard it so many times that I've almost learned to accept it ... I know I'm perfectly as capable of being swayed by a girl as by a boy. More and more people feel that way and I don't see why I shouldn't.'

But still Dusty's lesbianism was never addressed in her music and some biographers have suggested that it was discomfort with her position and inability to be honest about her life that led her to abuse drugs and self-harm.

Visionary producer Joe Meek was a gay man at a time when it was still a crime. He shot himself the same year homosexuality was decriminalised (in 1967). He did leave behind an extraordinary piece of proto-gay pop, though. The B side of The Tornadoes' final single in 1966 is a track called 'Do You Come Here Often?', a kitschy jazzy organ instrumental that remains cheesily conventional for its opening two-thirds until there comes into the mix a bitchy conversation between two queenish, gay men trading gags, insults and innuendo. There's a closing mention of 'the Dilly', a reference to the infamous gents toilets at Piccadilly Circus. The conversation is actually between two complicit and straight members of The Tornadoes, but the intention couldn't be clearer, as pointed out by pop culture writer Jon Savage: 'I think Joe Meek wanted to get a slice of gay life on to a record. Nobody bought it. It was completely hidden, but it was still released on EMI ... It's almost like a hidden track, because you've got these two minutes of instrumental music, you're thinking, "OK, and?" Then suddenly it happens.'

Another Joe from the Midlands, this one a playwright from Leicester, called Orton, was perhaps a better augury of how gay pop and gay culture would be represented in the future. Defiant, pleasure-seeking, short-haired and physically robust rather than effete, he presented his sexuality as a revolutionary artistic act rather than a guilty secret. And his link with pop could have been forged in perpetuity had The Beatles gone with his script, *Up Against It*, for their never-to-be made third live action movie. Paul McCartney was a fan of Orton's and had invested £1,000 in the production of *Loot*, but, in the end, it wasn't to be for reasons that McCartney himself made clear in an interview with music journalist Roy Carr: 'The reason why we didn't do *Up Against It* wasn't because it was too far out or anything. We didn't do it because it was gay. We weren't gay and, really, that was all there was to it. It was quite simple, really. Brian was gay ... and so he and the gay crowd could appreciate it. Now, it wasn't that we were anti-gay – just that we, The Beatles, weren't gay.'

Before gay British pop could fully come out, though, it had to go through it's coy seventies bisexual phase, one in which established pop stars like David Bowie and Marc Bolan either dressed effeminately or made modish allusions to swinging both ways. As with issues of race and gender, punk was fiercely egalitarian. Tom Robinson's 'Glad to Be Gay' was unashamed in its lyrical directness but its pub sing-along musical setting owed nothing to the pop music that became enshrined in eighties gay culture, which was predominantly dance/pop oriented. Although it seems unthinkable now that neither Elton John, Freddie Mercury nor George Michael was ever discussed as a gay man in the media. Elton's 'Philadelphia Freedom' may have taken its title from his friend, lesbian sportswoman Billie Jean King's pro-tennis team, but Bernie Taupin's lyric and the finished song are a tribute to the Philly soul sound rather than a call to arms. Songs like 'Nikita' and Wham!'s 'Everything She Wants' and 'Young Guns (Go for It)' are explicitly heterosexual.

So one can imagine how it must have felt to grow up gay in a town in provincial Britain at a time when the only gay role models you would hear or see were a comedy pop troupe dressed as cowboys and motorbike cops singing kitsch wedding songs about joining the navy, or John Inman trilling 'I'm Free,' or Larry Grayson flouncing around the set of *The Generation Game*. Far away from the protected fakery of light entertainment, down dark streets where queer-bashers lurked, it must have seemed the only option was to leave town and head for the big city, 'With everything you own/In a little black case/Alone on the platform'.

Bronski Beat's 'Smalltown Boy' begins with one of British pop's greatest opening couplets, a bravura piece of scene-setting which hooked the pop listener but which must have particularly resonated with many gay and lesbian listeners. No one would call Glasgow a small town, but it was the city where Bronski Beat's singer Jimmy Somerville grew up. He was born into a conservative Protestant community, felt an outcast at school and, in a curious echo of John Travolta's Tony Manero in *Saturday Night Fever*, worked in a paint store by day and danced away his nights in the city's discos, as he wrote on his website:

> It wasn't what I wanted. I used to read and dream about London. Anywhere else but home really. Got [there] in the summer of '79. Only meant to be for the weekend. First stop, Earl's Court. Oh my! so many men, a return ticket, two days and so little time. Home – I'd found it! Bought the T-shirt and stayed. Hurt so many people in the process. It hurt me, but I was angry. I was looking after number one. This was my chance to start afresh, find out who I was. I could make up any old shite and who'd know what I was, wanted and needed.

In echoes of Joe Meek and 'Do You Come Here Often?', Somerville soon found himself 'on the dilly', the rent-boy circuit, before joining the squat scene and becoming immersed in left-wing and anti-Nazi politics. Eventually he fetched up in a Brixton flat with fellow gay musicians Larry Steinbachek and Steve Bronski, with whom he formed Bronski Beat, and brought to pop music a new politicised, militant gay aesthetic, one very different from the affected and faintly dishonest campery of the seventies, in which pub rock bands like Mott the Hoople had to grudgingly adopt what they called 'poovery' and hardened Northern blues band stalwarts like Woody Woodmansey and Mick Ronson donned Lurex jump-suits to fit in with Bowie's styled androgyny. Somerville was more skinhead than sissy, as he told journalist Barry Walters:

> I've always lived my life as an out gay man from the very beginning, so I don't feel any empathy with them. I was always using my situation for some kind of political agenda, whether or not it was everyone's cup of tea. I felt that everyone had an obligation to say something to condemn the hysteria, misinformation, and violence. We now have in England quite a few out celebrities, but they'd rather just show off their kitchen than discuss who and what they are.

'Smalltown Boy' became Bronski Beat's début single and an instant, massive hit, climbing swiftly to number three with its compellingly chilly ambience, motorik dance beat and the social realism of its lyric and video. Put alongside Bronski Beat the other major pop acts of 1984 – Frankie Goes to Hollywood, Culture Club, Wham! and The Smiths, plus the ubiquity of dance, disco and hi-energy in the charts – and it was clear that it was turning out to be the year of a very different kind of Big Brother from the one that Orwell had feared. Not a jackboot stamping down on a human face for ever, but a Doc Martin stamping down on a neon-lit dance floor.

It was the beginning of a brief golden age for gay pop, which in turn reflected a momentous and turbulent era for gay and straight society. As the spectre of AIDS loomed, issues surrounding sexuality became politically charged and invested with new significance and urgency. Clause 28 of the Local Government Act of 1988 dictated that schools 'shall not intentionally promote homosexuality or publish material with the intention of promoting homosexuality' or 'promote the teaching in any maintained school of the acceptability of homosexuality as a pretended family relationship'. Against this backdrop of governmental persecution, gay pop flourished with out gay performers such as Boy George directly addressing the Act in the song 'No Clause 28'. As the 1990s dawned, rock acts such as Nirvana, the Manic Street Preachers and Suede appeared, whose singer Brett Anderson claimed to journalist William Leith, 'I see myself as a bisexual man who's never had a homosexual experience ... I've never seen myself as overtly heterosexual, but then, I didn't see myself as gay. I sort of saw myself as some kind of sexual being that was floating somewhere.'

But it would seem that a decade of lad rock has reversed this trend and instituted a new blokey hegemony of birds, booze, football and, accordingly, a drab rock aesthetic that reflects this. For critics like Jon Savage, this is definitely a step backwards, as he wrote in the *Guardian* in 2008:

> Lad culture has been a disaster for pop music. That definition of a heterosexual man – beer and football, Nick Hornby – is so restrictive. It's important that pop musicians play around with gender and sexual divergence. The fact that it's gone back to Oasis from The Rolling Stones, Mick Jagger being very camp, is just pathetic, it's a complete failure. People are scared of nonconformity in music ... I think the crucial point about contemporary pop culture is that people are scared to be different because they'll be called gay. How has that happened? It's a reversal of everything that made British rock music great ... There's a current mode of solipsism,

where you don't want to be challenged, you just want to have your own life reflected back at you.

The furore over new star Frank Ocean's admission of a love affair with a man last year shows how rigidly heterosexist the world of hip hop and r&b is and, like the world of professional football, hard rock and metal is a suspiciously straight place to be, with only Rob Halford of Judas Priest defying convention by being an out gay man and, with his leather and studs stage outfits of the seventies, pretty much defining the modern metal look. Similarly, radio and TV presenters and comedians now use the word 'gay' and 'puff' as insults and defend it with guff about irony and 'banter'. As long as there are small minds, there'll be smalltown boys being pushed around and kicked around, leaving in the morning with everything they own in a little black case.

34. RADIO GA GA

When Marilyn Monroe was alleged to have been completely naked in a photo shoot, she replied, 'It's not true I had nothing on, I had the radio on.' A few decades later, the American writer Douglas Coupland also alluded to the power and ubiquity of Guglielmo Marconi's wireless device: 'I like doing radio because it's so intimate. The moment people hear your voice, you're inside their heads; not only that, you're in there laying eggs.'

As I have written elsewhere, there is no *Play Misty for Me* about TV presenters. However keen one may be on Ant, Dec, Holly Willoughby, Nick Knowles or whoever is currently the *grande fromage* of what Clive James called 'the crystal bucket', we know that TV is essentially artifice, an illusion arrived at precariously via lighting, make-up and camera angles. Radio, on the other hand, is an intimate, insinuating medium; it is a voice in your ear. And that voice may find you in your car, or in your bed, up a mountain, in your office, in the bath – not just slack-jawed and passive in front of the goggle box. Radio is close-up and personal, which perhaps explains why Clint Eastwood got quite such a hard time from that frighteningly keen fan, and why radio presenters get the most interesting and unconventional fan mail.

In 1901 Guglielmo Marconi invented the notion of broadcasting when his wireless transmitted the first radio waves across the curvature of the earth. The Italian entrepreneur's broadcast, from the Isle of Wight to Cornwall, sparked the beginning of the broadcast revolution. By 1922 the technology was sufficiently developed for the BBC to begin broadcasting regular radio shows on a network called 2LO. This was the moment when radio moved from the realm of the 'amateur enthusiast' to the first proper public broadcasting service in the world.

Music was integral to radio right from the beginning. The BBC broadcast orchestral concerts, dance bands, singers and the like long before it bothered with plays or discussions. Singers and dance-band leaders were the first real stars of radio: Al Bowlly, Joe Loss, Gracie Fields, Henry Hall. But the formats and the music were to remain fairly staid and conservative even as the rock and pop era loomed. A convention called 'needle time' agreed with the Musicians' Union and the Phonographic Performance Ltd restricted the amount of recorded music that could be broadcast in any one day. Records could only comprise five out of any twenty-four hours, which meant a busy time for the BBC's various orchestras, dance bands and individual crooners – pop singles being played was the exception rather than the rule.

Which is one of the reasons why British pop radio lagged so far behind its transatlantic cousin. There were no top-forty stations in Britain spreading the rock and roll message to eager youngsters in an exciting, fast paced format. We had no Alan

Freed, no Wolfman Jack, no fast-talking DJs with jingles and madcap personas. For most of the 1960s, pop music on the BBC meant the occasional oasis of beat music on the Light Programme: Brian Matthew's *Saturday Club* or David Jacobs's *Pick of the Pops*, presenters who were authoritative and suave rather than zany or sensationalist. Consequently, the canon of American pop is full of heartfelt hymns and incidental references to the joys of AM radio – from The Beach Boys to the Ramones, The Carpenters to Indeep's 'Last Night a DJ Saved My Life!' – whereas British pop songs about the radio come much later, are far fewer in number and often take a distinctly ambivalent or cynical view. There are, however, a few lovely nostalgic tributes to the domestic delights of the wireless: Van Morrison's 'In the Days Before Rock 'n' Roll' lovingly describes the young George Ivan down on his knees looking at the various stations on the illuminated dial, turning them into a mysterious incantation – 'Luxembourg/Athlone, Budapest, AFN/Hilversum, Helvetia' – with almost the same haunting power as the shipping forecast litany. Remember that Van the Man is singing of the days before rock and roll. With the coming of rock, it's the American pop songbook that begins to fill with the teenage love letters to radio.

The greatest may well be Jonathan Richman's 'Roadrunner', a simple, joyous romp which elevates a late-night drive along suburban Massachusetts Route 128 into a religious experience by the simple addition of pop songs on the radio. Richman was a teenage Velvet Underground obsessive, so he will have known their classic 'Rock and Roll' in which Jenny first hears rock and roll on the radio and her life is literally saved. In Richman's magical song the speed, the night and the radio stations combine to take on an almost mystical luminosity. 'Got the AM radio on,' he sings, entranced, 'Got the rockin' rockin' neon sound.'

'We used to get in the car,' remembers his Modern Lovers bandmate John Felice, 'and just drive up and down Route 128 and the Turnpike. We'd come up over a hill and he'd see the radio towers, the beacons flashing, and he would get almost teary-eyed. He'd see all this beauty in things where other people just wouldn't see it.'

Though the Sex Pistols often covered Richman's proto-punk anthem, there was no contemporary British equivalent of 'Roadrunner'. But the wind of change had begun to blow through the British media in the mid-sixties, borne on a tangy, salt sea breeze.

In 1964 an Irish music entrepreneur called Rohan O'Rahilly was running a hip Soho club called the Scene and managing several artists including r&b singer and organist Georgie Fame. He took the unconventional step of recording a Fame single on his own independent label, but when he tried to get this played on the BBC and Radio Luxembourg he found to his dismay that the major labels – EMI, Decca, Pye and Phillips – exerted a virtual stranglehold over the nation's airwaves. He came to an unusual but momentous decision: 'I have recorded the guy, so I can't get it played, so we have to start a radio station.'

O'Rahilly found a former Danish ferry, the *Fredericia*, refitted it is a basic radio studio, renamed it the *Caroline*, moored it just off the coast of Felixstowe and began broadcasting on 28 March 1964. Radio Caroline was born. The next month Radio Atlanta began beaming pop music to the UK from a former coaster anchored off Harwich. Radio Jackie and Radio London soon followed. Broadcasting from offshore ships or disused sea forts, the effect of these pirate radio stations on the cultural life of the mainland was electrifying. By 1967 twenty-one pirate radio stations were broadcasting to an estimated daily audience of 10–15 million listeners. Instead of the benign toleration of the kindly BBC, and the crumbs offered grudgingly on the Light Programme when needle time allowed, pirate radio brought non-stop pop to a music-mad, newly liberated teen generation. It was thrilling, it was new; the presenters sounded engaged and energised by the records they were playing. It was happening without the grown-up world's permission. In his book about Radio 1, *The Nation's Favourite*, writer Simon Garfield puts it like this:

> When Radio Caroline began in March 1964, the world of British pop was a contradictory place. The music was unprecedented, an extraordinary burst of energy and frustration that still reverberates. Within eighteen months, The Beatles, The Stones and The Who had thrown off not only post-war austerity and authority but also any notion that young people would ever be governable again. But the institutions that controlled the music – the stuffy record companies, the crewed ballrooms, the weary, disbelieving parents – tried to keep the dampers on everything. No one had a more moralising grip on entertainment than the BBC, which rationed pop to a few hours a week on the Light Programme. No wonder teenagers screamed at their idols at concerts: it was an orgiastic release, true unbound freedom even as they were being levered back into their seats.

Though they rejoiced in that rakish, buccaneering nickname, these so-called 'pirate' radio stations were not technically illegal since they were broadcasting from international waters. Harold Wilson's government had been slow to move against them for fear of alienating the popular vote. But, in 1966, the same month that an episode of the TV spy show *Danger Man* called 'Not So Jolly Roger' set aboard a pirate station was aired, the British postmaster general, Tony Benn, introduced a Bill to Parliament that outlawed unlicensed offshore broadcasting. This became the Marine Offences Act, enacted in August 1967. The pirates were scuppered, holed below the water line, headed for Davy Jones's locker instead of playing Davy Jones records.

But the landlubber establishment had been forced to listen to the audacious voice of the pirates and their audience. In 1967, the whole of BBC was restructured largely because of the pirates and the unstoppable rise of pop. The Home Service became Radio Four, the Third programme Radio Three and the Light Programme, Radio Two. A new network, Radio One, catering for youth and the pop constituency, was born at 7 a.m. on Saturday 30 September 1967, when DJ Tony Blackburn announced, 'Good morning everyone. Welcome to the exciting new sound of Radio One,' to the strains of Van Der Graaf Generator's stirring rendition of George Martin's 'Theme One' and The Move's 'Flowers in the Rain'.

Blackburn was one of the many ex-pirate DJs who'd jumped ship for a berth at Radio One, along with John Peel, Keith Skues, Kenny Everett and others. The legendary Johnnie Walker did not come ashore quite so pliantly or take the establishment shilling. He practically lashed himself to the mast, relishing his outlaw status and fearing that the Beeb's new pop network would be a pale imitation of the pirate's free-spirited brio: 'Everyone knew what would happen if the government legitimised an onshore radio station –

it's what we got when Radio One started, a terrible station to begin with. The government and the BBC were pretty much the same thing back then.'

Even if Walker had been as keen as his fellow pirates to take a berth at the new BBC network, he may have found the welcome not so warm at first. He recalls seeing a BBC memo from 1967 addressed to the Radio One controller: 'On no account should Johnnie Walker be employed for at least a year to let the taint of criminality subside.'

From out of all this tumult, though, there were no significant songs. When British pop writers have addressed the medium of radio, as they have sporadically down the last few decades, they've been at best melancholic, at worst splenetic. Out of punk came two stinging diatribes. Elvis Costello's 'Radio, Radio' found him in his full avenging nerd persona, denouncing the radio as a banal dictatorship 'in the hands of such a lot of fools/Tryin' to anaesthetise the way that you feel'. It was a much bigger hit in the States than here.

The Clash's Joe Strummer had often railed in interviews against the anodyne character of music radio in this country: 'I want to slag off all the people in charge of radio stations. Firstly, Radio One. They outlawed the pirates and then didn't, as they promised, cater for the market the pirates created. Radio One and Two, most afternoons, run concurrently and the whole thing has slid right back to where it was before the pirates happened. They've totally fucked it. There's no radio station for young people any more. It's all down to housewives and trendies in Islington. They're killing the country by having that play-list monopoly.'

Strummer condensed these feelings into one of the most punchy and venomous numbers of The Clash's early repertoire, a song attacking London's main commercial network and called, bluntly, 'Capital Radio', which eulogised the pirate stations, now all 'silenced, 'cos they ain't got a government licence', and mocked the new station high in its tower in the heart of London, and the DJ Aiden Day who 'had all the hits to play to keep you in your place all day'. Both songs, with the typical and perhaps justified conspiracy theory combativeness of the New Wave, saw British pop radio as bland mind control, dishing out a diet of docility for the drones.

Buggles' 'Video Killed the Radio Star' was much more nostalgic and reflective; a song bemoaning but not resisting the coming of video and the end of the dominance of pop radio, it was, rather smugly, the first record on MTV. Even more direct, though, was Queen's 'Radio Ga Ga', also a direct response to the coming of MTV and music video, and a lament for the passing of the golden age of radio, not just pop radio but radio in general. The song, written by drummer Roger Taylor, makes reference to major radio events such as Orson Welles's infamous 'War of the Worlds' broadcast and Winston Churchill's 'finest hour' speech. But its heart is a plea for pop radio not to become 'some background noise, a backdrop for the girls and boys'. Ironically, after being performed exultantly at Live Aid, it became a staple of MTV.

But in the end, such doom-mongering and hand-wringing proved to be unnecessary. If anything it's music TV that's become the wallpaper of modern life, left on inaudibly in hairdressers, hotel lobbies and office receptions. Radio is booming, proliferating across digital platforms and the internet. Pirate radio is still with us, beaming cutting-edge music from specialist genres across the night-time cities from transmitters on top of tower blocks.

Writer Dorian Lynskey put it well when he said, 'I'll know I'm old when I no longer listen to pop radio at all. Now that consumer choice is the media's prevailing obsession, there is something magical about hearing a song, old or new, that you haven't chosen, while knowing that thousands of unknown fellow listeners are having the same experience, far away yet intimately connected.'

35. DO THEY KNOW IT'S CHRISTMAS?

Dawn, and as the sun breaks through the piercing chill of night on the plains outside Korem, it lights up a biblical famine, now, in the twentieth century. This place, say workers here, is the closest thing to hell on earth.

Nearly thirty years on, the words and images have lost none of their wrenching emotional power. Huddled corpses, weeping children, skeletal animals lumbering across a parched expanse of smoke and ash. This does not look like something from our time or our world, and in a sense, of course, it is not our world. It is the world of the poorest and most vulnerable people on earth, poised on the edge of the abyss in 1984, sixteen years from the end of the twentieth century.

Michael Buerk's BBC report from the Ethiopian famine in early 1984 remains one of the most chilling and powerful pieces of television ever broadcast, and one of the most far-reaching in terms of impact. Like the TV footage from the battlefields and villages of Vietnam a decade earlier, it reached into living rooms with utterly shocking effect and ramifications, the most obvious being Band Aid and Live Aid, Bob Geldof and Midge Ure's 'global jukebox' that arguably set the tenor for the function and shape of modern rock and roll, and also ushered in the age of celebrity.

But it wasn't the first time pop music had discovered its social conscience or moral compass. In November 1970 the Bhola cyclone ravaged across East Pakistan and West Bengal, killing half a million people and displacing hundreds of thousands more, sending them scurrying across the subcontinent in search of food, shelter and safety at the same time that a bloody liberation war was raging that would result in the creation of Bangladesh. India's foremost classical musician, Ravi Shankar, heard about the unfolding humanitarian disaster in Los Angeles, but many in the Western world were oblivious. When Shankar's friend George Harrison came to visit him in LA, he was struck by his friend's sadness and helplessness. As Shankar later said: 'I felt I had to do something. I was in this terrible state of mind ... [George] saw I was looking so sad, he was really concerned, and so I asked if he could help me. Immediately he called his friends.'

So it was, with the power that only an ex-Beatle's little black book can muster, that on Sunday 1 August 1971 two concerts were staged at the Madison Square Garden, featuring Harrison and Shankar and some of those friends: Eric Clapton, Bob Dylan, Leon Russell, Ringo Starr – John Lennon was reluctant to interrupt his trip to the Virgin Islands and McCartney declined, feeling that the credit for an effective Beatle reunion would be taken by Harrison's manager, the notorious Allen Klein. Harrison would later talk of spending 'three months' on the phone organising the shows but most of the work seems to have been done in the final five or six weeks.

Musically, the shows were a staggering success. *NME* called it 'The Greatest Rock Spectacle of the Decade!' *Rolling Stone* said, 'Seeing Ringo Starr drumming and singing on stage has a joy in it that is one of the happiest feelings on earth still.' *Village Voice* rightly raved about Shankar, Ali Akbar Khan and the amazing line-up of Indian musicians. And at the chilly dawn of the seventies, post-Woodstock, post-Altamont, many saw the shows like *Rolling Stone*, as 'a brief incandescent revival of all that was best about the sixties'. Allen Klein gushed about the peaceful vibe of the shows and the total absence of the police. In fact, there was an altercation between club-wielding riot police and about 200 non-ticket holders who tried to rush the event.

Did it help the people of Bangladesh? The concerts raised a quarter of a million dollars, to which could be added the later worldwide sales of a live album, a boxed three-record set and a film of the event. It's now estimated that well in excess of $12 million was sent to Bangladesh, and the live album and DVD release of the film continue to benefit the George Harrison Fund for UNICEF. But, perhaps more importantly, as Shankar acknowledged, the event seared the name and plight of Bangladesh into the minds of the world. 'Overnight,' said Gary Tilley in his *Working Class Mystic* book on Harrison, 'because of their fascination with rock stars, masses of people became educated about geopolitical events they had not even been aware of the week before. The tragedy in Bangladesh moved to the fore as an international issue.'

Harrison himself soon encountered what would prove to be the major stumbling block of such admirable and well-intentioned gestures: making sure the funds get to the people who need them. Persistent rumours had it that some money went walkabout, even, said some, into Klein's accounts. Harrison became angry at the response of politicians and the American IRS, who initially refused to wave their (tax) cut from the shows' proceeds. Then treasury minister Patrick Jenkin told Harrison that the British taxman would be levying 'purchase tax' on the live album sales. 'Sorry!' Jenkin said. 'It is all very well for your high ideals, but Britain equally needs the money!'

But the Concert for Bangladesh did more than simply raise money: it put the idea into the collective psyche that rock music could be more than simply about hedonism, excess and personal gratification. During the next decade, similar ventures helped further the notion of pop philanthropy. Amnesty International began its long-running *Secret Policeman's Ball* series of shows featuring stars from the worlds of music and comedy. ABBA, The Bee Gees, Earth, Wind & Fire, Rod Stewart and others played a concert at the UN General Assembly entitled 'A Gift of Song: the Music for UNICEF Concert'. Over the Christmas period of 1979 at London's Hammersmith Odeon, the Concerts for Kampuchea raised funds to help the victims of Pol Pot's murderous regime in Cambodia.

But 1984, ironically a year whose ominous associations were of betrayal and suspicion, was to see pop music's most emblematic moment of fellow feeling, and a turning point in political and pop culture. In the era before multi-platform TV, the internet and social media, the big TV news shows still set and dominated the news agenda and regularly commanded over 20 million viewers throughout the day. About half the population of Britain saw Michael Buerk's haunting report. One of them was the singer with pop punk outfit The Boomtown Rats, Bob Geldof, who came home to find his wife, Paula Yates, watching, weeping, with their baby.

The next day Yates had stuck a note on the fridge door: 'Ethiopia. Everyone who visits this house from today onwards will be asked for £5 until we have raised £200 for famine relief.' An idea was soon hatched in Geldof's mind, a charity single for the African famine. Geldof was savvy enough to know that a single by the significantly past their peak Boomtown Rats wouldn't raise much, so he contacted his old friend, Ultravox singer Midge Ure, who asked, 'Have you got a song?' Geldof replied that he had a scrap of an idea called 'It's My World'. Ure promised to get some ideas together when he got back to London. In a taxi the next day Geldof jotted down an idea for a lyric. The following day a tape arrived from Ure, with the skeleton of a melody. At Geldof's house in Chiswick the two of them roughed out what would become the then biggest selling single of all time.

The recording of the Band Aid single sums up all the bizarre contradictions that critics of such ventures trot out to discredit them. In order to help starving children dressed in rags in a hellhole on the other side of the globe, the bouffanted, mulleted and often mullered peacocks of the fashion parade of eighties' pop convened in Notting Hill to make a pop record. Elton John claims to remember nothing of the day: 'I had a bloody good time,' he said, incongruously.

Radio One relaxed its normally strict playlist rules and played the single once an hour. BBC controller Michael Grade ordered every programme in the run-up to Thurday's *Top of the Pops* to begin five minutes early so that the Band Aid video could be shown. Jim Diamond, the Scottish singer whose single 'I Should Have Known Better' was number one at the time, told people not to buy his record but to buy the Band Aid single instead. Geldof, who hadn't had a number one for five years, and knew the importance of a hit, was greatly touched by this. 'Do They Know It's Christmas?' became the fastest-selling number one ever, and went to the top of the charts in eleven other countries. Geldof and Ure had hoped to make £70,000. They ended up making over 1,000 times that much.

But not everyone was swept up in the general hoopla. Band Aid had its critics from within the pop business, particularly from the alternative sector, which Geldof had largely overlooked for his celebrity choirs. The Housemartins' début single 'Flag Day' excoriated the whole notion of charity and suggested, 'Try shaking your tin in front of the Queen.' The ever-loquacious and controversial Morrissey questioned the entire philosophy that Band Aid enshrined in an interview for *Time Out*:

> The whole implication was to save these people in Ethiopia, but who were they asking to save them? Some thirteen-year-old girl in Wigan! People like Thatcher and the royals could solve the Ethiopian problem within ten seconds. But Band Aid shied away from saying that – for heaven's sake, it was almost directly aimed at unemployed people ... I'm not afraid to say that I think Band Aid was diabolical. Or to say that I think Bob Geldof is a nauseating character. Many people find that very unsettling, but I'll say it as loud as anyone wants me to. In the first instance the record itself was absolutely tuneless. One can have great concern for the people of Ethiopia, but it's another thing to inflict daily torture on the people of England. It was an awful record considering the mass of talent involved. And it wasn't done shyly, it was the most self-righteous platform ever in the history of popular music.

Such dissenting voices were largely drowned out in the clamour around Band Aid and its even more high-profile spin-off, the Live

Aid concerts of the following year which brought over 70,000 people to London's Wembley Stadium and close to 100,000 at the John F. Kennedy Stadium in Philadelphia. The events of July 1985 have been so well documented elsewhere in print and film that all we should say here is that while the day remains a musical hotch-potch drawn very much from the blandest end of the eighties pop spectrum (does anyone remember 'Virgin' by Spandau Ballet, Adam Ant's 'Vive Le Rock' or Sade's 'Is It a Crime?') its iconic status is assured for ever. Live Aid, for one thing, marked the birth of today's stadium rock: a drug free, anodyne, corporate retail opportunity enjoyed by smart, casual members of every generation.

There have been several attempts since Live Aid to re-stage such ventures, often by Geldof himself, but none has the symbolic resonance of that summer's day, that weird but compelling orgy of compassion and generosity at the very height of the rapacious dog-eat-dog eighties. Farm Aid, Ferry Aid, Live 8, Live Earth and others followed down the years, with a regularity that means any humanitarian disaster or tragedy nowadays must automatically generate its own charity single and concert. And, as cynics will point out readily, the benefits are not just for the benighted victims of whatever the disaster may be. Live Aid resurrected the career of Queen, who had been languishing in the wilderness, widely ostracised for their concerts in the South Africa of apartheid. Bono was elevated overnight from journeyman alt-rocker to the definitive rock star of the late twentieth century, taking his mullet walkabout into the crowd for a twelve-minute version of 'Bad', the over-running of which meant the rest of the band were annoyed at having to drop sure-fire crowd pleaser 'Pride (in the Name of Love)'. But it didn't matter: in the week after Live Aid, all of U2's albums went back into the UK chart. Soon Bono would have the

Pope on speed dial and be a permanent perma-shaded Zelig-like presence at the political courts of the world.

Critics say that benefit concerts are a salve to the conscience of the West, and reinforce an ethnocentric view of Africans, or the developing world, as powerless in the face of unstoppable natural forces, rather than victims of political and economic exploitation. A Young Conservative, Jo-Anne Nadler, celebrated Live Aid as the welcome return of the distinctly nineteenth-century notion of the charity entrepreneur and the privatisation of aid, 'rather than asking the state to help'.

But others talk of the benefits of what's called catalytic philanthropy – the subtle persuasive effect of seeing favourite pop stars helping a good cause; a soft power that is in its own way as important in the long run as the rattling of a tin. As Billy Bragg, a man who has sometimes been suspicious of the motives of the millionaire rockerati, points out: 'When pop stars recognise that there's a world beyond the end of their leotard, we should give them the benefit of the doubt. If you start attacking that, you end up looking at the village fête and thinking, "What's the point?"'

Michael Buerk, whose harrowing report was the impetus for Band Aid, didn't actually see the concert. 'I knew it was happening, but South African television didn't carry it. South Africa was the story of the day, with townships in flames and riots. On the day of Live Aid I was actually being tear-gassed by the police.'

Before Live Aid rock and roll was still to a large extent a feral, outsider art form unfit for the broadsheets or the high table of the establishment. Remember that punk rock had raged only seven years before. After Live Aid, pop usurped Hollywood to become the glittery heart of the world entertainment circus. Moreover, for better or worse, it made Brangelina, Bono and Madonna the go-to

Dystopian, alienated, futuristic.
Gary Numan ponders whether
'friends' are indeed electric.

Madness, The Selecter and The Specials enjoy an afternoon off on Brighton beach during the 2 Tone tour of 1979.

The Brothers Kemp at a party in their 80s pomp; indestructible and always believing that they were gold.

High Goth: a profound earnestness that trembles on the lip of camp.

Bob Geldof in 1985 with the woman he called 'a punk politician', Margaret Thatcher.

The eighties was the decade when a generation of 'smalltown boys' and girls brought gay culture into the heart of pop.

The most significant
British band of their
generation in iconic pose.

Bernard Sumner and guest rapper
John Barnes on set of the video for
'World In Motion' during Italia 90.
Note striking period shorts.

'Got any Veras?' The 'baggy' and 'sorted' world of rave culture captured by Kevin Cummins at the Haçienda in 1990.

'A new dawn has broken, has it not?' The heady first morning of Blair's Britain.

Nineties eco-warriors photographed in their natural habitat, protesting the building of Newbury bypass.

The perennially mad for it uber-lad Liam Gallagher.

The brassy Boudicca of Girl Power, Geri Halliwell.

The haunted and hunted Amy Winehouse near the end of her short life.

Leona Lewis overcome by the benevolent despotism of Simon Cowell.

A reveller soaks up the vibe of a typical Glastonbury.

guys for political change and the grand philanthropic gesture – not a suited bureaucrat in a UN back office. Live Aid changed everything. But it's not the world that was fed that changed. It's us. Famine remains, war remains. But the age of the celebrity began 'at twelve noon in London, 7 a.m. in Philadelphia' 13 July 1985.

36. HOW SOON IS NOW?

St Peter's Fields is a small corner of Manchester that is forever revolutionary. On 16 August 1819, cavalry charged into a peaceful gathering of 80,000 people demanding parliamentary reform. Eighteen people were thought to have been killed, hundreds injured and the Peterloo massacre became seared into our national consciousness. Later, the Free Trade Hall was built on the site, where in the summer of 1976 the Sex Pistols played two gigs in quick succession; the first cost 60p to get into, and around forty people were there.

Let's not get bogged down in the never-ending speculation and debate over who was actually there. The simple truth is that those present at the electrifying evenings were people who wouldn't just form the advance guard of the next wave of Mancunian music – Peter Hook, Bernard Sumner, Ian Curtis, Steven Morrissey, Pete Shelley, Mark E. Smith, Howard Devoto, Paul Morley, Tony Wilson – but would also bring forth an entirely new music scene in Britain, one built on a rejection of all that was slick, empty and metropolitan about the coming decade, which embraced mystery, individuality, melancholy, wit, kitchen-sink realism and, above all, independence.

One of the many curiosities about punk is that this tsunami of sonic rage against the corporate music business was, in fact, largely funded by the corporate music industry. The Clash were on CBS; the Sex Pistols did their best to get signed (and then swiftly dropped) by almost every major label in Britain; and Epic, Polydor, United Artists and the rest all had their share of punk acts. This sat uneasily with some, not least The Clash, whose 1980 single 'Hitsville UK' was a heartfelt tribute to the passion and principle of the emerging independent labels in Britain, as compared to the 'mutants, creeps and musclemen' of the majors.

By contrast, the new labels were often the brainchild of one committed visionary acting out of artistic zeal rather than greed. The ethic was not just DIY out of necessity, it was an explicit rejection of the London music biz. Even when the labels were based in London, such as Daniel Miller's Mute, Ivo Watts-Russell's 4AD or Geoff Travis's Rough Trade, they were a million miles, ideologically if not literally, from the West End offices of EMI and their ilk.

And just as many were located far from the capital, intentionally placed to celebrate local talent and cussedness. Furthest north, in Glasgow, Alan Horne intended Postcard Records to be a 'punk rock version of the Chic Organisation', a place where spikiness and hedonistic pure pop could meet and showcase 'the Sound of Young Scotland', a nod to Berry Gordy's Motown and their slogan 'The Sound of Young America'. Postcard Records had an aesthetic that was both glacially cool and infectiously silly. The records came in sleeves knowingly festooned with tea-towel and shortbread-Caledonian iconography and featured cats, bagpipes, kilts and tartan; the records themselves, by the likes of Orange Juice, Josef K and Aztec Camera, were oblique, elegant and charming. Along the M8 in Edinburgh, Bob Last's Fast Product put out influential early singles by the Gang of Four, The Mekons and The Human League. In Newcastle, Kitchenware had a small roster of bands like Prefab Sprout and Martin Stephenson and the Daintees, with songs that were crafted and quirky. From Liverpool came Bill Drummond's Zoo Records and bands like The Teardrop Explodes, Echo and the Bunnymen and Wah! Heat – heady, crazed and psychedelic.

These records were made in different cities by very different kinds of people but they shared more than just idealistic notions about payment, distribution and shareholders. There was also an indie sound. In contrast to the lush, padded-shouldered widescreen vision of transatlantic pop – the huge, gated reverb drum sound of Phil Collins, Pat Benatar, Duran Duran and their peers – indie was slim, spiky, jangly, skinny, and frequently harked back to a classic sixties template or the angular funkiness of post-punk. Indie offered a different narrative to the one that is generally seen as the story of the 1980s: vintage clothes, old records, bedsits, Penguin modern classics, black and white movies instead of the champagne, filofaxes and outsize mobile phones of Thatcher's children.

But back at the Lesser Free Trade Hall in 1976, there was a young man from Stockport present, Paul Morley. Writing in the *Guardian* in 2011, he remembers:

> I'd gone on my nineteen-year-old own. I'm not sure what I
> actually recall or what I filled in using data acquired later as
> the gig was talked up into legend. We, the yokel audience,
> were scruffy, isolated avant-garde music fans motivated to
> constantly search out new music. Many audience members

have since become well known. So well known it appears now that the show was attended by a host of rock celebrities – members of Joy Division, New Order, The Fall, The Smiths, A Certain Ratio, Ludus, Simply Red, Buzzcocks, Magazine, the producer Martin Hannett. It was, in fact, attended by unassuming nonentities drawn to the gig from within a twenty-mile radius of Manchester city centre, perhaps because they were extremely frustrated by their stranded nonentity status, and craving purpose.

Three of the four members of what would become Joy Division were present, though. Peter Hook and Bernard Sumner had been schoolmates since they were eleven, although they went to the show separately. It was a moment of epiphany. Sumner later said that the gig 'destroyed the myth of being a pop star, of a musician being some kind of god that you had to worship'. The following day Hook borrowed £35 from his mother to buy his first bass. Ian Curtis of Macclesfield saw the second Sex Pistols show and was similarly inspired. They formed a band called Warsaw and played their first gig on 29 May 1977 supporting The Buzzcocks. It was reviewed in *NME* by one Paul Morley. The burgeoning indie scene was an incestuous nexus of people and ideas.

Warsaw became Joy Division and their début album *Unknown Pleasures* became the tenth release on Manchester's Factory Records, the defiantly unorthodox and enigmatic label that grew out of the club night in Hulme run by another present at the Sex Pistols' shows. Tony Wilson was a Cambridge graduate who'd come back to his native city to work for Granada TV. Opinionated, mouthy, bright, fired up by punk rock, English literature and Situationism, his importance to the renaissance of Northern music and the indie culture cannot be overestimated. Yet another of those present in that tiny throng at the Lesser Free Trade Hall was Martin Hannett. His production on *Unknown Pleasures* was, along with the music, a revelation: austere, brooding, menacing, ghostly, melancholic and beautiful. Manchester in the late seventies still bore the dust and rubble of the Industrial Revolution and the Second World War, and this was the city that *Unknown Pleasures* enshrined in sound, haunted throughout by splintering glass, industrial hums, the whooshing and clanking of traffic in the rain on the Mancunian Way, lifts ascending desolate Hulme tower blocks. But there's more than that. Before moving to the inner city, Ian Curtis had lived near Macclesfield, and Jon Savage is right when he talks of the 'witchy emptiness' of the Pennines weighing heavily upon Joy Division, ensuring 'the definitive Northern gothic statement'.

Tony Wilson gave Joy Division their first TV appearance on Granada in July 1979. Two months later they appeared on the BBC live from Manchester's Oxford Road studios. They played two songs, 'She's Lost Control' and 'Transmission' through which Curtis, seemingly in another world, twitched and twisted his way, jerked like a puppet by the angular rhythms and riffs. Everyone who saw the show was transfixed. It remains one of the most extraordinary, visceral and compelling pieces of music television ever.

One would imagine that, as a music-obsessed Mancunian, Steven Patrick Morrissey, also present at the second Pistols show, was watching Joy Division that night. He was a well-known if unusual figure on the city's scene. He was obsessed with the New York Dolls and 1960s' girl groups, was an inveterate letter writer to the *NME* and had produced a pulpish biography of James Dean. Tony Wilson said of him to journalist Ian Watson in 2003 for *Mojo* magazine:

He was the speccy kid in the corner, the clever little swotty outsider boy, and very brilliant … He wrote a fantastic short play about eating toast, and I think he gave it to me and I lost it. Then, at some point, whenever it was in 1980, he phoned me up and said, 'Would you come and see me.' I drove out to King's Road, Stretford, to his mum's house, went to his bedroom upstairs and sat on the edge of the bed while he sat on the chair, surrounded by James Dean posters, and he informed me that he'd decided to become a pop star. I sort of went, 'Well, Steven, that's very interesting,' and inside I was thinking, 'You must be fucking joking. You're off your fucking head, you're the least likely rock 'n' roll star imaginable in the universe.'

Events were to prove Wilson wrong, of course, as he would happily acknowledge. A precociously talented guitarist called Johnny Marr knocked on Morrissey's door, said, 'This is how Leiber and Stoller met,' and suggested they form a band. One of their first decisions was that The Smiths would sign to an independent label. Marr said that this was an important aesthetic statement in itself. As the fledgling Smiths, hailed as 'the new Beatles' by New Order manager Rob Gretton, began to be courted by major labels, Marr said that he was 'immediately struck by the lack of records in these buildings. As someone who was a record freak, it made me want to get back to Rough Trade. On the few occasions that I'd been in the Factory flat, and certainly when I'd been around Rough Trade, they were like record companies trying to operate under mounds and mounds of vinyl. All they had in CBS and Warner Brothers were huge posters of their artists in reception.'*

---

* From Richard King's book *How Soon Is Now?*

The Smiths did not, as many predicted, sign to Factory. They went with the workers' co-operative Rough Trade, described by Richard King as the 'independent sector's conscience, shop floor and corn market'. The label grew out of the Rough Trade shop opened by Geoff Travis in West London in February 1976 and whose idealistic, leftist communitarian ethos had nurtured unorthodox rock and roll from the likes of Scritti Politti, Swell Maps and Vic Godard and the Subway Sect.

Few bands can have entered the public consciousness as swiftly, strikingly or as fully formed as The Smiths. Drummer Mike Joyce said of their very first rehearsal that he knew instantly he was in the best band in the world. They came draped in gladioli, diamante, beads and controversy, with songs about the Moors murders, vegetarianism and unorthodox, shadowy sexuality. They chose their name to be deliberately plain and unvarnished, in contrast with the glamour and flamboyance of their music. Their first single, 'Hand in Glove', began with a wailing harmonica, possibly a sly nod to 'Love Me Do' and the beginning of The Beatles' career. But it was their second single, 'This Charming Man', that seemed to be their earliest statement of intent: chiming, plangent, vivacious, unusual and with one of the great opening lines of all time: 'Punctured bicycle on a hillside desolate' – six words, of least four of which were rarely heard in a pop lyric.

The Smiths' records were immediately embraced by a generation shivering their way through the economic wasteland of the eighties, informed as it was by kitchen-sink drama, films like *Saturday Night and Sunday Morning* and *Billy Liar* and writers like Shelagh Delaney, Victoria Wood and Alan Bennett.

A couple of years earlier, the *NME* had produced a compilation cassette entitled *C81*, which distilled the post-punk mood into a collection of disparate indie tracks from the likes of Scritti Politti, Orange Juice, Wah! Heat, The Raincoats and Aztec Camera. By the time of a second compilation, five years on, indie had lost some of its earlier connotations of radicalism and innovation and had come to take on a mildly pejorative sense in some quarters as bloodless and twee, accusations that were often levelled at the *C86* bands such as the Shop Assistants, The June Brides and the output of Sarah Records, known wryly as shambling bands.

In between these two dates, The Smiths came to embody the independent guitar culture with one release in particular. 'How Soon Is Now?' is perhaps The Smiths' best-known song if not their most representative, hovering somewhere opaquely between psychedelia, r&b and the dancefloor. Johnny Marr himself has described it as 'possibly our most enduring record. It's most people's favourite, I think.' It combines The Smiths at their most imaginative and magisterial as a band: soaring, meshing guitars, drifting in and out like smoke and light over a shifting Bo Diddley groove, with perhaps the ultimate Morrissey lyric, a compressed oblique tale of unfulfillment and Northern night life, littered with casual gems of imagery and observation. Morrissey declares, 'I am the son/And the heir/Of a shyness that is criminally vulgar.'

Many years later, I asked Morrissey, by now a solo artist, whether he had heard the briefly notorious duo t.a.T.u.'s version of 'How Soon Is Now?'. 'Yes, it was magnificent,' he said. 'Absolutely. I don't know much about them.'

'They're the teenage Russian lesbians,' I replied.

'Well,' said Morrissey, 'aren't we all?'

By then indie had come to mean something else, something much less unusual and underground, much less vulnerable and outsider. The narrative arc of indie going over-ground is best illustrated by the tale of Alan McGee's Creation label. Its first release was a single by a music journalist, The Legend. Originally Creation was the home of all that was fey, weird and out of step, bands like The Jasmine Minks, The Jazz Butcher, Biff Bang Pow!, then Primal Scream and Felt, and eventually Oasis, who bestrode nineties pop like boorish colossi playing loud, laddish indie rock. When you're the biggest band in Britain and are being invited to receptions at Downing Street, clearly indie means something very different from what it did in 1979.

Tony Wilson died of cancer at the tragically young age of fifty-seven in 2007. The Union Flag on Manchester Town Hall was lowered to half mast as a mark of respect and as an acknowledgement of how Wilson had helped with the renaissance of the city, from benighted post-industrial wasteland to a glamorous, cosmopolitan centre, one of the artistic capitals of the world. Manchester has the largest student population in Europe, and many of them come from all over the world, drawn by the music and culture that Wilson and the independent pioneers forged and fostered, a process begun though seen by hardly anyone at the Free Trade Hall on a hot summer night in 1976.

37. WORLD IN MOTION

On the Tuesday after Christmas, 2008, Britain woke up to the shocking news that England football stalwart and sometime captain, Steven Gerrard, a clean-cut, crew-cut individual straight from the pages of *Roy of the Rovers*, had allegedly assaulted a DJ in a Southport bar.

If the attack was a shock, the reported reason was even more shocking (or possibly fairly predictable, depending on your point of view). According to reports, the trouble kicked off when the DJ refused a request to play something from Gerrard's favourite album, Phil Collins's *Greatest Hits*. Some reeled – it was 2008, weren't footballers all supposed to like Kanye West and Jay-Z? – others nodded sagely, remembering three decades of interviews in which football's favourite music, from John Denver to George Benson to Whitney Houston, had been exposed as badly out of sync with the cutting edge of cool in the world of pop.

The journalist and academic Martin Jacques once claimed that where music defined the sixties, and comedy the eighties, football came to define the nineties. I'm not entirely sure that holds water, but certainly football and music have both loomed large in our popular social history – sometimes singly, but often woven together. Both are essentially working-class pursuits that have gained a huge international audience, and both have offered social mobility to young people, mainly men, from industrial and post-industrial urban communities. Both have global reach and influence and both generate colossal sums; both depend on the passionate commitment and enthusiasm of a dedicated consumer who will spend money and time following their favourite artist, band or team.

Or, to put it another way, as Nick Hornby did: 'Televised football has become like music. It's on all the time and you can tune in or not. And most of it isn't any good.'

We know that Norwich City had a football song as early as the 1890s.

'On the Ball, City', 'the world's oldest football song', is still sung today. But we don't know whether the footballing stars of the 1890s – Preston North End's inaugural league-winning team or Luton's Frank Whitby, the first professional footballer, or the dominant Sunderland and Aston Villa teams of the era – we don't know whether they hung out in exclusive members' saloons buying stout for Marie Lloyd and Florrie Forde. It's doubtful. For most of the first half of the century, footballers were part-time journeymen and wage slaves, treated as cattle by chairmen and managers. Men who would draw thousands to watch their artistry every Saturday would mix and live among those crowds for the rest of the week. The biggest stars would travel to the match on the same public buses as the supporters. Tom Finney was known as the 'Preston Plumber', reflecting his proper apprenticeship. Dixie Dean, of whom Bill Shankly said, 'He belongs to the company of the supremely great, like Beethoven, Shakespeare and Rembrandt,' took a job as a porter at Littlewoods after his retirement. It was still like this until quite late into the sixties. Alan Mullery, who captained Spurs and made thirty-five appearances for England, spent Saturday nights at the Malden Tavern, a pub-restaurant in suburban Surrey. 'We mixed with the public, played with the public, travelled on the train with the public. They'd sometimes have a pint with us too.'

But as the sixties progressed the worlds of football and pop music became subtly intertwined. In 1965 beat poet Allen Ginsberg said Liverpool was 'at the present moment, the centre of consciousness of the human universe'. He was probably referring to The Beatles and the Mersey Poets Roger McGough, Brian Patten and Adrian Henri, but he may also have noticed Bill Shankly's Liverpool FC beating Don Revie's Leeds in the FA Cup Final. In any event the Cavern and the Kop were making the city a focus of global attention. Andrew Ward and John Williams wrote in their book *Football Nation*: 'The Kop had always been a noisy place. People shouted and roared and there was banter and bad language. In the early sixties, however, those noises changed. The Kop began to sing, and singing made the fan feel good. Music and football blended together on the Anfield Kop.'

The Kop famously fused quick-wittedness and pop songs. When an opposition winger collapsed, exhausted, into the arms of his trainer, the Kop sang, 'He loves you, yeah, yeah, yeah.' When Leeds keeper Gary Sprake threw the ball into his own net, the Kop serenaded him with Max Bygraves's current hit 'Careless Hands'.

By now, with TV cameras present and the minimum wage long past, footballers were becoming strangely glamorous creatures. In the case of George Best they even looked like pop stars. 'El Beatle', the Continental press dubbed him, after, aged nineteen, he had scored twice in a 1966 European Cup game against Benfica. He and Mike Summerbee of Manchester City both opened boutiques in the city. City fans would work the latter's name in a version of the Small Faces' 'Sha-La-La-La-Lee' that went 'Sha-la-la-la-Summerbee'. Koppites would turn 'Yellow Submarine' and many another Beatles' classic into terrace chants. And, most famously, in 1963, 'You'll Never Walk Alone' from *Carousel* was covered by Liverpool group Gerry and the Pacemakers and the Kop was filmed singing the tune by *Panorama*. By 1965, when Liverpool faced Leeds in that FA Cup final, match commentator Kenneth Wolstenholme remarked on the 'Liverpool signature tune'.

And yet only a year later England's victory in the World Cup was marked only by one rather risible ditty called 'World Cup Willie'. Through the seventies the hair grew more rock-starish, but football music still meant gormless if affectionately remembered songs, often sung badly by footballers themselves – 'Nice One, Cyril', 'Blue Is the Colour' or 'Back Home'. There were no footballing equivalents of Roy Harper's elegiac 'When an Old Cricketer Leaves the Crease'. Football was still seen as essentially brutish, philistine and deeply uncool, a view of the game taken by The Fall in their chilly, acerbic 'Kicker Conspiracy', where ' Under Marble Millichip, the FA broods/On how flair can be punished', a namecheck for the fabulously named seventies' footie commissar, Bert.

Things were about to change. In 1986 a small magazine called *When Saturday Comes* was launched, named after a song by The Undertones and billing itself with a very indie sense of self-deprecation as 'the Half Decent Football Magazine'. There was nothing like it around in the bleak, hooligan-haunted, underachieving world of eighties British football. As the *Guardian*'s Barney Ronay has pointed out:

There was no real mainstream football presence: in the broader media the game was usually portrayed as a kind of urban affliction ... Nobody expected the players to be role models or the face of a new range of edgy urban menswear, perhaps because they all looked like angry junior butchers. Football had been, by turns, assailed and ignored.

It was against this largely unanimous sense of righteous and hierarchically sanctioned alienation that *WSC* first emerged. It was a DIY-ish production, an echo along with its many fanzine contemporaries of the moment, ten years earlier, when punk musicians had decreed that lack of a recording contract, an instrument – and indeed talent – need no longer be an obstacle to getting yourself heard. Initially an offshoot of the music fanzine *Snipe*, this spiky, likeable, unashamedly cerebral football magazine struck a chord with an unexpectedly voracious audience.

It was a musical audience too. *When Saturday Comes* would run similar wry, informed pieces about long-forgotten indie bands alongside ones on long-forgotten centre-halves. It would talk of the Shay ground and Roots Hall as affectionately as the Northampton Roadmenders Club and Eric's. A revolution was underway. The five-year ban on English clubs in Europe imposed in the wake of the Heysel stadium riot was lifted and a year later Manchester United won the Cup Winners' Cup. A thaw was bringing a kind of football spring to Britain as a new decade dawned.

In 1990 the World Cup was held in Italy. Italia '90 was a poor affair as a football spectacle but it had a major cultural significance in Britain. It took place just as this football spring was bursting out across our national media and consciousness in a new-found sense of fun and intelligence, expressed by fancy dress and inflatables at grounds and a post-acid house peaceful hedonism.

The *NME* put football on the cover for the first time since it had profiled Pat Nevin as 'The First Post-Punk Footballer' almost a decade before when his love of The Smiths and Joy Division made him an oddity. Significantly, three former members of Joy Division, now the band New Order, had recorded the official England World Cup song for Italia '90. It was a revelation. Previously official football songs had been asinine knees-ups that had more in common with sitcom themes and novelty comedy records. This was a New Order record first and a football record second. In fact, as the black England international John Barnes stated in the song's rap section – itself a shock on several levels – 'We ain't no hooligans, this ain't a football song.' Significantly, on the chorus, Bernard Sumner told us it was love, not football, that had the world in motion, and the song had a remix called 'No Alla Violenza', a call for peace at matches taken from a hip T-shirt slogan seen in dance clubs.

England didn't win Italia '90. They went out on penalties in a semi-final best remembered for the tears of Paul Gascoigne. But the tournament marked a turning point for British football. Within a year a Frenchman called Eric Cantona had come to play for Leeds United and won them the First Division title. Cantona's flair, intelligence and attitude to training and technique made him very different from the typical British footballer of the past and a role model for a new generation. *Après Cantona, le déluge*; an influx of footballers from the Continent and beyond came, drawn by the glamour and rewards of the new Premier League. The nature of our national game was to change for ever. It has certainly globalised our football to a happy, almost comical degree. One of Sky Sports' anchorman Jeff Stelling's most famous one-liners celebrates the almost joyfully absurd juxtapositions this new-found cosmopolitanism has brought about: 'Darlington's equaliser has been scored by Guylain Ndumbu-Nsungu. Very much a case of local boy makes good.'

Premier League players may now come from all over the world but their musical tastes remain disappointingly dull and parochial. A 2005 album of Chelsea players' favourite songs was almost beyond parody, revealing Frank Lampard's home listening – Lionel Richie's 'Stuck on You' – while John Terry went for Luther Vandross's 'So Amazing'. Portuguese defender Ricardo Carvalho chose 'Fool's Gold' by The Stone Roses, who along with Oasis and The Smiths seem to be the officially sanctioned indie band it's OK for footballers to like. Ex-Manchester City footballer Joey Barton's fondness for The Smiths has convinced many to overlook his violent, criminal past and regard him as a troubled philosopher.

There may be a sociological reason why footballers traditionally like such similar, homogenised music. They lead very different lives from normal people. They rarely enjoy a regular adolescence since, from an early age, they're removed from school and placed in academies with other budding footballers, thus missing out on the normal teenage round of gigs, compilation tapes, under-the-bedclothes radio listening and the rest. These days, r&b and hip hop have replaced Vandross and Ritchie as, with the dizzying rise in players' incomes, footballers tend to relate to the bling culture espoused by the urban music entrepreneurs they admire, and even know.

'World in Motion' and 'Kicker Conspiracy' are the exceptions that prove the rule that music and football love each other, but it's the love that dare not speak its name and can't seem to express itself. Pop can learn something from the classical world here. Sir Edward Elgar cycled more than forty miles from Malvern to watch his beloved Wolverhampton Wanderers, something he had in common with Led Zeppelin's Robert Plant, and is commemorated with a plaque at Molineux. Dmitri Shostakovitch was a qualified referee and wrote a ballet about football. Hungarian composer Bohuslav Martinü wrote 'Half-Time, a Rondo for Large Orchestra' in 1925, and British contemporary composer Mark-Anthony Turnage includes a terrace chant in his orchestral piece 'Momentum', while Michael Nyman has produced several football scores, if you will, including one based around the commentaries of John Motson.

Pop music, though, still struggles to articulate its kinship with football in words. It ends up either clichéd and banal, like a post-match interview clotted with 'obviously's, 'over the moon's and 'as I said to the gaffer's, or surly and remote, like a millionaire teenage striker, sullen and silent, buried in his Dr Dre Beats headphones, or listening to the music of the ghetto in a car that costs more than the street he grew up in.

38. EBENEEZER GOODE

Stanley Cohen published *Folk Devils and Moral Panics* in 1972. As already noted, it was a landmark study in deviance, and a rare case of a sociologist's work crossing over into everyday popular culture. It chronicled how, from time to time, widespread fear over some youth cult had been stoked by rumour and hearsay to become utterly out of proportion to any real danger. Cohen drew parallels between the witch-hunts enacted during the chaos of the English Civil War and the hysteria over the mods' and rockers' seaside clashes of the mid-sixties. But a few years after Cohen's book hit the shelves, a new folk devil called Johnny Rotten leered out of every tabloid across the breakfast tables of an outraged, anxious Middle Britain; and a further decade on another moral panic gripped the UK – this time concerning a drug that been around, unnoticed, since the First World War but was now the engine of a new scene of repetitive beats and hedonistic zeal.

When Douglas Hurd became home secretary in the eighties he was told, he said, that 'a long heatwave meant trouble'. May 1989 was the hottest and driest May for 300 years, and for people like Douglas Hurd, bastions of the establishment, for whom summer indulgence meant perhaps Pimms on the members' roof terrace at Lords, what began to bloom that summer did indeed mean trouble. Others, though, would see the summer of 1989, which stretched into the new decade, as the wildest expression of generational solidarity since punk. All across Europe, borders were opening and walls were falling as the Soviet Union and its satellite states collapsed. But in Britain a sense of torpor seemed to have becalmed our youth culture. Champagne corks popped across the City, of course, but elsewhere our manufacturing base continued to crumble. But one factory at least was flourishing, churning out product day and night to satisfy a boom in sales.

Mel and Kim and Rick Astley, Sinitta and Roland Rat, Kylie Minogue and Jason Donovan … Stock, Aitken and Waterman's self-proclaimed Hit Factory had dominated the UK pop charts for the second half of the 1980s; a formulaic, relentlessly profit-driven, ruthlessly business-oriented concern that mirrored Berry Gordy's Motown in its methods if not, perhaps, in the quality of its output. Pete Waterman himself said that SAW represented, for some, 'the respectable face of capitalism'. Quite how respectable was a matter of debate. Although Waterman had been a Northern Soul DJ, although the SAW sound was rooted in hi-energy and although the groundbreaking sample-heavy club hit 'Pump Up the Volume' by MARRS had stolen a break from a SAW track, 'Roadblock', the triumvirat were deeply uncool with most opinion formers, loathed for their ubiquity, their supposed banality and their lowbrow populism. You could hear the processed fare from Stock, Aitken and Waterman's Hit Factory anywhere, they sneered, but the new dance sounds arriving from Chicago – house music, as it was called – had to be sought out, at least initially, through a network of clubs and

DJs that kept the music underground and word of mouth. To the casual observer, though, each was merely a different strand of pop dance, operating from the same basic template: songs about love and dancing, enjoyed by a weekend crowd of smart, casual city-nightclub enthusiasts. Each week on *The Hit Man and Her*, a cheap and cheerful late-night TV show intended to bring the nightclub experience into the living room, Waterman and co-host Michaela Strachan would play house, dance and club tunes to the clientele of Mr Smith's in Warrington or the Discothèque Royale in Manchester, a clientele stimulated by nothing stronger than Grolsch or Midori. That was about to change. The coming dance revolution would not be televised by *The Hit Man and Her*. It would not involve party games or hen nights, bouncers, bow ties or beer. It would look and sound very different, thanks in no small part to a small white pill.

MDMA, or to give it its Sunday name, 3,4-methylenedioxy-N-methamphetamine, was first synthesised during the First World War by a chemist called Anton Köllisch working for the German pharmaceutical giant Merck and interested in blood coagulants for the medical industry. But no one seems to have been interested in its recreational properties until the early 1970s when a chemist working at the University of California at Berkeley heard from his students of the unusual side-effects of MDMA. They reported feelings of relaxation, warmth and euphoria. One even said that it had cured his stutter. The chemist Alexander Shulgin tried some himself and soon became an occasional recreational user of what he called his 'low-calorie Martini'. When it became popular among the gay and dance clubs of Texas in the eighties it was known as Adam. But by the time it reached Britain and Europe in the late 1980s it had become known by a less cryptic name, a more straightforward acknowledgement of its effects. Ecstasy.

It wouldn't be right to say that ecstasy exploded on to the rave scene for the simple reason that there was no rave scene until ecstasy came along. Rave as a phenomenon – underground, faintly anarchistic, defiantly dayglo and non-smart casual – had ecstasy as its chemical turbine; it reduced inhibitions, heightened pleasure and turned those provincial beer boys from Mr Smith's and the Discothèque Royale into loved-up, loose-fit, lotus-eating, urban hippies. That is the received wisdom, at least.

But the roots of rave, a very British pop phenomenon, lie, misleadingly, in two decaying industrial cities on the Great Lakes and in the name of a different drug altogether.

'Acid Tracks' by Phuture, recorded in Chicago, Illinois, in 1987 is generally reckoned to be the first acid house record, an offshoot of the city's already booming house music scene. Acid house saw the melodic warmth of early house mutate into something darker and stranger: a bleached and minimal sound built around the unique squelching of the Roland TB 303 bass synthesiser. Acid, as in the slang for LSD, may refer to the disjointed, hallucinatory feel of the music; but it may also just be an attempt to evoke the twisted, corroded sounds – the icy, polar opposite of the lush, orchestrated sounds of disco and Philly that had once emerged from the clubs of the eastern seaboard. Detroit added its own electronic spin to the music, as heard in the techno tracks of Derrick May, Juan Atkins and Kevin Saunderson, whose hits with Inner City crossed the Atlantic on a wave of underground cool and nocturnal euphoria. The scene was set for what was to be called Britain's second summer of love, the summer of rave.

As we've noted, raving is a peculiarly British notion. Buddy Holly might have had a hit with 'Rave On', but the Texan was borrowing from the English. In the Middle Ages we talked of madmen raving, and the noun 'rave' had been used to describe illicit or wild gatherings in Soho in the 1950s. By the 1960s the Small Faces were referring approvingly of themselves as 'ravers' in 'Lazy Sunday Afternoon' and by the 1970s the 'right little raver', a dolly bird of hedonistic bent, was a fantasy figure of the overheated middle-aged imaginations of Reg Varney in *On the Buses* and Syd James in the *Carry On* films. Had they made *Carry On Abroad* in 1988 rather than 1972 they might have encountered something stronger than lager and lime on their package holiday to Spain. It was in the clubs of Ibiza, like Pasha and Amnesia, that many British clubbers first encountered not only the sound of acid house, the so-called Balearic beats, but also ecstasy. Some argue that, even back then, you could spot the hugely unfashionable package-holiday influence on the stylings of rave: baggy clothes, shorts, bandannas, smileys, shades – the type of gear that certainly wouldn't get you past the rope and 'security' in Warrington, Wakefield or Wigan. Not yet, anyway.

The rave look was somewhere between Timmy Mallett and Andy Pandy, and involved a rich strain of kitschy and surreal childhood nostalgia. In the same way that a dreamy, hallucinogenic nursery whimsy permeated the first summer of love in 1967 – Edward Lear, Lewis Carroll, scarecrows, picture books, nursery rhymes; *The Piper at the Gates of Dawn, Sgt Pepper, Ogdens' Nut Gone Flake* – so the early ravers regressed to their own seventies' childhoods. By the time the Ibizan ravers flew back to Manchester Ringway or Heathrow, they not only dressed like toddlers on holiday, they listened to tracks like The Prodigy's 'Charly', a manic rave version of a fondly remembered seventies public information film featuring a small boy and his mildly annoying cat.

The look was new, the sound was new, the drugs and the venues were new; and it was these latter two factors that brought the peaceful, non-boozy, beatific vibe of rave into direct conflict with the authorities. The new dance parties eschewed the sticky carpets, cloakrooms and overpriced bars of the traditional urban club night. Music writer John McReady captured perfectly just how different it all was in the *Observer*:

> It wasn't like anything you'd ever experienced in a club before. The clubs we'd been to previously were full of apprentices in pressed white shirts on the pull. Girls were huddled in groups like disorientated wildebeest. At the Haçienda it was almost as if a generation breathed a sigh of relief, having been relieved of the pressure of the chase. The baggy clothes de-sexualised the whole environment. The rising heat from two thousand people dancing, even at the bar, in the queue for the toilets, damped down everyone. We all looked crap.

As the crowds grew bigger and less conventional, so did the venues. Raves were held in car parks and warehouses, or in rural settings like barns and aircraft hangars. Sometimes these would be legal and licensed affairs, but more often not. Many of the parties took place around the outer regions of the M25, London's orbital motorway, which became nicknamed the Magic Roundabout. Techno/rave duo Orbital also took their name from the motorway. Information about these raves was spread quickly and clandestinely via a bush telegraph of pirate radio, phone numbers and secret flyers so as not to alert the police. The cloak-and-dagger nature of it all was an important part of the thrill of raving.

As indeed was another illegal element of the rave culture: ecstasy or E, now widely and cheaply available in the UK, was absolutely integral to the rave scene. According to its advocates it transformed what were merely late-night dance parties into almost tribal expressions of love, solidarity and self-expression. 'Es are good,' implied the new generation. And then in 1992, a dance act called The Shamen sang it.

Compared to the great euphoric pioneering tunes to come out of the rave and acid house scene – A Guy Called Gerald's 'Voodoo Ray', Phuture's 'Acid Tracks', LFO's 'LFO', Rhythim is Rhythim's 'Strings of Life' or numerous other great techno tunes from Detroit – 'Ebeneezer Goode' was pretty ordinary fare: a novelty-ish pop dance record with contrived lyrics full of arch jokes and rhyming slang delivered in a mockney Dickensian, geezerish way by one Mr C. It purports to be the tale of one Ebeneezer Goode – 'A gentleman of leisure/He's there for your pleasure' – but clearly the fictitious titular 'Eezer' is merely there to allow the chanted refrain of 'Eezer Goode, Eezer Goode' – an 'oo-err, Missus' allusion to the joys of ecstasy.

With its chortled asides 'Ebeneezer Goode' was always far too close to *Minder*, Mike Reid and Chas and Dave for many a listener, this one included. But, amazingly, given its cheesy knockabout silliness, that heavy-handed play on words in the chorus provoked the ire of ... well, the professionally provoked. Newspapers frothed; the record was initially banned by the BBC; certain stations refused to air the video unedited; and on *Top of the Pops* Mr C was told to tone down the supposed drug allusions. Despite, or perhaps because of all this, 'Ebeneezer Goode' climbed to number one, ironically during the BBC's drug awareness week.

Behind such Punch and Judy-ish fun and games real battle lines were being drawn between the forces of the state and this new youth culture; a battle that had pop music at its very heart. Widespread confrontations had taken place between police and ravers at illegal parties. Things had come to a head earlier in the same summer 'Ebeneezer Goode' topped the charts, during a week-long rave and free festival at Castlemorton Common in the Malvern Hills. Concerned over the growth of the rave movement and its links with the more politicised anarcho-crusty new-age travellers, a coming folk devil of the British media, the government decided to act.

In 1994, Conservative home secretary Michael Howard passed the Criminal Justice and Public Order Act, a piece of legislation seemingly directly targeted at outlawing rave culture. Sections 63, 64 and 65 stated that a 'rave' was defined as a gathering of 100 people or more, at which amplified music was played in the open air and at night. Police were given the power to order people to leave the land if they were believed to be: preparing to hold a rave (two or more people), waiting for a rave to start (ten or more) or actually attending a rave (ten or more). Ignoring this direction, or returning to the land within the next week, were both offences, liable to three months' imprisonment and/or a £2,500 fine. Section 65 allowed any uniformed constable who believed a person was on their way to a rave (within a five-mile radius) to stop them and direct them away from the area.

The Act defined 'music' as 'sounds wholly or predominantly characterised by the emission of a succession of repetitive beats' – a notorious definition which seemed so culturally specific, so subjectively defined to demonise rave (as opposed to, say, Glyndebourne), as to be laughable and clearly drafted in haste – Castlemorton had clearly sparked a major moral panic.

Many musicians found the legislation risible and responded in kind. Electronica act Autechre printed a 'Warning' on their next EP, 'Anti': ' "Lost" and "Djarum" contain repetitive beats. We advise you not to play these tracks if the Criminal Justice Bill becomes law. "Flutter" has been programmed in such a way that no bars contain identical beats and can therefore be played at both forty-five and thirty-three revolutions under the proposed new law. However, we advise DJs to have a lawyer and a musicologist present at all times to confirm the non-repetitive nature of the music in the event of police harassment.' A mix on Orbital's *Are We Here?* EP was titled 'Criminal Justice Bill?' It consisted of nearly four minutes of silence.

When, in 1995, Essex schoolgirl Leah Betts died after taking one ecstasy tablet in the family home another wave of moral panic grew up around the drug. However, even the notoriously conservative *Daily Mail* later advised caution. As Deborah Hutton put it in the paper's *You* magazine:

> Bad reactions from a single ecstasy pill are still exceedingly rare ... it is nearly always mismanagement (heatstroke as in the case of the recent London fatalities, or excessive water intake in the case of Leah Betts) that's to blame ... After fifteen years, the number of deaths from this drug is still in the order of dozens rather than hundreds. Our perceptions are skewed by the huge shock-horror headlines accorded to every ecstasy death ... By current estimates, around a million pills are being swallowed every weekend, which makes the risk of dying from a single ecstasy tablet even smaller than being struck by lightning or, perhaps, winning a substantial prize on the lottery.

Whatever the pros and cons, the Criminal Justice Bill was the nail in the coffin of the large-scale free event and, arguably, rave culture in general. The Act is still on the statute book today, and in 2009 was used by police to shut down a birthday barbecue in Exeter, held on legal property for fifteen people. The Shamen never had another sizeable hit and in 2012 Colin Angus of The Shamen said, '"Ebeneezer ..." was intended to be celebratory and cautionary, like holding up a distorting mirror to rave culture. The song went ballistic: Uncle Ebeneezer is still looking after me to this day.'

Why did rave grip Britain so fiercely in its manic, loved-up bearhug back in the early nineties? Then, and now, two trains of thought exist. If you were there, maybe you thought that it was a collective reaction to rampant consumerism and individualism – a world where Margaret Thatcher could say there was 'no such thing as society'. Instead of the ceaseless lust for money and power, rave celebrated empathy and intimacy; a kind of spirituality – the joys of sharing powerful feelings with your fellow humans.

Or perhaps, as Jarvis Cocker wondered aloud in Pulp's melancholic meditation on the comedown to a rave, 'Sorted for Es and Wizz', was it perhaps just an excuse to take drugs, drink, dance and get out of it for while with your mates? An experience that will ultimately leave you with an empty, hollow feeling, asking, as Cocker does, 'Is this the way they say the future's meant to feel?/ Or just twenty thousand people standing in a field?'

39. THINGS CAN ONLY GET BETTER

In the spring of 1971 a bright young student left his Scottish public school Fettes with two As and a C in his A-levels and decided, in a move rather ahead of its time, to take the then unheard of notion of a gap year to further his ambitions as a mover and shaker in the rock world. The music biz was something of a common ambition for young men in the late sixties and early seventies and unsurprisingly little came of it for our student. For a while he ran a rock promotions and management agency with a friend. Then, following a largely unsuccessful year putting on gigs that, at 20p a ticket, mainly attracted scoolchilden, he took a place at Oxford and centre stage as singer with a band called Ugly Rumours, named after a bit of graffiti on a Grateful Dead album sleeve.

Ugly Rumours only ever played six gigs, and now those are chiefly remembered for lead singer Anthony's swaggering Jagger impersonation during their stand-out cover of The Stones' '(I Can't Get No) Satisfaction'.

Ugly Rumours never made it. Not in the sense of record sales and huge success anyway. But they did achieve a kind of global fame. In 1997 singer Tony sent bassist Mark Ellen, by now a famous magazine editor and broadcaster, a postcard saying, 'Well, I guess we made it after all.' Ugly Rumours had finally become big because of what Tony had done next. Having failed to become the new Mick Jagger, he had done the next best thing: become prime minister of the United Kingdom.

Nearly two decades before that postcard was sent, in late 1978, Labour Prime Minister James Callaghan made the political miscalculation that would keep his party out of office for a generation. Had he called an election right then, he might well have won and Margaret Hilda Thatcher might have been destined to be a historical footnote, the shrill *hausfrau* education secretary who took away free school milk and then unexpectedly was elected leader of her party briefly and unsuccesfully rather than one of the most significant political figures of the century and the first female leader of a world power. Instead, over the next few months a wave of industrial action gripped the UK. Lorry and tanker drivers, ambulance workers, health service staff, refuse collectors and gravediggers all struck. Rubbish piled in the streets and the dead lay unburied in mortuaries. The UK was still battling with its 'winter of discontent' when Callaghan returned from an economic forum on the tropical island of Guadaloupe. He looked tanned and relaxed when an *Evening Standard* journalist asked him how he was going to deal with 'the mounting chaos in the country at the moment'.

His actual response was, 'Well, that's a judgement that you are making. I promise you that if you look at it from outside ... I don't think that other people in the world would share the view that there is "mounting chaos".' But, in a stroke of genius, and displaying an admirable familiarity with soft prog rock, he recast his reply by quoting the title of a recent Supertramp album. 'Crisis? What crisis?' was to become James Callaghan's political epitaph.

When the Scottish National Party (SNP) withdrew support for the Scotland Act, 1978, a vote of no confidence was held and passed by one vote on 28 March 1979, forcing Callaghan to call a general election and thus exposing his miscalculation in not going to the country sooner. 'Labour isn't working' claimed the famous Saatchi and Saatchi election poster for the Conservatives, and it seemed the public agreed. There was a huge swing to the Tories, the biggest since 1945, and Margaret Thatcher was swept to power.

Labour were to remain in opposition for almost two decades. Two decades of change and stasis, war and peace, boom and bust, all reflected elsewhere in the people's songs. Labour licked its wounds and convulsed itself in paroxysms of self-destruction. Michael Foot and the Militant Tendency made it largely unelectable for most of the next five years. Neil Kinnock and Roy Hattersley came in as leader and deputy on a so-called 'dream ticket' but they too failed to unseat the Tories. Gerald Kaufman, a Labour MP, described the party's hard left 1983 manifesto as 'the longest suicide note in history'. The Tories breezed through the 1987 election largely unscathed and when, a week before the 1992 general election, with Labour leading in the polls, the opposition decided to hold a huge, glitzy political rally at the Sheffield Arena, modelled along American lines, with much hoopla, waving of placards, celebrity endorsements, a light show and Labour's shadow cabinet welcomed to the stage by an adoring throng numbering some 10,000, Neil Kinnock commandeered the mic and began shouting, 'We're all right!! We're all right!' It looked to many voters liked ill-placed triumphalism. Kinnock later rejected the idea that this hubristic event lost them the election ('bloody rubbish') but it was unquestionably the kind of party you should hold after you've won. Of course, they didn't. Kinnock resigned, and the soul-searching went on.

Enter the Prince of Darkness, one Peter Mandelson, grandson of legendary wartime Labour cabinet minister, Herbert Morrison. Suave, astute and Machiavellian, there are many anecdotes about his saturnine and secretive ways, but here's one I can vouch for. I was once at a Westminster function when Mandelson came over and began to gently berate a journalist friend of mine for perpetuating this image of him as a shady manipulator, a Svengali pulling strings behind the scenes. 'I'm just a normal constituency MP and activist, doing what I can for –' At this point Mandelson's mobile phone went off. He answered normally, but clearly there was significant and sensitive news being imparted. His brows furrowed. He glanced at us, turned half away and in an icy whisper said, 'This must be suppressed.'

One thing not even Mandelson could have foreseen was the unexpected death of the Labour leader, John Smith, from a heart attack in 1994. He'd laid the foundations of a new Labour Party – one that explicitly called itself New Labour, in fact. A new star was waiting in the wings: that former Ugly Rumours Jagger-a-like and failed rock entrepreneur Anthony Charles Lynton Blair.

The rest is history. And several competing volumes of memoirs. And at least one TV drama. But on 1 May 1997 there was only triumph. Two hours after polls closed – with the early results indicating a landslide – Tony Blair, mindful of past mistakes, ordered supporters in the Royal Festival Hall to stop celebrating for fear of appearing complacent or 'triumphalist'. But it was hard to put a stop to the party. And the music that blared out, chanted lustily by young activists and old warhorses, volunteers and future cabinet ministers alike, was a catchy if faintly cheesy four-year-old dance-pop hit whose hands-in-the-air optimism had its origins in an altogether different political process in the divided cities of Northern Ireland.

D:Ream's singer Peter Cunnah grew up in Derry and formed a pop group called Tie the Boy with three schoolmates who put out an independent single before being signed to U2's Mother label. Cunnah said later, 'Being in Tie the Boy was magic. There was so little in the town at that time. Kids were wandering the streets; some left Derry entirely, others joined the IRA. We stayed and made music. It was the best rite of passage anyone could have. We did the single ourselves, out of complete frustration, as there was no other way to get it done. That entire scene had been atomised by the troubles.'

Ironically, one member of the band, Gerry Diver, later went on to become mayor of Derry. Tie the Boy soon fizzled out, however, and Cunnah moved to London where he threw himself into the club and house scene and formed D:Ream with a DJ called Al Mackenzie. The so-called 'handbag house' sound of M People, Sub Sub and the ilk was then popular on radio and on the dance floor, and D:Ream's blandly anthemic, catchily uplifting material was perfect for the times. One song, 'Things Can Only Get Better', became a huge hit at the end of 1993.

But 'Things Can Only Get Better' gained its place in history when it was chosen as New Labour's campaign anthem for the 1997 election. America has had campaign songs for as long as it has had political campaigns – George Washington's supporters belted out 'God Save Great Washington' in the spring of 1790 and John Quincy Adams commissioned an original song mocking his opponents, before the most famous original campaign song of all time arrived in 1952: Irving Berlin's 'I Like Ike' – but in our modern rock era no one used a campaign song more effectively than Bill Clinton's adoption of Fleetwood Mac's 'Don't Stop'. Though the soft-rock staple was two decades old by the time Bill Clinton personally chose it for his 1992 campaign, it was the perfect marriage between song and candidate. The lyrics brimmed with buoyancy and optimism and, even better, Fleetwood Mac, the AOR giants that gave us *Rumours*, were favourites with the boomer generation whose vote he was courting.

Nobel laureate Toni Morrison said that sax-playing Clinton was America's first black president. Tony Blair was certainly Britain's first rock prime minister. Ten years younger than his predecessor, John Major, who belonged to an era of Bournvita, Denis Compton and *Two Way Family Favourites*, Blair was clearly a child of the sixties, of The Beatles and The Stones, *Oz* and Tariq Ali, crashpads and student sit-ins. As he entered Downing Street early on the morning of 2 May 1997 as prime minister, he said, 'A new dawn has broken, has it not?'

That new dawn came to be known as 'Cool Britannia', an exciting and overdue renaissance in our national cultural vigour – or a shallow and illusory orgy of vapid pride and self-satisfaction over trivia, depending on your point of view. With its emphasis on youth, pop culture and the stereotypically British iconography of Union Jacks, London and the like, it was an obvious harking back to the mood and style of the swinging sixties. Even the phrase 'Cool Britannia' was first used in a Bonzo Dog Doo-Dah Band track of 1967. Later, it was often yoked with another phrase.

Britpop was first used, by me it seems, in a *Select* magazine cover story of 1993, bemoaning the lumpen nature of grunge culture and celebrating what I saw as a new mood of verve, wit and glamour in the sound and look of fledgling bands like Pulp, Blur and Suede.

Cool Britannia came to mean more than just pop music; it came to include fashion designers like Alexander McQueen and Stella McCartney (whose dad, of course, had been a prime mover of the first 1960s cool Britannia). It came to mean the Young British Artists movement of Damien Hirst and Tracey Emin; and the feelgood rom-coms of Richard Curtis, whom actor Rupert Everett said in his memoirs was to Blair's Britain what Leni Riefenstahl was to Hitler's Germany.

As if to prove his credentials as the first rock prime minister, within his first few years in office Blair invited the following to stay at Chequers: Sting, Elton John, Bono, David Bowie, Bob Geldof, Mick Hucknall, Richard Branson and Cilla Black.

The most public display of New Labour's courting of the celebrity and entertainment worlds was the reception held at Downing Street on 30 July 1997 for stars from the worlds of music, fashion, the arts and sport. Some of the images of that evening remain indelibly associated with Blair's early years: the smiling, youthful prime minister shaking hands and laughing with members of Blur, Noel Gallagher of Oasis, and Alan McGee, the man who discovered them. This may well have been Blair's way of making a clear break with the past eighteen years of conservatism; cultivating links with the creative industries rather than furthering the obsession with financial, industrial and legal spheres that had dominated political thinking for decades. But the lasting impression for the cynics was of a government obsessed with spin and surface rather than substance.

Two of the bands invited that night, Blur and Oasis, had come to embody Britpop. Like their peers, Suede and Pulp, and to a lesser extent fellow travellers like Sleeper, Elastica, Supergrass, Echobelly and Menswear, their music was a deliberate reconnecting with classic

British bands from The Kinks and T. Rex to The Jam and Wire – and the classic British pop values of economy and pep, smartness and intelligence – with an eye on both working-class street style and art-school modernism. Britpop declared an uneasy truce between the latter two, and it was at its uneasiest in the relationship between Britpop's two biggest bands.

The roots of Oasis's and Blur's rivalry may lie in obscure personal grievances, but things caught fire when Oasis's guitarist Noel Gallagher said in an interview that hoped members of Blur died of AIDS. Soon, a drooling press had talked up the spat into a clash of cultures and geography, with Blur as ciphers for the suburban South and Oasis for the streetwise North. In truth, it was just that Oasis were the kind of young men in bands who'd been saying stupid things since time immemorial. Though more sanguine about the whole thing, Blur rose to the fight by deliberately scheduling their next single, 'Country House', for release the same day as the new Oasis single, 'Roll with It', thus ensuring a clear popularity poll. A kind of minor national madness ensued, with the contest covered not just in the music press but on major news bulletins and current affairs shows. *NME* proclaimed, 'Yes, in a week where news leaked that Saddam Hussein was preparing nuclear weapons, everyday folks were still getting slaughtered in Bosnia, and Mike Tyson was making his comeback, tabloids and broadsheets alike went Britpop crazy.'

Blur won the battle of the bands, selling 274,000 copies to Oasis's 216,000, the songs charting at number one and number two respectively. Ironically 'Country House' and 'Roll with It' are two of the weakest songs in either band's catalogue, and it was while filming the crass Damien Hirst-directed video for 'Country House' that Graham Coxon began to think seriously of quitting the band. But both records still supply the flavour of those heady and ridiculous times: a silly, shallow but necessarily heady and brazen antidote to the dour monochrome era that had gone before, the grey anonymity of the Major years. In the end Blur would outlive New Labour and Oasis – just – and Britpop, Blair and Cool Britannia would become a piece of history ripe for revisiting in books just like this – one of those moments when pop music echoes through the corridors of power and pop singers have the ear of the powerful who walk them.

40. CIGARETTES & ALCOHOL

'Lad'; noun: a boisterously macho or high-spirited young man, first noted around 1300; 'ladde': a 'foot soldier' or 'young male servant'. The origin of the word is Scandinavian from the Norwegian for a stocking, which would be appropriate as, with the emphasis on pillage, rampage, binge-drinking and berserking, there's something vaguely Viking about the notion of laddishness. But 'stocking'? Well, here's a thing: the linguist Mark Liberman derives 'lad' from the Old Norse *ladd*, as in 'hose, or woollen stocking' adding, 'Words for socks, stockings, and shoes seem to have been terms of abuse for and nicknames of fools.'

So a fool, then, with a hint of mayhem and an appetite for the hard stuff and the wild life. Is it my imaginayshy-un, or does that sound like a template for the modern rock lad, that football-loving, beer-drinking, parka- and Perry-clad monster that pimp-rolled his way into our consciousness at the tail end of the twentieth century?

Upon first hearing 'Cigarettes & Alcohol' by Oasis, the man who discovered the band, Alan McGee, claimed that the song was one of the greatest social statements anyone had made in the previous twenty-five years. Alan McGee often used to say things like this, which was part of his charm. He had been putting out records independently for over a decade on his own Creation label, set up with money from his dad's redundancy cheque as a panel-beater in Glasgow. In the beginning Creation had specialised in rather fey, jangly guitar fare. But there had always been a darker mood of dissolution and excess swirling around the Creation camp and, as the eighties gave way to the nineties, so McGee and his charges such as Primal Scream had embraced the hedonism of the new club culture to an alarming degree. By the time he first heard Oasis on a midweek night in a poorly attended Glasgow club, he was maybe ready for something new, or rather something as old as rock and roll itself.

As manifestos go 'Cigarettes & Alcohol' is no *Das Kapital* or *Quotations of Chairman Mao* but its effect was just as electrifying on its own putative constituency. 'Is it worth the aggravation/To find yourself a job when there's nothing worth working for?'. Lairy, lazy, loud, here in a nutshell were the guiding principles of that very British nineties' phenomenon, the New Lad.

'Jack the lad', 'one of the lads', *The Likely Lads*, 'lads' night out', 'Britain loves a lad' ... the notion of the lovable rogue and the cheeky chappie reaches far back into our entertainment culture, to Mr Punch and the porter in *Macbeth*, drunkenly making knob gags in the midst of murder. The original Cheeky Chappie was Max Miller: a flashily dressed comic turn whose *risqué* material delighted audiences primarily in the South of England. The North had a different kind of cheeky chappie in George Formby, a more vulnerable and hapless type, a kind of underdog, but nevertheless one with a twinkling eye for the ladies and a popular line in priapic, smutty ditties.

During the 1950s and 1960s, while rock and pop stars honed and developed images increasingly based around brooding sexuality and mystique, it was left to the likes of the *Carry On* films and, later in the 1970s, Robin Askwith's dire *Confessions* series to celebrate the lad – even if, in the case of Sid James, it was a lad in his fifties who really ought to have been taking women somewhere nice for dinner or back to his flat rather than for a furtive snog in a Dormobile.

In the seventies, sociologists like Dick Hebdige argued that skinheads, further harbingers of laddishness, were trying to make their cultural mark by rejecting the soft, peaceable, floral femininity of the hippy and the intellectualism of prog – instead celebrating coarse, aggressive, hedonistic, old-school blue-collar masculinity; the no-nonsense machismo of the factory floor, the building site and the salon bar. Even the clothes were borrowed from the workshop and the warehouse: short hair, workboots, belts and braces.

The skins and the suedeheads appropriated the music of Jamaica for their anthems, tracks like Symarip's 'Skinhead Moonstomp', infectious, rhythmic and loutish.

And these lusty lads had their own literature too, through the pages of the New English Library. Richard Allen, or James Moffat to give him his real name, wrote a slew of exploitative pulp novels at the time: *Skinhead*, *Suedehead*, *Mod Rule*, the seventies equivalent of the penny dreadfuls in many ways, based around the culture of skinheads, suedeheads, bootboys and bikers, many featuring the anti-hero Joe Hawkins. The books ooze both a loathing and a grudging respect for the violence of these ultra-lads and throb with a hatred for all things liberal and left. Sexist, racist and politically suspect, they are in many ways nasty little books. But every schoolyard in the 1970s did a roaring trade in them, a fact Morrissey must have been nodding to when he named his début solo single 'Suedehead' in 1988.

As we've noted before, for all its belligerence, punk was in many ways an intellectual movement. It was anarchistic, not conservative, and defied race and gender barriers. Most of its principal players saw themselves as revolutionaries, not rank and file: they abhorred the workaday, and mocked the man in the street. Sid Vicious even said of him 'I've met the man in the street ... and he's a c**t.'

But there was something of the lad about it all, and some of the early punk bands used the proletarian vigour of the music to soundtrack the hopes and frustrations of working-class kids not in spitting distance of art schools or the squat politics of Ladbroke Grove. Chief among these were Sham 69, whose Jimmy Pursey was the likeable laureate of laddish punk. Their album *That's Life* is that rarity, a punk concept album. It's the story of one day in the life of a lower-class everyman – from breakfast to bookies to boozer, through losing his job along the way, then on to the nightclub and a council-estate hangover – a kind of safety-pinned *Saturday Night and Sunday Morning* that, in 'Hurry Up, Harry', gave the nation a hymn to lad culture before we even knew the phrase.

The odd punk sing-along aside, overt displays of crass masculinity had become deeply uncool by the time the seventies glided into the eighties. 'Medallion man' was a term of mockery for the wannabe stud with his fake tan and chest foliage that you could find in city-centre discos, while 'beer monster', 'lager lout' or, in Scotland, 'Ned' were abusive terms for low-life, unreconstructed males. There were no lad role models comparable to David Sylvian, Bryan Ferry or David Bowie.

Bowie had predicated his image and career on sexual ambivalence and androgyny. From 'Starman' onwards his appearance – the kimonos, make-up and snow-white tan – had been about as far from our modern notion of the lad as is imaginable. But Bowie's witty 'Boys Keep Swinging' is one of the best, most tongue-in-cheek pop celebrations of young maleness; one that asserts the joys of being a boy while playing with stereotypes and teasing the listener. 'When you're a boy,' sings Bowie, 'Clothes always fit ya/ [you can] Learn to drive and everything,' and, of course, 'Other boys check you out.'

'I do not feel that there is anything remotely glorious about being either male or female. I was merely playing on the idea of the colonisation of gender,' Bowie said later, in a very David Bowie kind of way.

Wham!'s 'Bad Boys' was altogether more earnest. After a run of absurdly great singles, they attempted an anthem of revolt, a sort of white funk *Rebel without a Cause*, which, addressing 'Mummy and Daddy' ends up sounding just clunky and petulant:

> *Don't try to keep me in tonight,*
> *Because I'm big enough to break down the door*

As the ever-acerbic Julie Burchill pointed out, if he felt like that, what the hell was he still doing living at home anyway at nineteen? Move out and get a flat, bad boy. We should point out that George Michael was only nineteen himself when he wrote the song, and was later hugely embarrassed by it, calling it 'an albatross round my neck' and removing it from future greatest hits collections.

Around this time, the concept of the 'new man' began to enter the discussion. New men, the theory went, were caring, in touch with their feelings, unchauvinistic, supportive and progressive. And while all of these were undoubtedly admirable and to be encouraged, the idea of the new man was ridiculed right from the off. The final nail in its coffin came in the 1990s when its nemesis, a rough beast in a replica football top with all The Jam albums, slouched into the limelight.

It's tempting to see the birth of lad culture in that moment in 1991 when, at the Edinburgh Festival, the prestigious Perrier Award went to one Frank Skinner, a working-class Black Country comic about as far removed from Ben Elton as one could imagine. (At least on the surface – Skinner is a devout Catholic and A.E. Housman fan, a more complex figure than one might think.) In a 1993 article for the old-school men's magazine *Arena*, still preoccupied with ideal dates, jet-skiing and brogues, Sean O'Hagan talked of the 'New Lad'. And a new sitcom was taking off: *Men Behaving Badly* featured Martin Clunes and Neil Morrissey being drunk, immature and mildly lascivious while their long-suffering girlfriends rolled their eyes in despair.

As writer Michael Bracewell put it in a 1996 edition of *Frieze* magazine,

> Women, faced with lads, are supposed to raise their eyes to heaven in mock despair, thus becoming matriarchal figures who grant their grudgingly but secretly amused blessing ('Boys will be boys!') to the sealed male world of laddism. As a heterosexual construct, in which men become little boys with adult desires, and women become their passive but sexually available mothers, laddism is straight from the darker chapters of a psychoanalyst's hand-book.

Enter *Loaded* magazine, the brainchild of the young and energetic Yorkshireman and former fanzine editor who had already shaken up a moribund *NME* by bringing in new writers, encouraging humour and irreverence and championing new Northern guitar bands.

Scenting the wind of change, James Brown's next venture, with the backing of IPC magazines, was what modern business parlance would call a 'game changer'. *Loaded* was launched with the subtitle 'for men who ought to know better', which immediately captured the knowing nature of the enterprise. Whatever horrors it unleashed, *Loaded* was smart and different and both rode and reflected the new mood. Gary Oldman, cigarette between his lips, was the first cover star, and Brown's first editorial ran:

> What fresh lunacy is this? *Loaded* is a new magazine dedicated to life, liberty and the pursuit of sex, drink, football and less serious matters. *Loaded* is music, film, relationships, humour, travel, sport, hard news and popular culture. *Loaded* is clubbing, drinking, eating, playing and eating. *Loaded* is for the man who believes he can do anything, if only he wasn't hungover.

Eighteen months after its launch, in the autumn of 1995, *Loaded* was the bestselling man's magazine in Britain, and put an oikish-looking type from Burnage, south Manchester, wearing a Ben Sherman on its cover. How much *Loaded* had changed the world of men's magazines is obvious from this alone. Once upon a time no one this patently laddish and ordinary would have been allowed anywhere near a style magazine cover. Afterwards, slightly grudgingly, these magazines would have to sully their hands with football, fanciable TV presenters and Northern rock groups.

That oik was Noel Gallagher. The rise of his band Oasis had been has swift as that of *Loaded* and freighted with the same kinds of cultural meaning. They'd been discovered playing to a tiny midweek crowd in Glasgow club King Tut's Wah Wah Hut by the indie label boss of Creation Records, Alan McGee, who later recalled the fateful evening to the *Independent*'s David Pollock:

> There were about twelve people there. I was there with my kid sister. I'd had four or five double Jack Daniel's and Coke so I was pretty drunk, and they played one song and I thought, 'This is great.' But then I thought, 'Oh, I'm drunk and I'm drugged.' But then they played another and that was great and another and I thought, 'I'm going to do it.' So when they came off they were hanging around and I said, 'I'm Alan McGee. Do you want a record deal?' And he gave me a demo tape and I said, 'I don't need a demo tape. You can have a record deal.'

'Cigarettes & Alcohol' was Oasis's fourth single from their début album *Definitely Maybe*, and peaked at number seven. It was written, as was the bulk of their material, by Noel Gallagher, though with a heavy debt to T. Rex's 'Get It On', and sung by brother Liam. The sleeve is practically a manifesto for this new laddism. There's a great deal of the two titular subjects, bottles of champagne and beer held aloft like football trophies or proffered with 'D'you want some?' bravado. Liam sits on the floor sullenly pulling on a B&H like he was back round smokers' corner at secondary school, shielding his precious tab from the wind. The clothes are all tracksuits and football casuals. Tellingly, there are two women present, but they are purely decorative; one lounges on a bed for the band's amusement, another seems to be making an earnest, inept attempt to play the guitar.

The genuine friction between the two siblings was at the heart of Oasis's undoubted feral appeal. Older and wiser head Noel said of his captivating frontman brother to *Mojo* in 1994:

We actually do not get on. Except that we're members of the same band. At the moment it's quite funny, but if it's like this in two years we'll have to put a stop to it. Our kid's not got the faintest idea what's going on, not a clue. I think that's so cool. He's fresh. He'll be one of the greats because he doesn't know. He's not trying to be a rock star. Brett Anderson and the rest of them can't hold a candle to him. He'll upset loads of people and just carry on and not give a damn. I just leave him to it. I give him the songs and say, Right, sing that and keep out of my way.

Candidly and compellingly Liam told *The Face*:

I'm on fire inside. I'm just getting to know myself, and there's things I don't like. Parts of me are evil, parts of me are good, but I'm locked up in chains so I can't get it all out. But I opened the doors in my head, threw the key away and let it all in: madness, badness, evilness, goodness, beautifulness … It's like that Guinness advert, my head – a universe in a glass.

1995 was the zenith of lad culture, but there are some who would argue that it has been with us ever since, in some form or other, and not for the better. It could be argued that it has left a legacy of uniform blokeishness between men, replacing the great turbine of generational conflict that brought us so much great music and art with stadiums of fathers and sons, lads together in their replica tops who enjoy the same music, sport and TV comedies.

More seriously, it has left us with a legacy like the worst excesses of those comedies: bullying misogyny masquerading as wit on TV panel shows; phenomena such as the odious Uni Lad website, a nasty platform for rape jokes and vicious sexism among male students. And, of course, all of this can be waved away as 'banter' should anyone – a woman, for instance – rightly object.

Boys will be boys; perhaps that is part of our charm. Whether we need to be lads is quite another matter.

41. WANNABE

In the spring of 1997 even the most loyal and committed Conservative probably knew that the curtain was coming down on almost two decades of Tory government in Britain. But there was still time for brave words and a few volleys of electoral bravado. On 4 March chancellor Kenneth Clarke gave a speech outlining his fiscal objectives that was less memorable for what he said than how he said it. 'I'll tell you what I want, what I really, really want,' said the portly, clubbable, jazz-loving, Hush-Puppied chancellor. 'I want to see healthy sustainable growth and rising living standards for the next five years. No one wants a return of the late 1980s – and not just because they never want to hear another Bros record or see another yellow Porsche.'

It's not the rather odd reference to yellow Porsches that leaps out here. It's that striking first phrase. Healthy sustainable growth is probably what Chancellor Ken did want. But did he really, really want it? And, by extension, did he really, really, really want to zigazig, ah?

It was one of those doomed, toe-curling attempts at appearing to be regular, down to earth, fashionable even, that politicians of every stripe are prone to: William Hague's teenage beer consumption; Nick Clegg's romantic conquests; Gordon Brown's love of the Arctic Monkeys; David Cameron: Smiths fan. Ken's gambit, or his speechmakers', had been to try to curry favour with the electorate by showing his familiarity with the works of Ginger, Sporty, Scary, Baby and Posh, the gang of five who were holding the balance of power – girl power – in late-nineties Britain.

Of all the ideas, concepts and slogans that pop music has lobbed into modern life, one of the most contentious must be 'girl power', the one that the Spice Girls came brandishing as they launched their assault on the charts and our consciousness in 1996. Almost immediately there were those of both genders who mocked and derided it, from female academics to male comedians. But it didn't need this kind of approval to take a hold of the popular imagination. To some young women, girl power became more than just a marketing tool. And if, as Karl Marx might tell you, the only kind of power that matters is economic power, then the Spice's girl power was a very real global phenomenon: half a billion pounds worth of power in the first two years of their benign rule alone.

Although she never recorded her biggest tunes, Marie Lloyd has a claim to be Britain's first female pop star, with sell-out shows, American tours and a whiff of scandal about her racy songs, performances and private life that shows there's nothing new in rock and roll. Lloyd's heyday came before the charts, singles and albums. But in what we might call the modern pop era the first British female pop star was undoubtedly Gracie Fields. Gracie's biography comes perilously close to parody. She was born above a fish and chip shop in Rochdale and was working in a cotton mill when she was discovered by an impresario called Archie Pitt, who gave her her first sip of champagne on her eighteenth birthday and told her he would make her a star.

That stardom came in the 1930s with a string of hit songs and associated films like *Sally in Our Alley* that played up to Gracie's cheery, Northern working-class persona. She found filming boring and turned down the chance to go to Hollywood, but it didn't stop her being one of Britain's highest-paid entertainers. Her marriage to an Italian meant that she spent the war in North America and then retired to Capri and consequently lost some of her popularity at home. This seems unfair when you consider that she travelled as far as New Guinea to entertain the troops and paid for all servicemen and women to travel for free on the trams and buses within the boundary of Rochdale.

The success of someone like Patti Page in the 1950s shows how female artists are often written out of conventional music history. She sold almost as many records as Elvis in the fifties, more than 100 million, a dozen of which sold more than a million and one of which, 'The Tennessee Waltz', topped the charts in America for three months. And yet when we think of fifties pop we think of greasy quiffs, Pomade, Elvis, Bill Haley, Little Richard and Jerry Lee Lewis, not the creamy alto voice that brought us 'Old Cape Cod'.

The pop diva as we know her – glamorous, imperious, seductive – emerged in the 1960s. In America, interestingly, it was often black singers who epitomised this, like Diana Ross, Dionne Warwick and Aretha Franklin. Here our girl pop stars often had something of the girl next door about them: there was a Sandie Shaw, Lulu or Cilla for every Shirley Bassey, Petula Clark and Dusty Springfield. Punk could legitimately claim to be a gender-neutral movement, one in which women like Siouxsie Sioux and Poly Styrene and bands like The Slits rejected the stereotype of the pliant, decorative pop poppet. Even so, the marketing of former bunny girl Debbie Harry of Blondie was still more *Playboy* than punk rock.

We had to wait until the 1980s for the first real global female pop icon, someone whose name and face and music would be known the world over, and whose celebrity would become an unstoppable cultural force. The title of the first Spice Girls single was 'Wannabe', released in 1996. But the word had been around since a *Time* magazine cover story of May 1985, and what they really really wanted to be was Madonna Louise Ciccone:

> The bright side of this trend is that these Wannabes (as in, 'We wanna be like Madonna!') could be out somewhere stealing hubcaps. Instead, all of them, hundreds of thousands of young blossoms whose actual ages run from a low of about eight to a high of perhaps twenty-five, are saving up their baby-sitting money to buy cross-shaped earrings and fluorescent rubber bracelets like Madonna's, white lace tights that they will cut off at the ankles and black tube skirts that, out of view of their parents, they will roll down several turns at the waist to expose their middles and the waistbands of the pantyhose.

The tone is mildly mocking, as is ever the case, but it acknowledges Madonna as a force in young women's lives. Debate raged about whether songs like 'Papa Don't Preach' and 'Like a Virgin' were anthems of empowerment and self-determination or just fetishistic soft-porn sales techniques. Madonna soon even had her own branch of cultural studies comprised of volumes such as Robert

Miklitsch's *From Hegel to Madonna: Towards a General Economy of 'Commodity Fetishism'*:

> *From Hegel to Madonna* presents a genealogical survey of
> the discourses of negation and affirmation associated with
> the work of Hegel, Adorno, Deleuze and Guattari; then,
> rotating from the philosophical to the political-economic axis,
> turns to the problem of a general economy of 'commodity-
> fetishism'. The author also analyses the phenomenon of
> Madonna Studies, reading the interest in the pop star as a
> sign of the academic times, a symptomatic figure not only of
> cultural studies in all its celebratory, cultural-populist excess
> but of a critical discourse responsive to postmodern culture
> in all its politically complex mutability.

Quite. It's easy to be cynical about such earnestness, but it reveals just how powerful Madonna, as a performer and a concept, was – much more so than as a musical force. Madonna's influence in terms of her being a strong, individual woman in the music industry made her a role model for musicians outside the dance-pop world. Madonna, some would say, brought feminism to the forefront of pop simply by being an ambitious, powerful and confident sexual entity without shame.

The 'Riot Grrrls' of nineties America sounded nothing like 'True Blue' or 'Holiday', but in some ways they were Madonna's punkish kid sisters. The movement's seed bed was the Pacific north-west around Olympia, Washington, and its pioneers a trio called Bikini Kill, led by activist, photographer and ex-stripper Kathleen Hanna. Their songs addressed feminism, sexual abuse, low pay, rape and domestic violence, and the title of their independent demo cassette of 1991 said it all: *Revolution Girl Style Now!* Hanna's fanzine *Riot Grrrl* spelled Grrrl in a way to replace the sometimes demeaning diminutive with a growl of rage. The movement was a genuine DIY culture of books, fanzines, protests, soundtracked by bands like Bratmobile, L7 and, in the UK, Huggy Bear. Bikini Kill's 'Don't Need You' spelt out the scene's attitude.

Riot Grrrl had some currency here in the UK, but the message was arguably diluted and declawed into something much more manageable and marketable. Certainly, the young British women who answered this ad needed and wanted someone to tell them they were cute and all right. That was the whole point:

> WANTED: R.U. 18–23 with the ability to sing/dance? R.U. streetwise, outgoing, ambitious, and dedicated? Heart Management Ltd are a widely successful music industry management consortium currently forming a choreographed, singing/dancing, all-female pop act for a recording deal. Open audition.

Out of this advert, through a fairly tortuous and convoluted process which included being sequestered for a while in a bungalow in Maidenhead, five girls would emerge as the Spice Girls under the tutelage of Simon Fuller's 19 Entertainment. Paul Gorman of *Music Week* was invited to Virgin Records' Paris office to meet the band. His piece was short but prescient:

> Smart, witty, abrasive and downright fun, the five-piece Spice Girls were signed to Virgin Records last year after a major-label feeding frenzy. But don't dismiss them as a packaged product. 'We are not some management-led

concept,' insists Geri Halliwell. 'We all sing, we all dance, we all write the songs and decide on the arrangements and the way we present ourselves. We call the shots.'

How much the Spice Girls called those shots has always been in dispute, but they have always said that the concept of five distinct types was not a management contrivance but their own idea that arose naturally out of their individual characters. It was, however, a *Top of the Pops Magazine* piece that gave them the famous labels, Sporty, Scary, Ginger, Baby and Posh.

Their début single entered the chart at number three in the summer of 1996 and climbed the next week to number one, where it stayed for seven weeks. In January 1997 it topped the *Billboard* Hot 100 for four weeks. By March 1997 it had been number one in thirty-one countries and become the biggest-selling single ever by a female group.

One can argue endlessly about the merits of 'Wannabe' as a song. Musically, it's no slighter or less well made than 'Imagine' or 'Cigarettes & Alcohol'. Predictably, the *NME* hated it. But that's to miss the point. 'Wannabe' was designed to be a hit, a brilliantly designed slice of skilful lo-cal r&b with an attached manifesto and guidance as ruthless as the targeting system of a Predator drone.

The message of 'Wannabe' is simple: 'If you wanna be my lover, you gotta get with my friends.' Simple, yes, but also radical in an age when media commentators were bemoaning the pressure on young women to become mere appendages and accessories for boys. 'Wannabe' said that girl friends were as important as boyfriends, and any bloke who didn't respect your choices was to be dumped forthwith. The girls backed this up with some vague but heartfelt words about 'girl power', a phrase last used in a fanzine by Riot Grrrl stalwarts Bikini Kill. As espoused by the Spice Girls in interviews, it was a slight but upbeat philosophy of self-belief and dynamism. *The Face*'s Sheryl Garrett was sniffy but even she had to concede the girls' appeal to their constituency: 'It's not much of a manifesto, really: having a laugh, being positive, going for it, wearing what you want ... But to insecure pre-teen girls, this really is the stuff of revolution. The Spice Girls are a girl gang who sing about putting their mates before boyfriends, about having confidence in themselves and not letting people put them down. And what's more, they seem to be having a brilliant time doing it.'

The Spice Girls continued to have a brilliant time for the rest of the decade, which they dominated. In a survey for Trivial Pursuit, they were the most recognisable popular cultural icons of the 1990s. Even after the departure of Geri Halliwell they continued to have hits, 'Holler' being their ninth and final one before they announced an indefinite hiatus in the year 2000.

The legacy of girl power is contentious. Doubting its validity, Amy McClure of North Carolina University claimed, 'An ideology based on consumerism can never be a revolutionary social movement. The fact that it appears to be a revolutionary movement is a dangerous lie that not only marketeers sell to us but that we often happily sell to ourselves.' Quite apart from being simply wrong – it was the consumerist desire of Russians for Levi's, Wham! records and McDonald's that brought down the Soviet Union as much as any arms race – it's typical of the superiority and wrongheadedness of academia when applied to the world of pop culture, a world where often trends and movements happen without the permission of the establishment, political, commercial or academic. Professor Susan Hopkins was more accurate when she saw a correlation between girl power, the rise of the Spice Girls and the glut of late twentieth century female action heroes like Lara Croft and *Buffy the Vampire Slayer*.

In the twenty-first century you can add to those fictional heroes successful and dominant real-life role models like Beyoncé and Adele, Lady Gaga as well as that of an older generation, Oprah, Roxanne, Madonna, and of course genuine outsiders such as Pussy Riot. Though they may not be what you really, really wanted, Scary, Sporty, Ginger, Baby and Posh should be in that list as well.

42. TUBTHUMPING

The British Phonographic Industry's annual awards dinner of 1998 – dress to impress, carriages at midnight, RSVP – was held in the Docklands. The London Arena, just refurbished to the tune of £10million, might have seemed an unlikely spot for a gesture of anarchist outrage and radical grassroots protest. Then again, maybe it was perfect. A swanky, several-hundred-quid-a-ticket industry jolly hosted by Ben Elton, with the Spice Girls and Dave Stewart all trotting up the red carpet. Oh, and deputy leader of the New Labour government, John Prescott. A bunch of ex-commune-dwelling squatter punks from Burnley via Armley, Leeds, decided to mark the occasion by throwing a bucket of water over Prescott in a gesture which, while of limited political impact or meaning, certainly guaranteed that Chumbawamba and their colourful talismanic water-chucker Danbert Nobacon received plenty of column inches.

Next morning, Nobacon and the band issued a statement saying, 'If John Prescott has the nerve to turn up at events like the Brit Awards in a vain attempt to make Labour seem cool and trendy,

then he deserves all we can throw at him.' But, in truth, the whole
incident was a fairly odd piece of political theatre. Chumbawamba's
label EMI issued an immediate apology and many wondered exactly
what an avowedly anti-capitalist outfit like Chumbawamba were
doing on a global multinational like EMI in the first place – what's
more, they'd happily performed as entertainers at the showbiz
party, hoping to win the award for best British single.

That single, 'Tubthumping', and Nobacon's little gesture
may well have been the most newsworthy moment of a vague but
influential movement that had been growing since the seventies.
'Peace convoy', 'new-age traveller', 'peace punk', 'anarcho-punk',
'crusty', 'soap dodger' or 'dog on string' – the names could be
disparaging but, far away from the glitter of the Brit Awards, at road
protests and pitched battles and the largest civil arrest in British
history a voice had been given to a part of the British people, their
politics and music, that refused to be knocked down.

Most music fans, most political activists, most rebels of any
stripe like to keep their enthusiasms within manageable boundaries
and fit them into a relatively conventional life, however passionate
and committed they feel. But for centuries some kinds of people –
strolling players, troubadours, gypsies, showmen, bargees, circus
families and the like – have chosen or been forced into lifestyles
and cultures that differ from the settled familial norm. They move
around, eschewing urban life and city domesticity, often providing
music, entertainment or casual work.

But from the hippy era of the late 1960s onwards, numbers of
young people not from traditional travelling communities began
to experiment with new lifestyles, motivated by a desire to leave
behind normal bourgeois suburban family living. They'd got a

taste of this at early free festivals like Stonehenge, Glastonbury or Windsor, and taken their cue from the freewheeling, neo-Beatnik nomad philosophy espoused in the movie *Easy Rider* and tunes like 'Born to Be Wild'. Compared to the wide-open spaces and endless freeways of the United States, Britain was small and crowded. But then that made it perfect for a small network of free festivals to develop, and like-minded individuals could spend the summer travelling to and fro in a ramshackle convoy of motorbikes, vans, decommissioned coaches, old buses and ambulances that became known, at least to itself, as the convoy. Within its raggle-taggle ranks were hippies, punks, anarchists and good old-fashioned drop-outs, unlikely bedfellows united by the musical upheavals of 1976 and coalescing around events like the Deeply Vale Festival, which convened annually in the Pennine foothills near Bury for the four years after punk.

The music may have been very different, as well as the hairstyles and dress, but there were the beginnings of a shared ethos and outlook concerning communal living, squatter politics, anarchism and pacifism, monadic and seasonal lifestyles, drugs, and, increasingly in the early eighties, vegetarianism and animal-rights issues. These found their way into songs like The Smiths' 'Meat Is Murder' and Robert Wyatt's whimsical yet chilling 'Pigs ... (in There)'. Wyatt also provided the soundtrack to *The Animals Film*, a hard-hitting anti-vivisection polemic seen by over a million viewers on the third night of Channel 4.

As punk moved into the eighties it spawned musical offshoots like hardcore and peace punk, which became rallying points for new, dissenting lifestyle choices and political views. American hardcore bands such as Black Flag – named after the anarchist emblem – /

Seconds and Minor Threat often espoused the no drugs or alcohol credo called 'straight edge'. In Britain, fans and followers of post-punk anarcho acts like Crass, Discharge and Flux of Pink Indians were equally engaged with the causes underpinning the music, an umbrella of connected concerns like veganism, pacifism, animal liberation, CND and, later, the poll tax and Criminal Justice Bill.

Out of this scene arose bands such as New Model Army and Chumbawamba. New Model Army came from Bradford and named themselves after Cromwell's well-drilled puritanical fighting force of ideological zealots from the Civil War, a telling choice of name. Their début album *Vengeance* set out their stall: punkish slabs of rage calling for retribution against all manner of supposed enemies, from drug dealers to Nazi war criminals. They soon established a dedicated fan community called The Family, which became genuinely multi-generational and gendered, who would travel around the country with the band.

Around this time Chumbawamba convened in the declining West Pennine milltown of Burnley, something of a hotbed for anarcho music and politics, and often a target for the National Front or newly formed BNP.

The first LP, the provocatively titled *Pictures of Starving Children Sell Records*, was an attack on Live Aid and Band Aid, which the band saw as a cosmetic gesture that failed to address the real causes of poverty and, worse, was simply a glorified PR stunt for ailing eighties pop aristocrats. Tracks included 'How to Get Your Band on Television/Slag Aid' and 'British Colonialism and the BBC'. Their second album, *Never Mind the Ballots* ... was released in 1987, the year of a third Margaret Thatcher election victory, and was an attack on the whole notion of parliamentary democracy.

By the mid-eighties, the convoy, that loose collective of activists, freaks, hedonists, disenfranchised punks and ex-squatters, was regularly travelling the roads of Britain, united by their dissatisfaction with regular society and the Tory government. They made their way from festival to festival, the most emblematic of these probably being the Stonehenge Free Festival, which had been growing since 1972, grudgingly tolerated by the police and bodies like English Heritage. In 1985 the courts banned the festival, claiming that it was detrimental to the site's archeological importance, but around 120 live-in vehicles still turned up, only to be met, some seven miles from Stonehenge, by a police roadblock of three lorryloads of gravel. When they halted the convoy, the police, it was alleged, moved down along the line of vehicles, smashing windscreens and arresting occupants as they went. The convoy found themselves trapped in a field and the chief constable of Wiltshire, Donald Smith, ordered the arrest of the entire convoy on the grounds they 'intended' to breach the exclusion zone around the monument. It was the largest mass arrest in English civil history, but it was to be remembered for the brutality of the police operation, recorded on video and commented on by several journalists and news agencies. ITN's Kim Sabido spoke to camera on the evening news: 'What I have seen in the last thirty minutes here in this field has been some of the most brutal police treatment of people that I've witnessed in my entire career as a journalist. The number of people who have been hit by policemen, who have been clubbed while holding babies in their arms in coaches around this field, is yet to be counted. There must surely be an inquiry after what has happened today.'

Nick Davies of the *Observer* reported:

There was glass breaking, people screaming, black smoke towering out of burning caravans, and everywhere there seemed to be people being bashed and flattened and pulled by the hair. Men, women and children were led away, shivering, swearing, crying, bleeding, leaving their homes in pieces.

The miners' strike had ended three months previously, and the scenes reminded many of the clashes at Orgreave. The police themselves later commented: 'The police operation had been planned for several months and lessons in rapid deployment learned from the miners' strike were implemented.'

Local jails didn't have the room for all those arrested. Convoy members were transported throughout the Midlands and even to northern England, and children and parents were often separated. Photographic evidence of the day is scant. Both the aforementioned ITN and the *Observer* seem to have lost most of their film and photographs of the day. But the events in that Wiltshire field were commemorated in song called 'The Battle of the Beanfield' by the Levellers, perhaps the most successful band to emerge from the newly demonised culture of new-age travellers.

Despite being a genuine voice of a community, and a scene with music and self-expression at its heart, the weekly music press largely ignored or reviled the new-age travellers, referring to them as 'crusties' and mocking their 'dogs on strings'. But this didn't prevent the Levellers becoming one of the most successful bands of their generation; a huge live draw who enjoyed significant record sales, a success made all the sweeter by them having achieved it without the help of the supposed opinion formers in London.

Spiral Tribe's huge free party at Castlemorton Common followed, along with the Criminal Justice Bill in 1994 and the furore over 'repetitive beats'. And for three years through the mid-nineties, these crusty youths with their dreadlocks, piercings and colourful knitwear were at the heart of the protests against the proposed Newbury bypass. Seven thousand people in all demonstrated at the loss of 150,000 acres of mature woodland. They lived in the trees, chained themselves to diggers and constructed a complex series of tunnels. One of them, Daniel Hooper, aka Swampy, became the poster boy of the movement, appearing on *Have I Got News for You* and being offered a record deal by EMI to record a version of 'I Am a Mole and I Live in a Hole'.

EMI was seen by many as symbolic of all that was nakedly capitalist, a wicked corporate music monolith, not least for their former links with the arms manufacturer Thorn. Which made it all the more surprising when Chumbawamba signed to the label in 1997, especially as they had been involved with a compilation LP called *Fuck EMI* in 1989, and attacked the label in many early songs. The band responded to criticisms of hypocrisy by saying, 'Our previous record label, One Little Indian, didn't have the evil symbolic significance of EMI but they were completely motivated by profit.'

Even more unlikely was what came next. Their single, 'Tubthumping', was the catchiest thing they had come up with to date, perhaps a belated ackowledgement that a good tune will refresh the parts that dialectical materialism cannot reach. It was far less didactic, far more abstractly anthemic than less than snappy predecessors like 'Smash Clause 28!' 'Fight the Alton Bill' or 'British Colonialism and the BBC'. 'Tubthumping' at heart, and it was a big heart, was a defiant drinking song that knew the joys and limitations of alcohol as revolutionary kindling and, amazingly, went to number two in Britain and number six in America. Hence their appearance at the Brit Awards, with a version of 'Tubthumping' containing a lyric changed to 'New Labour sold out the dockers, just like they'll sell out the rest of us', and the subsequent dousing of John Prescott by Danbert Nobacon. Soon after band member Alice Nutter appeared on TV advising impoverished fans to steal their CDs from chainstores like HMV and Virgin, Virgin took the CDs off the shelf and put them behind the counter.

Chumbawamba were never to repeat the success, infamy or visibility of 1997 and 1998. Alice Nutter became a playwright and screenwriter, Dunstan Bruce runs his own film production company, and Nobacon lives in Washington State. They gave their blessing to a smaller acoustic version of the band recording a couple of albums in a folk vein before disbanding in 2012 with the statement: 'We do, of course, reserve the right to re-emerge as Chumbawamba doing something else entirely (certainly not touring and putting out albums every two or three years). But, frankly, that's not very likely. Thirty years of being snotty, eclectic, funny, contrary and just plain weird. What a privilege, and what a good time we've had.'

At the time of writing, 'crusty' is more likely to be heard with reference to an artisan bread than a youth movement. And yet, old and new new-age travellers or their children, literal and metaphorical, continue to be knocked down, rise again and be engaged and involved in direct action such as the G8 protests and the Occupy movement. Indeed, being kettled has become as much a part of the modern middle-class youth experience as a gap year in Asia.

John Prescott is still active in politics and has become something of a Twitter celebrity. Late in 2012 he tweeted: 'I might mark Chumbawamba's split by going out and buying their greatest hit album.'

43. BRIMFUL OF ASHA

Madison Square Garden, August 1971, and there's a lovely and very telling moment at the beginning of legendary Indian musician Ravi Shankar's set at George Harrison's Concert for Bangladesh. Shankar was the opening act, and Harrison asked the audience to 'try to get into the Indian section' just before Shankar and his fellow musicians took the stage. After the first section of music the crowd applauded and cheered enthusiastically. Shankar rather coyly faced them and said, 'Thank you. If you appreciate the tuning so much, I hope you will enjoy the playing more.' It was a sweetly awkward moment, but one that spoke volumes about how different cultures understand, misunderstand, baffle and allure each other.

George Harrison was just one of a generation of British pop musicians to be attracted to the otherness of Eastern music and philosophy. But long before the Beatle fell under the bewitching spell of the sitar and the raga, the culture, music, art and cuisine of the Indian subcontinent had been intoxicating the British. Initially, nineteenth-century travellers had mocked the strangeness of Indian art, science and literature, described by the historian and essayist

Thomas Babbington Macaulay as: 'Medical doctrines which would disgrace an English farrier – Astronomy, which would move laughter in girls at an English boarding school – History, abounding with kings thirty feet high, and reigns thirty thousand years long – and Geography, made up of seas of treacle and seas of butter.'

By the 1890s, though, poets like W.B. Yeats were becoming interested in Indian poetry and myth. We were quicker to embrace India's sensual delights. Around the same time Yeats was translating *The Upanishads*, Sir Richard Burton was causing a stir with his privately printed translation of *The Kama Sutra*, which was too spicy for some delicate English tastes. As was the fare on offer at the Hindoostane Coffee House at 34 George Street, near Portman Square, London, England's first curry house where 'all the dishes were dressed with curry powder, rice, cayenne and the best spices of Arabia. A room was set apart for smoking from hookahs with oriental herbs. The rooms were neatly fitted up *en suite* and furnished with chairs and sofas made of bamboo canes, Chinese pictures and other Asiatic embellishments.'

Indian people had been arriving in Britain in large numbers since independence in 1947, but the mid-sixties saw a huge upsurge in immigrants coming to work in the National Health Service, the railways, textile mills in the North and foundries in the Midlands. And a smaller, more elite group of UK residents began to travel, literally and musically, in the other direction.

During 1965 echoes of India began to be heard in the UK pop charts. The Yardbirds' 'Heart Full of Soul', written by Graham Gouldman, has a raga-like riff and The Kinks' 'See My Friends' was apparently inspired by the chanting of fishermen Ray Davies heard during a stopover in Bombay. George Harrison first picked up a sitar on the set of *Help* in 1965:

There were some Indian musicians in a restaurant scene and I kind of messed around with a sitar then. But during that year, towards the end of the year anyway, I kept hearing the name of Ravi Shankar. So I went out and bought a record and that was it. It felt very familiar to me to listen to that music. It was around that time I bought a sitar. I just bought a cheap sitar in a shop called India Craft, in London. It was lying around. I hadn't really figured out what to do with it. When we were working on 'Norwegian Wood' it just needed something, and it was quite spontaneous, from what I remember. I just picked up my sitar, found the notes and just played it. We miked it up and put it on and it just seemed to hit the spot.*

Harrison's sitar cameo was the first appearance of the instrument on a Western pop record, but it wasn't to be the last. Brian Jones got the bug round at Harrison's house and played one on The Rolling Stones' 'Paint It, Black'. Before long the sitar sound became a must-have on huge numbers of rock and pop songs, helped by Danelectro's manufacturing of an electric sitar – for what sixties rocker could resist the fusion of Eastern mystery and Western electricity? Traffic, The Animals, The Byrds, The Monkees, The Mamas and the Papas, The Moody Blues and The Move were just a few of the bands who included modish sitar strains on their records. The trend reached its apotheosis with The Beatles' 'Within You, Without You', five minutes of pop raga performed by George Harrison and a group of uncredited Indian musicians from the Eastern Music Circle of Finchley on swarmandal, dilruba, tabla

---

* From *The Beatles Anthology*

and tambura. Its inclusion on the *Sgt Pepper* album meant that this became the most widely owned artefact of Indian music in the Western world, and sparked a bizarre Bangalore via Bethnal Green version by Anthony Newley.

But the best of these crossovers between East and West was to appear a year later in 1968, tucked away on the B side of 'Lady Madonna'. 'The Inner Light' was the first Harrison composition to be featured on a Beatles single, with a backing track recorded in Mumbai during the sessions for Harrison's *Wonderwall Music* soundtrack album. The lyric was inspired by a letter from a Sanskrit scholar who suggested Harrison set some Taoist poetry to music. Harrison obliged with a beautiful, haunting setting in the south Indian Carnatic style for flutes, drums, banshuri, shehnai and harmonium that is both lovely and mysterious.

All of these experiments emerged from an era heady with talk of love, peace and spirituality. But by the time Asian communities had become well established in the UK in the seventies – the Sikhs in Southall; the Pakistani textile workers of Oldham, Bolton and east Lancashire; the Gujaratis of Tooting and Wembley; the Punjabi community of Wolverhampton; the East African Asians of Leicester displaced by Idi Amin – Britain was revealing a far less attractive face to its new citizens than the enigmatic, beatific smile of the quiet Beatle.

In an unwelcome perversion of their early love of ska, soul and reggae, some of the skinheads of the 1970s were less keen on multiculturalism. They added 'Paki-bashing' – unprovoked attacks on anyone of Asian extraction – to their notoriously noxious pastimes of hippy- and gay-bashing. But the racism wasn't always so overt. Comedy shows like Spike Milligan's and Johnny Speight's *Curry and Chips*, featuring the ex-Goon blacked up, showed that prejudice against Indians was still prevalent even among the supposedly enlightened. *It Ain't Half Hot Mum* and *Mind Your Language* had similarly stereotyped silly, lazy or devious Indian characters. Acting against type, though, it was Asian women who struck for equal pay at the Grunwick film processing plant and waged picket-line battles that became a fixture of the nightly news in 1976.

But it was almost the end of the twentieth century before Indian music made by Indians made inroads into the mainstream pop culture of the West. In 1982 a trio called Monsoon, led by Sheila Chandra, a teenage singer–actress of Indian descent, had a top-twenty hit with 'Ever So Lonely'. Wearing a sari, Chandra was the first Asian singer to appear on *Top of the Pops*, but Monsoon never repeated their success. However, it wasn't long before a new sound, Bhangra, began to emerge among the Punjabi communities of Britain. It was, in its own way, as guerrilla and DIY a music as punk or skiffle, melding the sounds and atmosphere of traditional Punjabi music with the dynamics and power of rock and dance, and using this to articulate the experience of urban British Asian youth. It was chiefly male Punjabis who found a voice through Bhangra, but as most of the records and tapes were bought in specialist Asian shops, few of which were chart-return shops, it maintained a pivotal, popular but underground image.

In the wake of Bhangra followed several, even more influential, Asian musicians: Apache Indian, Asian Dub Foundation, Nitin Sawhney, Bally Sagoo, M.I.A., and Talvin Singh, who won the Mercury Music Prize in 1999. But the biggest Asian pop success of all came from the Black Country, and a band who, like the popular Indian comedy series *Goodness Gracious Me*, reclaimed their name from a negative racial stereotype.

Cornershop, a multiracial quartet led by songwriter Tjinder Singh, had their roots in towns and cities like Wolverhampton and Leicester, with large, well-established, Asian working-class communities. Their début release came on curry-coloured vinyl and their early songs were imaginative, eclectic and polemical, and generally concerning the subject of race. After Morrissey had recorded a song called 'Bengali in Platforms' and appeared onstage draped in a Union Jack, Cornershop waded into the debate by burning a picture of the ex-Smith outside the offices of his label, EMI.

Their acclaimed album of September 1997, *When I Was Born for the 7th Time*, featured a Punjabi cover of The Beatles' 'Norwegian Wood', the song that had originally introduced the sitar to a British pop audience. Another of the album tracks was 'Brimful of Asha', a tribute to the Bollywood singing star Asha Bhosle, said to be the most recorded singer in history. But the song was also a modern cross-cultural celebration, name-checking Marc Bolan, the Trojan and Argo record labels, and two other great Indian singers, Mohammed Rafi and Lata Mangeshkar. The Asha of the title is not just the legendary Indian playback singer, though. 'Asha' also means 'hope' in Punjabi, underlining the song's infectious and positive vibe. The song was released in the same year that Tony Blair's New Labour effected a political revolution in the UK after a landslide general election victory, and a speech given by foreign secretary Robin Cook had a similarly upbeat view of modern multicultural Britain:

> It isn't just our economy that has been enriched by the arrival of new communities. Our lifestyles and cultural horizons have also been broadened in the process ... it reaches into every aspect of our national life. Chicken tikka masālā is now a true British national dish, not only because it is the most

popular, but because it is a perfect illustration of the way Britain absorbs and adapts external influences. Chicken tikka is an Indian dish. The masālā sauce was added to satisfy the desire of British people to have their meat served in gravy. Coming to terms with multiculturalism as a positive force for our economy and society will have significant implications for our understanding of Britishness.

Robin Cook's chicken tikka masālā became a much-discussed hit, and another Cook, Norman, the superstar DJ better known as Fatboy Slim, added his flavours and seasoning to Cornershop's 'Brimful of Asha' to similarly sensational effect. The first time around the single had peaked at number sixty, but Cook's Fatboy Slim remix turned a perfectly pleasant, slightly unusual piece of indie pop into a vibrant fusion of various cultures and genres, tastes and histories. 'Brimful of Asha' is a chicken tikka masālā of a song and it proved to be just as popular. The song topped the charts in Britain, was top ten in Italy and Ireland and a hit across the world. It was especially popular in America, reaching number sixteen on the *Billboard* chart and featuring in a Gap ad and several episodes of the hit TV show *Friends*.

Cornershop's success was brief but groundbreaking. In the decade and a half since 'Brimful of Asha', Coventry-born Indian artist Panjabi MC had a global hit with 'Mundian to Bach Ke' featuring rapper Jay-Z, M.I.A. has been nominated for two Grammies and an Oscar, and Bhangra–r&b artist Jay Sean, real name Kamailjit Singh Jhooti from Harlesden, had a US number one single with 'Down', which sold 4 million copies in the United States, making him the first UK Urban act ever to top *Billboard*'s Hot 100, the most successful male UK Urban artist in US chart history, and the most successful British male artist in the US charts since Elton John.

At home, the British Asian experience continues to be rich and complex. The summer of 2001 saw brief but intense rioting in the Asian communities of Oldham, Bradford, Burnley and elsewhere, across racial faultlines in divided communities. But personalities like Meera Syal, Amir Khan, Monica Ali, Hardeep Singh Kohli, Art Malik, Hanif Kureishi, Krishnan Guru-Murthy, Keith Vaz, Nasser Hussein, Monty Panesar, Anita Anand and Sanjeev Bhaskar have become part of the cultural landscape of modern Britain, even the establishment. Asha Bhosle herself now has a restaurant that bears her name in Birmingham, with plans for branches in London and Manchester, a potent symbol of a community and a relationship brimful of her name's other meaning: hope.

44. CAN'T GET YOU OUT OF MY HEAD

All pop is manufactured. No pop song or rock group has ever emerged from a flower like nectar, fallen from the sky like rain, or emerged fully formed from the sea on a scallop shell like Venus. Even the worthiest, deepest, most heartfelt music, and the sincerest, most committed artists, have patted their music into shape like butter, rehearsed it, marketed it, essentially manufactured it.

For the music snob, none of the music he likes – and it usually is a he – is ever manufactured, despite evidence to the contrary. Led Zeppelin had Ahmet Ertegun and Peter Grant working to market their brand. The Pistols had McLaren. Pink Floyd had Peter Jenner and the brilliant image makers at Hipgnosis design. The Beatles needed Epstein, George Martin and Derek Taylor as part of their backroom support of managers, producers and publicists. John Lennon acknowledged the importance of management at The Beatles' very first US press conference when, asked why they created such excitement and hysteria, he replied, 'If we knew, we'd form another group and be managers.' None of the above bands has ever been called manufactured. Manufactured pop is the trivial stuff that other people like.

In 1894 George Du Maurier published a novel called *Trilby*, the big *fin de siècle* literary hit, along with Bram Stoker's *Dracula*. It gave us two lasting concepts: the trilby hat as worn by the eponymous heroine, and a word for a malevolent, controlling mastermind, a puppetmaster bent on his own gain based on the novel's hypnotist villain, Svengali.

In *Starmakers and Svengali*, his history of British pop management published in 1988, music writer Johnny Rogan concluded that the age of the Svengali in British rock was over. His confidence was misplaced, as anyone who's ever seen a strange-looking cove called Simon Cowell will attest. But even when Rogan made his claim at the end of the eighties, it rang hollow. The bestselling album of that year was *Kylie*, by one Kylie Minogue, the product of a stable that dominated pop music in the late 1980s, Stock, Aitken and Waterman, just one of pop's many hit factories, an industry whose forges and belts and presses haven't stopped rolling and clattering this past half century.

How much manufacturing went into the young Elvis Presley is debatable. There was something protean and primal about this Tupelo truck driver's feral talent and appeal; and it's arguable whether his manager, the Dutch-born huckster Colonel Tom Parker, ever did much for him, besides stop him playing in Europe, force him into an artistic wasteland of hick movies and take half his earnings. But he is now seen as the archetype for the avaricious, music-industry puppetmaster. A few years after Elvis broke through, a very British story of music, marketing and manipulation emerged from the backstreets of the West End.

Larry Parnes was a teenage hustler in the garment business, or rag trade, as it was known, who moved into the seedy world of

Soho entertainment when he was eighteen. He ran a bar, put on plays and, in his most inspired move, became the manager of a young ex-merchant seaman called Thomas Hicks. Re-christened as Tommy Steele, Parnes steered Steele into becoming Britain's first teen idol. In the wake of this triumph Parnes set about creating the pop stable that would make him Britain's first and arguably greatest pop Svengali.

After Steele's success, the flamboyantly gay Parnes sought out other handsome, malleable male talent to mould into pop stars. He would change their image, control their careers and give them exciting new names. He spotted a young singer called Reg Patterson, born Reginald Smith, at London's Condor Club and transformed him still further into Marty Wilde with instantaneous success. It was a trick he adroitly repeated with Richard Knellar, Roy Taylor, John Askew and Ronald Wycherley, turning them into Dickie Pride, Vince Eager, Johnny Gentle and Billy Fury respectively. In his book *Revolt into Style*, the late George Melly suggested that the names Parnes gave the singers were meant to hint at their sexual temperaments. In one case, though, he failed to persuade his charge to change names. Vivacious cockney singer Joe Brown refused to become Elmer Twitch.

Usually, though, Parnes got his way. He employed the boys in his stable himself, rather than be employed by them, as was usual with managers, and paid them a weekly wage. When Vince Eager began to wonder why he wasn't receiving royalties Parnes told him he wasn't entitled to any. 'But it says in my contract that I am,' Eager protested. 'It also says I have power of attorney over you, and I've decided you're not getting any,' Parnes replied. Parnes became the subject of a mildly disapproving *Panorama* documentary in which he's referred to as 'Parnes, Shillings and Pence' and presenter

Christopher Cazenove interviews the young stars as if they were laboratory specimens or aliens. It is a vivid picture of the old and new Britain: the baffled, starched-shirt establishment and the new rising stars drawn from state schools and the provinces. Perhaps the ultimate accolade for Parnes came when he was parodied on Peter Sellers's album *Songs for Swingin Sellers*. In the skit he becomes Major Rafe Ralph, a colourful horse-dealer who's moved into rock and roll stars and who has personally discovered the likes of Lennie Bronze, Clint Thigh, Matt Lust and such vocal groups as The Fleshpots and The Muckrakers.

With the coming of the rock era, it became a badge of honour for bands to write their own songs and be masters of their own destiny, as opposed to toothsome puppets. Parnes's empire dwindled and he turned elsewhere, representing Joan Collins and ice-skater John Curry. Had he been a year or two younger, a teenage actor and singer from Manchester called Davy Jones was just the kind of performer Parnes might have groomed for stardom. As it was, he sought his fortune in America and became part of a curious but hugely successful attempt to merge the manufactured puppet pop of the Parnes era with the style and look of modern rock.

A producer called Bob Rafelson had been trying to sell the idea of a TV show about a pop group since 1962, but in the wake of The Beatles' *Hard Day's Night* he sold the concept of The Monkees to Screen Gems (the TV division of Columbia Pictures) in 1965. In September that year, the trade press ran an ad saying:

Madness!! Auditions. Folk & Roll Musicians–Singers for acting roles in new TV series. Running Parts for 4 insane boys, age 17–21. Want spirited Ben Frank's types. Have courage to work. Must come down for interview.

Out of 437 applicants, the four chosen were Michael Nesmith, Peter Tork, Micky Dolenz and the aforementioned Jones. Don Kirshner, Screen Gems' head of music, hired songwriters Tommy Boyce and Bobby Hart for the project. One of their first demos was '(Theme from) The Monkees' which helped secure the TV series commission.

The first long-playing album, *The Monkees*, containing '(Theme from) The Monkees' and their first hit single 'Last Train to Clarksville', spent thirteen weeks at number one and stayed on the *Billboard* charts for seventy-eight weeks in total. A string of hits like 'I'm a Believer', 'A Little Bit You, a Little Bit Me' and 'Daydream Believer' followed. But The Monkees themselves were expressly forbidden from playing on these early releases, though Mike Nesmith was allowed one song on the début album and some production input. In the liner notes to the Rhino records Monkees reissues, he commented:

> The first album shows up and I look at it with horror because it makes [us] appear as if we are a rock 'n' roll band. There's no credit for the other musicians. I go completely ballistic, and I say, 'What are you people thinking? You've crossed the line here! You are now duping the public. They know when they look at the television series that we're not a rock 'n' roll band; it's a show about a rock 'n' roll band ... nobody for a minute believes that we are somehow this accomplished rock 'n' roll band that got their own television show.'

Don Kirshner was The Monkees' musical Svengali, but he split with them over this, the group's desire to play and write their own music. His next band project was more malleable, though: an amiable bunch of kids going by the names of Jughead Jones,

Archie Andrews and Reggie Mantle, who were much less trouble. The Archies were the ultimate manufactured band: an animated TV cartoon whose music was made by anonymous session musicians. That didn't stop their first single, 'Sugar, Sugar', becoming a global hit and a number one in Britain and the US.

Both *The Monkees* and *The Archies* were TV shows that spawned hit music. But the most successful transition from TV to music was made so completely that few today may even remember that the star concerned was ever an actress – who didn't play a musician (cartoon or otherwise), but a young woman trying to forge ahead in the less glamorous, but equally male dominated, world of automotive repair.

Erinsborough is a fictional suburb of Melbourne in a TV series called *Neighbours* – Erinsborough being a loose anagram of *Neighbours* – that gripped the UK in a kind of national insanity in the late eighties and early nineties. A cute garage mechanic called Charlene, played by one Kylie Minogue, was one of the show's biggest stars. At a charity football match she sang a cover of Little Eva's 'Loco-Motion' with other cast members, and it became a hit in Australia. This caught the eyes and ears of the Stock, Aitken and Waterman self-styled 'hit factory', who'd enjoyed a couple of years' success with a clutch of singles marrying the sound of a burgeoning UK dance scene with resolutely light-entertainment values. Bananarama, Dead or Alive and Hazell Dean had all benefited from this approach. Kylie was to be next.

Was Kylie lucky, lucky, lucky to hitch a ride to stardom with the most successful pop production team since Chinn and Chapman? Or were the lucky ones Stock, Aitken and Waterman, who cashed in with the most recognisable and best-loved pop performer of her day, one whose appeal would outlive the formulaic SAW hit-factory formula? Over the next few years Kylie enjoyed a succession of hits: from the schmaltzy, dated 'Tears on My Pillow' and 'Je Ne Sais Pas Pourquoi' to the raunchy sound and look of the 'sex Kylie' era and harder, groovier tracks like 'Step Back in Time', 'Shocked' and 'Better the Devil You Know', a catchy tune saddled with perhaps the most reactionary, small-minded lyric since Peter Sarstedt's know-your-place anthem, 'Where Do You Go To (My Lovely)'

Was Kylie manufactured? Was Stock, Aitken and Waterman an artistic wasteland run like a car plant? Well, if it was, it had glorious antecedents. Pete Waterman claimed, a little grandiosely perhaps, that his stable was a modern Motown. Berry Gordy's label was explicitly modelled on that other great Detroit economic powerhouse, the motor industry; and, interestingly, both Waterman's and Gordy's home towns, Coventry and Detroit, were automobile boom towns that had fallen on hard times. Something of the factory conveyor-belt ethic informed both labels, but Motown had songwriters like Smokey Robinson, Stevie Wonder, Holland Dozier Holland and Whitfield and Strong, as well as performers like The Supremes, the Four Tops and The Temptations. Only the most generous pop fan would include Sonia, The Reynolds Girls, Mel and Kim and Rick Astley in that company. In fact, probably not even Sonia and Rick themselves.

But SAW and their stable had some of Berry Gordy's hard-nosed if occasionally tin-eared pop nous. (Gordy thought that Marvin Gaye's 'What's Goin' On' was a dud when he first heard it; too jazzy and too political.) Both understood the currency of a catchy tune, the power of radio, and the need to make hay while the sun shines. Stock, Aitken and Waterman had seven number ones in 1989, but 1990 brought their last UK number-one single, Kylie's 'Tears on My Pillow'. By mid-1990, with the notable exception of

Kylie, the Hit Factory was in trouble, and October 1990 saw the first UK top 75 with no SAW singles present in over two years. Their reign was brief but monumental.

Pete Waterman went on to become a familiar face on the nation's talent shows, while Kylie grew into a true pop icon, the nearest Britain had to a Madonna, at least until the coming of Adele. And almost fifteen years after she had come smiling out of Erinsborough in her dungarees with her dipstick and oil can, 2001 found her at the wheel of a sleek, futuristic supercar headed for a hyperreal space-age megacity in the video for her finest record, one of the greatest pop records of the new millennium, or any other era.

Both of the composers of 'Can't Get You out of My Head' had pop form. Rob Davis was the flamboyantly flared guitarist of seventies glam rockers Mud, seen sashaying on *Top of the Pops* to 'Tiger Feet' and 'The Cat Crept In', turned professorial songwriter. Cathy Dennis was a sort of East Anglian Kylie who had herself enjoyed a few hits at the end of the eighties but who'd turned to songwriting and production. The icy sensuality of the arrangement for 'Can't Get You out of My Head' was partly what made it so naggingly compelling. Later, Dennis would prove to be a master of the form by writing Katy Perry's 'I Kissed a Girl' and Britney Spears's 'Toxic'.

But 'Can't Get You out of My Head' was, in 2001, both utterly now and utterly of an era yet to come, its aching, narcotic physicality and eroticism set against the dreamlike futurism of the shivery electronic cloud of sound. As Mike Atkinson in *Stylus* magazine said, 'Like so many great pop records before it, "Can't Get You out of My Head" represents a graceful collision of contrasts.' The *Guardian* picked up an echo of an earlier electro-dance classic, believing, '"Can't Get You out of My Head" is sleek,

Arctic-blue minimalism, like an emotionally thwarted retelling of Donna Summer's "I Feel Love".' The peerless pop culture theorist Paul Morley went so far as to base a whole book, *Words and Music*, around its eerie, seductive sound and cultural import, placing it in a lineage of avant-pop from Satie via John Cage to Brian Eno and Kraftwerk.

Kylie's journey, from cute Melbourne grease monkey to enigmatic cultural cipher is, in many ways, the story of pop – that strange and alluring crossroads where commerce, art, sex, marketing and magic meet. Born or made, manufactured or not, we just can't get it out of our heads.

45. I BET YOU LOOK GOOD ON THE DANCEFLOOR

At the Conservative Party conference of 2012, Boris Johnson reduced his audience to tears of laughter by claiming that he had danced Gangnam Style with Prime Minister David Cameron at his country seat, Chequers. Most delegates assumed that the London mayor was merely indulging his customary fondness for buffoonish surrealism.

In fact, he was telling the truth. The PM had invited Boris to lunch to heal the supposed rifts between the two and defuse talk of a leadership bid from Johnson. After a good lunch at the Plough Inn, the men returned to the house in high spirits. Cameron then produced his iPad and began to play a video of Korean pop star Psy and his troop of girls, performing their global smash hit 'Gangnam Style' on YouTube. 'When you dance you've got to think you're riding an invisible horse in your lower body,' Psy had previously explained. 'This is the point of the Gangnam Style – dress classy and dance cheesy.' So to the delight of the assembled retinue the Prime Minister and Mr Johnson displayed an impressive familiarity with the famous 'horse-riding' dance moves and the various bizarre poses. 'It was uproarious – they completely brought the house down,' said one onlooker.

It's hard to imagine Churchill and Stalin in 1940 waltzing round the Chequers' library to Glenn Miller's 'In the Mood', though perhaps they did. But what is significant about this political vignette is not just that we don't think it odd that our modern political leaders lark about to the pop hits of the day, but how they experienced the music and how they came to hear it. 'Gangnam Style' became a worldwide hit thanks to its YouTube video which went viral during 2012, garnering over a billion views at the time of writing. It is the most watched internet clip ever – iPad, download, YouTube, viral, MP3. A decade ago these would have been meaningless pieces of esoteric jargon, but today they form the language of music. Some will grumble at this, and pine for an imagined golden age, but the truth is that, since the birth of recorded music, technological innovations have repeatedly altered both the nature of popular music and the way listeners experience and acquire it. For the past century a new technology has changed the music industry every quarter century or so. Pop music and technology have always gone hand in hand – all the way to the bank.

When Thomas Alva Edison invented the phonograph in 1877 he never intended his new device to record music. He thought his new technology would be used for the dictation of contracts, business letters and such. He actually resisted using it for music until his competitors proved there was a huge public demand for it. The invention of the music industry was a complete accident. Immediately, the nature of music changed to fit the new format. Songwriters shortened their compositions for them to fit on one side of a 78 r.p.m. record. Singers modified their vocal projection and enunciation to suit the primitive recording technology. Piano sales fell, and music lovers gathered around the horns of their Victrolas instead of having sing-songs at the old Joanna.

In the mid-1920s, new electric recording and amplification techniques meant clearer recordings and fewer demands on a singer's voice in terms of volume and projection. Crooners became the dominant vocalists in pop, and one in particular became the first pop singer.

Before Bing Crosby, singers tended to be big-voiced belters like Al Jolson, obliged to reach the back seats of theatres without the aid of the microphone. Crosby's relaxed, intimate style was entirely new; conversational, laid-back and contemporary. It was also hugely popular. After Crosby came the generation of singers who'd define the middle of the twentieth century: Frank Sinatra, Dean Martin, Tony Bennett and Perry Como, all singing slight variations of the style that dominated popular music until the coming of the rock and pop era ...

... An era that began in the fifties when three innovations – tape recording; the long-playing, high-fidelity record; and FM radio – led to what Jac Holzman, legendary founder of Elektra Records, has called 'the Big Bang': the ushering in of a new era of artistic expression. Thanks to magnetic tape, musicians now had the luxury of reworking and refining their art. Until the late forties there was no margin for error while making a record. If you hit a bum note in the second verse, or fluffed a riff, you either scrapped the recording by literally breaking the record or lived with the mistake. Now musicians could take chances; above all, they could relax. The other two major innovations, albums and FM radio, meant clearer, stereo sound and the emergence of longer songs. Rock culture had arrived.

That meant the dawn of the studio as a compositional tool, and a few grandiose statements. It led to albums like *Sgt Pepper*, *The Dark Side of the Moon* and *Tubular Bells*. But over the past couple of decades this trend has been reversed. Computerisation has seen the rise of the bedroom music boffin, and what would have taken hours and thousands of pounds in state-of-the-art studios is now achievable by anyone with a laptop and the right software.

But in the twenty-first century, technology has impacted on popular music in a way few could have predicted. It hasn't so much changed the music itself as revolutionised the industry built around it. Two of those revolutionaries were British: Tim Berners-Lee and Jonathan Ive.

Tim Berners-Lee was a young computer programmer working at the CERN institute in Switzerland who came up with the idea of linking a network of computers to share information. He was inspired by an old Victorian encyclopaedia called *Enquire Within Upon Everything*. Berners-Lee called his version the World Wide Web. 'Vague but exciting' was the comment his boss wrote on the initial report. Berners-Lee developed the world's first website in 1991, and before the decade was out the internet had changed the world.

Just as with Edison's phonograph, humanity quickly put the internet to uses its inventor had never dreamed of – like music. Ten years after the invention of the Web, another Brit working at Apple in California, Jonathan Ive, designed a piece of hardware about the size of a cigarette packet. The iPod was a device capable of storing thousands and thousands of songs on a portable hard drive – an entire music library in your pocket. Ive wasn't responsible for the science, but it was his striking, ergonomically brilliant design that ensured the iPod became the most desirable music artefact of its time. For maybe the first time, with the possible exception of the Sony Walkman, it was the hardware, not the songs, that listeners lusted after.

The iPod stored music as MP3s – compressed computer files which dispensed with some frequencies thought to be beyond normal auditory perception. A German scientist, Karlheinz Brandenburg, used the song 'Tom's Diner' by Suzanne Vega to develop the MP3, testing it again and again to make sure Vega's voice was reproduced accurately, and leading some to call Vega the mother of MP3.

In 1999 an American student called Shawn Fanning invented a music file-sharing system called Napster, which allowed listeners to share, peer to peer, as it was known, their MP3 music files Suddenly, Pandora's box opened and the whole music business was turned on its head. Initially, such peer-to-peer networks often specialised in the trading of long out of print items, obscurities or bootlegs. But soon the back catalogues of everyone from The Beatles to Beefheart, Radiohead to Rachmaninov to Racey were being distributed globally for free. The American heavy metal band Metallica took on Napster and ultimately destroyed it, but by then, to use another analogy, the genie was out of the bottle. A generation would grow up thinking that music should be as free as air, would no more pay for a record than they would pay to breathe.

The situation wasn't helped by the laggardly way the music labels responded to the coming crisis. Rather than develop workable, paid-for download systems, they concentrated on criminalising and threatening their core audience, in a panicked echo of the infamous Home Taping is Killing Music campaign of the eighties. When software like iTunes was put in place, it quickly became successful and popular. People, it seemed, did not want to steal provided they were given the chance to pay – well, some at least.

But the fast, easy sharing of information via the internet was to revolutionise music in another way. As bands themselves posted music and video online, so fans began to share new enthusiasms between themselves and, dispensing with the traditional networks, started making their own scenes, nurturing them virally without the permission of radio, TV or the music press. And, in a nice irony, the first band to break globally in this new way, the first superstars of the super-information age, specialised in songs that were vignettes of local life in the industrial North, inspired by the black and white kitchen-sink movies and the guitar sounds of half a century ago.

In the shadow of the Neepsend Gasworks, north-east of Sheffield city centre, four young men first worked on the songs that would later form the basis of the fastest-selling début album in UK history. At this stage the Arctic Monkeys had no idea what MySpace or Facebook were; indeed, had no idea how to put their music online. Their fans did, though. At early gigs the band would give away copies of a free CD, which became known as *Beneath the Boardwalk* containing fifteen songs. Posted online these became a word of mouth, or word of keyboard, sensation. Without ever playing in London, or releasing a note in the conventional manner, they established a passionately devoted fanbase. They had no records available, but A&R men who did make the trip north were amazed that the crowd knew every word to every song. While the conventional music industry wailed that the internet would destroy music, the Arctic Monkeys and their fans were showing how the Web could help music makers and music lovers. One of their early favourites was a song called 'A Certain Romance', in which lyricist Alex Turner commented wryly, 'There's only music so that there's new ringtones.'

At every turn, the Arctic Monkeys' rise reflected the new ways that pop music out-foxed the decrepit old regime. A Sheffield amateur photographer called Mark Bull posted a DIY video of the band playing 'Fake Tales of San Francisco' on his website, and it was picked up by MTV. In May 2005 the Arctic Monkeys included the song on 'Five Minutes with The Arctic Monkeys' , their first proper release, but on their own Bang Bang label, with just 500 CDs and 1,000 7-inch singles physically available. Significantly, though, it was also available to download from the iTunes Music Store. And there's the rub: generational, social and cultural. Once upon a time, owning the artefact would have been paramount, vital, the cute shot on the single sleeve lovingly gazed at, the album liner notes pored over while listening on headphones, or carried under the arm as a badge of cool. Now, as Prospero had predicted in *The Tempest*, the isle was full of noises:

> ... *a thousand twangling instruments*
> *Will hum about mine ears; and sometime voices*
> ... *the clouds methought would open, and show riches*

Music now came from the air, from things called clouds, and had no physical form at all. Which is actually how it had begun and how it had been experienced for centuries.

The Arctic Monkeys' first album, *Whatever People Say I Am, That's What I'm Not* took its title from a line in Alan Silitoe's slice of working-class factory life, *Saturday Night and Sunday Morning*. The Arctic Monkeys offered their own witty take on modern urban life, such as the 'Red Light Indicates Doors Are Secured', after-hours Sheffield seen blearily from the taxi rank, as the protagonists negotiate their ride home and discuss the event of the night.

In its early weeks at the top of the charts *Whatever People Say I Am, That's What I'm Not* was outselling the rest of the album chart combined. A spokesman for HMV said: 'In terms of sheer impact ... we haven't seen anything quite like this since The Beatles.'

So technology may have collapsed the existing business model and changed the way we consume music, and sadly put some people out of work, but music, in essence, remains unchanged – music that speaks directly to us about life, expressed with élan and vivacity, is still desired and enjoyed by pretty much all of us.

46. REHAB

Late 2003 and the guest on the *Drive Time* show on Radio Two was a young performer from North London whose début album had attracted much attention and praise. Amy Winehouse was a sultry, witty torch singer whose brassy, blowsy, broken-hearted balladry belied her nineteen years; and her lusty, late-night songs of romantic tribulations were a nicely dark and bitter alternative to the pale, tasteless fare emerging from the slew of TV talent shows that had come to dominate pop culture.

In 2007 Amy Winehouse won the Ivor Novello award for best song for 'Rehab'. Backstage at the Grosvenor House hotel, she had changed. For one thing, the voluptuous, vampish siren had become gaunt and bedraggled. She had lost a great deal of weight and was heavily tattooed. She was still amiable and co-operative, but the candid, cheeky, spunky girl I'd met a couple of years before had become somehow slacker and distracted, out of focus, blurry, disconnected, her sentences tailing off into nothing, her mind seemingly elsewhere. To be fair, she did have a lot to distract her, her struggles with a variety of drugs, her tortured, mutually abusive relationship – all of it somehow bundled and knotted together, like her birds' nest of hair, with the fame that had come her way and made her the ultimate tabloid fodder: permanently papped, stalked and doorstepped, her every high-profile binge, row and break-up captured in print, on film and across the internet.

A new kind of fame that led to an old kind of end: in Amy's case in a bedroom in Camden with three empty vodka bottles by her side, but a melancholy demise that had been played out many times before in the entertainment business, often by vulnerable young women caught in the spotlight of celebrity – from Judy Garland to Janis Joplin, Lena Zavaroni to Karen Carpenter. Amy Winehouse's life and death combined elements of the entertainment myth that were both old and new. As writer William Shaw put it, 'Uniquely, Winehouse welded the twenty-first-century idiom of the hedonistic, urban, vodka girl to classic twentieth-century songwriting of a Johnny Mercer or Lorenz Hart – those old songs of unbreachable sadness from before the rock and roll era. Amy sang about addiction, infidelity, masturbation and lust and made it all sound classy.'

Amy Winehouse flirted, dallied and stepped out with controversy all her short, crowded life. Many of her family were musicians. Her grandma was a singer and had been Ronnie Scott's girlfriend. Amy grew up steeped in the jazz songbook – Dinah Washington, Sarah Vaughan, Sinatra – so much so that her teachers in Southgate, London, would reprimand her for singing in class rather than studying. While still at junior school she formed an amateur rap group called Sweet 'n' Sour, indebted to her new love of feisty US r&b and rap from the likes of TLC and Salt N Pepa.

At twelve she was accepted into the Sylvia Young Theatre School, and a year later she received her first guitar. But by sixteen Winehouse was expelled for 'not applying herself', and for her pierced nose. She was briefly a showbiz journalist, in an ironic 'hunter and game' echo of what was to come for her. Then a schoolmate, singer Tyler James, passed her demo tape to his label, A&M, who were on the lookout for new, young, jazz-style vocalists during a jazz boom sparked by the likes of Jamie Cullum. A deal with Island/Universal followed.

On the Radio Two *Drive Time* show, making one of her first radio appearances in support of her début album *Frank*, she created a small controversy of a mild kind too. Several listeners texted and emailed in to say how refreshing her vocal style and personality were. But many others were less enthusiastic about her full-blooded, woozy, jazz-inflected vocals. 'Get this woman off' was a sentiment echoed in many of the interactions. But *Frank* was generally very well received and on songs like 'Take the Box' and 'Pumps' we saw the first evidence of a sad, sophisticated and sardonic take on human relations.

Frank might have been a critical success, but Amy was unhappy. She berated her record company publicly for forcing her to include tracks she didn't like. She felt it wasn't her own work and only partially represented her style. More crucially, *Frank*'s sales fell far short of its buzz. Amy's career hung in the balance. So, in March 2006, her management arranged a meeting in New York with a producer and DJ called Mark Ronson. Amy later described that initial meeting at his Mercer Street studios in Greenwich Village as a little like an awkward first date. Amy played Mark some Shangri-Las tracks and told him that was the sort of music she wanted to make for the new album. They met again the following day and the first fruit of this new sound was 'Back to Black', the first song recorded for the new album that would bear its name.

The song 'Back to Black' turns its back on the pop of its time, the bling and softcore of modern r&b, the slick, vocal gymnastics of Beyoncé and the multi-platinum divas of the day and turns its tear-stained, mascara-smudged face to the past: to Dusty Springfield, Aretha Franklin, The Shangri-Las and Peggy Lee, a canon of anguished, soulful, sexy female voices singing of joy and despair.

Energised by their collaboration, Amy's trip was extended and over a two-week period she and Ronson produced much of what would become the core of *Back to Black* the album, during which Winehouse poured out her heart to her producer. Her lyrics were centring around her troubled relationship with Blake Fielder-Civil, who had gone back to an ex-girlfriend leaving Amy to take refuge in drink and drugs. She told Ronson about an occasion when her family had been desperate for her to get medical help for her drinking and she'd refused. Everyone 'tried to make me go to rehab, and I said, "No, no, no."'

In true showbiz biopic fashion, Ronson replied, 'That sounds like a hook. We should go back to the studio and turn that into a song.' Three hours later, with Amy's lyrics set to a skilfully knowing retro-soul arrangement, they had 'Rehab'.

We mustn't let our over-familiarity with 'Rehab' obscure the fact that it is a pop confection of supreme skill and brilliance. It's finger-snapping, hip-swivelling beat hooks you instantly into its classic, uptown groove. Ronson's retro-soul arrangement is superb. And Winehouse's words are as complicated and quirky as she is. By turns the mood is defiant, then resigned, bolshy, then vulnerable. Quickly, deftly, and with the minimum of fuss, she pays homage to her musical heroes in a series of asides. Exactly who 'Ray' and 'Mr Hathaway' are is never spelled out. It's assumed that you know who Ray Charles and Donny Hathaway are, two great US soul voices and idols of Winehouse, and that you are part of the hipster world, at least for that three minutes the song conjures brilliantly.

That song made Amy Winehouse a superstar. And it provided the most eerie, poignant epitaph. After her death, much was made of Winehouse's age and her inclusion in the so-called 27 Club of musicians who had died young – Kurt Cobain, Jimi Hendrix, Jim Morrison and Janis Joplin. But of these it's the tale of Janis Joplin which has genuinely profound echoes of Amy Winehouse's sad end. Both were soulful vocalists steeped in jazz and blues, both had turbulent personal lives, both abused drugs and alcohol, leading to dramatic weight loss and infamously erratic onstage appearances. Whereas Hendrix's, Morrison's and Cobain's deaths were sudden and somehow very male, with their aura of debauchery and self-destruction, Amy Winehouse's narrative is a particularly female showbiz story of public fame and private sadness, vulnerability, loneliness and heartbreak.

We see it repeated in stories such as that of Karen Carpenter and Lena Zavaroni too. One of the most visible aspects of Amy Winehouse's struggles was her dramatic weight loss, and the pitiless media spotlight magnifies issues over body image. Karen Carpenter was one of the biggest pop stars of the seventies but suffered for years from eating disorders. Her death in 1983 was ascribed by the LA coroner to 'heartbeat irregularities brought on by chemical imbalances associated with anorexia nervosa'. For many people across the world, it was the first time they'd heard of this so called 'slimmers' disease' and the associated condition bulimia. Lena Zavaroni was a star in her early teens, bursting into the limelight thanks to her appearance on TV show *Opportunity Knocks*, the cheesy seventies template for the *X Factor*. At ten, she was the youngest person to have a top ten album and to appear on *Top of the Pops*, later she enjoyed her own TV series. But what the world didn't know is that from the age of thirteen Zavaroni suffered from anorexia nervosa brought on by early pressures to fit into stage costumes as she went through puberty. At one point, while at stage school (another echo of Winehouse), her weight dropped to four stone. Depression and anorexia dogged her through the seventies and eighties, by which time she was living on state benefit. She underwent drug treatment and electroconvulsive therapy in an attempt to beat her anorexia but, in October 1999, she developed a chest infection and died from pneumonia. She weighed less than five stone.

But the clearest parallels with Winehouse are perhaps earlier ones. Agonising vulnerability, heartbreakingly erratic onstage appearances, intensely emotional delivery and various debilitating addictions … Billie Holiday (whom Winehouse adored) and Judy Garland are sadly emblematic of the tragic female singer trope Amy Winehouse fell into.

Judy Garland perhaps embodies the female showbiz archetype that Amy Winehouse played out in her 21st century career. Again, the sadly predictable elements are there: youthful fame, abusive relationships, tabloid mockery, almost unbearable performances trembling on the brink of disaster, binges of booze and narcotics and beyond all this a voice that turns the pain into a pure musical truth.

Judy Garland, Billie Holliday, Janis Joplin, Karen Carpenter, Lena Zavaroni, Princess Diana, Whitney Houston, even latterly the brushes with self-destruction of Britney Spears and Lindsey Lohan: female showbiz tragedies are tales of private desperation, abusive and loveless relationships, press intrusion, self-harm, addiction and low self-esteem. They are very different tales from those of Jim Morrison, Jimi Hendrix or Keith Moon with their Byronic whiff of maverick poetry, excess and hedonism. These women's stories are sadder and somehow smaller. Of the young, male music-business casualties, only the cases of Kurt Cobain of Nirvana and Richie Edwards of the Manic Street Preachers seem to have an echo of Winehouse's demise. Both Cobain and Edwards were feminine figures, rejecting macho rock stereotypes. Edwards was glamorous and beautiful as well as being anorexic and alcoholic, and explicitly showed his kinship and solidarity with women in songs like 'Born a Girl' and 'She Is Suffering' from *The Holy Bible* album, whose cover artwork is a triptych by Jenny Saville entitled *Strategy (South Face/Front Face/North Face)*, depicting an obese woman reflected in mirrors – it's a stark meditation on female self-image.

Of that so-called 27 Club, only Kurt Cobain actively chose to take his own life. But, oddly, given that they sound so different, 'Smells Like Teen Spirit' is a strangely similar song in spirit to 'Rehab'. Two young people sing from the heart – 'from the pit of my burning, nauseous stomach' as Cobain's suicide note had it – about being thrust into the limelight and being bemused, shaken, even revolted by it. Both reject easy answers and assert a kind of defiant individuality and control.

Winehouse's travails, like those of Britney Spears and Lindsay Lohan, were mocked in a way no troubled male rock performer and his 'struggles' generally are. The comedian Russell Brand, a former drug abuser himself, who might have been expected to show some sympathy, once joked, 'Amy Winehouse – her surname's beginning to sound like a description of her liver.' Never hilarious, this cheap gag seems even less funny now.

Brand made his remark at the 2009 Brit Awards. By now Winehouse was becoming as much known for her chaotic personal life as her music. Her tortured marriage to drug addict Fielder-Civil seemed finally to be over after two years of high-profile turbulence. He told the *News of the World*, 'I made the biggest mistake of my life by taking heroin in front of her ... I introduced her to heroin, crack cocaine, and self-harming. I feel more than guilty.' *Spin* magazine reported that the couple had 'matching crisscross scars and scratches up and down their left arms'. During the same interview, Amy apparently started to carve the words 'I Love Blake' into her own stomach. Later, Fielder-Civil would be jailed for burglary and possession of an imitation firearm.

Winehouse admitted that she had been struggling with issues around food since 2004.

> I went through every eating disorder you can have. A little bit of anorexia, a little bit of bulimia ... I'm not totally OK now but I don't think any woman is ... I've had a flirtation with every eating disorder there is, I wouldn't tie myself down to one, and then I realise that I have to eat and I will fatten myself up and put on half a stone in a week, because I'm good like that.

The nadir was approaching. In 2008, footage appeared online of Winehouse seemingly smoking crack and sold to the *Sun* newspaper. Among those distressed by it was the legendary music writer Nick Kent, also a former heroin user, who wrote sympathetically of her plight in *The Times*:

> The grainy footage features the singer looking suitably out of it as she discusses having just taken six valium to counterbalance the cocktail of other drugs she'd consumed earlier in the evening. Then she lights up some crack and

becomes further glassy-eyed and incomprehensible ... The only genuinely shocking aspect to this latest lurid dispatch from the ongoing Winehouse meltdown industry resides more in the fact that the images under discussion were filmed by a supposed friend of the twenty-three-year-old apprentice diva. This same 'friend' is even quoted with undisguised glee masquerading as concern: 'Here is proof that she has pressed the self-destruct button,' he/she all but gloats. With friends like this, who need enemies?

Real friends were in short supply. By now Amy was a virtual prisoner in her gated apartment block in a converted warehouse in the East End, besieged night and day by reporters and photographers. She appeared onstage in Belgrade clearly distracted and intoxicated and was booed by the crowd and forced to cancel shows in Istanbul and Athens.

In his piece Kent identified what was so new and disturbing about the Winehouse narrative. From Billie Holiday to Keith Richards, musicians have always dallied with various dark, chemical pursuits, but theirs had been largely private tribulations. Thanks to the men camped outside Winehouse's apartment and the all-seeing eyes and ears and global reach of the internet, she wouldn't be so lucky. Amy Winehouse was no English rose but the relentless media interest in her breakdowns recalled the short life of Princess Diana. Kent's conclusion was chilling and prophetic:

If she manages to summon the presence of mind to combat her situation in the next few months she'll have a career to redeem and build on. If she doesn't, she will condemn herself to becoming a freakish joke-magnet, that skinny

Rehab girl who kept saying nonono to detoxification until
she polluted herself into the grave.

July 2011 and Amy Winehouse returned to her residence in
Camden after what appeared to be a lengthy drinking session. This
was her pattern: abstinence, followed by punishing binges. Her
bodyguard said that she seemed intoxicated and stayed at home
drinking steadily but modestly for the next three days. On Saturday
23 July he heard her around 2 a.m. 'laughing, listening to music
and watching TV'. At 10 a.m. he saw her lying on her bed. Shortly
after 3 p.m. he checked on her again and observed her lying in the
same position as before. He tried to rouse her, but she was not
breathing and had no pulse. At 3.54 p.m. two ambulances were
called and she was pronounced dead at the scene.

Amy Winehouse's final years have served to obscure her genius
as a performer and writer. She was a fabulous singer and a sharp
lyricist. But ultimately this became less important than her cartoon
status as public entertainment, not for the brilliance of her music
but the lurid waste of her last years. Her death, of course, was
the cue for an outpouring of sanctimonious moralising about the
dangers of drugs, even though it was the average pressman's drug
of choice, alcohol, that killed her.

47. BLEEDING LOVE

He is the king of the star-makers, the talent-show titan (or tyrant, some would say). There is something transatlantic about his voice, something slightly aloof about his black clothes and haughty demeanour. At each of his mass auditions for his ITV talent show, hundreds of hopefuls turn up desperate for a moment in the limelight. Most will be airily dismissed. He plays up to his image of arrogant superiority: 'Money is a hobby of mine. Some people collect stamps, I collect money,' he told a newspaper interviewer and, in the same story, the paper talked of how he has become 'the focus for every ocarina player, razor-blade eater and bird-song imitator' in England.

Yes, back in 1957 Carroll Levis was as ubiquitous, loved and loathed as ... whoever it was you thought I was talking about. His TV talent show *The Carroll Levis Discoveries Show* was a huge hit on ITV in the late fifties. It often topped the ratings, knocking *Sunday Night at the London Palladium* off its top spot, and among its alumni were Nicholas Parsons and Terry Hall (the ventriloquist handler of Lenny the Lion, not the deadpan singer of The Specials). So who could blame a young Liverpool group called The Quarrymen – at that point John Lennon, Paul McCartney, George Harrison, John Lowe and Colin Hanton – for entering the auditions for Levis's show at the Liverpool Empire Theatre on Sunday 9 June 1957 at 3 p.m. They didn't win, but impressed enough to qualify for the regional finals to be held in Manchester two weeks later.

This time the act comprised just Lennon, Harrison and McCartney, performing as Johnny and the Moondogs. The registration process in Manchester took all day – there was a queue of musicians carrying amplifiers and instruments stretching around the block. Lennon (without a guitar), McCartney and Harrison played Buddy Holly's 'Think It Over', but the last train left for Liverpool at 9.47 p.m., and at 9.20 there were still twelve acts to perform. As the trio only had £1 between them, it was impossible to stay for the 'clapometer' finale. As they were leaving, Lennon saw a cutaway electric guitar by the stage door, picked it up and walked off with it, later saying that the trip 'wasn't a total loss'.

Once again, history confounds us, especially those of us who talk of The Beatles as proper music as distinct from all the TV talent show rubbish of today. The Beatles themselves, it seems, were more than happy, desperate even, to sing populist cover versions in an attempt to win a TV talent show, a doorway to fame that has been open to the hopeful for longer than you might think.

Simon Cowell, Piers Morgan, Sharon Osbourne, Dr Fox: what do all these people have in common? Yes, they have all been made vastly wealthy and famous by TV music shows without ever having sung a note or having exhibited an iota of musical talent themselves. The phenomenon of the talent-show inquisition, with its almost medieval flavour, tells you much about how human nature conceals some ugly, ancient truths. Watching Morgan or Cowell presiding over their kangaroo court, sentencing their weak and foolish victims in front of a baying crowd, is surely a bloody assizes, a bear bait or witch trial for the electronic age.

But hang on! What snooty, elitist nonsense is this? Victoria Wood, Lenny Henry, Pam Ayres, Les Dawson – all of these national treasures emerged through TV talent shows, and a cursory trawl through the rock history books reveals just how many lauded and significant rock legends have a talent show to thank for a tipping point. Jimi Hendrix moved to New York in 1964, entered and won an amateur contest at the Apollo Theatre and was hired as a guitarist for the Isley Brothers. Bob Dylan entered the Hibbing Winter Frolic talent show in January 1959. He lost to Sharon Nelson, who sang 'Smoke Gets in Your Eyes', winning the $25 first prize. Elvis Presley won his first talent contest at the age of ten, singing 'Old Shep', and went on entering and winning contests all through his adolescence. U2's big break came at a talent contest in Limerick, Ireland, in March 1978, when they won a £500 prize and the studio time to record their first demo, which got them a deal.

The truth is that the talent show, far from being a modern indication of how pop music is going to hell in a handcart, has always been with us, quietly assuming its terrifying control over our culture with the help of its monstrous one-eyed friend in the corner of the living room.

Shows like Levis's and fellow Canadian citizen Hughie Green's *Opportunity Knocks* were, like their twenty-first century equivalents, *Britain's Got Talent* and *X Factor*, not just a showcase for music but a cavalcade of ventriloquists, dancers, comics and jugglers of varying degrees of quality. Future *Hi-de-Hi!* star Su Pollard was beaten into second place by a singing dog but, after the comedians, the bulk of *Opportunity Knocks'* contestants who went on to find fame were singers or musicians. There was Australian outfit New World, sensitive troubadour Berni Flint, singing miners Millican & Nesbitt, child balladeer Neil Reid, Mancunian soulsters Sweet Sensation, schmaltzy duo Peters & Lee, and in case all the above lack something in credibility, consider folk-tinged Welsh singer Mary Hopkin, recommended to Paul McCartney by Twiggy (who saw her on the show), later to marry Bowie producer Tony Visconti, be one of the first artists signed to The Beatles' Apple label and record McCartney-produced songs like 'Those Were the Days' and 'Goodbye'.

Opportunity Knocks' more racy seventies kid brother was *New Faces*. Its great innovation, and one that's at the heart of the modern glut of talent and celebrity shows, was the addition of a judges' panel as well as a studio audience. The panels included famed record producers and songwriters Tony Hatch and Mickie Most, as well as waspish journalists like Nina Myskow. Hatch, the man who wrote 'Downtown' and the *Neighbours* theme, was popularly known as 'The Hatchet Man' due to his abrasive way of judging, and was clearly the template for Cowell. In fact, *New Faces* was clearly the blueprint for the *X Factor*, although perhaps the most bizarre musical legacy of the show was Steve Bent's winning song of 1974, 'I'm Going to Spain', being later covered by Mancunian post-punk mavericks The Fall on their album *The Infotainment Scan* – a rather lovely and sad version.

We should mention that, during his wilderness years, Jonathan Ross briefly became the Hughie Green of the Britpop era, with a short-lived programme called *The Big Big Talent Show*. The series only ran for two years but alumni included Omid Djalili, Ed Byrne, Charlotte Church and the future *X Factor* winner Steve Brookstein. The monster pop-talent show of the modern era, though, began with *Popstars*, a London Weekend Television fly-on-the-wall

documentary following the formation of the manufactured band
Hear'Say. Whereas Hear'Say got their first single to number one
in the UK, it was the runners-up, Liberty X, who had the more
fruitful chart career. The show was followed by *Popstars: the Rivals*,
which brought us Girls Aloud. A year later *Pop Idol* was born – the
beginning of a global franchise and the rebirth of the *New Faces*-
style mix of public phone vote and coldly supercilious judging panel.

Enter Simon Cowell, a former A&R man and game-show
contestant himself (he appeared on *Sale of the Century* in 1990) –
who brought the world Curiosity Killed the Cat, Sonia and Robson
& Jerome, as well as releasing novelty records by Teletubbies, Zig
and Zag and, of course, the Mighty Morphin Power Rangers. But
Cowell's next move would even dwarf the cultural import of all that.

For the *X Factor* the hype, padding, false jeopardy, cruelty and
sentiment were ratcheted up to a level that was either unmissable
or unwatchable depending on your point of view. *X Factor* quickly
became the prime source of red-top content on a daily basis. The
judges' panel was retained from the *Pop Idol* franchise, though
there was greater emphasis on phone and online voting. To give
an idea of the show's once faintly terrifying might – in 2009
more people cast a vote for winner Joe McElderry than that of
the Scottish Conservative Party in the following year's general
election. Inevitably, it was sent up cosily by another populist TV
phenomenon, the comedian Peter Kay, in his programme *Britain's
Got the Pop Factor and Possibly a New Celebrity Jesus Christ Soapstar
Superstar Strictly on Ice*.

At the time of writing there have been nine winners of the *X
Factor*, of whom the most successful in terms of sales has been
Leona Lewis. She won the third series in 2006, her début album,
Spirit, was released the following year and sold over 8 million copies

worldwide. 'Bleeding Love', the flagship single, reached number
one in over thirty countries around the world, and was the world's
bestselling single in 2008, the year that *Billboard* proclaimed her
'Top New Artist'. What distinguishes 'Bleeding Love' from the
output of most talent shows is its undoubted quality. It may not
be the most innovative or brilliant pop song ever written, but it is
clearly a classy, crafted r&b ballad, sung with genuine power and
conviction. In other words, a record that could compete on its
own terms with Alicia Keys or Beyoncé rather than sound like a
Crackerjack-style cover from the winner of a British teatime talent
show. With hindsight, this was Lewis's crowning glory. Her sales
have never matched this, and by her own admission to the Mail
Online, the intervening years have not always been a pleasure:

> I've met some deplorable people over the past six years,
> who have done some really bad things, and I've seen their
> betrayal of my trust unfold before my eyes. But I've learnt
> from it and grown from it and I'm much better now at
> knowing who I should avoid. I believe I could have had a
> career in the music industry without the *X Factor*. But it was
> an amazing platform that propelled me to what's happening
> now. I won't listen to anything people say against it. I got
> up every week and sang on stage without that lip-syncing
> that a lot of artists do these days – that takes a talent that
> you can't fake.

Whatever you think of her music, that unfakeable talent was
certainly on display when a vulnerable, socially awkward, middle-
aged woman from West Lothian stood up to sing on another of
Cowell's contests, *Britain's Got Talent*, in 2009. The contrast

between Susan Boyle's homely appearance, as evidenced by the schoolyard sniggering from the audience and judges, and the astonishing voice that emerged from her frumpy frame made her an instant sensation. The moment may well have had its cheesy and staged elements, but the almost visceral power and shock of it was undeniable. It has the same kind of authentic *frisson* that occurred at the 2011 Brits when Adele sang 'Someone Like You' accompanied on the piano by co-writer Dan Wilson. The sincerity, sadness and power of the performance transcended the showbiz clutter of the framing. This was the real thing, and ordinary people didn't have to be the A&R man who discovered Zig and Zag to tell that. There was also a parallel in that Adele had been, it could be argued, created and shaped, not only by television but by the various talent academies that have become increasingly important this century in the development of bright new things. The Sylvia Young School, for example, has produced Billie Piper, three-quarters of All Saints, Emma Bunton, Matt Willis and most famously Amy Winehouse. And then there are the 'rock schools' like the BRIT school in Croydon, who've helped Adele, The Kooks, Katie Melua, Kate Nash and one Leona Lewis on their way.

The truth and passion of both Adele and Susan Boyle struck an immediate chord across the Atlantic. Adele, of course, has gone on to spend more weeks on the *Billboard* chart than Michael Jackson did with 'Thriller', and to make history by being the first artist to have a number-one album concurrently with three number-one singles – she also equalled the total number of Grammies won in a single night by any female artist. More jaw-dropping statistics over the months and years were to come.

Far from sniggering, something about Susan Boyle resonated with America too; with what we might call the American dream.

Here was a talented, poor outsider reaching the top by sheer effort and ability – log cabin to White House style. She was embraced by feminist commentators: Letty Cottin Pogrebin said that although people may 'weep for the years of wasted talent', Boyle's performance was a triumph for 'women of a certain age' over a youth culture that 'often dismisses middle-aged women'. At the time of writing, Susan Boyle's estimated worth is $22 million.

And she didn't win. That accolade went to a troop of hoofers called Diversity. Even for those who manage to win the popularity contest (as some will argue that it's not really about musical talent) very few manage to stay in the public eye for long; mostly because they'll quickly be replaced by the next winner of a TV talent show. Most winners are here today, gone later today. But Diversity's triumph represents, in some ways, the sublime, perhaps ultimately self-defeating paradox of the *X Factor* factor. As its ratings slide, the truth is that the biggest stars to emerge from the shows – Boyle, JLS, Olly Murs, Jedward and, of course, One Direction, the biggest British boy band since The Beatles – were all losers on Cowell's, Walsh's and Morgan's terms. How, one wonders, will they ever recover?

48. ONE DAY LIKE THIS

Around 600 years or so BC, they knew how to stage a music festival. The Rural Dionysia was a version of the wild Athenian celebrations in honour of the god of drunken revelry staged in fields out in the country. The Greeks loved a performance, and people would travel from all over to attend these festivals. They lasted for six days, and included processions, songs, dances and feasts. There would be musicians playing flutes and kitharas (an ancient stringed instrument), and often accompanied by singing.

And if you were really lucky, there'd be an *askoliasmos*, a contest to see who could balance longest on top of a greased, inflated wine-skin. Music, going nuts in the country, singing, kithara heroes, booze ... sound familiar? The music festival, that alfresco freak-out of music, free love and mind-bending stimulants, has been with us for at least two and a half thousand years. Some people bemoan that the free love and stimulants have been lost; the bacchic craziness of the original music festivals has been replaced by mobile-phone charging posts, designer yurts and corporate sponsorship. But freaking out on the cosmos, however politely and expensively, is more than ever a core part of the British music experience.

Across the Atlantic, the corporate face of festivals has tended to be slicker than here. The Newport Jazz Festival is these days 'The Atlantic Jazz Festival presented by Natixis Global Asset Management', but when it began in 1954 it was a very different beast and arguably the prototype for the modern music festival. The very 'First Annual American Jazz Festival' was held at Newport Casino, Newport, Rhode Island. It was a fascinating mixed bag: talks, academic panel discussions and live musical performances from luminaries like Billie Holiday, set outdoors on a lawn. Thirteen thousand people turned up over two days and the feeling was that event was a great success and something of a first. It wasn't all plain sailing, though. The weekend wasn't a big hit with the casino management as the festival did rather wreak havoc with their lawn. They refused to host another. The affluent strata of Newport society weren't so taken with an event organised by younger Newport scenesters, either; one which drew huge crowds from out of town – students and young jazz fans who slept rough outdoors and made too much noise. And, of course, it was jazz, and so many of the artists and fans were black, and decidedly non-U (although, as seen in the fabulous *Jazz on a Summer's Day* movie of the 1958 festival, white hipsters comprised the bulk of the audience). Right from the start, then, modern music festivals encountered the kinds of problems that would dog them in the States and the UK until the nineties when, over the course of just a few years, they became as much a part of the genteel bourgeois summer calendar as Henley, Glyndebourne or Ascot.

It certainly wasn't like that in the 1960s. At the 1960 Newport festival, where John Lee Hooker, Ray Charles and Muddy Waters headlined, rowdyism and drinking led to crowd disturbances and the National Guard being called. A menacing unpredictability had started to darken the sunny skies of the big outdoor music event in the United States. That storm would break appropriately at the very end of the peace and love decade, and The Rolling Stones would soundtrack its violent death throes.

On 6 December 1969 The Stones headlined a festival at the Altamont speedway track in northern California; in theory, a legitimately organised event, inspired, in part, by the largely positive reception for their free gig in Hyde Park the previous summer, and not, as *Rolling Stone* later put it when discussing Altamont, 'the product of diabolical egotism, hype, ineptitude, money manipulation, and, at base, a fundamental lack of concern for humanity'.

Hyde Park in 1968 had been semi-officially policed by Hell's Angels, and the decision was taken to do it all again, but not this time in one of London's finest royal parks, rather on some parched scrubland in a dry, hot state, with the American Hell's Angels as security. Mick and the rest were either unaware or had perhaps forgotten that, while British Hell's Angels were at heart motorcycle enthusiasts, the US version were essentially a violent criminal gang.

A third of a million people turned up, not quite as many as had been present in Woodstock, New York state, earlier that summer. But Woodstock, for reasons both practical and somehow vibrational, had been an enormous success; a celebration of the power of pop music and a totemic moment for the counter-culture, immortalised in Joni Mitchell's beatific song about the day. Altamont, by contrast, was a catastrophe. The day was as much about violence as it was about music: the Grateful Dead, one of the event's prime movers, actually refused to take the stage. The crowd, fuelled by beer, amphetamines and acid, turn ugly, as Hell's Angels prowled the arena (and even the stage), roughing people up. Marty Balin of Jefferson Airplane was punched unconcoious while actually performing onstage, during a mêlée. And later, a young and very high black man called Meredith Hunter was stabbed to death by one of the Angels as he waved a gun around during The Stones' performance of 'Sympathy for the Devil'. If Woodstock was the zenith of the age of Aquarius, Altamont was its nadir.

Over in Britain the sixties swung rather differently, but even our first festival, a jazz gathering organised by Lord Montagu of Beaulieu, was marred by fights and flying beer bottles during Acker Bilk's set. Undaunted and inspired by Newport's eclectic mix of jazz and blues, the manager of London's famous Marquee club, the un-racily monikered Harold Pendleton, organised 'The National Jazz Festival', held in England's very own Newport, Rhode Island, Richmond upon Thames, and soon became 'The National Jazz and Blues Festival', reflecting the blues boom that swept through the kids of middle-class England at the time. It wasn't long before the jazz element practically disappeared, relegated to earnest afternoon sets, while the likes of Cream, Jethro Tull, Fleetwood Mac, Jeff Beck and The Nice proved the big draws. Eventually, in the mid-seventies, the festival transmuted into Reading rock festival and largely featured hard rock and heavy metal. Though a more sanitised affair than it once was, Reading – with stiff competition from T in the Park – remains the gnarliest, most grebo of the summer festivals. It's seen legendary sets from Nirvana and Slade and, infamously in 1989, Hell's Angels threw bottles filled with urine at Meat Loaf and Bonnie Tyler.

Free festivals became part of the culture of British hippiedom, with the most famous at Stonehenge and Windsor becoming crucibles of communal living, anarcho-hippy ideals and what would become the new-age traveller movement. And, of course, a young dairy farmer called Michael Eavis so enjoyed Led Zeppelin's set at the Bath Festival of Blues that he decided to host his own free festival on his farm at Pilton, Glastonbury, in September 1970. Eavis and thirteen others clubbed together to stage the Pilton Pop, Blues & Folk Festival. It wasn't quite a free festival; tickets were £1, which included free milk from the farmhouse. A couple of thousand people turned up to see the headliners, who were to be Wayne Fontana and the Mindbenders and The Kinks, who pulled out late to be replaced by Tyrannosaurus Rex, Ian Anderson of Jethro Tull, Quintessence, Al Stewart and Keith Christmas. In a TV interview of the time Eavis sits with an earnest BBC reporter on one of the makeshift latrines that he was building and responds to a question about the suitability of the Vale of Avalon for a big pop jamboree by saying, 'It's a super place, it ... there's a euphoria down here.'

By the next year they had in place the famous pyramid stage, a one-tenth replica of the Great Pyramid of Giza built from scaffolding and metal sheeting and positioned over a spring which was found by dowsing. And that same summer, just off the south coast, the genteel Isle of Wight hosted the most extraordinary concert ever staged in these islands.

Fiery Creations Limited, basically three brothers, Ron, Ray and Bill Foulk, had been staging festivals on the Isle of Wight since 1968. Bob Dylan and The Band had appeared in 1969, when some quarter of a million attended, just days after Woodstock. At the time, Dylan was living near the festival site in upstate New York and, as the event was on his doorstep, it was assumed he'd put in an appearance. As it was, he was just across the Solent from Portsmouth. A year later, the 1970 event was one of the largest human gatherings in history: the island's population of 300,000 doubled; more people than Woodstock, Live Aid and the modern-day Glastonbury witnessed, among others, The Who, Jimi Hendrix (just three weeks before his death), Miles Davis, The Doors, Leonard Cohen, Jethro Tull, the first appearance of Emerson, Lake and Palmer, Free, Donovan, Joni Mitchell and Tiny Tim. England had its own Woodstock, but it also had more than a touch of Altamont. The event was not a free festival, at least initially, and some of the more anarchistic, hedonistic elements – militant hippies and stoned freaks who were camped out on 'Desolation Row', an area of hillside outside the corrugated fence enclosing the festival grounds – were not happy about the coming of capitalism to the Age of Aquarius, and wanted in free. Simmering discontent, actual fires and sporadic violence threatened to disrupt the concert. Kris Kristofferson mistook the angry noises for booing directed at his performance and cut his set short. Joni Mitchell, clearly upset at having been accosted on stage by a mad hippy, tells the audience an anecdote about going to a Hopi Indian ceremony recently – well, it was 1970 – and berates them with 'I think you're acting like tourists – give us some respect,' before launching into an emotional 'Big Yellow Taxi'. Master of ceremonies Rikki Farr was even more blunt: 'And if you come to this country and we have to charge you three pounds, if you don't want to pay it, don't fucking well come! We put this festival on for you bastards with a lot of love. We worked for one year for you pigs. Now you wanna break our walls and you wanna destroy it? Well, you go to hell!'

In more placatory mood, the organisers gave Desolation Row residents cans of paint and some brushes, hoping they'd do some decorating, cheer the squalor up and spread some good vibes. Instead, they drew swastikas and provocative slogans. 'This festival business is becoming a psychedelic concentration camp,' said one. Soon the fences were pulled down entirely and Desolation Row got the free festival they thought, oddly, was now their moral right.

Forty years on, and the smouldering ash heap of Desolation Row, with its brawls, wire-cutters, bonfires and swastikas, is of another age. By early 2013 the Glastonbury festival was looking to firm up advance bookings of luxury yurts:

Breakfast will be served Monday 1st July before striking camp Monday afternoon. Prices range from £5,395 inc. VAT for two, with yurts for four/families available. We also supply stageside hospitality tickets at cost with each accommodation booking: 2011 prices were £390 each inc. VAT. The yurts boast 'luxury showers and toilets to rival hotel standards', a private access road, passes into the inter-stage area, a gourmet restaurant and 24-hour security.

It's easy to sneer at this extract from a recent ad. (Which doesn't, of course, mean you shouldn't do it.) It's just as easy to mock the cosy liberal gentility of the new range of boutique festival – I love Simon Armitage's affectionate description of Suffolk's wonderful Latitude festival as Latte-Tude – but this writer would much rather be enjoying the intimacy, diversity and general civility of these new festivals than being shouted at through a loudhailer by a dog-handling security guard in a sea of mud that is nothing so much as a giant outdoor Ikea or Old Trafford for lads 'n' dads in matching replica tops. So what happened? Live Aid, at least that's my theory. Prior to Geldof, Ure and Goldsmith's defining powerplay of rock logistics, a pop festival had meant a gathering of marginalised weirdos on the fringes of respectable society: freaks, heads, punks, outsiders, drop-outs. Now go to YouTube and look again at the crowd who charge across the turf at Wembley on that summer's day in 1985. Laundered, keen, fresh-faced, sober. This isn't Desolation Row. This is Henman Hill, Murray Mound, the queue for Les Mis or Cliff Richard. This is a new kind of rock and roll crowd: the day-tripper, the family ticket holder, the coach party.

Is that so bad? Not at all, say the people who love their festivals and plan their summers around them. Britain has become the land of the festival. Arrive at an English airport these days and you'll see a huge piece of national branding, a corporate poster with an image of a young woman on her boyfriend's shoulders, swaying and waving her arms to the sound of a laser-lit band far in the distance: the Festival Calendar website lists some 110 UK festivals between early summer and the end of September.

And a song that has rung out at many of them, from tents and luxury yurts, and frequently from the main stage, is Elbow's 'One Day Like This'. It was included on their breakthrough album *The Seldom Seen Kid*, which won them the Mercury Music Prize. It's a song about waking up a little hung over on a beautiful morning and relishing the ongoing brilliance of life. It is in some ways the quintessential Elbow song, lyrically typical of Guy Garvey – big-hearted yet intimate, tender and uplifting – but, more than this, played by the band at the biggest UK outdoor events during the summer of 2008, when they broke into the national consciousness, it became Britain's festival anthem – grand but not grandiose, with a surging, tidal 'Hey Jude'-like climax over several minutes; an elated, mesmerised celebration of the joy of living, and living in the moment, ideal for the carefree hedonism of your summer festival. It is, in some ways, very much like David Bowie's 'Memory of a Free Festival', which paid tribute to the Beckenham Arts Lab free festival of August 1969. Or, to reach back even further, to a sun-soaked, booze-soaked afternoon in the hot fields and pine-scented meadows of ancient Greece, singing lustily in communion with a chorus of your fellow humans, watching a drunk bloke balanced precariously on a greasy, inflated wine-skin.

49. BONKERS

Late July 2012 and the eyes of the world are on what was, until a year ago, a stretch of derelict wasteland in an unlovely and abandoned part of East London. Now it has been transformed into the Olympic Park, the centrepiece venue of the 2012 London Olympics. Danny Boyle and Frank Cottrell Boyce's eccentric, dazzling opening ceremony has been the talk of the country. One Conservative MP, Aidan Burley, has described it on Twitter as 'lefty multicultural crap' and found to his embarrassment that hardly anyone has agreed with him. With its celebratory tableaux of British industry, technology, sport, welfare-state provision and culture, the opening ceremony has been universally hailed a triumph. Music was at the heart of it, from Elgar to Bhangra, Evelyn Glennie to the Arctic Monkeys; and a track that managed to offend a *MailOnline* writer called Rick Dewsbury who defined it as a 'form of awful electronic music popular among black youths in east London' electrified the Olympic Stadium with its manic energy and edge.

In the VIP enclosure, Prince William turned to Prime Minister David Cameron and said, 'I don't know if you know, Prime Minister, but my grandmother is a great fan of Dizzee Rascal.'

We don't know whether this was a wry joke from the future king, or indeed whether the Queen is actually a big fan of Dizzee Rascal, but we do know that Dylan Mills was born down the road from the Olympic Park in Bow, and that, since 2002, has gone from being the feral, semi-criminal inner-city youth of tabloid nightmares to a kind of 'national treasure' (*Daily Telegraph*), has debated politics on *Newsnight* with Jeremy Paxman, performed at an Oxford University black-tie ball, won the Mercury Music Prize, and had several number-one singles, all without hugely compromising the sound premiered on the single he made in his bedroom as a troubled teenager, and which writer Simon Reynolds termed 'one of those epoch-defining moments, on a par with Sex Pistols' 'Anarchy in the UK'.

Dizzee Rascal now lives in a country house in leafy Chislehurst, Kent. But when he made 'I Luv U', one of the most original and pioneering tracks to emerge from early twenty-first century Britain, he was just sixteen and called Dylan Kwabena Mills, raised by a single mother on the notorious Crossways estate in Bow after his father died when he was two. In 2009 he told the *Independent*'s Ian Burrell:

> I was frustrated, I was a hoodrat, man! I liked the streets more than school so I would always bunk off. I was disruptive … I've always been troublesome, I was one of those kids that couldn't get on with anyone. I never liked school, never liked anyone telling me what to do. Now I'm older I understand that you have to take orders to get anywhere. The worst thing was that I was smart, which meant I didn't get what I should've out of it.

In some interviews Dizzee has hinted at a criminal past, robbing pizza-delivery men and stealing cars. What is a matter of record is that Mills was expelled from four schools in as many years; an exasperated teacher was the first to refer to him as Rascal. In the fifth, Langdon Park comprehensive in Poplar, he was barred from all classes except music, in which he got an A in his GCSE.

But, alongside all this, Mills was also involved with a theatre group in Islington, making music at school and at workshops run by Tower Hamlets Summer University and the pirate radio networks that are a central part of youth culture and indeed 'the People's Songs' in East London. He cites an unusual mixture of early influences: Sham 69, the Sex Pistols and Kurt Cobain:

> I sense such a free spirit from someone like Kurt Cobain. I didn't really know what he was talking about, but he was a bit messed up, y'know! People like him look rough and they smash things up. 'Smells Like Teen Spirit' was a tune, man! But then I look at my own stuff and I can see some similiarities. They were just supposed to be grunge, innit? But they weren't. Music is music, no matter where you come from. Everyone should be able to make any kind of music.

Of course, part of the rich musical stew that the future Dizzee grew up on was US hip hop. From its roots in the beatbox and rapping culture of American inner cities, hip hop had become the lingua franca of modern pop, the seam of black running through every pop chart in the world. But by the time Dizzee Rascal was starting to make his own music, hip hop had ceased to be the primitive, stark, angry voice of the streets, as heard in the early tracks of Grandmaster Flash, Ultramagnetic MC's and the Bronx hip-hop crews, but a multi-million dollar industry wherein besuited moguls like Puff Daddy and Kanye West boasted on disc of opulent lifestyles of champagne and limousines and launched their own brands of toiletries and sunglasses.

But in the spirit of the pioneers of hip hop, a very British offshoot of hip hop and techno was bubbling up during the mid-1990s in the depressed areas of inner-city London, nurtured by illegal block parties and 'raves' and the bush telegraph of pirate radio stations transmitting from the tower blocks of Dalston, Peckham, Hackney, Harlesden, Limehouse, Stepney and New Cross. They called it 'jungle', and it was uniquely modern and British, reeking of stairwells, takeaways, flyovers, nightclubs; the whole noisy, clamorous, stressful, exciting, dangerous and non-stop sensory jangle of urban life. Junglist DJs took the six-second drum break that had often been used in hip hop – the so-called Amen break from The Winston's 1969 B side, 'Amen, Brother' – and sped it up to form the distinctive skittering, panicked rush that became the sound of jungle.

Jungle had a Sunday name, 'drum and bass', a more refined instrumentally experimental version of this new urban sound, played by white musicians like The Black Dog, Spring Heel Jack and Squarepusher. It became respectable, inspiring cerebral think-pieces in the broadsheets, and Roni Size and Reprazent's *New Forms* even scooped the Mercury Music Prize in 1997. There was more than a little of what we might call middle-class tourism about all this: liking jungle conferred a street kudos and offered a taste of inner-city edginess for middle-class white music critics who would never dream of visiting Broadwater Farm or the Aylesbury estate after dark. But jungle was authentic too, the hyperkinetic, visceral soundtrack to the lives of marginalised kids from the inner city, like Dylan Mills, now Dizzee Rascal.

Dizzee Rascal's early recordings are extraordinary in their visceral untutored originality. First single 'I Luv U' was a tale of teenage pregnancy and adolescent sex welded to a clatter of electronic beats, squelches, booms and general *Sturm und Drang*. This was no pose. Dizzee's life was as turbulent and disjointed as his music. Soon after 'I Luv U' was released, he visited the holiday island of Ayia Napa, where unknown assailants for unknown motives dragged him from his moped and knifed him several times within centimetres of vital organs.

This was a momentary setback, however. His first album, *Boy in da Corner*, was full of bold, manic sonic experimentation: 'I'd try to build a tune in fifteen minutes using the most obscure sounds I could find ... put a microphone next to a frying pan and knock it – just to see how they'd fit together. Considering how rough it sounds, I am surprised people get it in the way I wanted.'

Get it they did, and not just on the walkways of the Crossways estate. *Boy in da Corner* won the Mercury Music Prize in 2003 and the *Independent on Sunday* described it as

> like walking through London's busiest, most multi-cultural streets, absorbing every noise, from the bhangra or dancehall reggae coming from a car to the constant trebly chirp of mobile ringtones and car alarms, and making it into a polymorphous music, as irritating yet as stimulating as the sounds of the inner city.

As yet this new sound didn't have a name. It was variously described as a new style of UK garage, or maybe '8-bar', 'Nu Shape', 'Sublow' or even 'Eskibeat'. In fact, one of Dizzee Rascal's peers and fellow pioneers made the minefield of terminology the subject of his first single, 'Wot Do U Call It?' But, confusingly, it was another track by Wiley 'Eskimo' – that was first described as 'grime'. With its connotations of the cracked, distressed and dirty life at the bottom of the pile, grime was the perfect label for this new sound. And it stuck.

Sasha Frere-Jones of the *New Yorker* told his uptown readers of how grime had developed into something from modern hip hop:

Hip-hop, even at its harshest, is dance music. By contrast, grime sounds as if it had been made for a boxing gym, one where the fighters have a lot of punching to do but not much room to move ... a fierce, antic sound [made] by distilling the polyrhythms of drum and bass or garage to a minimal style sometimes consisting of nothing more than a queasy bass line and a single, clipped video-game squawk. Today, the music's choppy, off-centre rhythms are blanketing London. Some tracks are beginning to show the influence of American hip-hop genres like crunk, but the m.c.s' cadences are unmistakably black and British, indebted to Jamaican dancehall music and West Indian patois.

Grime culture transmits itself on the ground informally and outside of the usual music biz structures. There are homemade DVDs featuring wobbly footage of showdowns and contests between rival DJs and MCs, 'a little like spelling bees, but louder', as Frere Jones puts it. These are sold and swopped in barber shops and takeaways across East London, some are played on pirate radio stations like Raw UK and Rinse FM and on the cable network Channel U.

Grime not only sounds utterly its own beast, it is distinctly the voice – smart, humorous, threatening, defiant, dark – of a young

British subculture, one that may have begun in the sink estates but has reached Balmoral estate. The patois of grime is West Indian in origin and has become ubiquitous among young people of every class. It is the language of the street, the text message, the prison, even. It is not always pretty and its prevalence among young Britons and its preoccupations with sex, casual violence and criminality are not to everyone's taste.

In 'Sirens', a track on *Maths + English*, another Mercury Music Prize nominated album, Dizzee Rascal offers a scene from his daily routine ...

> *1 to the 2 to the 3 to the 4*
> *Limehouse police knocking at my door*
> *12 black boots on my bedroom floor*

... before launching into a lurid depiction of a street mugging, seemingly drawn from life.

But this is surely not Dizzee Rascal's everyday life on his Chislehurst estate. Since *Maths + English* he has become a genial fixture of the pop charts with his more anodyne dance hits with DJ Calvin Harris. His biggest hit to date, 'Bonkers', though a collaboration with the hugely successful mainstream dance producer and DJ Armand Van Helden, still sounds engagingly crazy, a brash, hyperactive, noisy celebration cum complaint about the energising insanity of the daily grind.

In the wake of Dizzee Rascal have come new British rappers like Tinchy Stryder and Tinie Tempah. And the influence has stretched beyond the Black, Asian and Afro-Caribbean communities. Professor Green and Plan B offer a white take on the grime template. In the case of Plan B – real name Ben Drew of Forest Gate, East London – it is an explicitly political take. His track 'Ill Manors' was inspired by the UK riots of 2011 and what Plan B saw as 'society's failure to nurture its disadvantaged youth'. Described in the *Guardian* as the 'the first great mainstream protest song in years' it seethes with sarcasm and mistrust – 'Keep on believing what you read in the papers/ Council estate kids – scum of the earth' – rails against the insulting use of the word 'chav', and does all this to a brooding incendiary grime track, with a little borrowing from Dmitri Shostakovich's *Leningrad Symphony.*

In 'Ill Manors' Plan B excoriates little rich boys like David Cameron. At the same time he stars in glossy movie adaptations like *The Sweeney.* Dizzee Rascal raps about life at the bottom of the pile, while performing 'Bonkers' at the glitzy opening ceremony of the Olympics and appearing at Oxford black-tie dinners. The two Britains of 2013 sit side by side uneasily, queasily some would say, raising interesting questions about culture, class and power. In the cracks, gaps and faultlines between the generations, the classes, the races, the haves and have nots, subcultures like grime continue to breed and multiply in the dark corners, before teeming into the light.

50. THE PEOPLE'S SONG: MERRY XMAS EVERYBODY

And that was almost it. But right from the very inception of The People's Songs, *over those pints and crisps in a Salford pub, I'd decided that to be true to the spirit of the book, the final song should be chosen by the people themselves. So, soon after the series that accompanies this book began, we asked via all manner of media, social and otherwise, for suggestions for the final song: song 50. We asked listeners to think of an era, a concept, an issue or event that we had perhaps overlooked, announcing that that would become the subject of the final show to be broadcast in December 2013. Among the topics we received were everything from James Bond to JFK, pirate radio to anarcho-punk, and songs from John Lennon's 'Imagine' to 'Spike Milligan's Tape Recorder' by The Membranes. In the end, there was a clear favourite though, a classic of British pop that was nicely fitting given the show's broadcast date …*

Whether angels have the same authority in the pop world as *The Guinness Book of British Hit Singles* is debatable. But they do have their own opinion on what was the first Christmas hit. The first noel, the angels did say, was to certain poor shepherds in fields as they lay. But that's only if you take that particular Cornish carol, its modern incarnation written by Rev. Henry Ramsden Bramley and arranged by John Stainer, as gospel. Some say that Christmas goes much, much further back into human history than those famous events in the Middle East a couple of millennia back, involving babies, camels, swaddling clothes, censuses and myrrh.

As Christians spread their new religion into Europe in the first few centuries AD, they ran into all kinds of people, tribes and cultures living by a variety of local religious creeds, which Christian missionaries lumped together under the umbrella term 'pagan'. Midwinter festivals, with their deep, dark pagan roots, were widely celebrated around the late December winter solstice, which made for a pleasing and convenient philosophical fit. 'O, how wonderfully acted Providence that on that day on which that Sun was born … Christ should be born,' wrote Cyprian, a third century bishop of Carthage.

The early Christians wanted to convert the pagans, but they were also fascinated by their traditions, which is why they incorporated so many into their new monotheistic creed. It's well known that Christmas trees were popularised by Queen Victoria's German born beau Prince Albert who brought the tradition from his native land, but the roots, if you'll forgive the expression, go deeper, to the pagan practice of bringing greenery indoors to decorate in midwinter. Centuries later Albert installed a decorated Christmas tree at Windsor Castle in 1841; soon woodcuts of it appeared in London magazines and a new fashion took hold.

Midwinter was the perfect time for a celebration in the ancient world. In an agricultural society, the harvest is done for the year and there's little left to be done in the fields. But despite the spread of Christianity, midwinter festivals did not become Christmas for hundreds of years. The Bible gives no reference to when Jesus was born and it wasn't until four hundred years after the birth of Christ that the notion of celebrating Christmas as the birth of the messiah occurred to church leaders in Rome.

But as soon as Christmas did get going as a festival, music was at the heart of the celebrations. Chants, liturgies and hymns in Latin were the early Christmas hits. Then, in the thirteenth century, under the influence of St Francis of Assisi acting as a sort of early George Martin come Tony Blackburn, the carol, a kind of circle dance with lyrics sung in ordinary vernacular language, started to become popular.

Christmas was banned by Oliver Cromwell and his Puritans who loathed the excess, the mystery and the musicality of it in much the same way that today's Taliban despise a good tune. But the human need for fun and warmth and revelry at the darkest time of the year won out over Oliver's army and with the restoration of the monarchy, music was enshrined again at the very centre of the Christmas celebrations. William Sandys' *Christmas Carols, Ancient and Modern* of 1833 contained the first appearance in print of many now-classic English carols and these rousing, uplifting songs contributed greatly to the Victorian revival of the holiday, helped along a little by one Charles Dickens and *A Christmas Carol*.

Christmas as we celebrate it today – gift giving, fairy lights, work holidays and music – is a largely twentieth century invention though. But there's a brilliant irony at work here. There's a theory that holds that Christmas as we know it was largely invented by people who didn't actually celebrate it. As the writer Robert Everett-Green put it, 'Jewish songwriters didn't just jump on the sleigh. They set it running in the first place, and helped create the nostalgic mythology needed to transform Christmas into a secular consumer festival.'

In the years immediately following the Second World War, the largely Jewish songwriters plying their trade on Broadway and Tin Pan Alley created a new canon of holiday pop tunes. Songs like 'Chestnuts Roasting on an Open Fire' or 'The Christmas Song', 'Silver Bells', 'Let It Snow! Let It Snow! Let It Snow!', 'Rudolph the Red-Nosed Reindeer', 'Santa Baby' and of course the best known Christmas song of all, and indeed the biggest selling record ever, 'White Christmas', written by Irving Berlin in hot dry La Quinta, California one night in 1940. 'Grab your pen and take down this song,' he told his secretary. 'I just wrote the best song I've ever written – heck, I just wrote the best song that anybody's ever written.'

Another Jewish songwriter and producer, Phil Spector, also looms large in the canon of Christmas music. His album *A Christmas Gift For You*, now usually known as *Phil Spector's Christmas Album*, gave the Wall of Sound treatment to a selection of secular Christmas standards. It was released on the same day that President Kennedy was assassinated and, perhaps for this baleful reason, was largely ignored until its re-issue on Apple in 1972 made it a Christmas stalwart. Spector's inspired move with *A Christmas Gift For You* is to simply add a seasonal twist to his already established glorious pop template, making it the first real Christmas record that modern beat pop fans could enjoy. It was a Christmas album for a generation weaned on Elvis, street corner soul, r&b and the new sounds of The Beatles and The Supremes rather than the typical yuletide schmaltz. It is Beach Boy Brian Wilson's favourite album.

That year that Apple re-issued the Spector Christmas album and sealed it in the pop consciousness, the Christmas number one in the UK was Jimmy Osmond's distinctly un-festive 'Long Haired Lover From Liverpool'. But that same year as esteemed a personage as Beatle John Lennon was trying his hand at a Christmas ballad, the preachy, wildly optimistic 'Happy Xmas (War Is Over)'. By the next year, the golden era of the British Christmas single was ushered in, and reached its zenith with Britain's favourite Christmas single, a record that the PRS – or Performing Rights Society – estimate has been heard by 42 per cent of the world's population.

In the bleak, strike-bound midwinter of 1973 Slade were the biggest band in Britain. Over the spring 'Cum On Feel The Noize' and 'Skweeze Me, Pleeze Me' had both entered the chart at number one, practically unheard of at the time. Drummer Don Powell then suffered a horrific car crash in which his girlfriend was killed and he was left in a coma. Happily, he recovered and returned in time to be part of the plans to produce a Christmas hit. They turned to their old notebooks and tapes for inspiration and dug out a whimsical hippy ditty called 'Buy Me A Rocking Chair', written in a previous incarnation as the N' Betweens. After a night out in Walsall, Holder re-worked the song overnight at his mum's as, in his words, a 'working class family song' with an eye on the nation's current gloomy situation.

'We'd decided to write a Christmas song and I wanted to make it reflect a British family Christmas. Economically, the country was up the creek. The miners had been on strike, along with the grave-diggers, the bakers and almost everybody else. I think people wanted something to cheer them up – and so did I. That's why I came up with the line "Look to the future now, it's only just begun". Once

I got the line "Does your Granny always tell you that the old ones are the best", I knew I'd got a right cracker on my hands.'

He was right. Oddly though, this wintry tune designed to melt the hearts of a frozen Britain was recorded at the height of a heatwave at New York's Record Plant during an American tour the previous summer. Next door John Lennon was recording *Mind Games* and they borrowed his harmonium, which manager Chas Chandler suggested. It took five days to record, with the band standing in the corridor to get the right echo-laden effect chorus.

The genius of 'Merry Xmas Everybody' is that it has become the sound of the British Christmas but the song itself never resorts to any of the musical tropes of the season; there are no children's choirs, sleigh bells, yo ho ho-ing. It's actually a very good driving classic folk song with just the right touch of Beltane fire and winter solstice in its modal tune and harmonium chords.

Unbeknown to each other, several of Slade's pop peers were also planning a yuletide assault on the charts. That same year, Elton John recorded 'Step into Christmas', Wizzard offered their very own festive homage to Spector with 'I Wish it Could be Christmas Everyday', which was only kept from number one by Slade themselves.

Thus began what might be called the golden age of the Christmas single; none it seemed could resist having a go. The next year – 1974 – saw Mud release their Elvis pastiche 'Lonely This Christmas' while The Wombles enjoyed a 'Wombling Merry Christmas'. By the following year, even earnest rock artists such as Chris de Burgh and ELP's Greg Lake offered sci-fi and seriousness with 'A Spaceman Came Travelling' and 'I Believe in Father Christmas'. For the rest of the decade, no one was immune. Paul McCartney, Kate Bush and

Queen all entered the fray. One of the quirkier Christmas hits was Jona Lewie's 'Stop the Cavalry', a bizarre Crimean War-flavoured Christmas ditty only kept from number one by the tribute records released in the wake of John Lennon's murder.

Perhaps the lure for all these artists, famous and obscure, was the hope of a Christmas number one and an appearance on the pop fixture of the year. The *Top of the Pops* Christmas special was as much a part of the seventies' Christmas day as the Queen's Speech and *The Morecambe and Wise Show*. Indeed, it came sandwiched somewhere between the two, in the post-presents, pre-blow out hiatus, where in wrapping paper and tinsel strewn living rooms across Britain the nation would watch a review of the year's bestselling singles culminating in the Christmas number one, the biggest pop prize of the year. The accolade was both symbolic and arithmetic. The Christmas number one would be the most talked about and high profile chart-topper of the year, and it would also enjoy the huge increased sales boost of the holiday period when tills would ring on a tide of record tokens and Christmas money.

After Live Aid's 'Do They Know Its Christmas', the nature of that prize and the Christmas number one was to change. For every straightforwardly festive number like Shaky's 'Merry Christmas Everyone' or Cliff's 'Mistletoe and Wine', there was a 'Reet Petite', 'Bohemian Rhapsody' or 'You Were Always on my Mind'. By the turn of the century, oddities like Mr Blobby, Bob the Builder's 'Can We Fix It' and Robbie and Nicole's 'Something Stupid' were typical Christmas chart-toppers. Then came the real cold snap, with the emergence of Britain's anti-Santa; a baleful Scrooge-like miser, a White Queen if you will, who'd turned Britain's pop Narnia into a place where, like C.S. Lewis's fairyland, 'it was always winter, but never Christmas,' a presence whose greed and lust for fame has taken all the simple fun out of Christmas. Simon Cowell's *X Factor* programme, with its grand finale timed for the Christmas season, is seen by many as the Tone Deaf Grinch Who Stole Christmas. For four years in the late noughties, *X Factor* winners Shayne Ward, Leona Lewis, Leon Jackson and Alexandra Burke had Christmas number ones. Eventually, in 2009, a campaign was launched to stop Cowell's domination of the Christmas market with the re-issue of Rage Against the Machine's 'Killing in the Name' in direct competition with the *X Factor* effort by Joe McElderry.

A much-discussed phenomenon of recent years has been what the Americans call 'Christmas creep', the ever-earlier start of the commercial onslaught of Christmas through shop decoration, gift advertisements and, of course, the ubiquity of Christmas singles in shops and on the radio. In the UK, it was traditionally felt that no mention of Christmas was acceptable before Bonfire Night, and in the US before Thanksgiving. But in recent decades the music and seasonal decor have been appearing increasingly early. It's become an annual lament as regular as Christmas itself, and a national pastime as fixed as listening out for the first cuckoo in spring; the hearing of the first 'Merry Xmas Everybody' in B&Q or Argos.

Even though the *X Factor* factor is mercifully on the wane, ill-feeling towards it continues to stoke resentment. For many people, the leverage provided by what is essentially free prime TV advertising, gives Cowell's protégés an unfair advantage and has taken the fun and competitive edge out of the annual race. Thus, each year since the Rage Against the Machine, various Facebook campaigns have been waged on behalf of various songs, but largely with the same aim in kind, to thwart the evil Cowell. Of course, the irony is that it isn't Cowell who buys the records and whether you like the *X Factor* records or not, it is a genuine People's Song. Although perhaps not so much as the song that was written in a Walsall living room forty years and a different Britain ago.

Slade's 'Merry Xmas Everybody', then, provides us with a fitting conclusion to our journey through seven decades of British life and the songs that soundtracked them. It is perennial and memorable, celebrated not so much for its critical acclaim or the approval of an elite, but for the affection and esteem it was held in by the people and the flavour of the times it continues to give. Like its 49 companions in this book, it will be remembered when hipper, more modish, more lauded music has been forgotten. It is the sound of the country we live in, one among many of the People's Songs.

PHOTOGRAPHY CREDITS

First picture section:
(1) Both Popperfoto/Getty Images (2) Getty Images (3) Getty Images (4 & 5) AFP/Getty Images (6) Getty Images (7) Redferns (top) Getty Images (bottom) (8) Redferns (top) Time & Life Pictures/Getty Images (bottom)

Second picture section:
(1) Popperfoto/Getty Images (2) Hulton-Deutsch Collection/ CORBIS (3) Neal Preston/CORBIS (4) Ray Stephenson/Rex Features (top) WireImage (bottom) (5) Popperfoto/Getty Images (6) Getty Images (7) Both Getty Images (8) Getty Images

Third picture section:
(1) Waring Abbott/Getty Images (2 & 3) Getty Images (4) Getty Images (5) Getty Images (6) Gamma-Keystone via Getty Images (7) SSPL via Getty Images (top) Getty Images (bottom) (8) Redferns

Fourth picture section:
(1) Getty Images (2 & 3) Getty Images (4) Matthew Polak/Sygma/ Corbis (top) Getty Images (bottom) (5) Getty Images (6) Adrian Fisk/PYMCA/Rex Features (7) Rex Features (top) Fremantle (bottom) (8) Redferns